A number of leading British and Australian historians have cited that a comprehensive study of Field Marshal Lord Birdwood is long overdue. He was a very significant general at Gallipoli, commanding the Anzacs, and leading the successful final evacuations. Throughout his life he displayed great diplomatic acumen and his later years were both militarily and politically significant.

FM Lord Birdwood was born in India in 1865. His father, from a West Country landed family, was under-secretary to the government of Bombay. Birdwood was educated at Clifton and Sandhurst, and joined the Indian Army in 1886. His early service in close relationship to Indian cavalry soldiers made a strong impact on his life. During this time, he effected his first viceregal connections and joined the viceroy's bodyguard. Success in the Boer war and a developing professional relationship with Lord Kitchener brought steady career progress in the first decade of the new century, including success on active service; command of an independent brigade; and work at the highest levels of Indian life. Before the World War he fulfilled two very prestigious appointments in India.

Soon after the start of hostilities, Kitchener personally asked for him to train the Australian and New Zealand forces in Egypt prior to going to the Western Front. However, they were deployed instead to Gallipoli with Birdwood as their commander. He emerged from the Dardanelles campaign with a deservedly enhanced reputation. He was confirmed as the Commander of the Australian Imperial Force. He led 1 Anzac Corps to France in March 1916, and to yet another baptism of fire. He had a proven ability to lift his men to face action time and again with determination. He commanded throughout the challenges and setbacks of the two years, 1916-17 – the Somme and Passchendaele – and the Australians showed the depth and value of both his leadership and training in the decisive battles around Villers-Bretonneux. He was promoted to command the Fifth Army in May 1918, while still retaining the administrative command of Australian forces at the strong personal request of the Australian prime minister.

In 1920 he made an acclaimed tour of Australia and New Zealand. He then returned to India, commanding Northern Command and in 1925 became commander-in-chief, as a Field Marshal, which neither Roberts nor Kitchener achieved. Birdwood left India in 1930. A desire to become governor general of Australia was not realised due to the Australian government's insistence on having an Australian in that post, much to the King's annoyance. Instead and surprisingly Birdwood became Master of Peterhouse, Cambridge. In his later years, he became a prominent man of the British Empire. He fulfilled a number of roles with distinction, all of which continued to generate the hallmark affection with which he was regarded by those serving under him or working with him. He gave substantial encouragement in writings and broadcasting to Australia and its World War 2 leaders

He died in 1951 at Hampton Court and was buried with full military honours.

Author at site of Birdwood's Headquarters at Anzac, Gallipoli.

Richard Farrimond served with the Royal Signals in Germany, England, Northern Ireland and Canada. Between commanding an independent signal squadron in Londonderry and a regiment in Germany, he trained as a back-up NASA Payload Specialist to launch a Skynet 4 military communications satellite from the Space Shuttle – cancelled following the 1986 Challenger disaster. This led him into the British space industry and involvement in defence and security programmes, with much time spent in Australia. Following final retirement, he undertook a Master's degree in World History and Cultures at King's College London and completed his PhD at King's in December 2021

Birdie

More than 'Soul of Anzac'

Field Marshal Lord Birdwood of Anzac and Totnes 1865-1951

Birdie

More than 'Soul of Anzac'

Field Marshal Lord Birdwood of Anzac and Totnes 1865-1951

Richard Farrimond

Helion & Company

Helion & Company Limited
Unit 8 Amherst Business Centre
Budbrooke Road
Warwick
CV34 5WE
England
Tel. 01926 499 619
Email: info@helion.co.uk
Website: www.helion.co.uk
Twitter: @helionbooks
Visit our blog at blog.helion.co.uk

Published by Helion & Company 2023
Designed and typeset by Mary Woolley (www.battlefield-design.co.uk)
Cover designed by Paul Hewitt, Battlefield Design (www.battlefield-design.co.uk)

ISBN 978-1-804512-36-4

British Library Cataloguing-in-Publication Data.
A catalogue record for this book is available from the British Library.

For details of other military history titles published by Helion & Company Limited contact the above address or visit our website: http://www.helion.co.uk.

We always welcome receiving book proposals from prospective authors.

Dedicated to the memory of my grandfather
Second Lieutenant Joseph Farrimond, Northamptonshire Regiment,
attached 1st/5th Battalion Gloucestershire Regiment. Missing, believed killed,
during night of 20/21 July 1916 in Mash Valley in sight of Pozières, that was
attacked by 1st Australian Division on night 22/23 July 1916.
Now remembered on the Thiepval Memorial to the Missing.

William Riddell Birdwood, 11th (Prince of Wales's Own) Bengal Lancers by Alfred Crowdy Lovett, c. 1894. (National Army Museum 1957-06-28).

Contents

List of Illustrations

List of Maps

In Colour Section

Abbreviations & Glossary

A & NZ	Australian and New Zealand
AAG	Assistant Adjutant General
ADB	*Australian Dictionary of Biography*
ADC	*Aide-de-camp*
AG	Adjutant-General
AIF	Australian Imperial Force
AMS	Assistant Military Secretary
ANZAC	The Australian and New Zealand Army Corps
Anzac	Any Australian or New Zealand soldier of the War and similarly as an adjective[1]
AWM	Australian War Memorial
Bashi Bazouks	Irregular Ottoman soldiers
Bde	Brigade
BEF	British Expeditionary Force
BGGS	Brigadier-General, General Staff
BGRA	Brigadier-General, Royal Artillery
BL AAS	British Library, Asian & African Studies
Brig	Brigadier
Brig-Gen	Brigadier-General
C-in-C	Commander-in-Chief
Capt	Captain
CGS	Chief of the General Staff
CIGS	Chief of the Imperial General Staff
CO	Commanding Officer
Comdg	Commanding
CRA	Commander, Royal Artillery

1 Bean provides six uses of this term in C E W Bean, *The Official History of Australia in the War of 1914-1918 Volume 1* (Sydney: Halstead Press, 1921), 609.

daffadur	Indian Army cavalry sergeant
dak	Traveler's rest house
DDMS	Deputy Director Medical Services
Div	Division, divisional
durbar	A community gathering with leader(s) – regimental, provincial, Viceregal or Royal
FAHA	Fellow of the Australian Academy of Humanities
FM	Field Marshal
FRCS	Fellow of the Royal College of Surgeons
GCB	Knight Grand Cross of the Most Honourable Order of the Bath
GCMG	Knight Grand Cross of the Most Distinguished Order of St Michael and St George
GGBG	Governor General's Bodyguard
GGO	Governor-General's Order
gharry	Horse drawn cab
GHQ	General Headquarters
GOC	General Officer Commanding
GSO 1	General Staff Officer (Grade 1)
HL Deb	House of Lords Debates
HMSO	Her/His Majesty's Stationery Office
HQ	Headquarters
IA	Indian Army
IO	Ondia Office
IWM	Imperial war Museum
jirga	Tribal council
KCMG	Knight Commander of the Most Distinguished Order of Saint Michael and Saint George
KCSI	Knight Commander of the Most Exalted Order of the Star of India
KGO	King George's Own
KMA	Kippenberger Military Archive, National Army Museum (NZ)
kopje	Small isolated hill (*Afrikaans*)
LHCMA	Liddell Hart Centre for Military Archives
LofC	Lines of Communication
Lt	Lieutenant
Lt Col	Lieutenant Colonel
Lt Gen	Lieutenant General

Maj Gen	Major General
masjid	Mosque
MD	Doctor of Medicine
MEF	Mediterranean Expeditionary Force
MI	Mounted Infantry
MP	Member of Parliament
MS	Military Secretary
munshi	Native language teacher
NAM	National Army Museum
NCO	Non-commissioned officer
NLA	National Library of Australia
NSW	New South Wales
NZ	New Zealand
NZEF	New Zealand Expeditionary Force
NZMR	New Zealand Mounted Rifles
OC	Old Cliftonian
OG	Old German – regarding trench lines at Pozières
ODNB	*Oxford Dictionary of National Biography*
PWDRO	Portsmouth and West Devon Record Office
Q'land	Queensland
QMG	Quartermaster-General
RA	Royal Artillery
RAF	Royal Air Force
RAMC	Royal Army Medical Corps
Regtl	Regimental
RFA	Royal Field Artillery
SALH	South African Light Horse
sepoy	Indian Army infantry private soldier
Silladar	Cavalry formed of soldiers providing their own horses and equipment
Sowar	Indian Army cavalry private soldier
syce	Indian groom
TA	Territorial Army
Tent pegging	Mounted game with ground targets
TMI	Thorneycroft's Mounted Infantry
TNA	The National Archives

VE	Victory in Europe (Day)
WA	Western Australia
WO	War Office
I ANZAC	I Anzac Corps
II ANZAC	II Anzac Corps
XI BL	XI (Prince of Wales's Own) Bengal Lancers
XIIth Lancers	XII (Prince of Wales's) Royal Lancers

Acknowledgements

While enjoying Professor Richard Drayton's Masters course on World History and Cultures at King's College London, Dr (now Professor) Sarah Stockwell encouraged me to consider undertaking a PhD. Professor Carl Bridge later stirred my interest with his modules on both Australian and Settler histories. My own fascination with Birdwood led me to a possible subject for research. I am extremely grateful to the three of them for their initial encouragement.

I was most fortunate to be able to speak with Lord Birdwood, the Field Marshal's grandson, before his death in July 2015, when the barony and baronetcy became extinct. The family assistance then came from Lieutenant Colonel Gordon Birdwood, retired, who could not have been more helpful about his great-uncle. Gordon was a long-time supporter of the Gallipoli Association and his early death in January 2017 was untimely sad. I am grateful to first Gordon's niece, Victoria Ellis, *née* Birdwood, and subsequently David Archer, one of Birdwood's three great grandchildren, for continuing the family link with me.

My first taste of archives was a number of years ago at the Australian War Memorial which is both a humbling and an inspirational place. I am personally indebted to Ashley Ekins, Michael Kelly – who together led a ten-day Gallipoli battlefield tour, which I attended as the sole 'Pom', – Peter Burness, and Emma Campbell of the Military History Section, and to Theresa Cronk, Sue Drucker and Jane Robertson of the Research Centre, for all their unstinting and comprehensive help over a number of years. The assistance at both the National Gallery of Australia and the National Library of Australia was likewise forthcoming and detailed. Numerous Australian historians have been helpful and Professor Peter Stanley has typified this approach above all others. I am particularly grateful to him for writing the foreword to this book.

It was exactly the same across the Tasman Sea. Audrey Waugh and Donal Raethel of the Archives New Zealand; Denise Roughan, Shaun McGuire and Delores Hoy of the National Library of New Zealand; and Anna Beasley of the delightfully impressive National Army Museum at Waiouru could not have done more to accommodate my own schedule and make so much of their individual archives available. The Auckland War Memorial Museum and small museums from Invercargill to Russell were all fascinating. For New Zealand the individual who gave me most help is of course Lieutenant Colonel Christopher Pugsley, retired.

I am grateful to Squadron Leader Rana Chhina, retired, of the United Service Institution of India for sharing some of his comprehensive knowledge of the pre-1947 Indian Army and introducing me to the archives of his Institution.

In England, assistance has likewise been unsparing, friendly and supportive. The National Army Museum is the major depository of Birdwood archives. Much of my research took place while the Museum's Chelsea premises were being rebuilt. A day a week at the off-site store at Stevenage was a joy, with ready access to papers, uniforms and photograph albums. Sarah

Horne, Rob Fleming and Ben Fellowes were always welcoming and generous with their time. Curator Jasdeep Singh has an in-depth knowledge about the Museum's vast Indian collection and was instrumental in directing me to a number of Birdwood 'gems.'

Everywhere else was exactly the same: Clifton College – Dr C S Knighton, Principal Assistant Keeper of Archives and Paul Wigginton, photographer; Royal Military Academy Sandhurst – Dr Anthony Morton, Curator and Andrew Orgill, Senior Librarian; Peterhouse – Dr Roger Lovatt, archivist, and Erica McDonald, librarian; Hampton Court Palace – Sue Whittaker; Totnes Museum and Image Bank – Sue King and Val Price; National Portrait Gallery – Paul Cox, Associate Curator; the Cavalry and Guards Club – David Cowdrey, Club Secretary; together with the many staff of the Asian and African Studies Reading Room of the British Library; Cambridge University Library; the Institute of Historical Research; Imperial War Museum; the Liddell Hart Centre for Military Archives; The National Archives and the Royal United Services Institute. Everyone showed interest and gave of their time with warmth and a positive willingness to help.

Finally, it was a great honour to visit the Royal Archives and be granted permission of Her Majesty Queen Elizabeth to make use of some unique material. I am grateful to Alison Derrett for her personal assistance.

At many seminars and conferences, countless historians of all ages and standing have shown kindness and support. To them all I am very appreciative. Through such events, I first met the cartographer Barbara Taylor, and I am so pleased that she undertook producing my maps. Meeting Emma Dolman was a delight, as was delving through her Grandfather's treasured suitcase, with its wealth of souvenirs of the 1936 cruise on the *Lancastria* for 600 people to Gallipoli and Salonika.

My supervisor, Professor Carl Bridge, has been a constant and experienced source of encouragement and advice. He has definitely become an Australian friend. When he was ill, Professor William Philpott could not have done more to step into the breach. I am very grateful to the Menzies Australia Institute at King's College London for the focus it has provided me on Australian history and studies.

In conclusion, continuing and sustaining help has been given to me by my wife, Annette, and without this I would have never succeeded. I am lovingly and deeply grateful to her.

Foreword

Richard Farrimond's *Birdie* deals with one of the most long-lived of the senior British officers of the Great War, William Birdwood (1865-1951). Born into a British Indian community which had lived through what they called the Mutiny, Birdwood then lived into the atomic age, and indeed, was still writing his diary in the life-times of some of this book's potential readers – certainly that of its author, former Royal Signals officer turned aerospace expert and now qualified historian. Birdwood is seemingly easy to pigeon-hole: classic Indian Army officer, protégé of Kitchener, somewhat indolent corps and army commander who seemed to avoid the catastrophes and controversies which queered the careers and reputations of his fellows; commander-in-chief in India and field marshal, enjoying a long and apparently fulfilled retirement.

Farrimond's biography – the first study of Birdwood's entire life – complicates that easy characterization, in the most productive way. Like all good biographies, it obliges us to reconsider whether the image we have picked up of Birdwood is justified by the evidence which the author puts before us. Birdie, for all that he surely was personable and charming (as the nickname suggests), could not just have been the amiable good fellow or harmless old buffer as he has so often been dismissed. (I must say that I harboured doubts that the real dynamo of command in I Anzac Corps was its secretive chief of staff Cyril Brudenell White, who surely dominated his rather lazy corps commander, who (I thought) preferred pinning medals on subalterns' tunics to doing the hard work of trying to work out how to break through in the next big push. Perhaps not …)

Richard Farrimond has not been content to merely reproduce or replicate evidence that would allow us to continue to accept that easy dismissal. He shows that Birdwood matured from the inattentive schoolboy at Clifton College in the early 1880s into a competent Indian cavalry officer, and then into an effective staff officer. Appreciated by Lord Kitchener, who used Birdwood's ability to frame new answers to the problem of how to best use the valuable resource of the Indian Army. Birdwood then gained commands, chosen for the unpromising responsibility of directing an amateur 'colonial' force in one of the most doubtful campaigns the British empire's armies have ever attempted. As Farrimond shows, he survived the graveyard of generals' reputations to command a corps on the Western Front, becoming an army commander by the war's final year. Returning to his beloved Indian Army he saw it through difficult post-war years, carrying out his own further reorganization of it – essentially bequeathing it the form in which it approached the Second World War and independence.

This was a career which did not rely merely on luck, patronage or amiability, though Birdwood benefitted from all three: he could easily have been killed at Colenso in South Africa or on

Gallipoli. As Farrimond shows, Birdwood worked hard (he mastered *five* of the Indian Army's languages) and possessed a solid core of competence and command which belied his agreeable style. That he successfully commanded Australians and New Zealanders, gaining and retaining their respect and affection, testifies to the qualities, and the depths, which Farrimond brings out. There was indeed more to Birdwood than we might have assumed.

Writing a book such as this has demanded stamina, not just in consulting a mass of often contentious sources in British archives but also (it has to be said, unusually for a British historian) doing justice to the Antipodean sources, and visiting the sub-continent which formed the core of Birdwood's life. Farrimond has used that diverse range of evidence to produce an authoritative study which takes us from the north-west frontier and the heights of Chunuk Bair to the conference rooms of Simla and Montreuil (and then back to Simla). It has demanded that its author become familiar with the Indian Army, with frontier and imperial conflicts and with major campaigns and controversies in the Great War. In taking us with him on this journey – riding alongside Birdie, as it were – Richard Farrimond proves a thorough and thought-provoking companion and guide. Thanks to his *Birdie*, we can never again look on Birdwood with such complacency.

Professor Peter Stanley, FAHA
University of New South Wales, Canberra
March 2023

Introduction

'Embarked on *Persia* to take over my command of the Australian and New Zealand contingents in Egypt,' so wrote the then Lieutenant General William Birdwood in his diary on 12 December 1914. 'My command' is a proud, positive and personal statement, and it would change his life. Nine days later he arrived at Suez and 'found a special train' for Cairo, where he was met by Generals Maxwell, Bridges and Godley, respectively commanding the troops in Egypt, the Australians, and the New Zealanders.[1] Birdwood was forty-nine years of age, the scion of a family with West Country roots and of civil and military service in India. He had attended a prominent Public School and Sandhurst. His successful military career had been built on sound foundations with the Indian cavalry, active service on the North-West Frontier and in South Africa, and staff work under his mentor, Lord Kitchener. A few years earlier he had been described as 'the *beau idéal* of what a British officer and English gentleman should be.'[2] Birdwood would take his Australian and New Zealand Army Corps (ANZAC) to Gallipoli, lead the fight in their sector and command the overall evacuation from those shores. He would take 'his' Australians to France and retain administrative command of them on promotion to Army Commander in 1918. As one of five such British commanders under Field Marshal Sir Douglas Haig on 11 November 1918, he would complete almost exactly four years of operational command.

Today Birdwood is very little known by either Britons or Australians. To the former he is merely the commander of Anzacs at Gallipoli and to the latter he falls between poor British senior commanders, who attract opprobrium, and native Australian commanders, who are avidly studied. After the Great War, Birdwood was fêted throughout Australia and New Zealand during his 1920 tour of both Dominions.[3] As an Indian Army officer, he then returned to India, eventually becoming the first Commander-in-Chief (C-in-C) to serve in the rank of Field Marshal.[4]

1 Birdwood diaries are held at the National Army Museum, [hereafter NAM] 6707-19 [Papers of Field Marshal Lord Birdwood (1865-1951)] -1 to - 56, except those for 1915-20 which are at the Australian War Memorial, [hereafter AWM] 3DRL/3376 [Papers of Birdwood, Lord William Riddell (Field Marshal, b.1865-d.1951)] 1/1 - 1/5. All diary references are hereafter made by year only, e.g. 1914 Diary.

2 *The Memorial to Old Cliftonians who fell in the South African War* (Bristol, 1904), 10-11.

3 Birdwood's name is honoured by the naming of the town of Birdwood, South Australia, and numerous Birdwood Streets and Avenues. There are over 70 geographical references to Birdwood in Australia.

4 For the 138 Field Marshals of the British Army, see T A Heathcote, *Dictionary of Field Marshals of The British Army* (Barnsley: Pen & Sword, 1999).

From early in his career Birdwood engaged with the upper echelons of the British Indian hierarchy. At the age of 27 he became Adjutant of the Viceroy's Body Guard and served at this viceregal level for six years. After the South African War, he spent a further ten years in prestigious Indian Army appointments. During the First World War, he corresponded regularly with the Defence Ministers of both Australia and New Zealand. All this was before his last ten years in India, after which his engagement at a high political level amounted to nearly thirty years.

In his personal relationships, there was a constant theme that most people seemed to like Birdwood. When he handed over command of the Kohat Brigade on the Frontier, his personal report from the General Officer Commanding (GOC) Northern Command observed: 'His tact is known to all and his personal charm of manner makes all men work for him and with him.'[5] When Birdwood reported to General Sir Ian Hamilton on 21 March 1915, Hamilton recorded that 'Little Birdie, now grown up into a grand general, turned up at 3 pm. I was enchanted to see him.'[6] In June 1918 after Birdwood had left the Australian Corps to become Commander Fifth Army, General Monash wrote of the relationship between Birdwood and Australian soldiers: 'General Birdwood's personality counts for everything in the AIF [Australian Imperial Force]. He possesses the complete confidence of the whole force. … He has been the chief factor in creating and maintaining its prestige and its spirit of unity.'[7] His interactions with people are recorded in his diaries. He kept a personal diary from his last year at school, 1882, until two years before his death, 1949 – sixty-one volumes.[8] Six are missing from his days as a young officer before he first met his wife. Perhaps he thought that entries about earlier dalliances were best politely discarded. Reading nearly 10,500 pages of diary has brought me close to my subject. He had dynamism and panache. He was fit and robust. He loved the profession of arms and was proud to be a leader. His tender affection for his wife reflected a gentler side of him. A full and objective study of these diaries produces a rich and varied portrait.

No full-scale study of Birdwood exists, apart from his own autobiography, *Khaki and Gown.*[9] No comprehensive research has been done on his whole life.[10] John Lee commented that 'there has been no modern biography and much of the writing on Birdwood has been in the context of wider studies of the Anzacs.'[11] Reviewing Australian military biographies, David Horner

5 British Library, African and Asian Studies [hereafter BL AAS], Mss Eur D 686 [Birdwood papers] folio 77, memo no 1855 dated 25/27 March 1912, from AMS to GOC Northern Army to GOC Kohat Bde.

6 General Sir Ian Hamilton, *Gallipoli Diary*, vol. I & II (London: Edward Arnold, 1920), 40. Birdwood stood five feet seven inches – calculated from the size of Birdwood's service dress jacket worn at Gallipoli, AWM RELAWM01099.

7 BL AAS, Mss Eur D 686 folio 77, letter from John Monash AIF Corps Commander to Senator Pearce, Defence Minister, 21 June 1918.

8 See fn. 1.

9 FM Lord Birdwood, *Khaki and Gown* (London: Ward Lock, 1941).

10 Birdwood appears in both the ODNB and the ADB: Robert Rhodes James, *Birdwood, William Riddell, first Baron Birdwood (1865–1951)),* Oxford Dictionary of National Biography, 2004, (https://wwwoxforddnd.com/view/10.1093 accessed 23 March 2021) and A J Hill, Birdwood, *William Riddell (Baron Birdwood) (1865–1951*), Australian Dictionary of Biography (ADB), (http://adb.anu.edu.au/biography/birdwood-william-riddell-5240 accessed 23 March 2021).

11 John Lee, "William Birdwood," in Haig's Generals, ed. Ian F W Beckett and Steven J Corvi (Barnsley: Pen & Sword, 2006), 33-35.

identified Birdwood as one of six persons for whom studies were required.[12] John Bourne stated: 'Birdwood, who not only commanded Fifth Army in 1918 but was also for three years GOC Australian Imperial Force, has been largely ignored and awaits a modern study.'[13] More recently Michael McKernan wrote that there is 'no full scale biography of this general.'[14]

Why has no study been made? The answer to this question has fascinated and challenged me. I attended the same school as Birdwood, Clifton College in Bristol, as did my father and my three sons. When my father first came to visit me there, he was horrified that I knew nothing of Birdwood, which just happened to be the name on the outside of the building that contained my form room. Now, even the name Birdwood has gone, replaced by that of a more recent generous benefactor. Like Birdwood my father served as an officer in the Indian Army. He instilled in me an admiration for that institution which Birdwood loved. In 2005, I had the privilege of visiting my father's old Regiment in Pakistan and caught something of the mystique of the old Indian Army that had attracted both men. Birdwood's old Regiment also transferred to the Pakistan Army on Partition.[15] My second career in the satellite industry took me to Australia on numerous occasions and to Canberra in particular. The Australian War Memorial (AWM), the creation of another Old Cliftonian, Charles Bean, overwhelmed me and it was there that I first delved into archives. Studying for a history Masters at King's College London gave me the opportunity to study a little of Birdwood. I found that I liked the man and was interested in what made him who he was. An academic study of Field Marshal Lord Birdwood beyond a biography was called for and this summation of all of my strands of interest is an answer to that.

While a study of Birdwood might concentrate on his year in command at Gallipoli, he commanded for just under a further three years on the Western Front. Dermot Millar produced an Australian-centric thesis, later published, which narrowly focussed on Birdwood's wartime corps command, identifying his inspirational leadership by example but with very little of the pre-1914 Birdwood.[16] Moreover, at the end of the war, Birdwood still had ten years to serve in two prestigious appointments in India. Those last ten years link back to his experiences with Kitchener and others in the Indian Army from 1902 to 1914. For a study of Birdwood to be comprehensive therefore his whole life of service should be addressed.

Birdwood was first and foremost a commander and command must be a theme throughout any study of him. Other historiographical themes must mesh with this. His leadership was the basis of his success at commanding, and the maintenance of the morale of those he led was vitally important to him. Leadership and morale are together a further theme. His service stretched across two major organisations – the British and Indian Armies. Understanding the politics of both of these and how they influenced his career are two more themes. Birdwood was a man of Empire and how the military cooperation between the British, Indian and the

12 David Horner, "Australian Military Biographies," in *Ranging Shots: New Directions in Australian Military History*, ed. Carl Bridge (London: Sir Robert Menzies Centre for Australian Studies, 1998), 88-89.

13 Simon Robbins, *British Generalship During the Great War: The military Career of Sir Henry Horne (1861-1929)* (Farnham: Ashgate, 2010), Introduction.

14 Michael McKernan, *Gallipoli: A Short History* (Crows Nest: Allen & Unwin, 2010), 50.

15 5 Horse, known as Probyn's Horse.

16 John Dermot Millar, "A study in the limitations of command: General Sir William Birdwood and the AIF 1914-1918," (PhD: University of New South Wales, 1993); *The Soul of Anzac* (North Melbourne: Australian Scholarly, 2015).

Dominion armies developed during his service must also be a theme – what one scholar has perceptively called the Imperial Army Project.[17] Anzac encompassed two of those dominion armies. Birdwood encouraged the wider usage of the term Anzac and thereby the foundation of the Anzac legend. This was a fundamental building block of the Australian identity and makes the final historiographical theme for this study.

The historiography of military commanders is vast but there are distinct variations of approach to it. Sir Hew Strachan provides a useful *entrée* to this in his introduction to the compilation of over one hundred military entries in the *Dictionary of National Biography* between 1900 and 1990, though sadly and notably this excluded Birdwood. Strachan identified the importance of 'administrative, political and cerebral qualities' as well as 'fighting attributes', recognising 'extraordinary courage, if not physical then certainly moral.'[18] It is interesting to note 'political' in the list of qualities and perhaps not surprising as earlier Strachan had himself written about whether the British Army was or had been truly apolitical. He concluded that the Army had acted politically in its own interests.[19] Also Mark Urban described how 'those British generals who left a great legacy combined military skill with a mastery of politics, of dealing successfully with the civilian holders of power.'[20] Birdwood was a politically astute officer and his ultimate position, Commander-in-Chief, India, was highly political. John Connell wrote about two later political C-in-Cs – Auchinleck and Wavell – taking a whole-life approach to both.[21] Auchinleck's appointment as C-in-C Middle East in June 1941 corresponded in career terms to Birdwood's arrival at Suez. Connell devoted nearly a third of his book to Auchinleck's life before this command, allowing Connell to assess Auchinleck at this crucial point. As Auchinleck and Wavell were in effect swapping jobs, Connell compared the two of them. [22] He then described the political challenges in Auchinleck's career and emphasised Auchinleck's staunch upright character, developed from childhood, and how this influenced his decisions. As Viceroy of India, Wavell had an even greater political role than Auchinleck. Connell died shortly after his book covering Wavell's life until June 1941 appeared, so how Connell would have treated Wavell as Viceroy will never be known, although Connell had planned and written the next stage as far as 1943. The book was completed by Michael Roberts. Wavell's early life was again considered important, as was his recognised intellectualism and strong love of poetry.[23] To read the preface of Wavell's own anthology of poetry, the chapter introductions and the occasional notes on individual poems is to gain an insight into the man himself.[24] Connell was less exhaustive in

17 Douglas E Delaney, *The Imperial Army Project* (Oxford: OUP, 2017). Delaney does acknowledge Darwin for this apt term John Darwin, *The Empire Project* (Cambridge: CUP, 2009), 3-4.

18 Hew Strachan, ed. *Military Lives* (Oxford Oxford University Press, 2002).

19 *The Politics of the British Army* (Oxford: Oxford University Press, 1997).

20 Mark Urban, *Generals: Ten British Commanders who Shaped the World* (London: Faber and Faber, 2005), 301.

21 John Connell, *Auchinleck* (London: Cassell, 1959). *Wavell Scholar and Soldier* (London: Collins, 1964). John Connell and Brigadier Michael Roberts, *Wavell Supreme Commander* (London: Collins, 1969); See also Philip Warner, *Auchinleck The Lonely Soldier* (London: Buchan and Enwright, 1981).

22 Connell, *Auchinleck*, ix, 237, 45 & 49.

23 Two small pamphlets show the depth of Wavell's study of his profession: General Sir Archibald Wavell, *Generals and Generalship* (Harmondsworth: Penquin Books, 1941); FM Viscount Wavell, *The Good Soldier* (Bombay: Times of India, 1947).

24 I treasure my father's copy of Wavell's anthology of poetry, A P Wavell, *Other Men's Flowers* (London: Jonathan Cape, 1971).

his quotations from letters and documents than with Auchinleck. Wavell had never kept a diary but on becoming Viceroy decided to keep a journal, later edited by Sir Penderel Moon.[25] Birdwood's diaries are not detailed enough to permit a similar approach. Certainly, taking stock of Auchinleck as he embarked for North Africa is an appealing approach by Connell, whose own biographer felt that more could have been made of Auchinleck 'the man, as opposed to the soldier' and suggested that it was Wavell's own writings that give more of 'a window on the man.'[26]

Beckett and Corvi's introduction to *Haig's Generals* provides a sound comparison in command styles, particularly regarding the balance between control and guidance.[27] It also draws attention to the importance of the commanders' key supporting staff, such as between Birdwood and Brudenell White. Other individual studies on Birdwood's fellow Army commanders – Byng, Horne, Plumer and Rawlinson – reinforce these points.[28] Haig, the commander of all these generals, has himself been studied at great length from Duff Cooper's admiring work onwards.[29] Haig was also an Old Cliftonian, a cavalryman, and successful in South Africa. Although an officer in the British rather than the Indian Army, he served for two years in India as Inspector-General of Cavalry and another two as Chief of Staff to the C-in-C. Birdwood served under him for three years, from 1916 to 1918. By 1963 Haig's reputation was as a commander who presided over unnecessary butchery but that year John Terraine produced a thoughtful masterpiece in Haig's defence.[30] Terraine carefully rebutted individual criticisms. Birdwood still suffers from a few well-worn criticisms, such as inability with staff work and Haig's dislike of him. These and others will be addressed in my study and refuted. Despite further positive works, Haig remained rather tarnished in the eyes of the public.[31] Seventy years after his death Brian Bond and Nigel Cave produced a balanced reappraisal.[32] Their collection of essays gave an insight into characteristics of a commander that can be applied to Birdwood. Haig had mental and physical robustness, and Birdwood saw himself as robust. He recorded that he 'must be among the very few who, landing on the 25th April, was able to stay and see things through without a day's absence till the final evacuation on 9th January, 1916; and my record is due entirely to the excellence of my digestive organs!' Accurate self-assessment and confidence in one's judgement, together with courtesy, self-control and religious belief are also cited in the essays and all feature

25 Penderel Moon, ed. *Wavell The Viceroy's Journal* (Oxford: Oxford University Press, 1973); See also, Bernard Ferguson, *Wavell Portrait of a Soldier* (London: Collins, 1961).
26 Robin Bryer, *Jack: A literary biography of John Connell (John Henry Robertson 1909-1965)* (Milton Keynes: AuthorHouse, 2010), 249-73.
27 Ian F W Beckett and Steven J Corvi, eds., *Haig's Generals* (Barnsley: Pen & Sword, 2006).
28 Jeffery Williams, *Byng of Vimy* (London: Leo Cooper, 1983); Robbins, *British Generalship during the Great War: the military career of Sir Henry Horne (1861-1929)*; Geoffrey Powell, *Plumer: The Soldier's General* (London: Leo Cooper, 1990); Robin Prior and Trevor Wilson, *Command on the Western Front: The Military Career of Sir Henry Rawlinson (1914-1918)* (Oxford: Blackwell, 1992).
29 Duff Cooper, *Haig* (London: Faber & Faber, 1936).
30 John Terraine, *Douglas Haig The Educated Soldier* (London: Hutchinson, 1963).
31 General Sir James Marshall-Cornwall, *Haig as a Military Commander* (London: Batsford, 1973); E K G Sixsmith, *Douglas Haig* (Worthing: Littlehampton Book Services, 1976); Philip Warner, *Field Marshal Earl Haig* (London: Bodley Head, 1991).
32 Brian Bond and Nigel Cave, *Haig: A Reappraisal 70 Years On* (London: Leo Cooper, 1999).

in Birdwood's life. Haig's admiration for hard work and 'canniness' are also highlighted, but canny does not describe Birdwood.[33]

Field Marshal Viscount Slim's Burma memoirs are obligatory reading for anyone studying leadership and morale.[34] On 7 and 8 August 1915, as a subaltern on Sari Bair, Slim led his company of Royal Warwicks in a joint assault with the Gurkhas, with whom he would later serve. His feats gained the personal recognition of Birdwood.[35] Slim was never C-in-C India but did become Governor-General of Australia, an appointment earlier sought by but denied to Birdwood. Slim's writings on *The Essentials of Morale* open the Sandhurst handbook *Serve to Lead*. There his thoughts on morale are developed into 'a fighting spirit for our men and a confidence in themselves.' These are what Birdwood strove for and achieved on both Gallipoli and the Western Front. Morale is ... 'based on leadership' and 'good morale is impossible without good leaders.'[36] Terraine well summarised British Military Leadership in the First World War, closing with the achievement of absolute victory.[37] Birdwood was focused on victory.

In South Africa and during the First World War Birdwood's service was under the command of the British Army and its politics, particularly patronage, influenced his career. Being an Indian Army officer, he naturally admired and had real affection for Field Marshal Lord Roberts. He was neither a member of the Roberts (Indian) ring, nor of Field Marshal Lord Wolseley's (African) ring. [38] Birdwood did, however, have his own powerful patron in Lord Kitchener, who from 1900 to 1916 considerably influenced Birdwood's career. There is a reverse to patronage and certainly Birdwood's interactions with Field Marshal Lord Nicholson – 'Old Nick', an unpopular character – were less than positive. This period also saw attendance at Staff College becoming increasingly important. Rapid promotion hindered Birdwood's attendance either as a student or on the staff. Birdwood was in India when in 1902 the position of C-in-C at the War Office ceased and four years later the General Staff was established. At Suez at the end of 1914 Birdwood returned to a different, and to him a less familiar, British Army.[39]

When Birdwood did finally leave India, he had served for close on 46 years. The changes that he had seen and overseen were remarkable in men, organisation, equipment and achievements. He had joined an army of 150,000. At the end of the War India had provided 985,000 combatants with 552,000 serving abroad. As C-in-C Birdwood oversaw the start of mechanisation.[40] His father's success in the Indian Civil service ensured that Birdwood met senior people from the start. These seem to have liked him and offered him attachments. He then made a success

33 See also J P Harris, *Douglas Haig and the First World War* (Cambridge: Cambridge University Press, 2009); Gary Mead, *The Good Soldier: The Biography of Douglas Haig* (London: Atlantic Books, 2007); Gary Sheffield, *The Chief: Douglas Haig and the British Army* (London: Aurum Press, 2011).

34 FM Sir William Slim, *Defeat into Victory* (London: Cassell, 1956). For reminiscences of earlier actions, see *Unofficial History* (London: Cassell, 1959).

35 Ronald Lewin, *Slim: The Standardbearer* (London: Leo Cooper, 1976), 22-3 and 42.

36 *Serve to Lead (An Anthology)*, (Camberley: Royal Military Academy Sandhurst, 1959), 3-8, 10.

37 Ann Clayton, ed. *Essays on Leadership and War* (Reading: Western Front Association, 1998), 43-54.

38 Tim Travers, *The Killing Ground* (London: Allen & Unwin, 1987), 6 & 8; Ian F W Beckett, *A British Profession of Arms: The Politics of Command in the Late Victorian Army.* (Oklahoma: University of Oklahoma, 2018), 74-98. Birdwood died in Wolseley's old bedroom in Hampton Court Palace.

39 David French and Brian Holden Reid, eds., *The British General Staff: Reform and Innovation c. 1890-1939* (London: Frank Cass, 2002), 41-45 & 144-45.

40 Kaushik Roy, *The Army in British India: From Colonial Warfare to Total War 1857-1947* (London: Bloomsbury, 2013), 46 & 82-85.

of each opportunity and these grew. As in the British Army, there was patronage, notably through the Viceroy and the civil administration. Early in his career Birdwood made Viceregal connections. The C-in-C India also commanded the British troops in India – 70,000 in 1885 – and the post usually alternated between British and Indian Army officers. In the Indian Army itself the number of British officers was small – seven serving in Birdwood's regiment at any time. Success on operations was a necessary stepping stone to appointments and promotion, and so such service was actively sought after by Birdwood and others. Many joined for this experience. The fact that life in the Indian Army was financially easier was an added bonus.[41]

In 1906 Staff College accepted its first Australian officer, Brudenell White – who was to be Birdwood's chief of staff for over three years. In 1909-12, White served as a staff officer at the War Office. His service typified the efforts to bring an imperial focus to the armies of Britain, India and the Dominions. The South African war had shown the need for a homogeneous army, directed by a general staff with common procedures – in effect an Imperial army. Delaney, a retired Canadian officer as well as an historian, details the Elgin Commission, the Esher Committee and Haldane's impact as Secretary of State for War as major drivers for Imperial reform.[42] Birdwood was in key positions during this period before 1914 and furthermore his patron, Kitchener, left India with invitations to visit Australia and New Zealand to advise on defence and army matters.[43] Jeffrey Grey described the transition of the new Australian Commonwealth forces into the imperial sphere as did Christopher Pugsley for New Zealand.[44] By 1914 all Dominions and India had prepared their mobilisation plans for possible war. The war saw Birdwood as a committed man of empire. After the war he built on this status, such that his appearances at the Royal unveiling of the Villers-Bretonneux Cemetery and at Ataturk's funeral were occasions, as will be shown, when messages were sent about international relationships.

During the war the Anzac soldiers created their own legend by their actions. Their commander and very much their leader was Birdwood. He encouraged personal pride in their achievements, including on the Western Front. Gallipoli and Anzac were, however, the two words always associated with national honour. Gavin Souter and Joan Beaumont trace the response of the homeland to the war.[45] It is sad that Souter ends his masterpiece in 1919, for in 1920 Birdwood toured Australia for five months and the pride of those who had served abroad was shared with widows, mothers, families and all varieties of communities. It became a national feeling, translated to the Second World War and with subtle changes of emphasis to the present day. Jenny Macleod has described how writers tried to capture the special nature of the Anzac struggle at Gallipoli and the ongoing commemoration.[46] New books and articles continue now, past the centenary of the founding event.

41 Philip Mason, *A Matter of Honour* (London: Jonathan Cape, 1974), 371-75. See also Heathcote, *Dictionary of Field Marshals of The British Army*; Daniel Marston, *The Indian Army and the End of the Raj* (New York: CUP, 2014).
42 Delaney, *The Imperial Army Project*, 7-43.
43 John Pollock, *Kitchener* (London: Constable, 2001), 343-46.
44 Jeffrey Grey, *A Military History of Australia* (Cambridge: Cambridge University Press, 1999); Christopher Pugsley, *Gallipoli The New Zealand Story*, 5th ed. (Auckland: Libro International, 2014).
45 Gavin Souter, *Lion and Kangaroo* (Sydney: Collins, 1976); Joan Beaumont, *Broken Nation* (Crows Nest: Allen & Unwin, 2013).
46 Jenny Macleod, Reconsidering Gallipoli (Manchester: Manchester University Press, 2004); For commemoration see, Gallipoli (Oxford: OUP, 2015).

How may these themes be applied to Birdwood? It appears that a whole life approach is beneficial in order to understand the man as well as the commander. A significant portion of the study should include the early years, as a number of the above works have shown. Connell's method of providing a review of the man as he embarks on his greatest or most life-changing challenge is an attractive one. Special emphasis on the political side is essential for Birdwood, and particularly his final ten years in India when he reached the zenith of military-political power. His qualities of command are essential for study, particularly on operations – the Black Mountain Expedition 1891, the Tirah Campaign 1897, the Second Anglo-Boer War 1899-1902, the Mohmand Expedition 1908 and of course Gallipoli and the Western Front.

With the exception of the Black Mountain Expedition, all are covered at length in his diaries. These are the major primary sources for this study. Turning a page, and discovering a dried snakeskin, one does wonder if anyone else has ever turned that same page, let alone studied its contents. The handwriting in the first diary, 1882, is easy to read but decipherment is harder as the writing deteriorates year by year. By 1915 it is definitely not easy to read. That diary has very probably been the most studied. Apart from in the National Army Museum and the Australian War Memorial, his personal papers are held at a national level at the British Library Asian and African Studies, the National Archives, the Imperial War Museum, and the Liddell Hart Centre for Military Archives at King's College London. At a more local and personal level, papers may be found at places such as Totnes Museum, Clifton College and Peterhouse, Cambridge.[47]

With these resources, my study takes three interrelated approaches to studying Birdwood's life and career. The first is to understand the man who arrived in Egypt just after Christmas 1914 to take command of the Australian and New Zealand forces and trained them there with a view to taking them to France. The man who arrived was a summation of his family heritage; West Country and India; his schooling; his military training; his first Regiments; his approach to language training; his operational experiences; his proficiency at the viceregal stratum of Indian life; and finally, his highly successful tour as an independent Brigade commander on India's North-West Frontier. The second approach is to study his wartime generalship, largely at Corps level but including his Army command from May 1918, exploring his personal impact on the planning stages, identifying when he had options, or perhaps should have sought options to influence events, and assessing his personal successes or otherwise. The third approach is an examination of his political performance as a commander both in wartime, with his extensive contacts with Australian and New Zealand politicians, subsequently as Commander Northern Command in India and finally as C-in-C India. The Twenties were a turbulent and challenging decade in India politically and it is of interest to explore Birdwood's involvement. Finally, and linking war and peace, there is an account of how Birdwood's hopes to become – and King George V's wishes that he should become – Governor-General of Australia were dashed by Prime Minister James Scullin's desire to choose an Australian. Through this matrix of approaches, Birdwood's successes and failures will be assessed in order to arrive at a considered evaluation of his public career.

Although he had many years of public service remaining, his wartime service was recognised in 1919 with a baronetcy and Birdwood chose as his title: 'Baronet of Anzac and of Totnes, in

47 Birdwood's Mastership at Peterhouse is the reason for 'Gown' in *Khaki and Gown*.

the County of Devon.'[48] Totnes was the focus of his family roots in the West Country and it is there that we begin William Riddell Birdwood's story.

48 *London Gazette*, 30 December 1919, 15988.

1

Origins

In August 1919, General Birdwood was granted the Freedom of Totnes. The Mayor 'noted that five of his [Birdwood's] ancestors had been made Freemen of the city since 1779'.[1] A study of Birdwood's family background reveals the legacies he grew up with and then took into his adult life. His first diary left to posterity covers the last year of his school days. This is the only one in which he makes any great use of the pages for notes. Here he wrote about his family and ancestors: a family quarrel in the first half of the eighteenth century: the change of 'u' to 'i' in Birdwood; the change of the coat of arms, and 'illegitimate sons' and 'disreputable brothers' who went to Australia.[2] Years later when the Field Marshal was finishing his time in India, *The Times of India* wrote a detailed article about his 'family connexions with India', which starts with his Devonshire ancestors, who moved to Plymouth and there became agents for the East India Company. Later generations moved to India and Birdwood's immediate forebears included distinguished civil and military personages.[3] This information came from Birdwood himself. So, he carried from his last days at school to his last days in military service a personal interest and pride in his family background.

The name of Birdwood is possibly a combination of the Anglo-Saxon *Birht* and *wuda*: meaning bright-wood.[4] Bodgewood, Bogewood, Byrdewood, Birdwood and Burdwood appear in early documents. Traditionally the Anglo-Saxon Bishop Burwould is linked to the origin of the name of Birdwood. King Canute granted the Bishop land using the following words: "I Cnut, do grant unto my most faithful Bishop who is called by the well-known name, Burwould …".[5] 'Bishop Burwould's nephew seems to have settled in Exeter; after which there is a complete blank until about 1500 AD, when the name recurs in occasional deeds of land to Birdwoods and others conjointly for public purposes.'[6] Burke's *Peerage* lists Birdwood's earliest predecessor as Richard

1 *The Mail* (Adelaide, SA), 23 August 1919, 1.
2 Diary 1882.
3 *The Times of India*, 28 November 1930, 10.
4 See <http://www.utexas.edu/cola/centers/lrc/books/asd/dict-G.html> (accessed 28 March 2014) Linguistics Research Center at the University of Texas online edition of T. Northcote Toller (ed.), *An Anglo-Saxon Dictionary, based on the manuscript collections of the late Joseph Bosworth* (Oxford, 1898).
5 *The Illustrated Western Daily News*, 9 May 1914, 26.
6 Plymouth and West Devon Record Office [hereafter PWDRO] 1390/17, Notes on the Family Birdwood, A R Birdwood, 28 July 1911. This was most likely to be Birdwood's cousin Alan Roger.

Birdwood of Preston, Devon, born 1536.[7] He was the great-grandfather of the Reverend James Birdwood 'of an ancient family which had an estate at Preston, in West Alvington, Devon, which hath been in the name of the Birdwoods for many generations'.[8] James was born in 1626. He was evicted for non-conformity from his parish of St Petrox, Dartmouth. After many further forced moves he was given hospitality in Totnes by Dr Richard Burthogge, a philosopher.[9] This is the first mention of Totnes.[10] James Birdwood is recorded as having a saying: "tis better to be preserved in brine than to rot in honey". He died in 1693. Calamy's lengthy description of his life and its troubles paints a picture of a man of principle and persistence. 'He was very humble, and eminently faithful, and yet prudent in reproving as there was occasion.'[11] Any descendant reading about a forebear like this would have good reason to take pride in his heritage and perhaps use such a person as an example to follow in some way. The *Times of India* article also stated that Birdwood 'inherited from his forbears … a fearless devotion to the truth', and then describes one of them, the Rev James Birdwood.[12]

James Birdwood 'had seventeen children but three only survived him. He was a very tender father to them, and greatly concerned about their souls; daily putting up earnest prayers for them with tears. All of them who lived to years of discretion, gave him ground to hope that a good work was wrought in them'.[13] The eldest, John, lived in Kingsbridge, a mile away from West Alvington, and so did his son, Roger. In the next generation, Richard Birdwood (1745-1810) was the Mayor of Plymouth and the first predecessor to become a Freeman of Totnes.[14] In 1796 he became the Agent for the East India Company in Plymouth. He held this post on his own until 1798 and then until 1810 jointly with his son, Peter, who himself held it solely until 1817.[15] The link with India had commenced. Peter Birdwood (1774-1839) was the great-grandfather of the Field Marshal. Peter was a Freeman of both Totnes and Plymouth. He 'raised and commanded the Plymouth Volunteers to meet Napoleon's threatened invasion in 1805'.[16] Three hundred years of family history in and around South Devon had passed before Peter's death. His descendants were to make a significant mark in India.

7 Leslie G. Pine, Burke's *Genealogical and Heraldic History of the Peerage, Baronetage and Knightage, Privy Council and Order of Precedence,* 99th Edition (London, 1949), 194-5. PWRDO 1390/13 'Birdwood family tree tracing from Richard Birdwood of West Alvington, born in 1550', does state that dates such as this one of 1550 have been verified from parish registers.

8 Edmund Calamy, *A Continuation of the Account of the Ministers, Lecturers, Masters and Fellows of Colleges, and Schoolmasters, who were Ejected and Silenced after the Restoration in 1660, by or before the Act for Uniformity* (London, 1728), 244-9.

9 Michael Ayers, "Burthogge, Richard (bap. 1638, d. 1705)." Michael Ayers In *Oxford Dictionary of National Biography,* edited by H. C. G. Matthew and Brian Harrison (Oxford: OUP, 2004). <http://www.oxforddnb.com/view/article/4120> (accessed 23 March 2014).

10 PWDRO 1390/17, Notes on the Family Birdwood, records that the house at Preston was sold around this time. When alterations were being made to this house 'circa 1900, names and initials of many of the Birdwood family were found on its stones.'

11 Calamy, *A Continuation,* 247-8.

12 *The Times of India,* 28 November 1930,10.

13 Calamy, *A Continuation,* 248.

14 *Totnes Times*, 23 August 1919.

15 H V Bowen, Margarette Lincoln, and Nigel Rigby (eds.), *The Worlds of the East India Company* (Woodbridge, 2002), 41.

16 Birdwood, *Khaki and Gown*, 26.

His eldest son, Christopher, entered the East India Company's service in 1825 and 'was in the Bombay Army for 52 years. For a long period as Commissary-General of the Bombay Army, he gave invaluable service during the Mutiny, organizing the bullock-train between Bombay, Wassind and Mhow. He married the daughter of the Rev Joseph Taylor (1790-1859), an agent of the London Missionary Society stationed for many years at Belgaum'.[17] General Christopher Birdwood died in 1882. His grandson, William Birdwood, first visited him, aged three, when he came home to England with his mother.[18] He later records that his grandfather was happy living at Bideford, though he was rather apologetic about not living 'in South Devon where, in the vicinity of Totnes, Kingsbridge, Plymouth and West Alvington, the Birdwoods had dwelt for many generations'.[19] General Christopher's eldest surviving son was George Christopher Molesworth, Birdwood's uncle. He was born at Belgaum in 1832, and 'educated at the new grammar school, Plymouth, the Dollar Academy, Clackmannanshire, and the University of Edinburgh. In 1854, he obtained the degree of MD and was admitted to the Royal College of Surgeons, whereupon he joined the Bombay medical service as an assistant surgeon.' Arriving in India in 1856 he shortly thereafter 'married the 24-year-old Frances Anne, eldest daughter of Edward Tolcher RN of Harewood, Plymouth, with whom he had three sons and two daughters'.[20] After serving as a surgeon in the Persian War of 1856-7, he held successively the professorships of anatomy and physiology, and of botany and *materia medica* at the Grant Medical College, Bombay, established for medical education of Indians in the Bombay Presidency.[21] In addition he was 'registrar to the newly founded University of Bombay, curator of the government museum, secretary to the Bombay branch of the Royal Asiatic Society, a founder of the Victoria Botanical Gardens, and a member of the municipality. These activities culminated in his election in 1864 as sheriff of Bombay'.[22] Unfortunately he fell ill in 1868 and had to return to England. He embarked on a new career both at the India Office and in authorship 'as an interpreter to his own countrymen of Indian life, art and culture and as a warm and constant friend of Indians'.[23] He was renowned for his kindness to anyone who showed an interest in India.[24] He died in 1917.[25] He clearly loved India and her people and left a lasting impression on his nephew.

Christopher Birdwood's second surviving son, Herbert Mills Birdwood – Field Marshal Birdwood's father, also made his career in India. Born in 1837, also at Belgaum, he was educated like his brother at Plymouth Grammar School and Edinburgh University where he read mathematics. In 1854, he entered Peterhouse, Cambridge, graduated in mathematics in 1858, and then passed the Indian Civil Service examination. He arrived back in India in 1859 and

17 *The Times of India,* 28 November 1930, 10.
18 1946 Diary, 11 May.
19 Birdwood, *Khaki and Gown*, 26.
20 Valentine Chirol, 'Birdwood, Sir George Christopher Molesworth (1832–1917)', rev. Katherine Prior, *Oxford Dictionary of National Biography* (Oxford, 2004) <http://www.oxforddnb.com/view/article/31896> (accessed 24 March 2014).
21 *The Indian Year Book 1908* (Bombay, 1908), 445.
22 Chirol, 'Birdwood,' *ODNB.*
23 *The Times of India,* 28 November 1930,10.
24 Chirol, Birdwood, Sir George Christopher Molesworth *ODNB.*
25 In 1915 it was noted that he had twenty-five nephews serving in uniform. *Pioneer*, 22 October 1915, 8. With thanks to Peter Stanley, *Die in Battle, Do Not Despair: The Indians on Gallipoli, 1915* (Solihull, 2015), 30.

served as an assistant collector in a number of locations in Western India. In 1861, he married Edith Marion Sidonie, eldest daughter of Surgeon-Major Elijah George Halhed Impey FRCS, of the Bombay horse artillery and postmaster-general of the Bombay presidency.[26] In 1863 he decided to follow the judicial line of the service and was appointed under-secretary in the judicial, political, and educational departments and secretary to the Bombay legislative council. His second son, William Riddell Birdwood, was born in 1865. Two years later Herbert was appointed Secretary of the Legislative Council and it was during this time that William went with his mother and elder sister and brother to England. Herbert then progressed from Acting Registrar of the Bombay High Court, to Judge of the Sadar Court, Sind and subsequently as acting Judge of the Bombay High Court, becoming permanent in 1885. This was the year in which his second son returned to India, and the anniversary of which Birdwood often referred to in his diary with affectionate comments on seeing his parents once more. Herbert was a member of the Executive Council of the Bombay Government from 1892 to 1897, including acting as Governor for a short period in 1895. Latterly he also served as the Vice-Chancellor of the University of Bombay, whose gardens benefitted from his enthusiasm.[27] He left India in 1897 with a farewell dinner at the Byculla Club, Bombay.[28] The Chief Justice included in his praises the 'large hearted hospitality' of Mrs Birdwood that all had enjoyed.[29] Herbert finally settled in Twickenham, writing on Indian matters, and was both 'a JP for Middlesex and a commissioner of Richmond Bridge.' Like his father, he 'enjoyed gardening'.[30] He died in 1907, by which time Birdwood was working for Lord Kitchener in India. In its obituary, *The Times of India* recorded at length both his judicial career and contributions to the University, but also portrayed him as a hard-working man, with only four years furlough out of his thirty-eight years of service, and whose 'good works, kind deeds, and a friendly accessibility to all who had claims upon his time… won him the good-will of all sorts and conditions of men'. He had a 'real liking for the people' and maintained at his own expense 'a school for servant's children' in 'his own compound'.[31] His son William described his father as 'the finest example of the English Christian gentleman' that he had ever known and was much saddened by his sudden death at the age of 70.[32] This West Country and Indian heritage – 'My family has also been very closely associated with India for five generations' – with a strong sense of duty and public service was inherited by Birdwood.[33] His life positively reflected this inheritance to such a degree that it could be considered that he proudly sought to be an echo of the past.

William Riddell Birdwood was born on 13 September 1865 at Kirkee, Poona, one hundred miles southeast of Bombay, where his father was Under-Secretary to the Government and his

26 F. H. Brown, 'Birdwood, Herbert Mills (1837–1907)', rev. Roger T. Stearn, *ODNB* (Oxford, 2004); [http://www.oxforddnb.com/view/article/31897, accessed 24 March 2014]
27 *The Times of India,* 26 February 1907, 8. He referred to his tasks as being of the 'Head Gardener'.
28 Samuel T Sheppard, *The Byculla Club, 1833-1916, A History* (Bombay, 1916) contains interesting accounts of such farewell dinners, and associated food and wine.
29 *The Times of India,* 31 March 1897, 5.
30 Brown, 'Birdwood, Herbert Mills', *ODNB.*
31 *The Times of India,* 26 February 1907, 8.
32 Birdwood, *Khaki and Gown*, 25 and 177.
33 Foreword by FM Birdwood of Anzac in C Lestock Reid, *Commerce and Conquest: The Story of the Honourable East India Company* (London, 1947), 11.

maternal grandfather was Postmaster-General.[34] William was the name of his uncle, his father's younger brother, William Spiller Birdwood, and was very much a family name.[35] Richard Birdwood, the first to be Agent for the East India Company in Plymouth and Birdwood's great-great-grandfather, had a nephew, William Ilbert, who similarly named his own son who later became Major General William Ilbert Birdwood Royal Engineers. The latter also gave his two sons the middle name William. Riddell, Birdwood's second Christian name, came from his maternal grandmother – Jane Anne Riddell, of Roxburghshire. Birdwood was the third child in the family: the oldest being his sister, Edith Jane, followed by a brother, Herbert Christopher Impey, born 1863. When William was three, the three children travelled with their mother to England. Subsequently three further brothers were born – Gordon Travers, 1867, Halhed Brodrick 1870 and Richard Lockington 1879.

Birdwood's papers do not include anything about his early years, during which time his parents continued to live in India. He attended a dame's school in Cheltenham, Miss Briggs at Vallombrosa (now Homespring House), Pittville Circus Road. Miss Briggs was a somewhat formidable lady whose educational standards were well regarded by Cheltenham College. There was by all accounts a distinct military atmosphere at Vallombrosa and Miss Briggs was known to organise sham fights for possession of a mound on nearby Battledown Hill, with the boys mounted on ponies. Captain W.P. Jeffcock, a pupil at Vallombrosa during the 1870s, reminisced:

> What must have been rather a unique spectacle, even in those days, was to see Billy Birdwood (later Field-Marshall Birdwood) and myself accompanying this fine old lady on occasions when she drove herself in her pony carriage through the streets of Cheltenham. We were mounted on young stock of her own breeding which she reared at her Buckholt farm. As she was the hostess, these invitations were to us of the greatest delight.[36]

Birdwood proceeded to Clifton College, where the entry book records only his and his father's details. Birdwood 'spent five happy years' at Clifton College in Bristol from 1877 to 1882.[37] His four brothers followed him to Clifton. Gordon and Halhed entered together in September 1878, his elder brother Herbert not until 1880 and finally Richard in September 1893.[38] Clifton had been founded in 1862. In preparation for the opening of newly constructed school buildings, a preliminary school had been started in September 1861 with just twenty boys at

34 Kirkee, now known as Khadki, is a northern suburb of Pune, known as Poona during British rule. The name Poona is still in use: diocese, golf club, etc. Khadki includes Kirkee Cantonment, one of the oldest in India.

35 BL AAS, Mss Eur D 686 folio 93, Birdwood family papers.

36 Mark Penfold, *Miss Jane Briggs – Maker of Men*, (Pittville History Works, 2018) <http://pittvillehistory.org.uk/bios/9920.html> (accessed 24 January 2022) and *Homespring House (formerly Vallombrosa and Deanwood House), Pittville Circus Road* (Pittville History Works) [https://pittvillehistory.org.uk/houses/HomespringHouse.html, accessed 21 January 2023]. Birdwood later rediscovered his old school during a trip to Cheltenham – 1933 Diary 29 March.

37 Birdwood, *Khaki and Gown*, 26.

38 F Borwick (ed.), *Clifton College Annals and Register 1862-1925* (Bristol: J W Arrowsmith, 1925); J A O Muirhead (ed.), *Clifton College Register, 1862 to 1947* (Bristol: J W Arrowsmith, 1948). S P Beachcroft (ed.), *Clifton College Register, 1862 to 1962* (Bristol: J W Arrowsmith, 1962).

the nearby 11 Arlington Villas. Interestingly one of those boys was Edwin Bean, the father of Charles Edwin Woodrow Bean who in January 1894 went to Clifton and was to become the Official Historian of Australia during the 1914-18 war.[39] The Registers of Clifton masters and pupils have been produced periodically since 1880 and its magazine, *The Cliftonian,* since 1865. Octavius Christie wrote in 1935 the first full history of the School detailing its formation and the story of its founding Headmaster, John Percival.[40] Derek Winterbottom, who taught history for nearly twenty years until 1994, has written five knowledgeable books on Clifton, including one on Sir Henry Newbolt, who was at school with Birdwood.[41] What attracted parents of boys such as Newbolt and Birdwood to send their sons to such a new school? The answer was the first headmaster: John Percival. In his sixteen years in post the School grew from 76 boys to 680. He had been recommended by the then headmaster of Rugby to the College Council, who were keen to 'provide an education of the type made popular by Dr Thomas Arnold during his Headmastership of Rugby'.[42] Percival created 'a *strenuous* school, one in which staff and boys alike were driven by the Headmaster's urgent desire that they should work hard, play hard and pray hard,' seeking 'to make adolescent boys live and think cleanly.' During Percival's 'time 50 scholarships to Oxford and Cambridge were won as well as forty admissions to Woolwich and Sandhurst and twelve to the Indian Civil Service, and it was this more than anything that brought Clifton recognition as a 'major' public school'.[43] He appointed 91 men to his staff, eleven of whom left to pursue distinguished careers in Universities, and four gaining election as Fellows of the Royal Society. About a dozen left to become headmasters'.[44] Birdwood arrived two years before Percival left and it is reasonable to assume that the

William Birdwood at Clifton College, 1882. (Clifton College archives)

39 AWM 3DRL 6673/12/ii/19, item 840, A sketch of the earliest days at Clifton College, E Bean.
40 O F Christie, *A History of Clifton College 1860-1934* (Bristol: J W Arrowsmith, 1935).
41 Derek Winterbottom, *Henry Newbolt and The Spirit of Clifton* (Bristol: Redcliffe, 1986), 7.
42 *John Percival: The Great Educator* (Bristol: Bristol Branch of the Historical Association The University, Bristol, 1993), 2. For comparisons between Arnold and Percival, see Brian Simon and Ian Bradley (eds.), *The Victorian Public School* (Dublin: Gill and Macmillan, 1975), 58-80.
43 Winterbottom, *John Percival: The Great Educator*, 4.
44 *Henry Newbolt and The Spirit of Clifton*, 19.

School's reputation attracted Herbert Birdwood and his wife, and led to them sending their son there.[45]

The only School record of Birdwood's time is his record sheet, which is a single page containing short comments at about quarterly intervals on a boy's performance in the senior School. The first entry is for October 1879 when he is reported as 'not satisfactory', 'idle' and 'not v[ery] strenuous.' A month later he is 'still not satisfactory' and in danger of going down if he did 'not do a fair exam.' He then started to improve, with December: 'better'; February: 'began well, falling off – inattentive and silly. Not quite sat[isfactory] but better than last term' and then April: 'much improved.' In his final year, reports cite weakness in both Latin and Greek, and in May: 'He must do better if he is [to make] Sandhurst.' By October it is stated: 'he ought to get into Sandhurst eventually, and pass the preliminary at once, every care is being taken to secure this. For the final, he will have to compete with about 450 candidates up to the age of 20 for 70 vacancies and it is not likely that he will succeed very easily perhaps not for 2 yrs. I think his leaving is somewhat premature and unnecessary.' His last entry was for December: 'very careless blunders but industrious.'[46] Birdwood described his own performance as 'keeping a steady place near the bottom of whatever form' he 'happened to be in.'[47] Latterly he was in the Military and Engineering Side, which 'was set up as a separate part of the School in 1875 as "the Woolwich Set". 'A special class was instituted for training boys for Sandhurst in 1879.' Mr H S Hall had 'charge of the "M and E" from its start.' 'In the 26 years of his Mastership 150 Cliftonians passed direct to Woolwich, 120 into Sandhurst and 15 into Coopers Hill [Royal Indian Engineering College].'[48] Birdwood's diary records his interest and prowess in swimming, running (fifth in Long Penpole, the School race and winning his House Cup), and rugby (he uses the term 'football'). Fives, tennis and riding also feature. These were the future basis of his physical fitness and robustness. Military affairs figure strongly with a guard of honour for the Duke of Edinburgh, command of a section, sergeant's exams and being photographed in uniform.[49] Any past or present Cliftonian would recognise the last weeks in his diary as he approached leaving: singing in Big School, walking round to say farewell, Chapel, and House Supper, at which he spoke.[50] His housemaster, Mr C M Oakley, wrote to him after leaving:

> I am much obliged for your note. Your leaving would anyhow be a great grief to me, and it is all the more so coming this early. However, in one way I am all the more glad to have had you in the house this year, and it is pleasant to hear that you liked it. Certainly, you have had every right to do so, for you have been, of course, worth your weight in gold to the School and the house and will be the same I trust to the next society you are thrown with whatever it is.[51]

45 Two more recent histories are: Cheryl Trafford (ed.), *The Best School of All* (London: Third Millenium Publishing, 2009); C S Knighton (ed.), *Clifton College: Foundation to Evacuation*, Bristol Record Society's Publication Vol 65 (Bristol: Bristol Record Office with Clifton College, 2012).
46 Clifton College Archives, 1882, Record Sheet Birdwood ma[jor] W R.
47 Birdwood, *Khaki and Gown*, 27.
48 Christie, *A History of Clifton College 1860-1934*, 39-40.
49 NAM 6707-19-62, Certificate in Engineering Duties awarded to Sgt W R Birdwood 2 Gloucester 'Bristol' Engineer Volunteers, 31 October 1882.
50 1882 Diary.
51 NAM 6707-19-59, Letter from C M Oakley.

The reason for his early departure is not explained but reading his diary demonstrates someone who was ready to move on in life.[52] Birdwood was fond of his time at Clifton. He stayed in contact with the School, finally becoming President of the College Council. He always noted if he was dealing with a fellow Old Cliftonian. He had a deep affection for the School. Douglas Haig was also an Old Cliftonian. He arrived the term before Birdwood but, being much older, left after two years. Birdwood named eighteen school friends in his 1882 diary. Six went on to serve in the Indian Army and two in the British Army.

Two other Cliftonians, not mentioned in his 1882 diary, feature prominently later. The first was Sir Henry Newbolt, who left the year before Birdwood. Newbolt would advance virtues such as 'Loyalty, Patriotism, Chivalry, dreams of ambition and imperial service' through his writings.[53] Two of his most famous poems are *Drake's Drum* and *Vitaï Lampada.* They were published together in *Admirals All* in 1897. The little book of twelve poems, which 'expressed the heartfelt sentiments of a patriotic English gentleman coached in manly ballad style,' was a sensational success. It sold 'no fewer than twenty-one editions of a thousand copies each in one year.'[54] Standing on the College Close today one can still bring Newbolt's words to mind:

There's a breathless hush in the Close to-night –
Ten to make and the match to win – ...
Then Newbolt takes his reader to an image of an imperial battle,
The sand of the desert is sodden red, –
Red with the wreck of a square that broke; –
The Gatling's jammed and the Colonel dead,
And the regiment blind with dust and smoke.
The river of death has brimmed his banks,
***
'Play up! Play up! And play the game!'
Before reminding the reader that such a message must be passed on,
... Every one of her sons must ...
Bear through life like a torch in flame,
And falling fling to the lost behind –
'Play up! Play up! And play the game!'[55]

At a dinner given in his honour after the invasion of Tibet in 1904, Francis Younghusband spoke of the fellow Old Cliftonians who had accompanied him: 'They all have that trait so characteristic of Clifton, and which has been so finely inculcated by Henry Newbolt, of playing the game. They may have nasty jobs to do but it is the game and they will play it through.'

52 I am grateful to Dr Duncan Anderson, the long-serving Head of War Studies at RMAS, for the suggestion that family financial reasons may have caused this early departure but I can find no evidence for this.

53 Winterbottom, *Henry Newbolt and The Spirit of Clifton*, 10.

54 Ibid., 43-44.

55 *Ibid.*, 86. *Vitaï Lampada* is from Lucretius, *De Rerum Natura,* Book 2 line 79 *et quasi cursores vitaï lampada tradunt* – 'and like runners they pass on the torch of life', a reference to a Greek relay race in which the runners carried a lighted torch.

After the invasion of Tibet, Newbolt had sent Younghusband a narrative poem 'honouring their schooldays together,' which included the following lines:

The victories of our youth we count for gain
Only because they steeled our hearts for pain,
And hold no longer even Clifton great
Save as she schooled our wills to serve the State.
Nay, England's self, whose thousand-year-old name
Burns in our blood like ever-smouldering flame[56]

The second Cliftonian of note was someone who started school with Birdwood. Henry (Harry) Plunket Greene, a famous baritone whose father-in-law, Sir Hubert Parry, put a Newbolt poem to music thus creating the school song:

It's good to see the School we knew,
The land of youth and dream,
To greet again the rule we knew
Before we took the stream:
Chorus: We'll honour yet the School we knew,
The best School of all:
We'll honour yet the rule we knew,
Till the last bell call.
For working days or holidays,
And glad or melancholy days,
They were great days and jolly days
At the best School of all.

***

To speak of Fame a venture is,
There's little here can bide.
But we may face the centuries,
And dare the deepening tide:
For though the dust that's part of us
To dust again begone,
Yet here shall beat the heart of us—
The School we handed on!

...

For working days or holidays,
And glad or melancholy days,
They were great days and jolly days
At the best School of all.[57]

56 Patrick French, *Younghusband: The Last Great Imperial Adventurer* (London: HarperCollins, 1994), 9-10.
57 Winterbottom, *Henry Newbolt and The Spirit of Clifton*, 46-48, 90-91.

So, this was the Clifton to which Birdwood bade farewell. He left with a positive view of his School, the ethos of which – spiritual robustness, manly sports and public service – were made internationally known by Newbolt and Parry. There is no reason to doubt that Birdwood embraced this same ethos with pride and shared the feelings so eloquently expressed.

Birdwood's parents had the intention that, on leaving Clifton, he should enter the Army through the Militia. Here one obtained a commission by nomination within the Militia and then transferred to the regular Army after a period of full-time service and having passed the Sandhurst final examination.[58] Through his mother's cousin – Lieutenant Colonel Tom Riddell-Carre – he obtained a commission as a lieutenant in the 4 Battalion Royal Scots Fusiliers.[59] He served from March 1883 to March 1885, completing 'a two months' course of recruit's drill with 2nd Scots Guards at Wellington Barracks,' and two Militia training camps. He considered sitting for the entrance examination to the Royal Military College Sandhurst while in the Militia and 'somewhat to his surprise he succeeded – though very low down in the list.' His father had earlier applied for a Queen's India Cadetship for him.[60]

Birdwood entered the Royal Military College Sandhurst in September 1884. Douglas Haig, who had gone to Oxford, was there at the same time, but was four years Birdwood's senior in age, and 'consequently seemed to belong almost to another generation.'[61] Purchase of commissions had ceased in 1871 and Sandhurst was set on producing professional officers. Its ethos was inline that of public schools, like Clifton. The Board of Visitors inspection of the College for 1884 took place in June, before the arrival of Birdwood, but its report can be taken as a fair representation of Sandhurst at that time. The Board saw 'classes of Cadets engaged in outdoor field work' and were 'much impressed' with the Cadets' 'muscular development and general healthy appearance.' The course consisted of tactics, fortification, topography and military administration and law. There were also parades, riding and gymnastics. The aim was to learn the elements of soldiering. The supporting Board data is interesting. As well as timetables, staff manning figures and hospital figures, there is a table showing the 'Parentage of the Gentlemen Cadets', distinguishing between sons of Peers, Baronets, Officers of the Army or Navy to finally 'Private Gentlemen, Merchants, Bankers, etc.' Another table shows the 'Distribution among the Public and other Schools of the Gentlemen Cadets.' Nine schools are listed by name, including Clifton, which had the third highest number of successful candidates after Eton and Wellington.[62] Birdwood was a very typical cadet, with connections through his school and his father's professional background.

Birdwood was commissioned six months early from Sandhurst, due to one of the periodical Russian war scares. A sudden attack had been made by the Russians on Afghan forces near Panjdeh, south of the Oxus River – the Panjdeh Incident. Fear of an invasion 'resulted, among other things, in orders for the first fifty of the 'juniors' at Sandhurst to be posted at once to regiments.' Thanks to his 'period of attachment to the Scots Guards' and his 'consequent thorough knowledge of infantry drill,' he had been made an Under-Officer, so was gazetted to

58 Angela Holdsworth and Christopher Pugsley (eds.), *Sandhurst : A Tradition of Leadership* (London: Third Millenium Publishing, 2005), 35.

59 NAM 6707-19-63, Commissioning Certificate as Lieutenant 4th Battalion Royal Scots Fusiliers.

60 BL AAS, L/MIL/9/293, Queen's India Cadetship Applications Vol A-A to D, 1882.

61 Birdwood, *Khaki and Gown*, 27-28.

62 RMC Papers WO 152/54 Box 105 90-5012, Report of the Board of Visitors in the Year 1884.

the XIIth Royal Lancers and ordered to be ready to embark for India. Three months short of his twentieth birthday Birdwood left behind his childhood, his school days and his initial military training, and sailed for Bombay on 3 June 1885.[63] To his heritage and connections, he had now added the ethos of both Clifton and Sandhurst.

63 Birdwood, *Khaki and Gown*, 28-29.

2

Return to India and early married life

Birdwood sailed for India on 3 June 1885, nearly seventeen years since he had left the land of his birth with his mother. On board ship, he found a fellow passenger whom he later described as:

> Captain Ian Hamilton … [who] already wore a halo of glory by virtue of his service in the Afghan War, the Boer War of 1881 (in which he had been badly wounded at Majuba), and the Nile Expedition. I was to see much of him as the years went by – in India, in South Africa, and at the Dardanelles. He is to-day [1941] the most distinguished of our veteran soldiers, and I am proud to count him, as I hope I may do for many years to come, among my best and oldest friends.[1]

Thirty years later Hamilton would be Birdwood's commander at Gallipoli.

Birdwood was to spend the next thirteen and a half years in India. During this period, he learnt his profession. He loved it and was successful at it. This benefitted him when he, through patronage, gained opportunities of both appointment and active service. During this time, he fell in love and was married. Birdwood and his wife returned to England with their first child. Above all throughout this period his character developed as both his professional and personal lives blossomed.

Birdwood's diaries are incomplete for his early years as a young bachelor. Marriage in April 1894 changed this. His future wife is first mentioned in his extant diaries on 6 February 1892.[2] Diaries exist for every year from that date until 1949, two years before his death, when it is probable that he ceased to keep one. Between his last year at school and his first mention of Jenny there are, however, only three diaries – 1886, 1889 and 1890. It is reasonable to presume that Birdwood disposed of the diaries for those missing six years.

All officers destined for the Indian Army served one year with a British unit resident in India before joining their Indian Army regiment.[3] Birdwood had been appointed to the British XII Royal Lancers, stationed at Bangalore: 'an excellent station, never very hot, and never very

1 Birdwood, *Khaki and Gown*, 29

2 Diary 1892, 6 February.

3 T A Heathcote, *The Military in British India: The Development of British Land Forces in South Asia, 1600–1947* (Manchester: Manchester University Press, 1995), 175.

cold,' together with British artillery batteries, an Indian cavalry regiment, and one British and three Indian infantry battalions.[4] Birdwood was there to study his profession. His copy of the Regimental Standing Orders still falls open at the page with the section for Subaltern Officers, who were required 'to be thoroughly acquainted with the men and horses of their squad of which they must have a descriptive roll,' and 'to acquire a perfect knowledge of the system of commanding a troop in every situation in all details.'[5] Most importantly he had to commence language training so as to communicate with his future Indian soldiers. He passed his first language exam, Hindustani Lower Standard, in November 1885. That August he embarked on a demanding seven-month course at the riding school and riding dominated the early months of 1886.

The year started with him falling off his horse on the New Year's Day parade – 'came off somehow … but remember nothing about it.' He was off sick for a week. Throughout his service, days off sick were nearly always for falls, bumps and blows of various kinds, although from the start he was a robust individual. His diary shows him as a typical young subaltern, with entries such as 'I don't remember,' 'was feeling most awfully seedy after that ball & didn't do much all day,' and 'had a real Europe morning in bed today as I was slightly strained after the exertions of yesterday.' The last entry is, however, followed by three hours of language work that afternoon with 'those blessed "*munshis*"'.[6] He failed his first attempt at the Higher Standard examination. He had 'ploughed the translation' and was 'stumped.'[7] *Munshis* appear more frequently in his diary after that and perhaps the failure jolted him. He passed, at his second attempt, and soon benefitted: 'Brigade parade: was interpreter & commanding the [Mysore] *Silladar* Horse, capital fun.' He celebrated his twenty-first birthday as 'orderly officer' sitting on a Regimental Court Martial, followed by 'a good game of polo' and 'a small dance'.[8] His time with the XII Lancers was fully occupied with military training, parades and duties, and his first command – a troop. Two officers had been killed in accidents and he commanded the funeral party at one of them. As well as polo, tent-pegging, steeple-chasing, hunting, golf and cricket all featured. He also enjoyed escapades, for example when two officers drove 'two polo ponies in tandem from Bangalore to Ootacamund [180 miles].' This was achieved 'by Christie-Crawford [*sic*] and a friend of his who joined the Regiment in 1885, and who was destined to win enduring fame. His name was Lt W R Birdwood.'[9] *Khaki and Gown* was dedicated 'to my oldest friend Arthur Christie Crawfurd' – proof of their lasting companionship. Above all Birdwood made connections, or in his own words 'valuable friendships.' Early on he met (the future Sir) James Lyall, then the Resident in Mysore, and acted as his ADC for the first of many occasions.[10] He developed an acquaintance with 'Major Stuart Beatson of the XI Bengal Lancers,' the Military Secretary to the C-in-C Madras. It was through Beatson's influence that Birdwood 'was

4 Captain P F Stewart, *The History of XII Royal Lancers (Prince of Wales's)* (London: Geoffrey Cumberledge, 1950), 163. British units had all British officers and men. Indian units had British and Indian officers and all Indian men.
5 NAM 6707-19-71, Standing Orders of the 12th Royal Regiment of Lancers (Madras, 1883).
6 Diary 1886, 1 and 21 January; 18 March.
7 Ibid., 20-21 April; 10 May.
8 Ibid., 13-14 September.
9 Stewart, *The History of XII Royal Lancers (Prince of Wales's)* 163; Diary 1886, 13-17 June.
10 Ibid., 4-12 October.

fortunate enough to get posted to the XI Bengal Lancers.'[11] In between regiments Birdwood visited his parents in Bombay where his father was a High Court Judge and so facilitated Birdwood meeting the Viceroy and other dignitaries.[12]

At the end of leave in December 1886, Birdwood left Bombay for a day and a half's train journey, followed by a further day by *gharry* and overnight stay at a *dak*, to join XI (Prince of Wales's Own) Bengal Lancers, (XI BL), at Nowgong – 'a very quiet little place'.[13] He had made a beginning with his profession but now had the opportunity to start afresh. He entered wholeheartedly into this new challenge. He stayed all his first week in his Commandant's (commanding officer), Colonel Prinsep's, bungalow. He was immediately into polo and tent pegging ('with the long spear').[14] Thirty-three years later, Birdwood was asked to write the Introduction to a book on the descendant Regiment – Probyn's Horse (5th King Edward VII's Own Lancers) and began with his memories of being 'most struck on joining' by the 'wonderful set of senior Indian officers,' one of whom as a boy had served with Ranjit Singh's troops.[15] He was now joining a different world that would have a great influence on him personally and on his approach to soldiers and soldiering.

In his seminal history of the British Indian Army, Philip Mason wrote about the character and *mores* of the British officers of that Army. Recalling that 'the half-century from the Mutiny to the Kaiser's war … covered the heyday of British Imperial rule' and saw its officers as 'an Imperial class, not a caste.' That class was 'extremely competitive; esteem within the class depended on a whole set of factors. Birth and money were not enough by themselves.' Whether in 'a good house in a good school,' or in 'a good regiment,' the individual had to contribute to excellence. This meant both 'tone and good form,' qualities not easy to define. 'Membership of the class was not quite hereditary, but to be born into it was undoubtedly useful', as Birdwood himself was. 'If your father and grandfather had been in the Queen's service, there would be many friends ready to give a young man a chance and it was permissible to write to them for advice and to apply for employment wherever military experience could be gained. A campaign on the Frontier, war in the Sudan, offered a chance of distinction – perhaps a brevet or a step-up in rank, perhaps a mention in dispatches, certainly experience of fighting – and a flood of applications from eager young officers would reach the Military Secretary.' Mason summed up that 'to get far, a man must be judged to be efficient at what he undertook, and he must be neither a mug (not sporty, went to bed early, or swotted) nor a bounder. The positive aspect of this was to be a good fellow; Birdwood was a superlatively good fellow, liked by everyone, but it was not a term that would have been applied to Kitchener, who achieved a good deal without it.'[16]

11 Birdwood, *Khaki and Gown*, 33-35.
12 Diary 1886, 9 November-16 December.
13 Birdwood, *Khaki and Gown*, 5.
14 For a short history of the Regiment see John Gaylor, *Sons of John Company: The Indian and Pakistan Armies 1903-91* (Tunbridge Wells: Spellmount, 1992), 68-70.
15 Major C A Boyle, *The History of Probyn's Horse (5th King Edward's Own Lancers)* (Aldershot: Gale & Polden, 1929), xi. Ranjit Singh (1780-1839) was the founder of the Sikh Empire.
16 Mason, *A Matter of Honour*, 362-4. This is the first, of only a few, references to Birdwood in the book and it is interesting that Mason specifically selected Birdwood as his example of 'a superlatively good fellow.'

When Birdwood joined XI BL at the end of 1886, his fellow British officers were his Commandant, the second-in-command, one captain as adjutant and four fellow lieutenants as squadron officers – just seven in all. The other five regimental officers were on furlough or staff appointments. Birdwood had joined an extremely small family. Following on from his year with the XII Lancers, he would continue on probation until August 1889.[17] Splendid photographs of three of Birdwood's fellow officers are in the NAM.[18]

Captain S B Beatson in officers full dress uniform of 11th (Prince of Wales's Own) Bengal Lancers, c. 1886. (National Army Museum 1972-11-7). Note: Beatson featured later at Wilmansrust, South Africa, 1901.

17 *The India List – Civil and Military* (London, 1887), 317.
18 NAM 1964-08-341, Six cabinet and *carte de visite* photographs, Major Carruthers, Captain Beatson and Lieutenant Delamain, c. 1886-7.

For five years Birdwood shared a bungalow with one – Delamain.[19] Indian Army Lists from 1891 included 'native officers' and that year, XI BL shows seventeen such Indian officers.[20] The XI BL was a *Silladar* regiment.[21] Each *sowar* (private soldier) owned the horse he rode and the equipment he wore. He paid a deposit on joining and then monthly deductions were made from his pay. At the end of his service he sold back his horse and equipment. He had, therefore, a financial interest in his regiment. The men were linked in pairs. Each pair had a pony and a tent, and hired a *syce*, who tended the horses and cut the fodder, making a self-contained team. A regiment with such teams could move at short notice and was independent of external logistical support and administration. A feature of a *Silladar* regiment was the *durbar*, when the British and Indian officers would sit facing the regiment, seated on the ground. Any man could raise a point or query regarding the administration of the regiment and receive an answer from his Commandant. The regiment was, therefore, in touch with its men and the men with their officers. Eighteen years later Birdwood, on the C-in-C Lord Kitchener's staff, wrote about the benefits of the *Silladar* system which was then under review, stressing that 'any such fundamental change as that now suggested will go far towards altering the magnificent spirit and *esprit de corps* which is universally acknowledged to exist in the *Silladar* Cavalry.'[22] This debate made the papers and *The Pioneer* added the comment that 'if we consider the spirit of resourcefulness and individuality which a training in a Silladar Cavalry regiment engenders in the British officers the loss to the Government from any change would be incalculable.'[23] A few years earlier Winston Churchill and Birdwood had been involved in different Frontier expeditions and Churchill wrote then:

> To the young man who wants to enjoy himself, to spend a few years agreeably in military companionship – to have an occupation – the British cavalry will be suited. But to the youth who means to make himself a professional soldier, an expert in war, a specialist in practical tactics, who desires a hard life of adventure and a true comradeship in arms, I would recommend the choice of some regiment on the frontier, like those fine ones I have seen, the Guides and the 11th Bengal Lancers.[24]

Such was to be the basis of Birdwood's regimental life, but experience gained on active service was doubly important. The first separate Indian Army List of 1891 included a complete section entitled War Services, detailing all officers who had gained campaign or battle experience. This was also included in each officer's Record of Service.[25] It was, furthermore, distinctly advantageous to be mentioned in despatches and a separate column in an individual's record gave the dates and the extracts of each mention.[26] Having served briefly on two campaigns,

19 Diary 1886, 28 December and 1892, 22 January.
20 *The Quarterly Indian Army List for April 1891* (Calcutta, 1891), 272.
21 Charles Chevenix Trench, *The Indian Army and the King's Enemies 1900–1947* (London: Thames and Hudson, 1988), 26; Mason, *A Matter of Honour*, 26, 376.
22 NAM 6707-19-312, Draft printed critique on *Silladar* cavalry by Birdwood 12 July 1904.
23 *The Pioneer*, 24 August 1904, 2.
24 Winston S Churchill, *The Story of the Malakand Field Force* (London: Longmans, Green and Co, 1898), 261.
25 NAM 6707-19-57, Record of Officers' Services – W R Birdwood, 1885–1930.
26 The oakleaf emblem was not introduced until 1919.

Birdwood made sure of a mention on his third, Tirah. Birdwood had joined an Army in which meritorious campaign service was vital for advancement. His desire to see active service was not unusual and valuable friendships did assist him when he pushed to join campaigns.

The aspect of a *Silladar* regiment that Birdwood loved was its ability to move at short notice and be self-supporting. In October 1888, XI BL departed Nowgong on line of march to its new barracks at Rawalpindi and Birdwood was the commander of the 4th Squadron, his first sub-unit command. Birdwood treasured the memory of that long march all his life, with each week consisting of three or four marching days of about twelve miles. Along the way he visited old acquaintances, including the Lyalls, and sites such as the Golden Temple at Amritsar. The Regiment reached Rawalpindi after a hundred and four days on the march. Two weeks later Birdwood became Adjutant. This 'brought hard work but also a great deal of pleasure, for it necessitated a great intimacy of contact with the men and enabled me to hear much about their homes, their ambitions and their troubles.' The Regiment was composed of Sikh, Dogra, Punjabi Mussulman and Pathan soldiers. Indian Cavalry Regiments had no Riding Master. The Adjutant supervised 'all the foot-drill, riding school, recruits, musketry and so on,' together with the 'training of all remounts – something like 70 [horses] a year.'[27] His diary describes months of continuous recruit training – riding school, drill and stables – and parades, as well as time for polo and coach driving. At the end of June, he went to Simla for ten days to act as ADC to Sir James Lyall, who had moved from Mysore to be Lieutenant Governor of the Punjab. Birdwood must have been a success as he was back again at the end of August 1889 for a further seven weeks. By the end of these periods he had dined at both the Viceroy's and the C-in-C's, escorted Sir James and Lady Lyall to numerous events, meeting various dignitaries and senior staff.[28] 1890 began with XI BL forming part of 'about 7,000 cavalry on parade' for 'Prince Albert Victor of Wales.' Birdwood again spent all of August and September at Simla with the Lyalls. They were very much his patrons now and Birdwood saw the family side of Simla life. Throughout he continued with his languages, passing Lower Standard Persian and embarking on Pushtu.[29] In 1891 he had his 'first chance of seeing active service.'[30]

As a result of the 1888 operations in the Black Mountain region, about forty miles north east of Attock where the Kabul River flows into the Indus, the British had acquired freedom to manoeuvre along what was then the north western border of India. This was tested in late 1890 and the column involved came under fire. A larger divisional size force was constituted and deployed in March 1891.[31] The XI BL were split between the divisional troops, south of Black Mountain, and the reserve at Rawalpindi.[32] The Expedition set off on 12 March and by 29 May the 'unconditional surrender of two tribes was tendered.'[33] To Birdwood, it was 'a somewhat

27 Birdwood, *Khaki and Gown*, 64.
28 Diary 1889, 23 June – 4 August, 26 August – 12 September.
29 Diary 1890, 9 August – 1 October.
30 Birdwood, *Khaki and Gown*, 71-73.
31 NAM 5501-14, Black Mountain Expedition Photograph album 1891. This contains sixty-seven expedition images but regrettably none of cavalry or XI BL in particular.
32 BL AAS, L/MIL/7/14698 Enclosure 11, Correspondence regarding march of a force to Black Mountain, Hazara in October 1890 and subsequent measures, in Black Mountain and Hazara Epeditions 1888-1893, GGO No 45 16 January 1891.
33 BL AAS, L/MIL/17/13/53, Captain Alexander Herbert Mason, *Expedition against the Hasanzai and Akazai tribes of the Black Mountain by a force under the command of Maj-Gen William Kidston Elles in*

unsatisfactory expedition, and little was effected by it.'[34] His next campaign, the Isazai Field Force in September 1892, was listed in his personal file but received mention neither in his diary nor in his autobiography.[35] This was not surprising as 'the expedition came to nothing, as the enemy not only put up no fight but cleared right out of the country.'[36] Meanwhile he had continued as Adjutant and in both 1892 and 1893 he 'won the silver shield for the Best Officer-at-Arms' in the annual Rawalpindi Military Tournament and Assault-at-Arms.[37]

In late 1892 Birdwood took part in a large Cavalry Concentration in 'command of a composite regiment of Imperial Service cavalry formed from squadrons of Lancers from the states of Jind and Nabha.' He was a Lieutenant in command of a regiment. Here he first met John French, then commanding 19th Hussars, but for this concentration given command of a brigade, which included Birdwood's Lancers. French considered that Birdwood had acquitted himself well. On the final parade Birdwood noted his own 'first appearance as a CO before the Chief [Lord Roberts then C-in-C].'[38] He returned to his Regiment at the end of January. On 3 May, celebratory red ink appears for the first time. He 'got telegram in afternoon from Beresford M S V [Military Secretary, MS to C-in-C] offering me the Adjutancy of the Body Guard. Went round & consulted everybody … I decided to take it but hate the idea of giving up the Adjutancy of these grand fellows here.' His appointment was confirmed four days later. It stated that he had been most successful as adjutant of his Regiment. He had had opportunities also to command at both squadron and regimental levels and was an experienced trainer. He had mixed at the highest levels of British society in India. But first there were the goodbyes. At a farewell dinner in the mess Birdwood recorded just six names – a reminder of what a small family he was leaving. The next day the 'men all came up in crowds to say goodbye' and 'everyone coming down to the station.'[39]

From 1889 until 1947 the Governor General's Body Guard (GGBG) kept a large paged and leather-bound Digest of Service, in which the Commandant or the Adjutant, the two British officers, wrote a handwritten annual report. The Guard consisted of one hundred and twenty immaculately turned out Sikhs and Punjabi Mussalmans, each over six feet in height, towering over the 'short' Birdwood.[40] Having joined on 24 May 1893, Birdwood departed for two months to take the instructional classes and examinations necessary to qualify for the Army Staff.[41] He passed and gained distinctions in fortification, military law and tactics, together with a Special Mention. This achievement was not unique but it placed him among the top five per cent of

1891, Simla: Intelligence Branch, QMG's Dept.

34 Birdwood, *Khaki and Gown*, 71.

35 Diary 1892, 16 August – 11 October.

36 Major General Sir Steuart Hare, *Annals of the King's Royal Rifle Corps: Vol 4 "The K.R.R.C." 1872-1913* (London: John Murray, 1929), 124.

37 Birdwood, *Khaki and Gown*, 68-9; Diary 1893, 28 March

38 Diary 1893, 1, 26 and 27 January. *Ibid.*, 67-68.

39 Ibid., 3, 7, 20 May.

40 *The India Year Book 1940-41* (Bombay: The Times of India, 1941), 319. Of the martial races, Sikhs and Muhammedans 'contributed the larger proportion to both the cavalry and infantry', with the Muhammedans 'unequalled as cavalry.'

41 NAM 5405-10, Governor General's Body Guard Digest of Services. In 1927, thirty-four years after he started, there is a photo of Birdwood, then C-in-C, visiting his old unit.

those that did qualify.[42] He was late starting his practical tactics examination 'as Godley didn't call for me till 9.'[43] Years later they shared practical tactics together on Gallipoli. On return to the GGBG Birdwood commenced his duties in earnest, responsible for the training of all the new recruits and remounts – generally fifteen of each, every year. The GGBG spent December through to March at Calcutta and the rest of the year at Dehra Dun.

A new commandant arrived in April: Captain Jim Turner, 2nd Bengal Lancers. He and his wife became life-long friends of Birdwood. The first weeks were filled with riding school, stables, kit inspections and parades. Birdwood was now focused on learning Gurkhali, with assistance from the local Gurkha regiment, and took the exam first on 5 October but failed.[44] He noted that 'a man offered me the paper before the exam but I refused to see it.'[45] He passed at his second attempt and was now qualified in five languages.[46]

The Viceroys, Lords Lansdowne and Elgin, changed over in late January 1894. By the end of that month Birdwood had taken tea, been to a dance and dined at Government House, sitting beside the new Viceroy. Before the Guard left Calcutta at the end of March there were two months of escorting the Viceroy and attendance at Government House. In mid-October he received news that his elder brother, Chris, was 'dangerously ill' at Umballa, about four hours away. Birdwood rushed there and found him 'awfully bad. Stayed with him whole day & the whole night.' On 15 October, 'Dear old Chris died at 8.15 am. I was with him all the time. Poor Ethel [Chris' wife] was over at the hotel changing & arrived at 08.30. Poor girl, she was of course frightfully done up.' Chris was buried the next day.[47]

Back in Calcutta, he 'dined at Commander in Chief' on 15 February 1895.[48] Thirty years later he would dine as the C-in-C himself. A month later he tried to get back to the XI BL for the Chitral affair but Turner was going 'which cuts me out.'[49] He had not let his duties drift and was acting Commandant from March until October. The Viceroy's Military Secretary, who oversaw the Guard, wrote complimenting Birdwood on 'the excellent condition of the Body Guard,' saying that 'things at Dehra reflects [*sic*] great credit on you, and I congratulate you in having done so well, and kept everything up so well to the high Body Guard standard.'[50] The 1896 Guard diary entry recorded a busy summer of work on the Dehra Dun lines. Rows of huts were pulled down and new barracks constructed. In September 1937 Birdwood wrote to the current Commandant thanking him for initiating a Regimental newsletter, commenting that it made him 'long to see our lines in Dehra again! All the years I was there I never had leave & spent my 6 summers trying to improve our lines.'[51] Also, from June to mid-September he

42 *The Quarterly Indian Army List for April 1896* (Calcutta, 1896), 688-94.
43 Diary 1893, 3 August.
44 Diary 1893, week beginning 21 September.
45 Diary 1893, 5 and 31 October.
46 *The Quarterly Indian Army List for April 1896, 154-78.*
47 Ibid., 13-16 October
48 Diary 1895, 10 February.
49 Ibid., 14 March.
50 NAM 6707-19-102, Letter H Durand, Military Secretary to the Viceroy to Birdwood, 23 October 1895.
51 NAM 5405-10, Governor General's Body Guard Digest, Letter Birdwood to Mostyn-Owen, 15 September 1937.

passed with credit a course at the Army Veterinary School.[52] He escorted the Viceroy on the New Year's Day Proclamation Parade, which was under the command of Brig-Gen Yeatman-Briggs, under whom Birdwood would serve on operations later in the year.[53] Back at Dehra Dun Birdwood was once again in command from the end of March, as Major Turner was in England for Her Majesty's Diamond Jubilee. By mid-summer the possibility of an expedition into the Swat Valley arose, and Birdwood as ever pushed for involvement, despite Turner's absence. The possibility of a road being built to Chitral was seen as a spiritual challenge and taken up by a fakir, known as the Mad Mullah.[54] Birdwood approached the commandant of XI BL, by then part of the Malakand Field Force, to no avail.[55] The impact, however, of the Mad Mullah had spread and the Afridis and Orakzais, two renowned and ferocious Pathan tribes, rose up. General Lockhart was charged with leading an expedition 'to exact reparation for the unprovoked aggression of the Afridi and Orakzai tribes … by the invasion of Tirah, the summer home of the Afridis and Orakzais which has never before been entered by a British Force.'[56] Birdwood persisted. On 22 September Yeatman-Briggs wrote saying 'there is precious little patronage in GOC's hands' but that he would 'be very glad to employ you & will give first wicket down as orderly officer.'[57] Turner was now due back from England and a wicket must have fallen as on 11 October, Birdwood 'left for Tirah Expedition,' as Orderly Officer to Yeatman-Briggs, in command of the Second Division of Lockhart's Tirah Expeditionary Force.[58] The Force consisted of two divisions of infantry, the same structure as that of the Australian and New Zealand Corps at Anzac Cove.

Birdwood travelled through Kohat and then around the foot of the Samana Ridge, which is the southern boundary of the Tirah region that lies to the southwest of Peshawar, catching up with General Biggs on 16 October.[59] The Forts along the Samana had been cleared and it was now necessary to break into the Tirah. Two days later General Briggs and his staff marched towards Shinwari, south of the Chagru Kotal, 5325 feet, where they would cross over the Samana Ridge. While en route they 'watched Dargai being stormed by Genl Palmer [First Division] … It was taken easily but we lost (60) killed & wounded retiring, including Bramley of the Gordons the troops got back very late.' Lockhart's staff had been calamitously ineffectual and no supply arrangements had been made to hold the position. Two days later Briggs' Division was directed to continue the advance to Karappa. The direct route via Chagru Kotal was chosen once again and for the second time the Dargai heights, the prominent bluff to the west of Chagru Kotal, had to be cleared.[60] 'Kempster's Brigade of 2nd Ghurkhas, Dorsets & Derbys in

52 NAM 6707-19-113, Command Order No 479 – pass at Army Veterinary School with credit; Diary 1896, 8 June; 16 September
53 Diary 1897, 1 January.
54 Churchill, *The Story of the Malakand Field Force*, 37-46; Arthur Swinson, *North-West Frontier* (London: Hutchinson, 1967), 234-38.
55 NAM 6707-19-114, Letter, General Elles to Birdwood, 9 July 1897; Churchill, *The Story of the Malakand Field Force*, 61, 94-97 and 325.
56 Captain L J Shadwell, *Lockhart's Advance Through Tirah* (London: W Thacker, 1898), 27.
57 NAM 6707-19-120, Letter, Yeatman-Briggs to Birdwood, 22 September 1897.
58 Philip J Haythornthwaite, *The Colonial Wars Source Book* (London: Caxton Editions, 2000), 116.
59 NAM 5405-10, Governor General's Body Guard Digest, 24. BL AAS, Maps 51820 (27), Rough Map of Tirah and surrounding Country, Simla: Intelligence Branch, 1897. Diary 1897, 11-16 October.
60 Colonel C E Callwell, *Tirah 1897* (London: Constable, 1911), 47-49.

reserve attacked. All got to within 500 yds all right, when rush had to be made over 100yds of open [ground].' The first rush failed. The 'Derbys & Dorsets then tried combined rush & were all shot. Gordons were then called up & rushed up in grandest style. 2 Pipers & Col Mathias leading them: cleared the dangerous zone ... They reached the crest with little further loss. The enemy abandoning it before they got up. Our loss was 8 officers, 137 men killed & wounded. Action of Gordons was <u>most</u> beautiful & heroic, as enemy were posted in perfect positions & real crack shots.'[61] Birdwood may well have recalled Dargai when he first viewed the cliffs of Anzac Cove. Photographs of Dargai from Shinwari and drawings detailing the route of attack show steep climbs in a way amazingly similar to Anzac.[62] There on that hillside Birdwood saw the value of preparations so that ground gained is held and of inspirational leadership to push home a charge. It was a triumphant final assault and the enemy melted away at the end. In August 1915, however, the Ottomans held on and counterattacked.

Briggs' Division continued to lead the advance, first to Karappa and across the Khanki Valley that ran eastwards towards the Kohat River, to Khangarbur. It was slow going for a force of 34,000 officers and men, and over 40,000 camels, bullocks, mules and other pack animals.[63] The enemy harried them – 'sniped at a good deal at night' and 'the camp was fired into all night from all sides & we must have had a lot of casualties.'[64] Birdwood liaised between headquarters for his Commander, accompanied foraging parties and chased up baggage and supplies. The advance north continued with the First Division leading through the Sampagha Pass into the Mastura Valley. Then on 30 October the Second Division broke through the Arhanga Pass into the Maidan, a large plain and the stronghold of the Afridis.[65] On his first day on the Maidan, Birdwood reconnoitred its small village, Bagh, but found only 'a miserable masjid with pine trees around it.' Lockhart summoned *jirgas* but the Government's terms were not accepted. Reparations were now exacted and photographs showed the Maidan with numerous columns of smoke such that an enveloping cloud sits over the scene.[66] In mid-November the Second Division moved over to Bagh and proceeded to reconnoitre to the north, where there was access to the Bara River valley leading to Peshawar. The burnings continued.[67] The climatic conditions, however, necessitated evacuation in early December.[68] The 1st Division exited the Tirah via the Mastura Valley, while it was decided that 2 Division would go via the Bara ensuring that this valley did not remain untouched by British presence. They made slow progress with a rear guard down a six-mile long defile whose stream had to be crossed and recrossed.[69] Birdwood commented that 'this, I always thought, was the most difficult operation that the troops were

61 Diary 1897, 18 and 20 October.

62 All the following provide fascinating views. BL AAS, Maps 15.b.39 [A series of 13 views illustrating the movements of the] Tirah Expeditionary Force, Simla: Intelligence Branch, 1897; NAM 1955-05-18, 28th Bombay Pioneers Tirah 1897-8; NAM 1957-05-28-1, Bombay Sappers and Miners, Photograph Album, Tirah Expeditionary Force 1897-1898.

63 NAM 7501-44, Letters from H B Abadie XI Hussars from Tirah 1897-1898, contains forty-seven photos and a map, with which it is possible to follow Birdwood's movements in Tirah.

64 Diary 1897, 21 and 25 October.

65 The route is well covered in NAM 1957-05-28-1, Bombay Sappers and Miners, Photograph Album.

66 Bombay Sappers and Miners, Photograph Album. Diary 1897, 4-10 November.

67 Diary 1897, 6 December.

68 Callwell, *Tirah 1897*, 140.

69 Diary 1897, 7 December.

called on to perform.' The Division now moved along the Bara River and eight days later reached the confluence of the Bara with the Kohat River. Peshawar was fifteen miles to the northeast. 'The march down the Bara was a sad, if heroic, operation,' according to Birdwood and for him, 'one lesson was burnt very deeply into my mind as a result of the experience through which we had passed – the impossibility of attempting to carry out any but the shortest daily marches in such country.'[70] Studying his diary and maps of the Tirah, it would appear those six miles was his considered limit for such marches. Birdwood rode into Peshawar on 21 December and for him the Tirah Expedition was largely finished. The Force had lost 1050 killed and wounded. He went on leave to Lahore.

From a personal viewpoint, Birdwood had witnessed at close quarters four generals on operations in the Tirah – Lockhart, Yeatman-Briggs, Symons of the 1st Division, and General Palmer of the Lines of Communication. The first two were sick. Briggs died on 4 January 1898. Lockhart had as his Chief Staff Officer, Brigadier-General Nicholson, who could 'wield a golden pen' but 'had never held any executive military command.' He had no 'faculty for mixing with the fighting men or keeping a finger on the pulse of the troops.' Birdwood 'could not help noticing and deploring the absence of anything more intimate than the necessary official contact between Force Headquarters and that of our Division. ... even when the two formations were close together, correspondence rather than personal discussion was the rule. ... As things were, there was a notable absence of that confident and happy spirit which is always so important in military operations.'[71] Birdwood would later display quite contrary personal methods of command and would become renowned for his approach.

As in 1897, from February until October 1898 Birdwood was in command. The Guard digest recorded the building of a mess house, a gymnasium, a second reservoir and a forge. During a two-week spell at Simla he had plenty of time and opportunity to discuss his future. Above all he was due home leave. He appeared before a medical board on 2 December. He did not record the reason but was 'invalided for a year.'[72] On 4 January 1899 he 'sailed for home', now married and a father.

In 1892 Birdwood had met his future wife – Miss Janetta [Jenny, Jen or Jane] Hope Gonville Bromhead – as 6 February is marked with 'Arrived in Peshawar ... Spent very pleasant morning with my little Jenny.[73] Drove down to polo ground in afternoon ... & went for ride with Jen afterwards,' and the next day he 'spent all morning with Jenny' before leaving for Pindi.[74] Jenny had come out to India as a young girl to be with her father, Colonel Sir Benjamin Bromhead who was renowned for his brave actions during the Hazara Expedition, 1888, and was later Governor of Aitchison College, Lahore.[75] On 4 November, he marked 'xxxx' in the margin of his diary. He 'sat with my little Jenny all morning, proposed to her & was accepted. Pray God we may be very happy & that she may really love me very much someday, which I can't believe

70 Birdwood, *Khaki and Gown*, 86 and 88.
71 Birdwood, *Khaki and Gown*, 83.
72 Diary 1898, 2 December.
73 Lieutenant Colonel Gonville Bromhead VC was her great-uncle.
74 Diary 1892, 6-10 February.
75 Aitchison College is today one of Pakistan's most prestigious educational establishments. Benjamin Bromhead's youngest brother was Gonville Bromhead of Rorke's Drift fame.

she absolutely does now.'[76] Their marriage was to last fifty-three years. At the end of 1892 Jenny returned to England. A year later Birdwood received 'Jenny's last letter from home' and on 12 November he met 'my darling Jen' at Lahore.[77] By this time his forthcoming wedding was on the horizon. It took place in Lahore Cathedral on 6 April, and afterwards at Colonel Bromhead's house. His daughter was in an 'ivory satin wedding gown, one's ideal of a bride – sweet, modest, and yet withal very happy.' 'Everything went off very well indeed' and Birdwood wrote a request in his diary that 'God grant my darling Jen & I may have very happy, noble lives.'[78] His good friend Captain Delamain was best man and 'as for the bridegroom, who wore the uniform of the Viceroy's Bodyguard, if the bride looked happy, he looked more than beaming.' Their gifts, 'over a hundred,' included those from the Viceroy and his wife, his predecessor and the Lyalls. They spent 'their honeymoon at Kapurthala, where the Maharaja' had 'most kindly placed his guesthouse at their disposal.'[79] Jenny then followed the regular moves of the GGBG between Calcutta and Dehra Dun, although some years she spent the winter with her parents in Lahore. In mid-1894, in the light of what was to follow, he and Jen made a sad visit to the cemetery at the hill station Mussorie, 'to look for the grave of her small brother & sister, which we found: Gonville James born August 67, died August 68. Mary Edith born July 68. Died August 68.'[80] On 20 July he noted that 'Jen not feeling well.' She did not go out all the next day and stayed in bed throughout the following day. That night she was 'in a good deal of pain & passing blood. R [Ruttledge – the doctor] thinks she must have miscarriage.' Both the diary entries for the following two days record 'a good deal of blood.' Finally, on 6 August Jenny 'put on some clothes and went to Turners for tea.'[81] September, with both their birthdays, provided a respite. On his, 'my darling Jen gave me such a nice birthday card, painted by her dear self.' It is a beautiful card of pink flowers with a small bird and inscribed 'God be wi' you with all my heart.'[82] On 30 September, he wrote: 'My Jen's 22 birthday. I hope she will always have very happy ones.'[83]

In the following February and March, he noted that Jen 'was too seedy' and 'not feeling well enough' to come out to dinner. He may well have been aware that his wife was pregnant again but his urge to go on operations was strong. By April, however, his focus was on his wife. The pages of his diary then exude devoted care and concern and demonstrate a depth of feeling that is unique among the sixty-one diaries. His wife spent months at Mussorie, with Birdwood riding up there whenever he could. On 4 October Jenny had been 'very restless all night. We neither of us got any sleep.' Later 'Jenny's little girl was born at 9 pm ... Jenny very brave & good & quite happy as soon as Baby appeared.'[84] The Viceroy and his wife sent their congratulations.[85] For the next six weeks his diary remained blank. It would appear that 1895, apart from a brief effort to get on operations, was a year focused on Jenny delivering safely their first child, Nancy.

76 Diary 1892, 4 November.
77 Diary 1893, 29 October and 12 November.
78 Diary 1894, 6 April.
79 *The Pioneer*, 11 April 1894.
80 Diary 1894, 21 June.
81 Diary 1894, 20 July – 6 August.
82 NAM 6707-19-89, Hand painted card.
83 Diary 1894, 13 and 30 September.
84 Ibid., 4 and 5 October.
85 NAM 6707-19-101, an Indian Telegraph.

Birdwood and his wife, Jenny, with Nancy, c. 1896. (British Library Asian and African Studies, MSS Eur D 686/98)

When he did return to work, riding or driving with Jen and tennis parties became regular entries. Jenny and Nancy become very much part of his dairies from this time.

She was a strong support to him, including at a distance during the long absences his operational service demanded. Selecting education in England for their children caused Jenny to choose trips home to see them and thereby more marital absences. Socially she was at home in the society in which Birdwood's career was developing and later Jenny, it will be seen, even won over Lord Kitchener. A stable marriage was an asset, as later as a brigade commander's wife at Kohat, in many visits to wounded during the war and during their Australia visit.[86] Some wives were outwardly ambitious for their husbands but this was not apparent with Jenny then or as Lady Birdwood later.[87]

86 See Chapter 4 for Birdwood's Kohat service.

87 See 'Wives' in Ian Beckett, *A British Profession of Arms: The Politics of Command in the Late Victorian Army* (Norman, Oklahoma: University of Oklahoma Press, 2018), 131-41. Throughout both the Boer War and First World War, Birdwood received regular letters from his wife. He replied expressing his gratitude but none of her letters are found in any archives.

On reaching Southampton on 26 January. He, Jenny and Nancy went by train straight to his father's house in Twickenham. It was Birdwood's 'first day in England since 3rd June 1885.'[88] He had left as a young officer embarking on his regimental training. He returned as a highly proficient military officer. He had been successful both as an adjutant and in squadron command. He had struck a rapport with his Indian soldiers by both his personal behaviour and by his industrious learning of their languages. He was a skilled trainer of men. His experience on operations had gained him vital recognition and a mention in despatches 'for his good service' in Tirah.[89] He had conducted himself successfully in the highest circles of Indian official society, both through his appointments and by his own manner. Despite being invalided for a year, he was a very fit man, involved in a number of sporting activities. His diaries suggest that he possessed a faith and a certain moral compass, both of which he applied in his life with ease. Finally, he had a stable home life with a wife whom he loved deeply, together with the blessing of their first child. Jenny had returned to England pregnant with their second child. After a good long break in England Birdwood could expect to return to a military post that ensured his continued progression in the Indian Army for which he now had great affection. Thus, Birdwood had taken his first steps in command. He had gained sight of the vital importance of leadership and morale and was now experienced in the politics of the Indian Army.

Birdwood and his wife set about visiting friends and welcoming them to his father's home. With no horse he found himself 'becoming a bicycle enthusiast, if only to get the exercise to which' he had 'always been accustomed.'[90] His first non-family visit was down to Aldershot to see the XII Lancers, who were back from India. He spent time at the Cavalry Brigade Chases, meeting 'Sir Redvers Buller & Genl French' there.[91] On 22 May, 'Baby Boy [Christopher] was born at 5 minutes past 8 in the morning – a very decent boy apparently & all going well – Jenny so brave & good.'[92] For the next month he usually spent half of the day sitting with his wife. After that Clifton beckoned and he set off to Bristol by bicycle for Commemoration.[93] He spent two nights with Lord Methuen halfway through his journey and the subject of South Africa could well have arisen. Commemoration took a familiar routine – chapel in the morning, then cricket, and finally dinner in Big School with speeches by Henry Newbolt and the Headmaster. He cycled back to Twickenham via Oxford – ten days of exercise.[94] In late August and early September the Birdwoods spent four weeks holidaying in Kent with members of Jenny's family. At that time, the British cabinet committed 10,000 troops under General Buller to South Africa. The XII Lancers were due to go but to Birdwood's pleas, Lord Airlie, their Commanding Officer, wrote back: "I am afraid we are full up.'[95] Birdwood wrote to others, including Lord Lansdowne, previously Viceroy but now at the War Office. Lansdowne 'sent in his name to the Military Secretary & said a few words in your favour but the number of applicants is legion &

88 Diary 1899, 4 and 26 January.
89 BL AAS, L/MIL/17/2/403, General Orders by the Government of Bengal, Government of India (Military Department) Simla, 1898, 252.
90 Birdwood, *Khaki and Gown*, 91.
91 Diary 1899, 20-22 March.
92 Diary 1899, 22 May.
93 Commemoration is the occasion each summer half term when the foundation of the school is celebrated.
94 Diary 1899, 16-26 June.
95 NAM 6707-19-146, Letter, Airlie to Birdwood, 21 September 1899.

I don't know whether there will be much chance for officers of the ISC [Indian Staff Corps].'[96] War was declared on 11 October and Birdwood believed Lansdowne did put in a word for him as on 27 October he 'got wire saying was selected for special service Natal & to appear before medical board.' Eleven days later he 'said goodbye to my sweet little Nancy & Christopher before leaving. We went by Waterloo to Euston where I said goodbye to my darling dear wife & dear old mother.' His father travelled up to Liverpool with him and Birdwood said, 'goodbye to my dear old father there.' Birdwood's leave in England was over. His ship sailed on Wednesday 8 November. On board was a party of military attachés, including one from France – 'Lt Col d'Amade' – who would later command the French Forces at Gallipoli.[97]

96 NAM 6707-19-146, Letter, Lansdowne to Birdwood, 3 October 1899.
97 Diary 1899, 7 and 8 November.

3

With Buller and Kitchener in South Africa

While Birdwood was at sea much had happened. The news of 10,000 men being dispatched and further British mobilisation forced the Boers' hand. War was declared on 11 October and the Boers crossed from the two republics, Transvaal and the Orange Free State, besieging both Mafeking and Kimberley. By 2 November, commandos from both Republics linked up and besieged Ladysmith. Meanwhile, General Buller's corps had started arriving. He split his forces in response to the major sieges: a division, under Lord Methuen to relieve Kimberley and Mafeking; and a central force, under Major General William Gatacre, to secure the central railway; while Buller himself would advance with the majority of his Corps to relieve Ladysmith.[1] Birdwood landed at Durban on 1 December. As well as through luck and good fortune, his professional performance over the next two-and-a-half years in operational and staff appointments was to transform the trajectory of his career. He earned rapid promotion, found in Kitchener a lifelong patron and commenced nine years of service to him. Birdwood was, furthermore, now serving with the British Army and would learn to be aware of its politics.

Birdwood left Durban for Pietermaritzburg with written instructions 'to report yourself to Col Lord Dundonald for duty with an Irregular Corps.'[2] He found he 'was appointed Staff Officer B to Lord Dundonald Comdg all the mounted forces in S Natal – a better billet than I had ever anticipated.'[3] Dundonald's command had only been created two weeks earlier and when eleven months later it was broken up, Birdwood, by then its Brigade Major, acquired the unit War Diary and kept it.[4] On 10 December Dundonald's force was 'constituted a Mounted Brigade', with Major Graham 5th Lancers as Brigade Major; Birdwood as staff officer; and Captain Hubert Gough 16th Lancers, as Intelligence Officer.[5] The Brigade consisted of: 1st Royal Dragoons; the 13th Hussars; and three recently raised irregular units, namely the South African Light Horse under Lieutenant Colonel Julian Byng; Bethune's Mounted Infantry (MI) and Thorneycroft's MI. Birdwood considered these Irregular units as having 'first-class

1 Haythornthwaite, *The Colonial Wars Source Book*, 196-8; Thomas Pakenham, *The Boer War* (London: George Weidenfeld & Nicolson, 1979), 104-06, 53-55.
2 NAM 6707-19-157, Handwritten orders from Major Heath AAG LofC, 2 December 1899.
3 Diary 1899, 28 November, 1-4 December.
4 NAM 6707-19-189, War Diary 3rd Mounted Brigade South African Field Force,1899-1900.
5 It was Hubert Gough whom Birdwood succeeded as GOC Fifth Army in 1918.

Commanding Officers.'[6] Major Alec Thorneycoft had raised his unit in October with personally selected officers including ex-Yeomanry, Indian Staff Corps, and 'a few Australians and other colonials.'[7] Major Edward Bethune raised his, also in October, with some Australian officers 'who had come over at their own expense, so as not to miss whatever fighting was going on.' Both were 500 strong. Byng's, raised at the Cape in November, consisted of 'eight squadrons, 600 strong.'[8] Buller now made his first bid to relieve Ladysmith with the attempted capture of Colenso to his front. The Mounted Brigade, strengthened by 7 Battery RFA, were to cover the right flank of the infantry frontal assault. 'The whole force marched to Chieveley not far from Colenso' on 14 December. Birdwood observed:

> Battle of Colenso. Force advanced at 4 a.m. Lyttleton's and Hart's Bdes were to cross the river [Tugela] well to our left & fall on the right of the Colenso position. Barton's Bde to hold it in front. Hillyard in reserve. We were on the extreme right to check a commando there going to the help of Colenso. Hart's Irish Bde had the Royal Dragoons under Burn-Murdoch on their left. B-M warned Hart that the enemy were strong, but he disregarding this, advanced in columns up to 1000 yds of the enemy who opened up on him with shrapnel & rifle fire. His Bde lost about 528 men during the day. In the centre Long had galloped up his 2 Batteries recklessly close to their Inf fire & in a few moments his horses & men were all out of action, the guns & horses lying about on the plain, where 10 guns had to be abandoned. The Inf had to be advanced to protect the guns & lost very heavily advancing splendidly over the open without firing a shot. Our guns very soon silenced all theirs with the exception of a beastly quick firing Nordenfelt which pumped lead all over the place & which could not be located. … Eventually Buller ordered a general retirement, we guarding the rt. Flank. Our Bde lost about 100. Colenso shelled us for some time & the whole time I hardly saw a Boer, the smokeless powder giving him a great advantage.[9]

It was the first time Birdwood had been under gunfire.[10] Colonel Long was the very same officer who on Attock manoeuvres in 1890 had galloped hard along the Grand Trunk Road and suddenly found an enemy battery to his front, forcing him to circle around and withdraw. The exercise umpires put his battery out of action. 'It was at the battle of Colenso long afterwards, that history repeated itself.'[11] When 7 Battery was tasked to help extricate Long's guns. Birdwood 'asked Reed, the Captain of the Battery, to take along three teams to see what he could do … After what seemed quite a short space of time Reed returned, looking rather white. He had been shot through his thigh, and had lost most of the teams and many of his men. For his gallant effort, he was awarded the V.C., as were other old friends of mine – Walter Congreve

6 War Diary 3rd Mounted Brigade, 22 November-10 December 1899. Birdwood, *Khaki and Gown*, 94.
7 Uitlanders, (Afrikaans: 'foreigners'), were the British or non-Afrikaner workers attracted to the gold fields of Transvaal and grew to be an awkward majority for the ruling Boers.
8 The Marquess of Anglesey, *A History of the British Cavalry, Volume 4: 1899-1913* (London: Leo Cooper, 1986), 70-72.
9 Diary 1899, 14 and 15 December.
10 Birdwood, *Khaki and Gown*, 97.
11 Ibid., 66-7.

(who had been at Sandhurst with me), dear Freddy Roberts (only son of Lord Roberts), and Babtie, [doctor – RAMC].'[12] Roberts was killed. Birdwood's first battle, in a form of warfare quite unlike that of the North-West Frontier, had ended in failure. He had seen two headstrong advances suffer dire results. Colenso was the third disastrous British failure in a few days – with General Gatacre surprised at Stormberg on 10 December, and Lord Methuen defeated at Magersfontein on 11 December – and consequently 10-15 December became known as 'Black Week.' Command and tactics had to change.[13] Lord Roberts was summoned from Ireland to take overall command and selected Kitchener as his Chief of Staff. Buller was retained in command of the forces in Natal.

The Mounted Brigade were now 'busy re-fitting and reconnoitring the surrounding country' and the 'staff at work reorganising the Brigade & making arrangements as to signalling, ambulances, etc.'[14] This was Birdwood's first lengthy opportunity to get to know the commanders, officers, and units of the Brigade. On Boxing Day, Winston Churchill arrived – both as a war correspondent and an officer in Byng's SALH – and recounted 'all about his escape from Pretoria & some very interesting conversation about the Boers & the war.'[15] The Brigade commenced to reconnoitre to the West. On 10 January, they reached Springfield on the Little Tugela river and finding the bridge there unoccupied, pushed on to Potgieter's Drift over the Tugela itself. On 12 January Major Graham was ordered to take command of a composite regiment formed from a number of MI sub units. Birdwood then became Brigade Major as a local major. The Mounted Brigade manoeuvred around the western end of the Tugela Heights that lined the north bank of the Tugela river, the eastern end of which looked down onto Colenso, twenty-five miles away.[16] This opportunity to turn the enemy's right flank from their position was halted by Sir Charles Warren, temporarily in command of the force. He was 'furious at our having gone so far & saying he wanted us to cling to him & between him & the heights held by the enemy, instead of rt. away to the flanks as we shd. have been.' He removed some of the brigade 'to keep up on the hills & said he didn't care what we did.'[17] The reduced Mounted Brigade was not involved in the subsequent battle – Spion Kop – but one of its commanders was most prominent. Warren had delayed selecting his point of attack on the Tugela Heights, prompting Buller to make visits forward and 'goad him into action.' Thorneycroft and 200 MI – dismounted for this action – led the night attack, under the overall command of Major General Woodgate. The six-mile approach march began at 8.20 pm and reached the base of Spion Kop around midnight. 'It takes a fit man a little more than an hour to get up Spion Kop but in the darkness and confusion of a tiring night march the troops took four and a half hours to make the ascent.' As the slope was beginning to flatten out voices were heard in the darkness ahead. A burst of fire and then a bayonet charge cleared the hill. Recalling Majuba and the lack of entrenchment there, the accompanying engineers laid out a 400-yard trench system. At 7 am the mist temporarily lifted and the British troops were able to observe that their field of fire only extended to the plateau's crest line – 200 yards away at best and only 80 yards at its nearest

12 Ibid., 96. 'Reed came out to Gallipoli as BGGS to General Stopford at Suvla.'
13 Pakenham, *The Boer War*, 246-7.
14 War Diary 3rd Mounted Brigade, 18-21 December 1899; Birdwood, *Khaki and Gown*, 97.
15 Ibid., 97-8; Diary 1899, 26 December.
16 War Diary 3rd Mounted Brigade, 10-18 January 1900.
17 Diary 1900, 19 January.

point. 'The full appreciation of their peril burst upon the British when the sun finally burned the mist away at about 8.30 am. A wide arc of enemy fire covered their position.' The tragic details of the stages of the fighting need not be recounted. First Woodgate was killed; then the next senior commander was injured; to be followed by the next, who sent 'a panicky message.' This resulted in Warren sending forward reinforcements. Buller, on the other hand, perceived conflicting evidence in the reports. Wanting a strong commander on the ground, he telegraphed Warren to put Thorneycroft, who he could see through his telescope prominently leading the fighting, in command. Thorneycroft was promoted to the local rank of Brigadier-General.[18] The day continued with both intense fighting and a lack of clear communication between those on the hilltop and their distant commanders. By sunset the British had secured their position but they did not know it. By then Winston Churchill had climbed up Spion Kop and in his words:

> I found Colonel Thorneycroft at the top of the mountain. Everyone seemed to know, even in the confusion, where he was. He was sitting on the ground surrounded by the remnants of the regiment he had raised, who had fought for him like lions and followed him like dogs. I explained the situation as I had been told and as I thought. Naval guns were prepared to try, sappers and working parties were already on the road with thousands of sandbags. What did he think? But the decision had already been taken. He had never received any messages from the General, had not had time to write any. Messages had been sent him; he had wanted to send others himself. The fight had been too hot, too close, too interlaced for him to attend to anything, but to support this company, clear those rocks, or line that trench. So, having heard nothing and expecting no guns, he had decided to retire. As he put it tersely: 'Better six good battalions safely down the hill than a mop up in the morning.' Then we came home, drawing our rearguard after us very slowly and carefully, and as the ground grew more level the regiments began to form again into their old solid blocks.[19]

Birdwood served with Thorneycroft until November and Churchill was with the Brigade for another month. The apparent lack of clear communications and understanding between commanders on the ground and their superiors that led to a regrettable withdrawal must have been an obvious lesson to Birdwood. Did this drive him to communicate clearly with Hamilton on the first evening at Anzac Cove? In doing so he ensured that everyone understood the situation on the ground and knew the resultant orders – stay, hold on and dig.

Buller resumed his command and decided 'to retire again across the Tugela to everyone's disgust & horror.'[20] On 1 February Buller divided the Mounted Brigade into two. The 2 Brigade was to consist of the SALH, TMI and the Composite Regiment, with Dundonald in command and Birdwood formally as its Brigade Major.[21] Birdwood now wrote up both his own diary and the Brigade War Diary. The siege of Ladysmith had yet to be relieved. Buller made his third attempt midway between Spion Kop and Colenso. This was the attack on Vaal Krantz, 4-8

18 Oliver Ransford, *The Battle of Spion Kop* (London: John Murray, 1969), 52, 63-69, 73, 78, 86-91, 98.
19 Winston Spencer Churchill, *London to Ladysmith via Pretoria* (London: Longmans Green, 1900), 139-40.
20 Diary 1900, 25 January.
21 War Diary 3rd Mounted Brigade, 1 February 1900.

February, during which Birdwood watched successful attacks followed once more by inaction. At the end he wrote: 'had we stuck to it after taking Vaal Krantz, all wd. I am sure been well ... we simply sat down & did nothing,' concluding with 'Gough & I bathed in Tugela.'[22]

Meanwhile, Roberts, having advanced in the centre and in the west, had drawn forces away from Natal to the Orange Free State. Buller now planned his fourth attempt on Ladysmith, to the east of his first but using the Hlangwane feature where Dundonald's Brigade had first gone into action two months earlier. On 27 February, attacks were launched on a series of hills northeast of Colenso and Dundonald's 'dismounted men & machine guns lined the ridge running from Hlangwane parallel to the Tugela & completely swept the whole face of the enemy's positions with fire.'[23] They 'crossed the Tugela in early morning ... & began reconnoitring.' Finally, Gough 'scouted towards Ladysmith & reported all clear. Lord D, self, Winston Churchill & Saint Clowes [ADC] rode on, sending back the SALH & TMI. We had a never to be forgotten mad gallop into Ladysmith ... across Klip river, where Brocklehurst [Cavalry CO in Ladysmith] met us, & on to Sir G White's Hd Qtrs.' This was an historic event for Birdwood and Gough to share together. Birdwood met up with General White whom he had last seen in 1898 in Calcutta as C-in-C India. On White's staff was Hamilton. Buller entered Ladysmith the next day but Birdwood had 'left at dawn with our 2 Squadrons & met up with the rest of the Bde.' No further advance took place and once again Birdwood recorded in his diary: 'Sir R lost grand opportunity of pursuing. Cavalry might easily have captured lots of wagons, stores, guns, etc, but he wasn't for it. Nobody did anything.'[24] Hamilton left Ladysmith for Roberts' HQ and Churchill went with him as ADC. Birdwood wrote to his wife about Churchill:

> He is an awfully good little chap, & will undoubtedly make his mark, but not I think a very big one, as has little power of self-restraint – if he is thirsty he must drink – if has nothing to talk about, he still must talk – the same with his writing. He has just left us to join Ian Hamilton as ADC. Before going, he came up to say good bye & took me aside & said "Well, goodbye my dear Birdwood. I am so glad to have served with you & having seen everything as I have, I know perfectly well that Lord D owes every bit of success he has had entirely to you, & if he doesn't see that you are very well looked after, he ought to be ashamed of himself." Wasn't it nice of him?

The Brigade pushed out patrols during March but did not advance. By the end of the month Birdwood had been confirmed as a local Major and been mentioned in Dundonald's despatch as having 'proved himself to be a valuable staff officer and has done very good work both in "B" duties and as Brigade Major to a mounted brigade.'[25] This was to be the first of three mentions for Birdwood that year. His overview of the Brigade's organisation, deployment, state of health and administrative position written for the war diary is comprehensive.[26] With an increase in cavalry regiments, two cavalry brigades were formed and Dundonald's became the 3 Mounted Brigade. Birdwood wrote to his wife, stressing that 'You needn't be afraid little pet of my doing

22 Diary 1900, 7 February.
23 War Diary 3rd Mounted Brigade, 27 February 1900.
24 Diary 1900, 27 and 28 February, 1 March.
25 *London Gazette*, 8 February 1901, 942
26 War Diary 3rd Mounted Brigade, 1 April 1900.

anything rash as I have already promised you I won't, even if I wanted to Lord D wd never let me lead any gun capturing expedition or such like things.' He noted 'how much you have given up for my sake in my coming out here at all, so don't you think I forget it.' He described his relationship with Dundonald, who clearly appreciated Birdwood, as one of growing affection and increased understanding, although he was not confident that Dundonald had the courage to push things like promotion. Birdwood noted that it was 'impossible' for him to succeed in England after the war, as he was an Indian Staff Corps officer.[27] He was, of course, to succeed in India with patronage that linked him to England. Birdwood had had a bout of dysentery in mid-February and then on 19 April, was sent down to a hospital ship at Durban. He had extended convalescence, returning to his Brigade on 7 May. He was careful not to become so incapacitated again, having only one very short bout of dysentery at Gallipoli.

Buller's forces now advanced northwards, along the line of the railway leading ultimately to Johannesburg. The Boers 'fought a really first-class rear-guard fight, taking up one position after another … as they retired they burnt the veldt everywhere & the whole country for miles was blazing & dense smoke.'[28] The three-day truce at the start of June ended with 'the Boers refusing to have anything to do with Sir Redvers' terms.'[29] The Brigade was then at Ingogo Drift.[30] On 20 June Dundonald's Brigade was strengthened with the addition of Strathcona's Horse, recently arrived from Canada. Buller took Laing's Nek pass and his force entered Transvaal. On 4 July at Vlakfontein, Buller's forces 'joined hands for the first time with Lord Roberts,' and then moved north-eastwards in the direction of Machadodorp. As they fought ridge by ridge, Birdwood was injured. He wrote the next day to Jenny that he

> … saw Strathcona's Horse going out in front of a kopje where I was sure they would be certain to come under a heavy shell fire from the ridge beyond, so I galloped on to see if I couldn't get them under cover & was just getting them behind a hill & a piece of the railway embankment, when sure enough the shells came down on us like billy-oh! The very first one burst with a tremendous crash just in front of my horse & I just had time to think that it was precious close & wonder if I was going to be hit, when I felt my horse give a great lunge forward … jumped off before my horse fell, to find that he had been hit through the jugular vein by part of the shell & another piece had gone into his chest & out behind the shoulders & into my leg just below the knee.[31]

The horse was killed. Birdwood considered that the horse's shoulder wound saved his leg from far worse damage.[32] But to his mother he wrote; 'they aren't yet quite certain if the bullet is still in the bone or not,' annotating this with the comment, 'Don't tell Jenny this.'[33] After a couple of days in the small hospital at Machadodorp he was put on a train with other wounded to Pretoria.

27 NAM 6707-19-228, Letter, Birdwood to his wife, 12 March 1900.
28 Diary 1900, 12 and 14 May.
29 Ibid., 2 and 5 June
30 NAM 6706-19-229, Letter, Birdwood to his wife, 6 August 1900, for which Birdwood invited Captain Molyneux, who was out there 'on purpose to be able to paint a realistic war picture for next year's academy,' to add four water colours, including a delightful view of Ingogo Drift.
31 NAM 6707-19-230, Letter, Birdwood to his wife, 29 August 1900.
32 Ibid.
33 NAM 6707-19-249, Letter, Birdwood to his mother, 30 August 1900.

Lord Roberts missed seeing him as the train passed by very late but 'Sir H Rawlinson stopped to say that Lord R had wired on to Pretoria about me.' On arrival in Pretoria he found that 'Lady Roberts had sent up to ask after him.' His wound looked 'rather nasty but not dangerous.' 'Roe[n]tgen … showed no signs of any bullet in the leg but a split down the tibia.'[34] He remained in hospital until 18 September, receiving many visitors. Lady Roberts sent her carriage for Birdwood to come out and have tea with the family on occasions. Following what might be considered a lucky wound, connections had benefitted him once more. After recuperating in Johannesburg, he returned to the Brigade on 2 October, finding to his great regret that his 'days of daily treks across the veldt had come to an end, for the Natal Force, as such, was broken up, and Sir Redvers, Lord Dundonald, and most of the staff returned to England. For nearly a year I had led a life that I loved: scarcely ever sleeping in a house, and almost every day passing long hours in the saddle.' Buller having earlier mentioned Birdwood 'as having performed good service' now stated that Birdwood

> … has served as staff of the 3rd Mounted Brigade since November 1899. He is an admirable staff officer from every possible point of view. I desire to give him, as he well deserves, the highest possible commendation. His duties during the campaign have been exceptionally difficult and severe and have been discharged with exceptional skill. In the interests of the Army, I strongly recommend him for advancement.[35]

Birdwood was not to go home with the others.

Rather, he was summoned by Kitchener, who was to take over from Roberts. Birdwood described the meeting to Jenny:

> Kitchener was awfully nice & after all one has heard of his being such a brute, I was quite astonished how very nice & easy he was to get on with. He said he had heard I had been doing very well, & that consequently he couldn't spare me, but wanted me to take up work under him at once as DAAG Army Headquarters. He gave me no time to answer, or think of anything, but plunged into it at once, gave me files of papers & explained what he wanted me to do & sent me off, to at once start on them, before I had settled up my old job with the Bde.[36]

Forty years later Birdwood wrote:

> I now had orders to report to Lord Kitchener at Pretoria, and thus it was that I met, for the first time, the man who was to have the greatest influence on my life. If I may say so, we seemed to take to each other at once, and for the next nine years I was scarcely ever away from him.[37]

34 Diary 1900, 1-4 September.
35 *London Gazette* 2 February 1901, 959 and 972.
36 NAM 6707-19-231, Letter, Birdwood to his wife, 16 October 1900.
37 Birdwood, *Khaki and Gown*, 117.

To his old friend Crawfurd, he said 'they have put me in charge of the interests of all the Mtd troops in the country – Cavalry, Colonials & MI – a big job, their mounting, equipment & movements, & I have to raise & organise a new force of 4000 MI at the same time.'[38] He realised that 'with Lord K coming out to India as C-in-Chief, it is really a great chance for me, being able to do this work under him.' Birdwood was naturally very disappointed not to be going home to his wife and family, watching his children growing up from photographs alone. Kitchener had not realised that Birdwood was married. When Lady Roberts did mention to Kitchener that Birdwood was married, Kitchener 'nearly bounded out of his chair with a shout of "What Birdwood married! Married!!" She said she had never seen him so excited & it was just as if a Bombshell had fallen on him!' Lady Roberts 'finished up by saying "I told him you would be far more useful to him as a married man than as a bachelor, on which we had a great argument, as I have always maintained that a good soldier is only improved by marrying!"'[39]

The Boers continued with their guerrilla warfare and movements over the veldt, against which Kitchener employed mounted columns. Birdwood remained busy and had not 'a second to myself, for besides all my office work to get through Lord Kitchener likes to keep constantly sending one flying off to see how the various new corps we are raising are getting on, or to go out with some of the many columns.' Birdwood had still over a year to serve in South Africa and much more strain on individuals to observe. In three months of staff work, '5,000 new MI & about the same number of Irregular Horse' had been raised.[40] Birdwood exercised regularly, riding most days – often with Kitchener. There was 'a very pleasant mess' and it was there Birdwood first made friends with Kiggell 'an exceedingly able staff officer' and Haig's future CGS.[41] Hamilton had returned as Kitchener's Chief of Staff and was a frequent companion for morning swims.

Since his arrival in South Africa Birdwood would have been aware of 'Colonials,' a general term for white Britons from other parts of the Empire. At the end of November 1899, Australia, together with New Zealand, had sent its First Contingent of 1,200 formed troops. These had served with the western and central forces, as they advanced northwards. The Second Contingent had been recruited post Black Week and had served likewise. The demand for more mounted forces and the willingness of men in the Australian colonies to serve resulted in the Third Contingent, entitled the Citizens Bushmen – funded by public subscription, and the Fourth Contingent, the Imperial Bushmen Corps – so named as they were funded by the British Government. The Third and Fourth arrived from April until mid-May and were the contingents with which Birdwood now had dealings.[42] Australia's official centenary historian of the Boer War, Craig Wilcox, has commented that the destinations of the contingents 'were largely determined by William Birdwood, an obscure staff officer and acolyte of Kitchener's who would make his name commanding Australians during the Great War.'[43] Twenty thousand

38 NAM 6707-19-261, Letter, Birdwood to Capt Christie Crawfurd, 28 November 1900.
39 NAM 6707-19-231, Letter, Birdwood to his wife, 16 October 1900.
40 NAM 6707-19-262, Letter, Birdwood to Capt Christie Crawfurd, 28 November 1900. Diary 1901, 7-11 January.
41 Birdwood, *Khaki and Gown*, 120.
42 Grey, *A Military History of Australia*, 55; R L Wallace, *The Australians at the Boer War* (Canberra: AWM and Australian Government Publishing Service, 1976), 61, 77, 231-36.
43 Craig Wilcox, *Australia's Boer War: the war in South Africa, 1899-1902* (South Melbourne: Oxford University Press (in association with AWM), 2002), 193.

Australians served in South Africa.[44] In March Birdwood went down to Cape Town to see off the First Contingent, after its year of service. Mounted troops, however, were still increasingly needed and Birdwood told all elements of the Contingent how much Kitchener wanted them, explaining the terms of reengagement on offer. Quite a number responded and reengaged for a further year.[45] Birdwood wrote later that he 'always felt that my close contact with these excellent fellows laid the foundation of my very happy relations with the Australian and New Zealand troops throughout the War of 1914-18. Indeed, it was because he realised how well we had got on together in South Africa that Lord Kitchener selected me to command' the Anzacs in 1914. Birdwood's autobiography makes no mention of a later incident involving Australians and the now Major General Beatson, a column commander, whose troops included the Fifth Victorian Mounted Rifles. His Brigade Major was Major Waterfield, an XI BL officer of Birdwood's vintage.[46] On 12 June at Wilmansrust, a detachment of 250-350 under Major Morris, also XI BL, was returning from a sweep south of the main column. When they camped for the night, they stacked their rifles in piles and posted pickets, which were spotted by the Boers. Beatson, ignoring local experience, had enforced the outpost system. [47] A group of 150 Boers totally surprised the Victorian camp, killing eighteen and wounding forty-one. Around eighty prisoners were taken and released some distance away. A hundred horses were killed and a further hundred taken off by the Boers. It was a humiliation.[48] Three days later Birdwood wrote that 'heard that Beatson had detached a wing of his Victorians 250 strong with 2 Pompoms [small guns] under Morris S of Middelburg & that they had been attacked & all mopped up by Moller detached from Viljoen.'[49] The humiliation and subsequent debacle came to be known as The Wilmansrust Incident. After the attack, Beatson came up to the site and apparently remarked to another officer that the Victorians were 'a fat-arsed, pot-bellied, lazy lot of wasters.' Challenged about these words, Beatson replied 'you can add that in my opinion they are a lot of white-livered curs.' Such opinions filtered out among the Victorian Contingent. It was later stated that an officer overheard one Private James Steele say 'We'll be a lot of fools if we go out with him [Beatson] again.' As a result, a Field General Court-Martial tried Steele and two others for inciting mutiny. On 11 July, all three were found guilty and sentenced to death.'[50] On 8 July Birdwood noted in his diary that Beatson was 'in the "muck tub" with Lord K!' Beatson had been ordered to give up his Victorians and was tasked with the Inniskillings & Royals. Beatson 'said he wd start when he found an objective! This delay annoyed Lord K.' In the end Beatson was left with just the Victorians.[51] Then on 9 August Beatson visited Kitchener's HQ for two days and stayed with Birdwood. He wrote later to Crawfurd: 'Beatson, I am very sorry for him, for I am sure he really is a good man & I should have most awfully liked to have seen him get a chance but he has never had one. He came out too late in the war, that's about what it

44 Grey, *A Military History of Australia*, 55.
45 Diary 1901, 14, 15 and 18 March. NAM 6707-19-263, Letter, Birdwood to Capt Christie Crawfurd, 15 April 1901.
46 Max Chamberlain, "The Wilmansrust affair", *The Journal of the Australian War Memorial,* 6, April (1985), 51.
47 Wilcox, *Australia's Boer War: The War in South Africa, 1899-1902*, 205, 208.
48 Wallace, *The Australians at the Boer War*, 328-33; Souter, *Lion and Kangaroo*, 58-59.
49 Diary 1900, 15 June.
50 Souter, *Lion and Kangaroo*, 59-61.
51 Diary 1900, 8 July.

was and by the time he had learnt the game, his opportunities had gone.'[52] Kitchener, as C-in-C, did confirm the guilty verdicts but 'commuted the sentences to prison terms of ten years in the case of Steele and one year with hard labour for each of the others.'[53] On 28 September the news of Beatson's comments and the resultant trial and verdicts reached Australia. The Melbourne *Age* published an anonymous letter from a soldier of the 5th Victorians.[54] Its readers heard the news before the British Government had informed Australia.[55] Volunteering in loyal support of the Empire conflicted with understandable concern about the fighting performance of troops, but the incredibly offensive comments by a British general gave rise to understandable doubts concerning the British leadership of Australian troops. Suffice it to say, Beatson's words and approach caused public upset and debate.[56] Birdwood would meet up again with Beatson in India and as members of the XI BL family they would stay in touch.[57] Birdwood must have known in detail about the Wilmansrust Incident and all its ramifications. Perhaps this contributed to his treatment in December 1914 of Anzacs with equanimity on his arrival in Egypt, and subsequently his extremely careful handling of relationships with Dominion governments and their ministers.

Throughout 1901 Birdwood wrote home to Jenny telling her how much he missed her and the children and expressing hope about coming home. By September, he unenthusiastically remarked that 'time drags on dreadfully & I fear we are all feeling a bit depressed at present with no immediate prospect of the end of the war.'[58] Already in the Honours gazette at the end of April Birdwood had been 'noted for promotion to Lieut Colonel on becoming a substantive Major, i.e. 4 years hence unless anything else turns up meanwhile!'[59] In October it did. 'Fancy – Lord K has made me a Lt Colonel out here! He didn't say a single word about it & the first I saw or knew of it was when I suddenly saw it in orders.' He added: 'shan't you feel very ancient my dear, when it is "Col & Mrs B"! just think of it.'[60] His letters expressed a private confidence to Jenny that he would go to India with Kitchener, but that the position and the rank were still to be determined. Birdwood frequently rode with Kitchener and was often a guest at dinner. These contacts gave Birdwood time to appreciate the demands on a very senior commander, noting occasions when Kitchener was tired or depressed, and frustrated with his own staff; Birdwood would face similar pressures in the future.[61]

On New Year's Day 1902 Birdwood wrote sadly that he 'had hoped a good many of Botha's men would have come in & surrendered today. Rather disappointing, as I suppose we may now

52 NAM 6707-19-238, Letter, Birdwood to Capt Christie Crawfurd, 22 September 1901.
53 Wallace, *The Australians at the Boer War*, 333; Craig Wilcox, "Australia's South African War 1899-1902", *Scintia Militaria*, 30, 1 (2000), 1.
54 *The Age,* 28 September 1901, 13.
55 On 1 January 1901 the process of the Federation of Australia was completed and the original colonies became the states of the Commonwealth of Australia.
56 *Argus*, 30 September 1901, 5; 1 October 1901, 5.
57 Diary 1902, 24 November. The Birdwoods went straight to Simla on return to India and on their second evening Mrs Beatson was one of two visitors to their home.
58 NAM 6707-19-236,2377,238 and 240, Letters, Birdwood to wife, 2 May, 25 July and 22 September 1901.
59 Diary 1901, 26 April.
60 NAM 6707-19-239, Letter, Birdwood to his wife, 25 October 1901.
61 Diary 1901, 18 October. 'Lord K still very seedy & depressed.'

have to go on again indefinitely.'[62] But thankfully, 'February, 1902, found us full of hope that the end of the war was at last in sight.' Key Boer commanders, Steyn and De Wet, 'were in the net,' but slipped out.[63] 'Those were nerve-racking days.'[64] Birdwood's qualities had been noted. In late February he turned down an offer to command all the volunteer forces of Natal, in the rank of Colonel for five years at £1,000 per annum. His rejection received this response:

> As you know, it is not given to every man to possess the qualities suitable to make a Commandant of Volunteers, and if you will permit me to say so we, one and all, spotted you as the only Imperial Officer of our acquaintance who had in the highest degree the qualifications so much required. ... Speaking for the Vol Brigade we will ever look back with pride & pleasure to the time when we served with Dundonald, and more especially to the harmony and good feeling which existed between his Lordship's Chief Staff Officer & the OCs and Adjutants of the Brigade.[65]

These were the qualities that he would display on meeting the Australians and New Zealanders in Egypt and he had twelve more years in which to develop them. At the end of March, he was able to write to his 'darling old mother' that there had 'just been a visitation from the so-called Transvaal Govt. which may or may not lead to something important.' And a month later to Jenny:

> [W]e can't expect anything till after the 15th May ... de Wet who has been visiting all the different commandos in the O.R.C. [Orange River Colony] has been strongly advising them all to vote for peace when they send in their representatives to Vereeniging next month.

He was positive about the prospects. He had recently said goodbye to Byng who had returned for three months' leave. Byng had written to Jenny and Birdwood asked her to buy Byng 'a little wedding present from me: a gold pencil case engraved "Bungo from Birdie. South Africa 1899-1902." Birdwood ended the letter with his own news that Lord K. had been asked for 'some names for a Coronation honours list – don't say anything about it to anyone but he has recommended me for my Brevet Lt. Colonelcy.'[66] As the war dragged on Jenny had considered going out to South Africa herself, but on 31 May Birdwood began his letter to her that 'today at last everything will be actually settled definitely one way or the other.' He stopped his letter to write: '11P.M. PEACE HAS JUST BEEN SIGNED !!! and in the room too where I do all my work. What do you think of it all, my own darling dearest? Wasn't I quite right now in writing to you to stay at home?'[67] His letter went in the very mail that carried the Peace Treaty, escorted by Colonel Hubert Hamilton, Kitchener's Military Secretary. Birdwood then temporarily

62 Diary 1902, 1 January.
63 Diary 1902, 7 February. Birdwood, *Khaki and Gown*, 126.
64 Birdwood, *Khaki and Gown*, 127; Diary 1902, 9 and 10 March
65 NAM 6707-19-224, Letter, Deighton to Birdwood, 28 February 1902.
66 NAM 6707-19-243, Letter, Birdwood to his wife, 26 April 1902.
67 NAM 6707-19-243, Letter, Birdwood to his wife, 31 May 1902.

assumed that post.[68] In addition Birdwood telegrammed his wife: 'Hymn 135,' which starts: 'The strife is o'er, the battle done.' As Military Secretary, he lived 'in a state of siege – for every single officer in the place is bothering me & as far I can see everyone's Mother is bound to die, or his wife to have a baby, or he is certain to lose all his property if he can't get home during this next week or so! A serious epidemic seems to have set in.' Birdwood embarked for home on 24 June 1902, having not seen Jenny, Nancy and Christopher since 7 November 1899. He had left as a Captain, well versed in the Indian Army, with the hope of gaining his substantive Majority in 1903. He returned as a substantive Captain, but he had been both Local-Major and Local Lt Col, and been awarded both Brevet Major and Brevet Lieutenant Colonel. He had, furthermore, gained and developed his knowledge of the politics of the British Army. Kitchener wrote in his final despatch:

> This young officer has held a difficult position as Assistant Adjutant General, Mounted Troops, and responsible adviser as to the distribution of remounts. In carrying out these duties he has proved himself to possess exceptional ability, and he has shown, moreover, remarkable tact in dealing with and conciliating the various interests which he had to take into consideration.[69]

His ability to get along with people, not just socially but particularly under the stressful demands of active service, had become a regular comment made about him. He had spent two and a half years on operational staff matters and learnt how to operate successfully for commanders. Birdwood had seen at first hand the interaction of various imperial troops and this was the basis for the forthcoming drive for commonality between dominion and Indian forces. He had been severely wounded. On active service for two and a half years with the British Army he had observed the ebb and flow of the operational environment His career had leapt forward.

On Saturday 12 July, Kitchener and his staff arrived home to great celebrations all the way from Southampton to Paddington, where the Prince of Wales, Duke of Connaught, old Duke of Cambridge, Lord Roberts and others met them. They 'drove in great state in royal carriages through the Park to St James Palace' where they lunched with 'the principal members of govt.' Finally, he 'got away about 3' to meet 'my little Jenny Jane … we went down to Richmond … & the children all looking very well. The latter of course very much grown.' Two days later Birdwood took his wife up to meet Kitchener and they lunched at the Cavalry Club with friends such as 'Mrs Jim Turner, and the Brat & Conk' – Kitchener's ADCs.[70] They dined with fifty others at Lord Roberts' home to meet Kitchener once more.[71] The guests included Sir Dighton Probyn, after whom Probyn's Horse was named.[72] Birdwood knew this illustrious old officer of his Regiment from India who was now part of the Royal Household and resident at Hampton

68 Diary 1902, 2 June.
69 *The London Gazette*, 29 July 1902, 4836.
70 'The Brat' was Major Frank Maxwell 18th (KGO) Lancers, Indian Army and Major Raymond Marker Coldstream Guards was known as 'Conk'.
71 Diary 1902, 12 and 14 July.
72 'It was one of my proudest distinctions to follow him [Sir Dighton] as Colonel of Probyn's Horse, the name by which the XI Bengal Lancers became known after amalgamation with the XII Bengal Cavalry.' Birdwood, *Khaki and Gown*, 135.

Court. Birdwood had been writing to him from South Africa and Sir Dighton wrote back that 'I must tell you that 2 or 3 of your letters – those that I felt I might – I have shown to the King.'[73] Birdwood's ability and confidence to correspond with high-ranking personalities is apparent from then. It had been fixed for some time that he would accompany Kitchener to India as Assistant Military Secretary and Interpreter to the C-in-C. Before leaving, he, Jenny and the children had six weeks' holiday. Birdwood went up to London only very occasionally, including for the coronation of King Edward VII to act as ADC to Sir Ian Hamilton commanding the Yeomanry & Volunteers.[74] Latterly Birdwood worked with Kitchener in preparation for India. Just before leaving, Kitchener and his staff were invited to the Palace to be 'presented with our King's African Medal by the King, who on giving me mine said, "I am very glad to know that you are going to be with Lord Kitchener in India."'[75] The Viceroy, Lord Curzon, was keen to see Kitchener as C-in-C, as Curzon saw a great need for change in the Indian military, observing it as characterised by: 'absurd and uncontrolled expenditure', 'a lack of method and system' and 'slackness and jobbery'.[76]

73 NAM 6707-19-226, Letter, Probyn to Birdwood, 30 May 1902.
74 Diary 1902, 9 August.
75 Diary 1902, 13 October.
76 Letter, Curzon to Kitchener, 31 March 1899, *op. cit.* in Philip Magnus, *Kitchener: Portrait of an Imperialist* (London: John Murray, 1958), 176.

4

Return to India once more

Since leaving India Birdwood had advanced in rank and in the coming ten years he would advance still further, through his own hard work and association with Kitchener. On the return voyage Birdwood 'worked on schemes on unification.'[1] These would bring the armies of Calcutta, Bombay and Madras into a single entity. Having taken his family straight to Simla, he returned to Bombay to welcome Kitchener, now aged fifty-two, and accompany him to Delhi to view the site of the forthcoming Durbar. During these first weeks, Kitchener aired his ideas of a renumbering scheme for the Indian Army. Birdwood later kept his working notes on the constitution, present title, proposed title, and alternative of the Indian native regiments.[2] It was an extensive piece of staff work. He had cut his teeth on the twin demands of volumes of data and the need for very careful detail concerning mounted forces in South Africa. Now working on four different schemes, Birdwood was pleased when Kitchener accepted in principle the most conservative one, which brought the entire Indian Army – the term was now firmly in use – on to a common list.

Birdwood was appointed secretary of a unification committee to undertake the staff work himself.[3] Names and numbers are sources of regimental pride and so renumbering and renaming inevitably become emotive issues. Nonetheless in January 1903, his proposed scheme was well received by the senior generals.[4] In June the details were sent out to Colonels of Indian Regiments and views were returned in July and August.[5] It was promulgated by the end of September and Birdwood was considered to have achieved success in a most difficult and challenging task. General Duff, Adjutant-General (AG), wrote to Birdwood:

> I write to let you know about the Chief's remarks yesterday at the meeting of the Advisory Board regarding the renumbering of the Native army. He spoke of how very

1 T R Moreman, *The Army in India and the Development of Frontier Warfare, 1849-1947* (Basingstoke: Palgrave Macmillan, 1998), 184.
2 NAM 6707-19-547, MS notes by Birdwood on renumbering the regiments of the Indian Army.
3 Moreman, *The Army in India and the Development of Frontier Warfare, 1849-1947*, 184.
4 NAM 6707-19-550, Printed replies on proposed scheme.
5 NAM 6707-19-555 556, 557, Circular to Colonels of Indian Regiments, 8 June 1903; Circular seeking suggested amendments, 31 July 1903; Printed 'Remarks by Commanding Officers on the new numbers and titles of Native Regiments,' 6 August 1903.

Kitchener, C-in-C India with his personal staff: Colonel Hubert Hamilton ('Hammy'), MS, Birdwood, AMS and left to right in back row three ADCs – Captain Victor Brooke DSO 9th Lancers, Major Raymond Marker DSO Coldstream Guards ('Conk') and Major Frank Maxwell VC DSO 18th Lancers ('The Brat'), Delhi, 1902, (National Portrait Gallery x 193210)

> well it had been received and how pleased he was about it and ended with a public expression of thanks to Colonel Birdwood to whom full credit was due for having arranged the scheme in such a way as to make it acceptable to the army. He does not often praise so it is just as well that you should know that in this case he has made an exception.[6]

At the same time Birdwood had reorganised the composition of the *Indian Army List* – the quarterly list of all officers, appointments and regiments – and improved the quality of its production. This also drew praise, particularly in the press: 'The editorship of the Indian Army List has lately been transferred … to the office of the Commander-in-Chief … What is more

6 NAM 6707-19-562, Letter General Duff, Adjutant-General, to Birdwood, 29 October 1903.

manifest is that under Lord Kitchener's inspiration many alterations have been devised and perfected by someone in warm sympathy with the Indian Army and in touch with its inner sentiments.'[7] Both these achievements received public acclaim when in 1905 Birdwood was appointed as Kitchener's Military Secretary.

> Colonel Birdwood has shown what tact and consideration can accomplish in the face of obstacles. The scheme for renaming and renumbering the two hundred various units of the Indian army (under Lord Kitchener's direction) fell virtually into Colonel Birdwood's hands, and the fact that so difficult and delicate an operation should have been conducted at every stage with unbroken smoothness and at last brought to a harmonious conclusion speaks volumes to those who know the sentiment of cherished tradition that cluster round regimental nomenclature. The fact too that under Colonel Birdwood's virtual though unclaimed editorship the *Indian Army List* has been unostentatiously transformed from an incomplete and unsatisfactory periodical, which was the standing butt of miscellaneous criticism, into a really proud and useful compilation is another testimony to his good sense and good feeling.[8]

Both were clear demonstrations of sound staff work.

The Proclamation Durbar for the King's Coronation took place on 1 January 1903 and was presided over by the Viceroy.[9] The reviews, parades and celebrations lasted for ten days.[10] Shortly afterwards, Kitchener set off on the first of his tours accompanied by his Military Secretary 'Hammy' Hamilton, Birdwood, and two ADCs. Kitchener's many tours over the next seven years would cover 65,000 miles, often over challenging country and by various means of transportation.[11] This first tour was to South Waziristan and thence to the areas near the Tirah engagements of 1897. After a month back in Calcutta, Kitchener was off again to the Northwest Frontier, riding through the Khyber Pass, considering options for roads and railway, and finally looking into Afghanistan.[12] From Peshawar they travelled north to Malakand. On all these tours Birdwood was interpreting between Kitchener and native leaders, officials and soldiers. This gave Birdwood a close understanding of Kitchener's thoughts and intentions, observing a senior commander seeing things for himself and then developing his plans.

When he and his party returned to Simla for the summer, Kitchener addressed an issue that had been raised by his predecessor when they met at Bombay.[13] It concerned the Military Member of the Viceroy's Council and the associated small Military Department responsible for

7 NAM 6707-19-310, Press cutting on Indian Army List of July 1903. The List detailed all headquarters, formations, units and individual officers in India.
8 NAM 6707-19-348, Press announcement of Birdwood as Military Secretary.
9 NAM 6707-19-299, Letter, Kitchener to Birdwood, 15 November 1902, inviting Mrs Birdwood to be Kitchener's official guest for the Durbar.
10 Diary 1902, 20-23 and 29 November, 3-20 December. Diary 1903, 1-10 January; R W Paul, "Coronation Durbar at Delhi" (British Film Institute Library, 1903). see extract at <https://www.youtube.com/watch?v=oKF_lie2Wc8> (accessed 19 April 2016).
11 BL MS 52278, 1898-1914, folio 95, Kitchener-Marker papers Vol III, General Correspondence, Kitchener's farewell speech at Simla Club, 20 August 1909.
12 Diary 1903, 2 March.
13 Birdwood, *Khaki and Gown*, 161.

supply, transport, ordnance and general organisation. While the C-in-C controlled operations and training, the Viceroy had overall civil control of all matters, including military ones, with his Military Member, then Major General Sir Edmond Elles, as his personal staff officer.[14] In May a question arose about the issuing of a Governor-General's Order (GGO) which if published would 'increase the powers of the Military department.'[15] On 25 May Birdwood noted in red ink:

> On the proposed publishing of a GGO giving much power to M D [Military Department]. Lord K wrote a very short memo & as a side issue the question arose as to whether the M D cd publish GGO's without the Chief's authority. Curzon having written to say they could, Lord K answered that as this took the command of the army virtually out of his hands, it only remained for him to tender his resignation. Curzon then climbed down & said he had never given such a ruling & wd support the Chief in any such question which must go to Council.[16]

The matter was resolved but it was 'the first faint ripple on the waters of what, later on, was to develop into the great storm popularly known as the Kitchener-Curzon controversy,' which Birdwood treated more gently in his autobiography than did the newspapers of the time.[17] A less controversial event was the 'Peace Dinner' held by Kitchener on 31 May for 'all those who were in South Africa on 31 July 1902.' This may have included both Beatson and Byng as they are mentioned in Birdwood's diary at this time. Another subject which occupied Kitchener's attention throughout the year was his residences. Twenty-seven years later, as he completed his own period as C-in-C, Birdwood wrote a small volume entitled *Residences of the Commanders-in-Chief in India*.[18] Kitchener embarked on rebuilding the Simla residence, 'Snowdon', and 'also took Wildflower Hall, situated a few miles out in the hills.' He executed no major work on this latter house but 'had every member of his Staff busy each week-end in the garden, under his personal supervision.'[19] This included Birdwood's son – 'At Wildflower Hall & Christopher came out for day. Lord K playing with him & teaching him to dig.'[20] In mid-August Kitchener embarked on a 1,600-mile trip taking over two months to view all the strategic passes on India's beautiful north-western frontier 'wild flowers beyond imagination, the whole place being a mass of them.' Birdwood later pasted stunning photos of this trip into an album.[21] The journey was hard-going – 'Lord K had a man pulling him by each arm & another holding on to his belt & shoving him up or holding him back when going down hill.' They crossed suspension bridges,

14 John Pollock, *Kitchener* (London: Constable, 2001), 264-5; C Brad Faught, *Kitchener Hero and Anti-Hero* (London: I B Tauris & Co, 2016), 150.
15 Birdwood, *Khaki and Gown*, 148.
16 Diary 1903, 25 May.
17 Birdwood, *Khaki and Gown*, 148.
18 FM Sir W R Birdwood, *Reminiscences of the Residencies of the Commanders-in-Chief in India* (Bath: Pagoda Tree Press, 2006 (reprint of 1930 edition)).
19 Birdwood, *Khaki and Gown*, 148.
20 Diary 1903, 5 and 7 June.
21 NAM 6206-29, Visit of Viscount Kitchener to Jind State interspersed with other photographs compiled by Col William Birdwood, 1903-1907

forded glacial streams, and even hung onto yaks' tails to ascend in places.[22] Kitchener wanted to see for himself the challenges faced by both any attacking forces and his own defensive forces. They returned down the Khagan Valley, reaching 'Abbottabad and civilisation on 19 October.'[23]

Back in Simla, the proposed reorganisation of the overall structure of the Army was finalised. The balance of Indian and British units in a brigade was altered from two plus two, to three plus one. Having allocated the units necessary for internal security, the remaining eight divisions, capable of serving anywhere, were grouped geographically with permanent commanders and staff.[24] Having been instrumental for nearly a year in the comprehensive restructuring of the entire Indian Army, Birdwood had shown himself to be a most capable staff officer. Kitchener wrote: 'an excellent staff officer – energetic. Gets on well with everyone.'[25] At the end of October Colonel Douglas Haig had arrived in Bombay to become Inspector of Cavalry. Subsequently Birdwood visited the XIIth Lancers at Umballa and recorded meeting and dining with Haig there.[26] In the middle of November tragedy struck Kitchener. While returning alone from Wildflower Hall, his horse was startled coming back through the dark Sanjouli tunnel. Kitchener's leg was trapped against the wall and his ankle snapped. He was found and put in a rickshaw. Birdwood was alerted and 'seized a bottle of brandy and met the Chief half a mile off.'[27] Kitchener was bedridden in Snowdon for a month and only reached Calcutta for Christmas.[28]

1904 proceeded much as the previous year for Birdwood: Calcutta, a spot of leave with his brother, C-in-C inspection visits, Simla, 'a beastly cropper at polo,' and an August tour towards the Tibetan border.[29] By this time Kitchener was keen on the Indian Army establishing its own staff college and on 8 September he informed Birdwood that he was to move to the Army Department as 'AAG [Assistant Adjutant General – a colonel's position] to get it sanctioned.' Birdwood moved across a week later but was still 'collared by K on my way back in afternoon to help layout the garden!'[30] From leaving India as a captain in 1898, Birdwood had become a substantive colonel in less than six years and just before his fortieth birthday. He had been an acting squadron commander only occasionally and now would never serve as a regimental commander. He remained with the Army Department in Simla for most of that winter, during which time Jenny and the children went home to Lincolnshire. The debate regarding dual-control of the Army – C-in-C and Military Department – had simmered throughout the year, only widening its area of friction as the Viceroy had returned to England at the end of April.[31] Curzon returned to Calcutta in December to be joined later by Kitchener after his tour of

22 Diary 1903, 15 August.
23 Diary 1903, 19, 22, 27, 29 and 30 August, 2 September.
24 Birdwood, *Khaki and Gown*, 143-4.
25 Birdwood, *Khaki and Gown*, 155. Diary 1903, 18-20 October.
26 Douglas Scott, (ed.), *Douglas Haig: The Preparatory Prologue Diaries & Letters 1861-1914* (Barnsley: Pen & Sword, 2006), 228. Diary 1903, 30 November.
27 Pollock, *Kitchener*, 279-80. Diary 1903, 15 November.
28 Soon after the tunnel was widened, whitewashed and provided with electric lighting, E J Buck, *Simla Past and Present* (Shimla: Minerva, 1925), 232-3.
29 Diary 1904, 20 May.
30 Diary 1904, 8, 14, 19 September.
31 This period is well-documented in Pollock, *Kitchener*, 287-96.

Burma. Kitchener submitted his proposals on dual-control, sending a copy to Conk (Marker) in London, who wrote on the envelope:

> Lord Kitchener's Memorandum on the Administration of the Army in India – which was so vehemently combated (& with such extraordinary methods) by Lord Curzon of Kedleston. The latter did not hesitate to suppress the truth, to tamper with telegrams & to make false statements in official correspondence, in order to try & deflect Lord Kitchener. He failed in spite of these tactics & resigned the Viceroyalty.[32]

Conk had been corresponding with Charles A'Court Repington, *The Times* military correspondent, and these letters confirm that Birdwood was also writing to Repington.[33] Presumably, therefore, Birdwood shared Conk's views. Studies since have revealed Kitchener's deviousness.[34] Kitchener's paper was debated in the Viceroy's Council, then referred to the India Office for resolution and finally sent to the Cabinet for endorsement.[35] In the interim, modifications had been introduced and the 'Prime Minister wired to Curzon asking why K agreed to certain modifications. Curzon sent for K in morning before Council to see if K wd not accept retention of old title of "Military Dept." This K refused to have & Curzon eventually gave way but wired to Prime Minister that unless Govt now agreed to the modifications, that K & he would both resign!'[36] The Military Member would be sacrificed but there was to be a compromise – a Military Supply Member with a considerably smaller span of responsibilities and with no Military Department. Both Curzon and Kitchener had candidates for the post. 'K told me Curzon says he will resign if he cannot have Barrow [Major General Sir Edmund Barrow] as supply member.'[37] In the ensuing debate Kitchener's view held, so 'Lord Curzon resigned, as Sec of State [India Office] refused to let him have Barrow as Mil Member. Lord Minto apptd Viceroy vice Curzon.' At the end of October 'we all went round to Viceregal Lodge for public farewell to Lord & Lady Curzon. They both shook hands with K but neither said a word!'[38] Birdwood had achieved so much through tact and diplomacy, and although temporarily not on Kitchener's staff, watched this great rivalry proceed between two powerful men over a small issue.

In November Birdwood 'went down to Snowdon to see the Haigs [him now a Major General, recently back from England and married] who had arrived last night.'[39] in March 1906 General Duff told Birdwood that the Staff College would open on 1 July and Birdwood would become Kitchener's Military Secretary – the personal staff officer to the C-in-C and very much involved

32 BL MS 52276A, Kitchener-Marker papers Vol II A Letters, Folio 41, Memorandum on the Administration of the Army in India, 1 January 1905.

33 BL MS 52276B, Kitchener-Marker papers Vol II B Letters, Folios 29 & 35, Letters, Marker to Repington, 2 & 26 January 1906.

34 See Faught, *Kitchener Hero and Anti-Hero*, 162-6; The case against Kitchener is also well summarised in Peter King, *The Viceroy's Fall* (London: Sidgwick & Jackson, 1986), 254.

35 BL AAS, Mss Eur D 686 folio 58, letters, from Kitchener to Birdwood, 3, 12 & 20 March 1905.

36 Diary 1905, 29 and 30 June.

37 Diary 1905, 7 August.

38 Diary 1905, 21 August, 23 October.

39 Diary 1905, 18 November; Scott, *Douglas Haig: The Preparatory Prologue Diaries & Letters 1861-1914*, 243-44.

with the selection of officers for posts across the Indian Army.[40] Birdwood's opportunity to attend Staff College, either at Camberley or Quetta, had passed and now, with this new appointment, any chance of being on the College staff to gain the passed staff college qualification – *psc* – also disappeared. This was as the significance of the qualification was growing and the graduates showing their worth. Just before Christmas Birdwood finally took over from Hamilton, who had been in the post for six years.[41] Birdwood had served closely with Kitchener for over five years. He had been part of a close-knit family supporting their Commander but now Birdwood was the key personal staff officer. Having a strong rapport with his chief, Birdwood was in a powerful position. January 1906 saw the usual Proclamation parade at Calcutta with both the new Viceroy and the Prince of Wales attending and later that month Birdwood was honoured as an ADC to the King.[42] Haig left India that spring.[43] Both he and Birdwood wrote in their diaries about Haig's farewell lunch at Wildflower Hall, together with their wives and young Christopher Birdwood.[44] Tours and inspections filled that year: Darjeeling and surrounds in March; Delhi, Lahore and across the Indus to Baluchistan in April; Abbottabad and Kashmir in September; and finally, Nepal in November. The contrast between the varying standards of Indian and British units, their commanders, unit training, equipment and above all the diverse geographical locations provided Birdwood invaluable experience that he would be able to apply when judging his commanders on first meeting in Egypt and subsequently. 1907 commenced with the usual festivities but on 23 January: 'Heard of my dear old Father's death, which I can't realise at all or believe … The best example of the Christian gentleman you cd meet in the world without an unkind thought, word or deed for anyone' and 'to think we shan't see him again & here have I all these years been out here, picturing to myself years with him at home in time to come.' The following day Birdwood wrote: 'a blank – a complete blank. I can never see dear old Father again.' His diary remained empty for a week.[45] Birdwood subsequently wrote some of the most moving entries in his diaries suggesting that he aspired to the standards he admired in his father. In April, Kitchener got a wire 'asking him to accept 2-year extension – which he did.'[46] Birdwood would serve as Military Secretary until the end of Kitchener's tenure.[47] Reorganisation of the Army had continued and '"Commands" were abolished in India & Northern & Southern Armies took their place.' This would change again just as Birdwood returned to India in 1920.[48]

As trouble was rumbling on the Frontier, the Viceroy and the Secretary of State were discussing whether to mount an expedition and for how long. Major General Sir James Willcocks was tasked with a punitive expedition against the Zakha Khel Afridis in the Bazar Valley which

40 Diary 1906, 16 March.
41 Diary 1906, 15 November, 8 and 21 December.
42 NAM 6707-19-356, Telegram, Viceroy to Secretary of Sate for India, 20 January 1906.
43 Haig's time as Inspector General is well described by Andrew Winrow, 'Reactionary or Reformer? Major General Douglas Haig: Inspector General of Cavalry India 1903-1906', *Durbar, Journal of Indian Military History Society,* Volume 26, No 4, Winter 2009.
44 Scott, *Douglas Haig: The Preparatory Prologue Diaries & Letters 1861-1914*, 250. Diary 1906, 6 May.
45 Diary 1907, 24, 25 and 26 February.
46 Diary 1907, 3 April.
47 During this period Jenny would go home from November to March each year, leaving Nancy in England in 1903 and then Christopher in 1907.
48 Diary 1907, 1 June. Birdwood would command Northern Command 1920-24.

runs south-west from Fort Jamrud, the gateway to the Khyber. This was executed swiftly and decisively but despite this, one morning Birdwood had to go 'round to Govt House & see the Viceroy in his pyjamas with a wire about Willcocks remaining longer in the Bazar Valley.'[49] In April Kitchener and Birdwood left for the Frontier. Their visit was cut short at Quetta because of 'reports from Peshawar what looks like large general rising, so Chief decided to leave for Simla at once.' 'The Chief went to see Viceroy in afternoon & on return told me he wished me to go up as CSO [Chief Staff Officer] to Willcocks for the Mohmand Expedition. I said I thought this would do him no good, nor me any good, as all would say it was a job [biased preference] of both of ours. He said he did not mind what was said in such a case as he had discussed it with Viceroy & both were decided there was no one so well suited. After that I could say nothing & it is of course a great honour, but I fear many will be furious at my luck.'[50] The Mohmands had been conducting 'incessant raids.' Willcocks called for Jirgahs to resolve matters but this only produced 'evasive or defiant replies.' He moved promptly to secure the Khyber but further action was delayed due to an outbreak of cholera and subsequent reorganisation. On 10 May Birdwood left Simla and three days later he was advancing with the two leading Brigades ten miles north of the Khyber, into Mohmand country.[51] Birdwood's diary at this point is fascinating. Brief entries about tennis, polo and dinners, with short mentions of the developing situation are replaced with detailed daily accounts of operations in his familiar small operational hand-writing. In 1897 in the Tirah he had been an orderly officer to a commander of two brigades (plus a reserve). He was now CSO of a comparable force with a similar objective of inflicting punitive damage on the offending tribes – 'burnt 5 villages' and seven the next day. At times, they were attacked in force – 'a devil of an attack again at night firing going on for several hours, a bullet coming into my tent & striking alongside of my foot.'[52]

The destruction, with diplomacy from a most experience Political Agent, Robert Warburton, had its desired effect.[53] 'As the Utmanzai and Dawizai sections still refused to submit to our terms, … the sappers and pioneers had been all ready for blowing up the towers, the [Utmanzai] Jirgah came in hurriedly and submitted in full. Four towers were destroyed, at the sight of which the Dawizai Jirgah, which had been watching the proceedings from a neighbouring hill, also arrived and paid its fine and agreed to our terms.' The original instigators of the rising were dealt with and 'by 1st June all troops had left Mohmand country and demobilisation of the Force commenced.'[54] He noted that the 'greatest difficulty throughout the operations was lack of water, and arrangements for supplying this were hard to make.'[55] Similarly at Gallipoli he would issue strong advice about water.

49 Birdwood, *Khaki and Gown*, 182-3; Diary 1908, 20 February.
50 Diary 1908, 16, 23 & 25 April. No discord appeared to have been forthcoming.
51 NAM 6707-19-398, Despatches of Major General Willcocks in *Gazette of India*, 26 June 1908, 219-221.
52 Diary 1908, 15, 16, 18 and 20 May.
53 For the balance between punitive action and direct diplomacy with tribes, see Charles Miller, *Khyber: British India's North West Frontier* (London: Macdonald and Jane's Publishers, 1977), 271, 77-8.
54 NAM 6707-19-398, Despatches of Major General Willcocks, 224.
55 Birdwood, *Khaki and Gown*, 187.

Birdwood must have been gratified to read in Willcocks' report that 'the elasticity of the Divisional and Brigade systems, each with its own permanent peace staffs, proved well adapted to all requirements.'[56] Willcocks wrote that Birdwood was

> … an able and resourceful officer who never acknowledges difficulties and by his influence and tact secured the smooth working of the entire Staffs and of the Force. He was always in the right place during a fight and rendered most valuable service throughout the operations.[57]

Birdwood was awarded the Distinguished Service Order, which he felt he 'had done little to deserve.'[58] He had been away from Simla for just over three weeks on this his single operational deployment between 1902 and 1914.

Birdwood returned to a summer of office work, sport and dinners, which included one for Old Cliftonians.[59] Kitchener made a further two tours before leaving India. At the end of October, he and Birdwood left via Karachi to tour the west coast. At the southernmost tip of India – Cape Comorin, Birdwood took his obligatory swim.[60] They travelled inland up the east coast, reaching Calcutta on 21 December. In early 1909, Kitchener travelled out to the Sunderbans, the vast mangrove forest covering the delta of the Ganges, Brahmaputra and Meghna rivers, now largely Bangladesh. At the beginning of May, all were back in Simla where Jenny and Birdwood were reunited. Birdwood was soon to be made temporary brigadier-general and given command of an independent brigade at Kohat. On Sunday 4 September, he and Jenny 'rode out to Wildflower Hall & had our last lunch with dear old Lord K there. Both very sad to think of it.'[61] Kitchener left for a tour of inspections in Australia. He wrote in his last report on Birdwood: 'I cannot speak too highly of the ability, tact & discretion with which he has carried out his duties during nine years on my staff. He is quite fit to command a brigade and will no doubt eventually go higher.'[62] Kitchener's patronage was to continue. Birdwood's performance had never let Kitchener down. Together they benefitted each other. After nine years together, Birdwood was a Kitchener man.

In September, the Birdwoods arrived in Kohat, their home for thirty-two months until April 1912. The Kohat District of the North-West Frontier Province stretched from the Indus in the East to the Khyber tribal area in the west and from the Peshawar District in the North to Bannu in the South.[63] It encompassed the area that Birdwood had fought over in the Tirah Campaign. His life was taken up with training, interspersed with two trips to England. The Kohat Brigade was – as its title indicated – independent. Birdwood did not report to a divisional commander but instead directly to Northern Army, commanded by Willcocks for the majority of Birdwood's time. The Brigade consisted of a cavalry regiment – the second-in-command was

56 NAM 6707-19-398, Despatches of Major General Willcocks, 225.
57 Diary 1908, 27 June. A red ink entry.
58 Birdwood, *Khaki and Gown*, 191.
59 Diary 1908, 8 September.
60 Diary 1908, 26 November.
61 NAM 6707-19-398, Despatches of Major General Willcocks, 225.
62 NAM 6707-19-402, Note 'Lord K's CR [confidential report] on me 15.5.09.'
63 Christian Tripodi, *Edge of Empire* (Farnham: Ashgate, 2011), xi and 37.

an old friend from Clifton, Leslie Younghusband – and four Indian Army infantry battalions, with supporting artillery and medical subunits.[64] 'He was junior to just about every commanding officer in the brigade and many expected trouble. But within three months, during which he was chiefly remembered for his passion for gardening and reading the newspapers, he had won the affection and respect of the entire brigade and demonstrated that quality of leadership for which he would become renowned'.[65]

Birdwood inspected every unit in his first month. He rode, and played polo and tennis, later adding cross-country running. Soon a regular diary entry appeared: 'Church in evening. Jenny played the harmonium & I read the lessons!'[66] The new C-in-C, General Sir O'Moore Creagh, came to visit in November and stayed with the Birdwoods. A new Chief of the General Staff, CGS – Lieutenant General Sir Douglas Haig – had arrived in late October.[67] Captain Philip Howell had served as a staff officer in the War Office with Haig and they still corresponded. Haig once commented: 'What stories we hear of Birdwood's ill deeds [as Military Secretary], and Duff too comes in for much unfavourable criticism! I am really appalled at some of the appointments which they made.'[68] This contrasts with the view of Birdwood so far but as will be seen, it was not the only critical comment. Birdwood continued to train his Brigade with regular field days and in the New Year he 'carried out experimental mobilization of the Bde.'[69] After participating in the Brigade Assault-at-Arms, he went on leave, reaching his father-in-law's home at Thurlby, Lincolnshire, two days after the birth of his second daughter: 'to see my darling, little Jenny & the new daughter … both of them going on capitally.'[70] While on leave, King Edward VII died and, as an ADC to the King, Birdwood participated in the funeral ceremony. He also visited Clifton College for the annual Commemoration celebrations and saw for the first time its South African War Memorial. Henry Newbolt's inscription read:

Clifton, remember these thy sons who fell
Fighting far over sea,
For they in a dark hour remembered well
Their warfare learnt of thee.[71]

At the unveiling Lord Methuen had spoken of two Old Cliftonians, saying of Colonel Haig, 'the right-hand man of Sir John French during his successful career and all the time he was in South

64 Leslie Younghushand was the younger brother of Francis Youghusband, renowned for his Tibetan and Central Asian exploits. Francis also features in Birdwood's diaries.
65 John Lee, "William Birdwood," Ian F. W. Beckett and Steven Corvi (ed.), in *Haig's Generals* (Barnsley: Pen & Sword, 2006), 26.
66 Diary 1909, 31 October.
67 Scott, *Douglas Haig,* 288.
68 Liddell Hart Centre for Military Archives (hereafter LHCMA), Howell, Brig Gen Philip (1877-1916) Papers, 2/27, Letter, Haig to Howell, 18 November 1909. Lieutenant General Sir Beauchamp Duff was Haig's predecessor as CGS and had been an advocate of Kitchener's organisations, which Haig was about to change.
69 Diary 1910, 12 January.
70 Diary 1910, 7 March. She was christened Judith Horatia Maud – Horatia in honour of her godfather, Lord Kitchener.
71 Derek Winterbottom, *Henry Newbolt and The Spirit of Clifton* (Bristol: Redcliffe, 1986), 97.

Africa,' and of Birdwood, 'intimate friend and constant companion in the Tirah campaign, and the *beau ideal* of what a British officer and English gentleman should be.'[72]

On return to Kohat in October 1910, Birdwood welcomed the 59th Scinde Rifles, Frontier Force to his Brigade, with a full-dress parade and the presentation of their Mohmand Expedition medals. Their Commanding Officer wrote: 'The men very much appreciated the honour you did them in personally handing out the medals and the presence of the rest of the Brigade was a source of great pride and satisfaction to them & added much to the honour.'[73] In January 1911 a change-over took place with his cavalry regiment. The departing Commanding Officer wrote:

> ... I say that everyone deeply regrets leaving the Brigade which you command, because you command it. For other reasons many of us are glad to go – it is hard to keep up the efficiency of a Cavalry Regt in a small station, ... If we have not deteriorated since we came to Kohat ... it is entirely due to the interest shown in & advice given to us by our Generals & none of these have done half as much for us as you have done. You have competed on equal terms with the best of us at games. I know, & no one knows better than themselves, how good you have been to the NOs [Native Officers] – I could quote you many accidental remarks in proof of this & I am convinced that the Rank & File have appreciated & been bucked up by the fact you have taken a constant interest in their daily work. It would be a bad Regiment that did not respond to your sympathy, & I can assure you that the 23rd wish for nothing better than the chance of serving under you again, not in Kohat but in a Division. We would try to do you well & know that we should be done well, whether in cantonments or, for choice, on service.[74]

The new regiment, 31st Lancers, would have received copies of the *Military Report on the Kohat Brigade Area* 'for the use of officers coming new to the Kohat Brigade.'[75] Birdwood must have overseen its ninety detailed pages. At his Brigade Rifle Meeting the Birdwood Cup was won by the 26th and again at the Brigade Assault-at-Arms, Birdwood participated in tent-pegging and jumping.[76]

In 1911 Birdwood was present at two further Royal occasions. As an Indian ADC to the King, he made a short trip to England for the coronation of King George V. On the day he landed, he 'drove Mother over to Twickenham Cemetery to see Father's grave' – his first opportunity to do so.[77] Then in December the King and Queen came out to India for the Delhi Durbar. Birdwood was on duty with the King for a week at Delhi and then a further ten days at Calcutta. Haig had remained in India for this event and it is probable that he and Birdwood met again here, though there is no mention in their diaries. The King made two significant announcements: the capital was to move from Calcutta to Delhi and Bengal was to be reconstituted as a single province. The King spoke to Birdwood: 'He was very nice to me on leaving – saying he was glad to know

72 O F Christie, *A History of Clifton College 1860-1934* (Bristol: J W Arrowsmith, 1935), 147-9; *The Memorial to Old Cliftonians who fell in the South African War* (Bristol: J W Arrowsmith, 1904), 10-11.
73 NAM 6707-19-467, Letter, Lt Col Carruthers to Birdwood, 31 October 1910.
74 NAM 6707-19-448, Letter, Lt Col Kennedy to Birdwood, 10 January 1911.
75 NAM 6707-19-446, *Military Report on Kohat Brigade Area* (Simla, 1911).
76 Diary 1911, 9, 20 and 25 March.
77 Diary 1911, 10 June.

I was promoted again to be QMG [Quartermaster-General in India] but sorry I was no longer to be ADC.'[78]

At the beginning of April 1912, Birdwood and Jenny left Kohat. It was reported that 'during their three years here, General and Mrs Birdwood have endeared themselves to all in a manner which suggests "god-gifted," since it is so rare.'[79] His closely written diary entries over five days reflected how much the farewells meant to them both. The 1911/12 Annual Training Report of the Kohat Brigade read that 'training has been carried out on very practical lines. … Major General Birdwood always does everything thoroughly and his Brigade manoeuvres have been realistic and instructive.'[80] He left with a glowing report:

> General Birdwood is an officer of quite exceptional merit. Keen, active and far beyond the average in professional zeal. His tact is known to all and his personal charm of manner makes all men work for and with him. He is well fitted for and will surely rise to the highest rank.[81]

Having only ever been an acting squadron commander and never having commanded a regiment, he had now commanded a brigade with success and transitioned his own ability as a trainer from subunit to formation level.

At the age of forty-six Birdwood was QMG, who with the CGS (aged fifty-seven years) and the AG (fifty), advised and supported the C-in-C (sixty-four). Birdwood 'was now responsible for the feeding, quartering, equipping, and general well-being of the Army in India, both British and Indian.'[82] A newspaper commented that although 'no doubt young for his responsible post … it would be difficult to find a man at the present time better suited to his post.' It went on, however, that 'as Military Secretary it was a matter of complaint against him that he was so much in Lord Kitchener's confidence that he was too absorbed with the large questions that were then on the tapis so that too much was left to the permanent officials of his proper department.'[83] An echo perhaps of earlier private comments by Haig. At this point news of his mother's death brought personal sadness: 'I cannot believe I shall never see her again – she whose love for us all was infinite.'[84]

A major focus for 1912 was the Army in India Committee led by Field Marshal Sir William Nicholson, who had come out from England charged to review and consider the size and organisation of the forces in India. Due, however, to the posting of the incumbent, Birdwood was selected by the Viceroy to become Secretary to Government in the Army Department. His duties were 'to see that all military matters of importance were brought to the notice of the Governor-General-in-Council.'[85] Lord Minto, the previous Viceroy, had described the post as 'being the constitutional go-between between an over-bearing soldiery! [*sic*] and the constitutional govt as

78 Diary 1912, 8 January. As CGS, Haig would have been party to this promotion.
79 NAM 6707-19-484, Newspaper cutting, no details.
80 BL AAS, Mss Eur D 686 folio 74, Annual Training Report of the Kohat Brigade 1911-12.
81 BL AAS, Mss Eur D 686 folio 74, Confidential Report by GOC Commanding Northern Army.
82 Birdwood, *Khaki and Gown*, 216.
83 NAM 6707-19-480, Cutting from *The Broad Arrow*, No 2275 Vol LXXXVIII.
84 Diary 1912, 7 August.
85 Birdwood, *Khaki and Gown*, 164.

represented by the Viceroy.'[86] The C-in-C had recently produced a ten-page minute in response to a note by Nicholson on the conduct of business at Army Headquarters. It noted that the current system had been 'conceived in strife' and went on to outline the intervening history, with some critical personal comments on previous office holders. It stated that the incumbent Army Secretary was to be 'succeeded by Major General Birdwood … an able and most tactful officer who will carry out his duties, I feel confident, with sympathy and discretion, and under whose regime all will go well.'[87] Birdwood would have anticipated a three-year tour in this post, until the end of 1915 when he may have expected to become a divisional commander. In early December, he started work 'in the temporary offices at Delhi' and a week later 'joined the other members of the Viceroy's Legislative Council' for the formal handing over of Delhi to the Government of India. 'After a long wait & after head of procession had arrived, we heard a bomb had been thrown into the Viceroy's *howdah*,' wounding the Viceroy and killing a jemadar. The ceremonies continued without the Viceroy but the speeches did allude 'to the dastardly attempt on the Viceroy's life.'[88]

The XI BL were stationed in Delhi and – as Jenny was back in England – Birdwood lived with them, often riding in the morning with Cole, commanding XI BL, playing polo, tent pegging and participating in the riding school, just as he had done as Adjutant twenty years before.[89] At the beginning of February 1913 he attended his first Council Meeting, by which time the Viceroy, now Lord Hardinge, had recovered. Nicholson and some of his Committee had left in April but the discussions were still on-going.[90] In June he received his confidential report from the C-in-C, the last in his files before the start of the First World War:

> Good manners & tactful beyond average. Has good health. Has great technical knowledge & skill in imparting it. His reasoning powers, judgement, self reliance, and decision of character leave nothing to be desired especially as the latter is formed by cautious foresight. He is an officer with plenty of originality of thought. I have the highest opinion of his capabilities. He is a most excellent staff officer in any position and would make an admirable Divisional Commander. He is most popular with British and Native ranks, universally so with the latter whom he thoroughly understands.[91]

In November as he was also Secretary in the Marine Department, he left for a tour of the Persian Gulf, where India administered a number of representative outposts. His stops included: Muscat, Bushire, Bahrein, Shat-el-Arab, Basra, Kut and finally Baghdad. As well as departmental matters, the Viceroy had asked him to look into issues of slavery and oil. This was a forerunner of future roles as a man of Empire. He then returned via Babylon and Karbela

86 BL AAS, Mss Eur D 686 folio 61, Letter, Minto to Birdwood, 15 September 1913.
87 NAM 6707-19-499, Minute by His Excellency the Commander-in-Chief with reference to Note by Lord Nicholson and Sir William Meyer on conduct of business at Army Head-Quarters, 20 September 1912.
88 Diary 1912, 13 and 23 December and memoranda pages.
89 Diary 1913, January – March.
90 Diary 1913, 9 April, 24 June and 18 July.
91 NAM 6707-19-517, Notes of Confidential Report by Sir O'M Creagh, C-in-C, June 1913.

to Basra, arriving back in Karachi on Christmas Day.[92] He had visited many of the places, in Mesopotamia, and Kut in particular, where the Indian Army – though not he himself – would serve in the coming years. In early 1914 he was working on the necessary actions resulting from his visits.[93] In March, he welcomed, Sir Beauchamp Duff as C-in-C, attended the unveiling of Kitchener's statue in Calcutta and met Jenny, Nancy and Judith's ship at Bombay.[94]

His second year in post was proceeding well, when on 1 July, 'we were to have gone to a dance … but everything put off for court mourning on account of assassination of the Archduke Francis Ferdinand & his wife in Bosnia.' He recorded nothing further until 29 July and then 'heard Austria had declared war on Serbia. Nabokoff, Russian Consul-General thinks Russia must join.' Later he 'was called up in night with wire from Sec of State saying we were to take precautionary measures for War = [against] power or powers to be notified later.' The next day it was 'decided that 6th, 7th & 3rd Divs & 9th Cav Bde should be the ones to go to Europe if necessary.' On 5 August, he was 'wakened at 3 am saying ultimatum had been presented to Germany which expires at midnight 4th-5th which almost certainly lead to war. Called up at 7am to say war had been declared. In office till very late.' The next day he 'heard Lord K had been apptd Sec of State for War vice Asquith, of course <u>the one</u> thing to do – the best piece of work Govt has done for a long time.' Kitchener did not take long to wire Duff: "Tell Birdwood I want him here more than I did ever at Pretoria."[95] Birdwood was not released by the Viceroy and stayed in India over the next three months, while two infantry divisions and two cavalry divisions were despatched from India to France. Two further divisions were sent to Mesopotamia, the equivalent of a division to Egypt and more than a brigade to East Africa. Birdwood could justifiably take pride in his considerable contributions to the reorganising and readying of the Indian Army. Haig had also attempted to prepare it 'for major operations outside of India.'[96] Both had enabled the speedy despatch of such forces. The regular British infantry battalions also departed for England. These were to form the 29th Division and eventually land on the beaches of Gallipoli. Both the recently arrived British territorials and the newly raised Indian troops required training.

On 18 November Birdwood received a wire from Kitchener:

> I should very much like to obtain your services. I think Egypt would be the first step, where I propose to land and train Australian and New Zealand contingents, which you could look after. Let me know if there would be any chance of getting you by formal application.[97]

Duff thought that Kitchener wanted Birdwood to work at the War Office but Kitchener came back 'saying I was nominated to command Australian & New Zealand Contingents: former

92 Diary 1913, 7 November – 25 December. National Archives of India, Foreign Department, External-B, Nov 1913, Nos 427-428 outlines the visit but no reports of the visit have been found in national archives in either London or Delhi.
93 Diary 1914, 7 January. A few days later on 16 January he recorded 'dining with Lutyens & Baker the architects of New Delhi.'
94 Diary 1914, 9, 21 and 27 March.
95 Diary 1914, 1, 29 July, 5, 6 and 7 August.
96 Gary Sheffield, *The Chief: Douglas Haig and the British Army* (London: Aurum, 2012), 61.
97 Diary 1914, 18 November.

18,000 men, latter 8,500 with status of Corps Commander & temp rank of Lt Genl to train in Egypt prior to taking them to France.'[98] Duff did not stand in his way. Birdwood recorded these two wires in red in his diary. Sadly, on an intervening day he also wrote in red that during fighting against the Turks on the right bank of Shat-el-arab, 'my dear [youngest] brother Dick had been killed in action on 17th: he was struck with 3 bullets from a shrapnel one through the brain. … I feel his loss much.'[99] Eighteen days after his appointment, Birdwood 'embarked on *Persia* to take over my command of the Australian and New Zealand contingents in Egypt' – very proud and confident words from a man at the threshold of the most crucial challenge of his life.[100]

Birdwood's career to date had prepared him for contingents such as he was about to command. He had trained recruits over many years and a formation for over two years. Initially and most importantly, he would need to get to know the officers and men of his command. He had established relationships with his men in the past by learning their languages and speaking with them. Subsequently he was able to interpret for Kitchener, who never learnt to speak any Indian language, as they visited units across India. Birdwood confidently and fluently spoke with soldiers and locals and in this way, came to understand them. Having been a very successful staff officer himself, he knew the value of a sound staff team. He quickly selected the best of those he could avail himself of in India and they sailed with him. Fit and robust, Birdwood brought personal experience of battle and sound views on the command of brigades and regiments. Above all, he got on with people and knew the many attendant benefits.

98 Diary 1914, 24 November.
99 Diary 1914, 19 November.
100 Diary 1914, 12 December.

5

The Anzacs make their landing and their mark

On 1 November 1914, the fleet transporting the 1st Australian Division, the New Zealand Infantry Brigade, two mounted brigades and supporting troops left Albany, Western Australia.[1] The first battalion arrived in Cairo on 3 December and over the next fortnight all were encamped.[2] On 21 December Birdwood landed at Suez, 'saying farewell to my Jenny Jane & little Judith.' At Cairo Birdwood 'was met by Sir John Maxwell, General Bridges & Godley Comdg the troops in Egypt, the Australians & New Zealanders respectively.' The next morning, he went out to see the Australians at the Pyramids and in the afternoon visited the New Zealanders. Two days later the High Commissioners for Australia and New Zealand, Sir George Reid and Mr Thomas Mackenzie, arrived in Egypt.[3] The year closed with Birdwood appointed Knight Commander of the Order of the Star of India.[4] As in South Africa, he was now back with the politics of the British Army and in four months about to face his greatest command challenge to date.

Birdwood would have expected a reasonable length of time to prepare his embryonic corps. The Australians, for example, had had about six weeks training in Australia. But still they required further basic training before exercising as subunits, units and formations.[5] Birdwood now gained his first impressions of these men. Charles Bean, the official war correspondent to the Australian Imperial Force (AIF), commented: 'Such men could not easily be controlled by the traditional methods of the British Army. The fact that a man had received a good education, dressed well, spoke English faultlessly and belonged to the "officer class", would merely incline them, at first sight, to laugh at him …'[6] Bean wrote about Birdwood:

1 In November 1913 at the Staff College at Camberley, an exercise had been set on the notional raising and movement of a 10,000-strong force from New Zealand to Egypt for training and further deployment. Lt Col J T Burnett-Stewart, "Scheme for Special Expeditionary Force", Staff College 1913. Exercises, notes etc. issued. Senior Division. CR/1913/2 JSCSC.

2 C E W Bean, *The Official History of Australia in the War of 1914–1918, Volume 1* (Sydney: Halstead Press, 1921), 98-99, 115-6.

3 Diary 1914, 21-27 December.

4 NAM 6707-19-546, Telegram from Viceroy, 30 December 1914.

5 Bean, *The Official History of Australia in the War of 1914–1918, Volume 1*, 135-6.

6 Ibid., 48. One of the first twenty boys that in September 1861 had gathered as a 'preliminary school' for Clifton College was Edwin Bean, the father of Charles Bean, who was also a Cliftonian, 1894-8.

> Many an Englishman of the period before the war judged things by the conventional outward signs with which he was familiar. The Australians might have found themselves under a commander who would have summed up a man by the boots he wore, or the roughness of his voice, or the manner in which he parted his hair, and who would have laid a horrified insistence upon the correct manner of saluting or addressing an officer, or upon insignificant points of dress. To such details of dress and manner British officers ordinarily attached great importance. It was Birdwood's nature to look past the forms at the man himself.[7]

Immaculate dress and impressive bearing had been his currency when Adjutant of the GGBG. He demanded neither of these. A biographer of Sir John Monash commented that 'Birdwood realised from the start that these were not men to be treated in the same way as the soldiers to which he had long been accustomed. To take up time in insisting on the niceties of dress and the cardinal importance of saluting would have been a disaster in this army. His new charges met him more than halfway, for they were sound judges of a man and had no difficulty in distinguishing between the genuine and the spurious.'[8] Birdwood got it right first time and it was a pivotal decision by him to establish the relationship in this way. He wrote to an old Clifton College master expressing thanks for a letter of sympathy about his brother Dick's death and he continued:

> They [the Australians] are a really magnificent lot of men, but alas! So far little trained or disciplined. The junior officers & NCO's are the difficulty – they have not & cannot have the necessary control & authority, and without that, can hardly expect to be able to give men much instruction – they are full of enthusiasm but as only a small percentage are professional soldiers they cannot have the knowledge … However, they are really good fellows & are doing their very best & working most loyally & willingly for me – In fact I have found no difficulty in "getting on" with the Australians about which I had received many warnings.[9]

Birdwood's days commenced with an early morning ride followed immediately by visiting the men training: battalions marching or on musketry practice, artillery field firings, sapper exercises and mounted troops at stables. Church parades also featured. He invited two officers to dine with him most evenings. By the end of January, he was dining with commanding officers, and, as ever, carefully recording their units – 'Lee 9 Q'land & Johnston of 11th WA.' He had observed the power of command on operations and now he had to assess his subordinate commanders. By the middle of February brigade exercises were starting to appear in his diary. His last formation – 4th Australian Infantry Brigade under then Colonel John Monash – arrived in early February. Birdwood allocated this to Godley, together with his New Zealand Infantry Brigade and the New Zealand Mounted Rifles, NZMR. The Australian and New Zealand

AWM 3DR/ 6673 item 840, Papers of C E W Bean, Origines: A Sketch of the earliest days at Clifton College, E Bean.

7 *Ibid.*, 119-20

8 A J Smithers, *Sir John Monash* (London: Leo Cooper, 1973), 53.

9 Clifton College Archives, letter, Birdwood to Pearson, 24 January 1915.

Army Corps, now named ANZAC, consisted of Bridges' three-brigade 1st Australian Division, and Godley's New Zealand and Australian Division.[10] Birdwood had seen service with similar groupings in both the Tirah and Mohmand Forces.

The AIF mythology was forming, in which the prowess, physique of the soldiers and their sense of mateship were already prominent. The historiography of this mythology may be considered to have started with Australian war correspondent Charles Bean's *The Anzac Book*. He compiled this from contributions 'prepared, in small dug-outs, with shells and bullets frequently whistling overhead.' Birdwood wrote in the volume's introduction about 'all the inhabitants of our little township,' in reality Anzac Cove. At Anzac and in the Australian popular imagination, people and place had become linked. Bean's works influenced the mythology for the next half century, but he clearly had told Australians what they wanted to hear about themselves. Historian Ken Inglis' writings based on personal interviews and letters reintroduced Bean and this was followed by one of his students, Bill Gammage. He described his major work as 'an emotional history of the AIF.' The mythology is based on individuals. The viewpoints may have changed but the focus is still of that of a select body of men who created their legend and whose nation has treasured it and the accompanying historiography.[11] This explains why Anzac Day has now widened to embrace all Australians from those who have made the ultimate sacrifice to those serving today, or indeed all Australians *in toto*. As Prime Minister Paul Keating said at the entombment of Australia's unknown soldier and is now inscribed at the entrance to The Hall of Memory, 'He is all of them. And he is one of us.'[12]

On 20 February, Kitchener telegraphed Maxwell concerning possible operations on the Gallipoli Peninsula, informing him that forces were being concentrated on Lemnos Island to assist the Navy and, 'to give cooperation and to occupy any captured forts.' Maxwell was to 'warn a force of approximately 30,000 [of the] Australian and New Zealand contingent under Birdwood to prepare for this service.' Troopships would be despatched to 'arrive in Alexandria about March 9th.' Furthermore, Maxwell was instructed to 'communicate through Navy with Admiral Carden, commander at the Dardanelles, as he may require a considerable force before that date and in order that you may send him what he most requires.'[13] Maxwell duly communicated with Carden who replied on 23 February that he had been directed 'to prepare for a landing of 10,000 men, if such a step is found necessary' and that his instructions went 'no further.' If sent, he proposed to land at 'Sedd-el-Bahr, with the object of occupying the peninsula as far east as the line Suandere river—Chanalvasi.'[14] This is a line running northwest to south east, about three miles north of Achi Baba, which is the major hill feature four miles north of the tip

10 Diary 1915, 5, 15 and 18 January; 1, 7 and 15 February.

11 C E W Bean (ed.), *The Anzac Book*, 3rd ed (Sydney: University of New South Wales, 2010); K S Inglis, 'The Anzac Tradition', in John Lack, K S Inglis and Jay Winter, *ANZAC Remembered: Selected Writings by K. S. Inglis* (Melbourne: University of Melbourne, 1998), 14-28; Bill Gammage, *The Broken Years: Australian Soldiers in the Great War* (Canberra: Australian National University Press, 1974). For a comprehensive discussion, see Graham Seal, *Inventing Anzac: The Digger and National Mythology* (Brisbane, University of Queensland Press, 2004); Carolyn Holbrook, *Anzac: The Unauthorised Biography* (Sydney: NewSouth, 2014) provides a more up-to-date view.

12 *Remembrance Day 1993* <https://www.awm.gov.au/commemoration/speeches/keating-remembrance-day-1993> (accessed 6 July 2021)

13 AWM 3DRL/3376 11, Incoming Cablegrams, Kitchener to Maxwell, 3180, 21 February 1915.

14 AWM 3DRL/3376 11, Outgoing Cablegrams, Carden to Maxwell, 23 February 1915.

of the Gallipoli peninsula, Cape Helles. This hill was subsequently the objective for the actual Cape Helles landings. That same day Birdwood received his first instructions from Kitchener: 'Proceed by the earliest possible opportunity to consult Admiral Carden on the spot as to nature of combined naval and military operations to be undertaken in connection with forcing of the Dardanelles and report result to me.' Birdwood was to 'ascertain from local observation and information the numbers and composition of the Turkish garrison on the Gallipoli Peninsula'; whether Carden thought that troops should be employed to take the forts, and if so what force would be needed; whether a landing force would be required to take the forts in reverse, and generally projected employment of such troops. Finally, Birdwood was asked whether the Bulair lines have to be held and if operations on the Asiatic side would be necessary.[15] Kitchener further expressed his strategic thinking to Birdwood in a telegraph dated 24 February, stating that the 'object of forcing the passage of the Dardanelles' was to gain 'possession ultimately of Bosphorus and overawing of Constantinople.' He saw it mainly as a naval operation, adding that it did 'not appear a sound Military undertaking to attempt a landing' where 'there is reported to be a garrison [of] 40,000 troops,' until forts have been reduced 'and passage forced.'[16] Birdwood left Cairo in the afternoon of 24 February with his GSO 1, Lieutenant Colonel Andrew Skeen. They should have arrived at 'Lemnos at 7 a.m.' on 28 February, but instead 'it was a beastly day,' and 'it came on to blow like the devil', so they made their way to Imbros, arriving instead 'at 4 p.m.' This was Birdwood's first experience of the vicissitudes of the local weather.[17] The next day he landed at Mudros to select the site for the Advanced Brigade – Colonel Sinclair-Maclagan's 3rd Infantry Brigade – together with Rear Admiral Wemyss, responsible for establishing a base on the island. The overall force was growing to include potentially the Anzac Corps, the Royal Naval Division and a French Division, with Birdwood in overall command. On 2 March he commenced his reconnaissance with Carden's second-in-command, Vice Admiral de Robeck, and made an initial survey of the Gallipoli coastline

The Anzac historiography of Gallipoli started with Ashmead-Bartlett dispatches on the Landings to the Australian press. In the post-war years personal works, such as General Hamilton's and Winston Churchill's, and then the official histories dominated. After World War II, Rhodes James consulted papers previously unavailable and produced one of the lengthiest comments on Birdwood in any book:

> His nickname, "Birdie', suited him admirably. He had something of Hamilton's alertness and vivacity, without its gentleness. Small, pugnacious, practical and determined, it was difficult not to like him. But his considerable flair for self-advertisement had the result that there were some officers who felt that there was something not quite genuine about him. There was undoubtedly a considerable element of jealousy in this: Birdwood was a 'Kitchener man', and extremely ambitious.

15 AWM 3DRL/3376 11, Incoming Cablegrams, Kitchener to Maxwell, 3229, 21 February 1915.
16 AWM 3DRL/3376 11, Kitchener to Maxwell, 3261, 24 February 1915.
17 Diary 1915, 28 February.

And on Birdwood's relationship with the Anzacs:

> Nevertheless, it was a happy accident which gave Birdwood the command of the Australian and New Zealand Army Corps. He had a real feeling for his Anzacs, and a quick appreciation of their great potentialities beneath what was, at that time, a rather rough-and-ready exterior.

Rhodes James maintained a positive view of Birdwood throughout but sadly his work is without references in the text.[18] Like Gammage, Patsy Adam Smith introduced study of individual soldiers. In the last decade of the twentieth century the literature grew with works embracing new sources, narrative approaches and focus on specific episodes. Winter, Carlyon, very much a journalist rather than an historian, and Crawley typified these three approaches. The value of new approaches using newly sourced material has continued to enhance the historiography since the centenary and is exemplified by Hurst.[19] It is noteworthy, however, that all accounts, except Bean's, underplay Birdwood's role at Gallipoli. His voice is an important one. Whereas the Western Front has many studies of principal generals, those of Gallipoli do not. Birdwood was the significant commander and the following chapters will reveal his important voice and the vital role he played.

Since the 'Young Turks' government seized power in 1908, Ottoman Turkey had changed from being a British ally to becoming friendly with Germany. When Britain seized two battleships, *Sultan Oman* and *Reschadich,* paid for by the Turkish people, and Germany delivered a battle cruiser, *Goeben,* and a light cruiser, *Breslau,* to the Golden Horn, the transfer of allegiance was complete. After the Turkish shelling of Russian Black Sea ports and the British Aegean Squadron shelling of the forts at Sedd-el-Bahr and Kum Kale – on the urgings of Churchill, the First Lord of the Admiralty – war was declared. Possibilities for military action had originally been presented in 1906 to the Committee of Imperial Defence, suggesting a feasible offensive could be undertaken from the Sinai, through Palestine and Syria, and thence into Anatolia. A joint naval and military operation against the Dardanelles was not recommended, as secrecy

18 *Hobart Mercury,* 12 May 1915 reported 'a brilliant description of the landing of the Australians and New Zealanders on Gallipoli Peninsula by that experienced war correspondent, Mr Ashmead-Bartlett. It is a thrilling story, a story that will make us all feel proud of our soldiers. They have shown that, though transplanted to these southern skies, the breed is still the same as that of the men of Mons and Waterloo, and a hundred other great battles.' General Sir Ian Hamilton, *Gallipoli Diary*, vols. I & II (London: Edward Arnold, 1920); The Rt Hon W S Churchill, *The World Crisis 1915* (London: Thornton Butterworth, 1923); Robert Rhodes James, *Gallipoli* (London: Papermac, 1989). In her detailed analysis of earlier works, Jenny Macleod, *Reconsidering Gallipoli* (Manchester: Manchester University Press, 2004), 219, described Rhodes James' work as the 'best history of the Gallipoli campaign.'

19 Patsy Adam-Smith, *The ANZACS* (Southbank, Victoria: Thomas Nelson, 1978); Denis Winter, *25 April 1915: The Inevitable Tragedy* (St Lucia, Queensland: University of Queensland Press, 1994); Les Carlyon, *Gallipoli* (Sydney: Pan Macmillan Australia, 2001); Robin Prior, *Gallipoli: The End of the Myth* (New Haven and London: Yale University Press, 2009); Rhys Crawley, *Climax at Gallipoli: The Failure of the August Offensive* (Oklahoma: University of Oklahama Press, 2014) and James Hurst, *The Landing in the Dawn: Dissecting a Legend* (Solihull: Helion, 2018).

could not be achieved and a force of 100,000 'will be found to receive the joint expedition when it appears off the coast.'[20] By late 1914 such thinking had been forgotten.

On 2 January 1915 Russia sought allied assistance to relieve pressure from successful Turkish actions in the Caucasus. Churchill, considered the prime mover for the Dardanelles approach, posed a leading question to Admiral Carden:

> Do you consider the forcing of the Dardanelles by ships alone a practicable operation? It is assumed older Battleships fitted with minebumpers would be used preceded by Colliers or other merchant craft as bumpers and sweepers. Importance of results would justify severe loss. Let me know your views.

Carden responded that the Dardanelles could not be rushed but 'might be forced by extended operations with a large number of ships.'[21] The first naval bombardment of the Dardanelles forts took place on 19 February, with later successful follow-up destruction by marine landing parties.

Birdwood entered the Dardanelles with De Robeck, on 2 March, going 'in past Besika Bay', where the Turks had 'made extensive trenches, past forts at Eastern entrance and across to Helles Point, and then down past Sadl-Bahr [*sic*] and up the straights.' He observed 'forts on both sides completely destroyed and all guns knocked over.' 'After reconnoitring beyond Morto Bay', they 'turned when Turks opened fire … from where they could not see.' The wind was 'so strong' that they 'could hear nothing.'[22] Twenty years later at Peterhouse, Birdwood recalled this reconnaissance:

> The wind was blowing very hard down the Straits and we had got no distance at all when shells came in from all sides. You might have thought that you could have said "That has come from here or there", but you could not. It was almost impossible to tell from which side the shells were coming. We also came near one of the minefields. I may mention that the Turks had a wonderful searchlight … which was so strong that on the bridge of the "*Irresistible*" I could read the newspaper quite distinctly. Coming back I said to the Admiral – there was a certain amount of lapping of the waves on to the shore – "On a sea like that could you land us and keep us supplied on shore?" "No, I certainly could not: my small craft would be smashed to pieces."[23]

They returned to Tenedos and after a further meeting with Carden, Birdwood returned to Egypt, crossing with some of the transports of the 3rd Brigade sailing from Alexandria to Mudros.[24] He wrote to Kitchener, displaying his affection for his patron:

> My dear old Chief, I cannot tell you how deeply grateful I do feel by the confidence you have placed in me in giving me this command. I am really almost overwhelmed in

20 TNA CAB 17/184 General Staff memo (copy), 19 December 1906.
21 The Rt Hon Winston S Churchill, *Sandhurst Edition of The World Crisis* (London: Thornton Butterworth, 1933), 139-40.
22 Diary 1915, 2 March.
23 Sir William Birdwood, *Gallipoli* (Cambridge: Peterhouse Historical Society, 1936), 8-9.
24 Diary 1915, 4 March.

> my feelings as of course I well realise that no one but you would ever have done such a thing with so many senior men to be provided for. I know you must have found it difficult to ride out their claims. I can only promise in return that I am ready and will do my very best to work for success …[25]

Birdwood telegraphed Kitchener on 5 March that:

> I am very doubtful if the navy can force the passage unassisted, at all events it must take considerable time. Forts taken so far have been very visible and easy, as the ships could stand off and shoot from anywhere, while inside they are bothered by unknown fire. No troops could be landed in the present weather. … I consider cautious advance from Helles Point to be best line of action.[26]

The next day he added that he considered Carden to be 'very second rate', and having 'no "go" in him, ideas or initiative,' and that he doubted 'if the Navy can force the passage unassisted.'[27] This was a very sound analysis by Birdwood but it had no impact on immediate plans.

Birdwood, his staff and Maxwell then started detailed planning for a landing at Cape Helles, with a feint at Bulair. Staff had made map studies of both the Suvla and Bulair options. Birdwood intended a rapid advance on the Achi Baba ridge and the Kilid Bahr plateau. The future site for the Anzac landings was not considered at this point. On 10 March Kitchener finally decided to commit the 29th Division and as a consequence of the increased size of the force sought a more senior general as commander. General Sir Ian Hamilton was appointed and received his directions from Kitchener on 13 March. Constantinople was still the firm goal in Kitchener's mind. Hamilton left that evening with a hastily assembled staff. Birdwood took his altered circumstances with good grace.

Having seen off two Indian brigades for Mesopotamia with Maxwell, Birdwood visited 29th Indian Brigade, that would later serve under him during the August Offensive. On 17 March, he left for Mudros, where Hamilton had arrived that same day – the last day on which the military commanders had any confidence in naval ships being able to force the Dardanelles on their own. The Turkish victory of 18 March through the sinking or damaging of five battleships changed all that. On 20 March, Birdwood met Hamilton who agreed with Birdwood's planning.[28] An exodus to Alexandria followed, as both the 29th Division and the Royal Naval Division required adequate port facilities to re-embark themselves for tactical use. The French Division also went to Alexandria. While returning there himself, Birdwood wrote to his wife that he did not expect a swift victory, rather 'you can take it, this will be a long business & [I] can't think how Churchill can ever have thought – as I fancy he must have – he could rush it through with the Navy.'[29]

25 John Pollock, *Kitchener* (London: Constable, 2001), 433.
26 AWM 3DRL/3376 11/7, Telegrams between Kitchener and Birdwood, 685 E Maxwell to Kitchener, 5 March 1915.
27 Magnus, *Kitchener*, 322.
28 Diary 1915, 20-24 March.
29 AWM 3DRL/3376 8/1, Letter, Birdwood to wife, 25 March 1915.

Discussions and appreciations now turned to options beyond landings at Helles, Suvla or Bulair. A major factor was the perceived logistical difficulty of landing all of Hamilton's forces on the limited area at Helles. The stretch of beach from Gaba Tepe to Fisherman's Hut was mentioned for the first time in an appreciation for Hamilton by Captains Aspinall and Dawnay:

> extensive but narrow, spurs from Saribair [*sic*] ridge running close down to the sea. The exit is not good, and the only alternative to passing from the beach across a series of pathless spurs is the road along the shore, which appears to have been covered in places by landslides from the sandy spurs above it. The actual landing would seem, however, hardly likely to be very seriously molested by the enemy's artillery. A force moving south from the beach would advance astride the main "road" to the north-west of the Kilid Bahr plateau – about 4 miles. Such a force would, however, have to make specially effective provision for the protection of its left flank.[30]

This was a perceptive appreciation based on reconnaissance from the sea and maps.[31]

Birdwood arrived back on Mudros on 12 April and then his diary showed a marked change in tempo. He mentioned 'Admiral Thursby who is to cooperate with my Army Corps in attack,' visited 'Sir Ian H & talked over plans for our operations,' and finally, he 'steamed slowly all down the coast of Gallipoli Peninsula past Ejemler Bay, Cape Suvla & Gaba Tepe looking at places for landing.'[32] Birdwood was now aware of the separate plans for his Corps. Both the Force Order No 1 and the specific 'Instructions for GOC A & NZ Army Corps' had been issued.[33] Birdwood and his staff produced their final detailed plans which were completed by 17 April.[34] There was a 'meeting of all Generals & Admirals to discuss operations & settle date of starting date' and on 21 April, 'Admiral Thursby & all naval & military concerned came on board *Minnewaska* at 10 & we discussed all plans.'[35]

The objective given to the ANZAC was 'the ridge over which the Gallipoli – Maidos and Boghali – Kojadere roads run, and especially Mal Tepe.' Such a position would threaten the Turkish line of retreat on the Kilid Bahr plateau, the overall objective of the landings, and prevent reinforcement from Maidos, Gallipoli or Bulair. In the 1913 Manual for Combined Naval and Military Operations, 'a necessary preliminary to the disembarkation of an army on an enemy's coastline' was 'always' to be based on 'the successful landing of a covering force' and 'by a secret landing at night' if 'practicable.' The covering force was 'to effect a lodgement, and to make such dispositions for the protection of the beach and anchorage' to enable disembarkation of the main force.[36] Correspondingly, the objective for Birdwood's covering force was given in

30 LHCMA, Hamilton 7/4/14, Appreciation, 23 March 1915.

31 See Peter Chasseaud and Peter Doyle, *Grasping Gallipoli: Terrains, Maps and Failure at the Dardanelles 1915* (Stroud: Spellmount, 2005) for both hydrographic charts and operational maps.

32 Diary 1915, 12-14 April.

33 AWM4 1/25/1 Part 5 – April 1915, HQ ANZAC, war diary [AWM4 is First World War unit war diaries series. Hereafter 'war diary' not included], Order and Instructions dated 13 April 1915.

34 Brigadier General Cecil Faber Aspinall-Oglander, *Military Operations: Gallipoli Volume 1 Maps And Appendices* (Edinburgh: R & R Clark, 1929), Appendices 3 and 5.

35 Diary 1915, 19 & 21 April.

36 *Manual of Combined Naval and Military Operations (A1674)* (London, 1913), 29. This Manual is referred to in the ANZAC Op O No 1.

the overall Force Order as 'a covering position on the south-western spurs of the hill' [Sari Bair Ridge]. Moreover:

> The first essential for the covering force will be to establish itself on the hill … [Sari Bair Ridge] in order to protect the landing of the remainder of the Army Corps. From the ridge … spurs run north-west and south-west to the sea. This semicircular system of ridges seems to lend itself to the establishment of a strong covering position. Whether it will be necessary or not to include the crest of the mountain must be left to your discretion. [37]

These orders cannot be fairly described as prescriptive but the ridges were the objective and not the summit itself. This is reflected in Birdwood's instructions to Bridges, with the covering force having to 'advance and occupy the ridge running first east from Gaba Tepe and then North East' the ridge now commonly termed the Third Ridge.[38]

The line due west from Mal Tepe to the coast, through the Third and Second Ridges, leads to a landing position south of Anzac Cove. Hamilton ordered a landing in force 'on the beach between Gaba Tepe and Fisherman's Hut' but Birdwood's orders were more southerly: 'to land North of Gaba Tepe and occupy the heights covering the beach.'[39] In his Peterhouse talk, Birdwood stated that instead of landing where 'we meant to do, the destroyers missed their exact way in the dark and went up a bit north.' Acknowledging that 'a great many people have wondered' whether it 'was fortunate or unfortunate', he personally recognised 'the hand of Providence' and the resultant 'cover from view and enfilade fire.'[40] There is a great difference between the ground due east of Anzac Cove to that due east of the mid- point between Gaba Tepe and Hell Spit. Study of maps then available to Birdwood and his own reconnaissance from the sea would not have identified the severity of ravines and gullies, in which groups and individuals could, in effect, disappear. The more northerly landings did draw the covering force into more difficult country, and away from its original objectives.[41] The other variable was the timing of the landing. Birdwood strongly advocated surprise and decided to land in the dark, without a naval barrage. The moon would set at 2:57, dawn would start to break at 4:05 and sunrise would be at 5:15. In order that the moon could not silhouette the approaching landing vessels, the first wave was set to land about 4:30.[42] The darkness contributed to the confusion as the boats and tows approached the shore before dawn broke. After planning the landing and advance of his covering force, Birdwood had to define the detailed objectives for his main force from those he received from Hamilton. Disembarkation of the second division should be once the first division was landed. Then with both divisions ashore, further advance

37 AWM4 1/25/1 Part 5 – April 1915, HQ ANZAC, Instructions dated 13 April 1915, para 6. Topography.
38 AWM4 1/25/1 Part 7 – April 1915, HQ ANZAC, Instructions to GOC Australian Division, 19 April 1915, para 4; Chris Roberts, *The Landing at ANZAC 1915* (Sydney: Big Sky Publishing, 2011), 62-64. This well describes the interactive planning process between commanders.
39 Aspinall-Oglander, *Military Operations: Gallipoli Volume 1 Maps and Appendices*. Appendices 5 and 14. I am grateful to Robin Prior for drawing my attention to this intended southerly shift.
40 Birdwood, *Gallipoli,* 17.
41 AWM4 1/23/3/1 Part 1 – August 1914 – June 1915, 3rd Infantry Brigade, Op O No 1, 21 April 1915. This is demonstrated in Hurst, *The Landing in the Dawn*, 70.
42 Carlyon, *Gallipoli*, 166.

should be possible, with 'an effort' to be made 'to storm Mal Tepe.'[43] This direction is reflected in subsequent lower level orders but not with quite the same impetus as suggested by the word 'storm.' With his orders disseminated, Birdwood worried that 'I am beginning to fear the delay may defeat my plans of being able to land as a surprise in the dark, as the moon may now give away our approach.'[44] Having struck a real rapport with his men and their commanders, he was about to commit his whole corps in an opposed landing and to attack over ground that was largely unknown. The ultimate objective, Mal Tepe, was just less than five miles away from the landing beaches but nothing in his orders suggest that Birdwood expected easy progress. He now had to trust the Navy and his covering force brigade.

On the evening of 23 April Birdwood joined Thursby on board HMS *Queen* for 'the start of operations.' They left Mudros the next afternoon. One last minute change had been thrust upon Birdwood. Colonel F E Johnston, the New Zealand Brigade Commander, had fallen sick and was replaced by Birdwood's Chief of Staff, Brigadier Harold Walker.[45] At 02:30 on 25 April HMS *Queen* and *Prince of Wales* were off Gaba Tepe and 'each discharged their 500 men of the covering force into boats in silence – followed by 7 destroyers each with 400 men on board. Boats missed their bearings in the dark & inclined about 2 m [miles] to North getting us under the very difficult country there.'[46] Each battleship provided a steamboat towing four tows.[47] As the Corps Commander, Birdwood cannot be faulted for positioning himself with his associated naval commander on board a ship carrying part of the first echelon of the covering force. At this stage Colonel Sinclair-Maclagan became the commander on the ground and had the responsibility of making decisions in the light of circumstances, the first of which was that the tows had become bunched up and intermingled. On landing, the forces that made the immediate assault became mixed up. Prior described the developing situation, suggesting that some rudimentary sorting of men took place on Plugge's Plateau, after the climb from Ari Burnu. Hurst's detailed analysis suggests this was an optimistic view. Roberts describes mixed groupings as generally from 9 and 10 Battalions advancing south towards Gun Ridge and men from 11 Battalion attacking towards Battleship Hill.[48] Birdwood's Covering Force had been landed and now his instructions were that speed was essential.

The ground was nightmarish. From Plugge's Plateau the First Ridge runs north west through Russell's Top, The Nek, Baby 700 and Battleship Hill to Chunuk Bair, and finally to Hill Q at 918 feet. The Second Ridge develops southeast from Baby 700 through Pope's, Quinn's, Courtney's, and across 400 Plateau where it splits into: Bolton's Ridge in the north and Pine Ridge to the south. The valley formed by the two ridges from Baby 700 is Monash Gully. The Third Ridge runs southwest from Chunuk Bair, finishing just east of Gaba Tepe. Such a simple description of the ground fails to convey that connecting Plugge's Plateau to Russell's Top is little more than a razorback ridge and each gully had its own myriad of smaller gullies. Any

43 Aspinall-Oglander, *Military Operations: Gallipoli Volume 1 Maps And Appendices*, Appendix 15, 42.
44 Diary 1915, 15-21 April.
45 Christopher Pugsley, *Gallipoli The New Zealand Story*, 5th edition (Auckland: Libro International, 2014), 111.
46 Diary 1915, 23-25 April.
47 In 1914 the Navy List contained 634 steam pinnaces – steamboats. Only one remains – *Steam Pinnace 199* at National Museum of the Royal Navy (Portsmouth).
48 Roberts, *The Landing at ANZAC 1915*, 73-78; Hurst, *The Landing in the Dawn*, 89-97; Diary 1915, note 106.

approach from north of Anzac Cove to the north side of Russell's Top faced the Sphinx, with its near vertical cliff faces. Maclagan reached Plugge's Plateau and made his way to the area of the future Quinn's Post, from where he could look clearly across to the Third Ridge. He realised that the ground had defeated his orders. If he had followed them, it is probable that his brigade would have in effect disappeared. He decided to consolidate as best he could on the Second Ridge and introduced a defensive approach thereafter. This decision was made before 09:00 and the Anzacs never made it beyond the Second Ridge for the remainder of their stay on the Peninsula, although individuals did achieve it. Birdwood had positioned himself correctly but the ground irreversibly changed his plans four hours after the first landings.

Bridges 'went ashore about 9 am' and Godley 'landed about 1 pm.' Birdwood himself 'went ashore at 3 pm, conferred with commanders, inspected the beach arrangements – He apportioned fronts to commanders and received their reports. The troops ashore were not secure but the situation was not such as to cause great alarm at that time.'[49] Birdwood arrived after his subordinate commanders had had some time to establish themselves, so that he would receive their informed views. But should he have gone ashore around midday? Bridges' division was ashore by then and Bridges himself had been there for three hours. Birdwood's instructions to Bridges state that the remainder of his division was to assist the covering force to secure the line of its objective. Then Bridges was 'to be guided by the situation' whether to make a further advance or consolidation 'until the landing of the bulk of the Army Corps permits the development of an advance towards its objective.' Birdwood could have influenced matters and added impetus to the situation that had consolidated on the Second Ridge. In his autobiography, he states that he went ashore as soon as he could. He got as far forward as 'Walker's Top [*sic*],' demonstrating his typical desire to see for himself, but should he have gone further? By not doing so and by not pushing his commanders harder, he must be judged to have accepted the line of the Second Ridge. By this time the 2nd Bde had been deployed to secure the right flank, instead of developing a thrust towards the Sari Bair ridge – its primary objective. Some elements of 1st Bde had been sent in this direction to stem the Turkish attacks, but were not a force sufficient to secure that objective. As Battleship Hill and Baby 700 had seemed to be under greatest threat, the elements of Godley's division that had landed were sent there. Thus, both Battleship Hill and Baby 700 were lost - never to be regained. Such was the situation when Birdwood first met Bridges and Godley.

Birdwood was not expecting the next summons. 'Both the divisional generals represented that the GOC's presence was necessary on shore' and Birdwood arrived around 8 pm. They urged Birdwood to seek re-embarkation. Birdwood described how the men 'all afternoon had been subject to awful shrapnel fire which reminded one of Spion Kop,' where Buller and Thorneycroft lacked communication and mutual understanding.[50] Birdwood contacted Hamilton and all parties were informed. The Manual of Combined Operations called for re-embarkation plans. Thursby had issued short instructions on 24 April, which Skeen had forwarded to Birdwood, with the comment that 'The Rear Admiral anticipates no difficulties in meeting your wishes should you desire to reembark all or part of the troops.'[51] Thursby now interjected that re-embarkation would be most difficult and so Hamilton's order came back to

49 AWM4 1/25/1 Part 1 – April 1915, HQ ANZAC, 25 April.
50 Diary 1915, notes 106-7.
51 AWM4 1/25/1 Part 8 – April 1915, HQ ANZAC, Covering note and memorandum, 24 April.

'hang on and dig.' Birdwood decided to stay ashore and 'spent an awful night on the beach with thoughts that morning might bring disaster.' Sniping went on all night. It rained a little and Birdwood recorded thankfully that wounded men were got away. He longed for the daylight so that he could go around his troops.[52]

In just over two months Birdwood had first learnt about possibly supporting the Fleet to force the Dardanelles, then achieved an opposed landing in the face of an aggressive enemy, and finally spent a disastrous day on the shore. He had been about to be overall commander of the force and then reverted to commanding his Corps. He had shown his customary ability to work with others and gain the respect of his immediate subordinates as well as his men. Training in Egypt, under Birdwood and their national commanders, had produced aggressive fighting soldiers. The ground over which his Anzacs had fought had defeated their progress and would remain an ongoing issue. In many respects Birdwood should have been proud of what he had achieved but at the end of the first day, the precarious nature of the toehold gained dogged his thoughts. By dawn he would face an immediate challenge. How he responded to this test would be a measure of his character and abilities.

52 Diary 1915, notes 107.

6

Trapped and how to break out

Morning did not bring the disaster that Birdwood had dreaded. His troops were still ashore and he set off to visit them.[1] 'The enemy were evidently exhausted as a force – but snipers and machine guns kept up a continuous fire ... The flat tops of hills were also searched with shrapnel, as was the beach at times.'[2] His original plans had called for the covering force to be on the Third Ridge. Twenty-four hours after landing, 3rd Brigade should have been there fighting, with its own reserve 12th Battalion, and reinforced by the 1st Division. The vital ground of Sari Bair should have been secured or still fought over. Behind both of these actions there should have been sufficient ground for manoeuvre, gun positions, support and supply. Instead of mentioning failure he issued a Special Order recording 'his appreciation of the gallantry and dash with which the 3rd Australian Brigade carried out the difficult operation entrusted to it – in landing in face of opposition on an open beach.'[3] The coming three months, would demonstrate Birdwood's command abilities and his desire to maintain an aggressive posture.

Birdwood was heartened to see the morale of his men. 'Early in the morning the general line held was straightened out. The men, taught by the experience of shrapnel fire in the previous afternoon, had dug themselves well in, and feeling secure in the morning were in better heart.'[4] A 'much happier spirit pervaded all ranks.'[5] Three days later he described that day to his wife. Finding small groups of men, he would ask 'them their Reg[imen]t, they would reply that we 20 are all that are left' of the so-and-so battalion. 'All the others have been cut up.' He 'of course chaffed them & told them that just across the valley there were another 500…! This did a lot to cheer them up.' He found that 'many men would quietly slip away from the ranks & lie up in the sands to take an easy [*sic*] when they were wanted to fight.' As he went 'round the trenches, the shrapnel came pouring in' and everywhere he 'saw men scattering – simply because it was new to them.'[6] He 'found the best method to adopt to reassure them was to saunter quietly on swinging [his] stick, just to let them see it wasn't anything so very awful!' He believed that 'the

1 Diary 1915, 26 April.
2 AWM4 1/25/1 Part 1 – April 1915, HQ ANZAC, 26 April.
3 AWM4 1/25/1 Part 8 – April 1915, HQ ANZAC, Appendix 2.
4 AWM4 1/25/1 Part 1 – April 1915, HQ ANZAC, 26 April.
5 Diary 1915, 26 April.
6 These were the 'stragglers' about whom there would be vigorous debate between official histories and that still features in current histories. See Alistair Thomson, 'Popular Gallipoli history and the

men began to think it was much more ordinary than they had imagined.' He perceived that 'they have found that they are more or less safe when dug in,' and so were 'in quite good spirits again.'[7] These personal visits confirmed to him the need for some relief for exhausted troops and above all reorganisation. This was made possible with the arrival of the 4th Brigade.

Monday 27 April saw heavy shelling of the beach and was devoted to very necessary reorganisation. Birdwood 'went up to Walker's Bde on hill over camp with Godley & got Monash up there to show him [the] country around & arrange definite sectors of defence.' Then he 'went with Bridges up [a] valley in rear of camp to Maclaurin's HQ & arranged sectors there.'[8] Just after they left, Maclaurin and his Brigade Major were killed. Birdwood had lost his second brigade commander in a matter of days. The 3rd Brigade was pulled out and replaced by the 4th Brigade.[9] The third day ashore also produced a clearer picture of the enemy facing the Anzacs. Three prisoners produced information on German officer numbers assisting the Turks and some encouraging points about adverse Turkish morale. The next report confirmed the presence of 19 Division and that its commander was Kaimakum (Colonel) Mustafa Kemal Bey.[10]

That night, however, the Turkish troops showed their resolve. They 'made several determined attacks to turn' Birdwood's troops out, 'advancing to the attack in masses along the line blowing bugles and shouting "Allah".' More than one Anzac battalion 'retained its fire until the Turks were nearly on them, when they poured in rapid fire, and then went for them with the bayonet.' Birdwood emphasised 'the utmost importance of' retaining at all costs the positions that the Anzacs had 'so gallantly taken.' Digging hard was encouraged 'to improve the present position and make the troops immune from shell fire.'[11] On ammunition Birdwood was clear:

> I appeal to all officers and N.C.O.'s to do all that they can to control the expenditure of ammunition so that we may retain it all for its legitimate purpose – the destruction and defeat of the enemy – and not risk running out of it by useless waste.[12]

'Destruction and defeat' typified Birdwood's goals and he reflected these throughout the war. Sir Ian Hamilton now visited Anzac Cove, going up to Plugge's Plateau, and Birdwood would have learnt from him the overall situation. On 29 April, he wrote to his wife: 'We have <u>very</u> much yet before us & have only just begun, though it is something to have managed the landing.'[13]

Birdwood now focussed on aggressively pushing forward. The arrival of the Royal Naval Division provided opportunity for relief in line. To Hamilton, Birdwood summarised his attempted advances: 'On the night of 2nd May an attempt was made … to seize the knoll on spur 700 [Baby 700] from which sniper fire could fire down Monash Gully, but this position was found to be too strong, and the original position was reoccupied with a loss of 800 men.' The same day a party of New Zealanders was sent north of Anzac Cove to a suspected observation

representation of Australian military manhood', *History Australia*, 16:3 (2019), 518-533, for an overview of this ongoing debate.

7 AWM 3DRL/3376 8/1, Letter, Birdwood to wife, 29 April 1915.
8 Diary 1915, 27 April.
9 AWM4 1/25/1 Part 8 – April 1915, HQ ANZAC, Operation Order No 1 dated 27 April 1915.
10 AWM4 1/27/2 – April 1915, Intelligence, HQ ANZAC, Appendices VIII and IX.
11 AWM4 1/25/1 Part 8 – April 1915, HQ ANZAC, Appendix 5.
12 AWM4 1/25/1 Part 8, Appendix 6.
13 AWM 3DRL/3376 8/1, Letter, Birdwood to his wife, 29 April 1915.

station, successfully capturing twelve and killing three enemy. On the morning of 4 May 'an attempt was made to seize Kaba [sic] Tepe but was not successful.'[14] That afternoon brought all such efforts to a halt. Orders were received to provide two brigades for Cape Helles. Birdwood 'sent off 2nd Aust & NZ Inf Bdes – also 5 Batteries Artillery after dark to join Sir Ian's force at Cape Helles to join in big attack on Achy Babi [*sic*].' This left him very weak: '1st and 3rd Bdes only about 2300 each & Monash's 4th Bde about 1700 – while Naval & Marine Bdes – 2 Bns each – practically useless.'[15] To Birdwood's staff the 'reembarkation proved a useful rehearsal for the operation of reembarking the whole force should that be necessary.' The Anzac perimeter was arranged in four sections, from South to North: I – 3rd Bde; II – 1st Bde; 3 – Marine Bde and 4th Aust Bde, and 4 – Naval Brigade.[16] Birdwood's forces had achieved a landing, held on and shown aggressive intent, but were now purely defensive under constant enemy fire. Withdrawal was still on the cards.

On 9 May Hamilton sent Captain Guy Dawnay to see Birdwood. Dawnay told him that 'the attack on Acha Babi [*sic*] had failed & suggested [the] idea [of] my embarking as I might not be able to hold out at Anzac Cove.' Birdwood added: 'To this I am much averse as withdrawal would have worst possible effect in every way & I hope I can hold out.' The next day Birdwood went 'to Cape Helles to see Sir Ian *re* situation and decided to hang on' at Anzac.[17] The decision was made but hanging on was not sufficient. That would result in a negative attitude and the initiative would be handed to the Turks. The burden was on Birdwood to prevent this and continue to instil aggression. Despite being a Corps Commander, he had lived and slept in a dugout in a ravine by the beach for two weeks, setting a personal example of accepting hardship. His whole corps was packed into an area no bigger than 3.25 square kilometres (1.25 square miles), constantly within range of enemy guns. The Anzac area was a salient jutting uphill from the beach into enemy territory.[18]

The next ten days saw further reorganisation as the two Brigades returned from Cape Helles and the requested reinforcements came from Egypt. These included four mounted brigades as complete units but without horses.[19] All arrived by mid-May. The Marine and Naval Brigades were replaced and left to re-join the Royal Naval Division at Helles. Additionally, 2nd Brigade and the New Zealand Brigade returned from the Second Battle of Krithia.

Hamilton informed both the fronts that 'a brief pause to recoup, refit and prepare for fresh exertions' was called for and the first step was 'to consolidate effectively' positions 'against hostile attack by strengthening and improving trenches … Commanders should foster the offensive spirit by every means in their power and every effort should be made to gain ground at night by sapping, or by advancing and then digging in.' The orders mentioned future possible capture of Achi Baba, but nothing about progress towards Chunuk Bair or its surrounding features.[20] 'Offensive spirit' aligned with what Birdwood was undertaking. He was already thinking of

14 AWM4 1/25/1 Part 8 – April 1915, HQ ANZAC, Appendix 14.
15 Diary 1915, 5 May.
16 AWM4 1/25/2 Part 1 – May 1915, HQ ANZAC, 5 and 7 May.
17 Diary 1915, 9 and 10 May. This ended the debate on withdrawal which features little in the historiography.
18 AWM4 1/25/2 Part 2 – May 1915, HQ ANZAC, Appendix 1.
19 Christopher Pugsley, *Gallipoli The New Zealand Story*, 5th ed (Auckland: Libro International, 2014), 194.
20 AWM4 1/25/2 Part 3 – May 1915, HQ ANZAC, Appendix 29.

Chunuk Bair. On 13 May Birdwood wrote to Hamilton wanting more troops to achieve a 'better position' than that which he occupied. He particularly sought the 29th Indian Brigade to make a 'sweeping movement round my left in the direction of Biyuk Anafarta, and its right to Point 971.' He finished his letter with thoughts that 'it might be advantageous to land a really large force' using his Anzac bridgehead' and gain a position covering Kilia Bay, in the Dardanelles.[21] Thus the concept that led to the first stage of the August Offensive was hatched by Birdwood at Anzac. On 15 May, just three days after their own landing, the Commanding Officer of the Canterbury Mounted Rifles Regiment sent out his second-in-command Major Overton to 'reconnoitre the enemy's position.'[22]

> On this his first enterprise he took with him Corporal Denton, and crossing from No. 1 Outpost to the bed of the Sazli Beit Dere, followed its northern branch to the foot of the long ridge which, falling down from Chunuk Bair, reaches the sea at No. 2 Outpost. This ridge he named Rhododendron Spur, the scrub which grew there much resembling bushes of rhododendron. He followed up the spur until he reached the saddle at the head of the Sazli Beit, and from there made notes of the country to the north as far as the great Abdul Rahman Spur, locating "The Farm" and the several branches of the Aghyl Dere. There were no enemy visible, but on the way back Major Overton and his companion had to lie low several times as they came across parties of Turks. The information gained in this daring reconnaissance, combined with that gained from the later ones carried out by or under the supervision of this enterprising officer, formed the basis for the operations which were carried out against Chunuk Bair in August.[23]

Overton's hand-drawn map described the beds of the streams as 'smooth and passable for troops at night' but that the ridges have 'very steep razor backs.' The detail of the ridgeline is less accurate – particularly regarding Hill 971 – than that of the gullies.[24]

On 14 May Kitchener enquired from the War Council 'what force would be necessary to carry through the operations' on which Hamilton was engaged.[25] Hamilton visited Birdwood on 16 May who further expanded his ideas, following up with a letter showing a willingness to consider bold ventures:

> Land Cox's brigade at Anzac Cove where it would be joined by one of my Australian Brigades and the two to march via Fisherman's Hut and Inam Chai [a watercourse running West from Biyuk Anafarta to the sea] to attack [up] the big spur running South East … almost immediately on to point 971. I understand from scouts whom I have had about the hill that there are practically few if any trenches facing down the hill in that part. Simultaneously with the advance of these two brigades I would send

21 AWM 3DRL/3376 11/5c Part 1, Letter, Birdwood to Hamilton, 13 May 1915.
22 Diary 1915, 15 May.
23 Colonel C G Powles (ed.), *The History of the Canterbury Mounted Rifles 1914-1919* (Christchurch: Whitcombe & Tombs, 1928), 29 31.
24 AWM4 1/27/3 – May 1915, Intelligence, HQ ANZAC, Appendix 14.
25 *Final Report of the Dardanelles Commission* (London: HMSO, 1919), 24.

> up to spur running South East from the well at Fisherman's Hut [towards Baby 700]. These two flank attacks I would make in conjunction with an attack of two brigades … up along the main ridge of the hill [Russell's Top]. With this force I should hope to take the whole main ridge … While this attack was going on I would land at Anzac Cove any new divisions you were sending me, and bring them on to my right. … I would endeavour to make a joint advance down the ridge leading to Kaba Tepe … I would be holding the line I want along the main spur of the Sari Bair Hill and commanding Kojadere and country beyond.[26]

Hamilton's response to Kitchener arrived during the political turmoil leading to the Coalition Government, so without changes Birdwood continued with his same forces.

One of the dominant features of Birdwood's diary during these days is the personal immediacy of the casualties. On 9 May, he recorded how an 'orderly had his head taken off near my bivouac.'[27] Then four days later Birdwood himself was injured, as he recounted to his wife:

> I had only posted a letter to you yesterday when I appeared to catch a bit of a bullet – most likely a very slight one. I was going my round of the troops as usual & on getting up to one of the trenches was quite upset at hearing bomb after bomb being thrown into it by Turks from their trench only 30 yds off. Men were being brought down fearfully & mucked about by bombs & no one seemed at all able to put a stop to such an intolerable state of things, which is not only most demoralising to the men but by gradually incapacitating so many makes us so weak. So I saw the only thing to do was to go up – the trench is right on top of a cliff at the head of the valley – and see to matters & try to devise a plan. I got into the trench & was making a most careful survey around in, I thought, complete safety, as of course I was using my periscope when to my annoyance I found myself nearly knocked head over heels with a bullet. The men in making the trench had done – what they so often will do in spite of all orders – put a sort of top layer of earth on the parapet which was not bullet proof. I thought I was quite safe behind it, when a bullet came through – aimed at the periscope as they always are – and just grazed along the top of my head. Luckily I had my head rather thrown back to use the periscope so it only just grazed along & did us no harm. At first it was of course impossible to know what had happened, as it naturally bled a lot & gave one a buz [sic]. But I realised at once it was nothing & got up & came home to get bandaged.

After seeing the doctor, he was later further upset.

> To add insult to injury, & as if I hadn't had my share for the present – at all events – some rascal of a German gunner proceeded to hurl a large shell right into the entrance of my little dugout this morning – luckily that was all he could do, for he would

26 AWM 3DRL/3376 11/5c Part 1, Letter, Birdwood to Hamilton, 16 May 1915.
27 Diary 1915, 9 May.

> have to go round a corner to get further in, & that I am hoping that they not be able to do – But we will have to be altering our lodgings or perhaps I should say diggings.[28]

On 17 May General Bridges was mortally injured near Quinn's Post.[29] Birdwood 'was most distressed at Bridges being so seriously wounded – a great loss & such a nice fellow.' He went out the next day to see Bridges on a hospital ship and found him 'very bad – leg mortifying & Doctors little hope of him being able to stand an operation.' Birdwood wrote that he would 'find it hard to carry on without him.' He came back to hear that his 'beloved Villiers-Stuart had been killed – a bit of shrapnel through the heart.' Birdwood described him, one of his staff officers, as 'the best of fellows – a most devoted & loyal officer & best of soldiers,' and in a letter to Hamilton as 'a loss that I personally feel very much indeed, as he was with me for three years as a staff officer when I commanded the Kohat Brigade, and I had the most implicit confidence and trust in him, and I might also say affection for him.'[30]

'Where General Birdwood lived with his staff: The Headquarters at Anzac'. (*The Graphic*, 29 January 1916).

28 AWM 3DRL/3376 8/1, Letter, Birdwood to his wife, 15 May 1915.
29 HQ ANZAC had called for both Divisions to advise on the commonly used names for features. See AWM4 1/25/2 Part 2 – May 1915, HQ ANZAC, Appendix 28(a). Such place names featured regulalry in Birdwood's diary from 8 May.
30 Diary 1915, 14 - 17 May. AWM 3DRL/3376 11/5c Part 1, Letter, Birdwood to Hamilton, and Letter, Birdwood to his wife, 17 May 1915. After leaving Kohat Birdwood had been asked for his picture to add to a Headquarters collection, Villiers-Stuart wrote to thank him with a delightfully affectionate and newsy letter, NAM 6707-19-506, Letter, Villiers-Stuart to Birdwood, 2 December 1912.

Birdwood's picture of the enemy, although limited, was becoming clearer week by week. By 16 May four divisions and eight regiments had been identified. On 18 May, there were aeroplane reports of 'movements of troops South & landings of considerable numbers of troops near Maidos [and] Attack expected on ANZAC.'[31] A 'warning out to all troops to be on the alert' was sent. 'At midnight 18/19 a heavy rifle and machine gun fire broke out from the enemy positions at the head of Monash Gully and about Baby 700 directed chiefly on Quinn's Post. This fire was the hottest we have known as yet.' At about 5 o'clock 'the action became general along the line.' A planned counter attack 'coincided with the commencement of a Turkish attack from the direction of Baby 700 which held up the counter attack. This Turkish attack did not develop.' Fire 'continued strongly throughout the night' but after 5 a.m. activity ceased. The enemy's casualties were large. 'At least 3,000 are lying in the open view of our trenches while their own trenches are probably full of them.' Birdwood estimated his own casualties as 'about 100 killed and 9 officers and 400 men wounded.'[32] On 19 May his intelligence staff identified all twelve Regiments of the four Divisions arraigned against the Anzacs, with enemy forces estimated at least 35,000.[33] 'From a wounded prisoner' it was learnt that it was a "real effort to push our force into the sea, also that Liman von Sanders was in command.'[34]

There followed a series of 'white and red crescent flag' events. At first these were perceived as ruses as 'bodies of troops were observed massing in the rear of the enemy's positions.' The next twenty-four hours continued with the Anzacs beating off assaults in all sectors. A further white flag on 21 May brought in a Turkish envoy seeking burial of their dead. Birdwood, despite believing that the major purpose was for the enemy 'to get hold of the rifles on their dead as we hear that they are very short of them & reinforcements are coming down unarmed,' sent proposals for a cease-fire to Hamilton.[35] Deliberations went on for 48 hours and finally on 24 May an armistice commenced, with 'suspension of arms for the burial of the dead & removal of the wounded.' The day passed off without 'serious incident.'[36]

With the armistice over, Birdwood immediately returned to his planning for a break-out. Birdwood and the Canterbury Mounted Rifles Regiment diaries had recorded a visit by Birdwood on 20 May. Birdwood may have met Overton and discussed his further reconnaissance of 15 May.[37] On the day after the armistice, Birdwood went on board the destroyer HMS *Newmarket* 'to reconnoitre round Suvla Bay to look up the cliffs of 971.' He then writes that 'on the way back we saw torpedo strike *Triumph* on starboard side S[outh] of Kaba Tepe about 12.10, she soon keeled over, but remained on her side about quarter hour … we sped to her as did several destroyers.'[38] Watched by countless Anzacs on the beach and on the cliffs, the sinking of *Triumph* made a dramatic impact.

Sunday 30 May was a landmark day regarding Birdwood's future plans. Hamilton came over from Imbros and made a lengthy description of his day:

31 AWM4 1/27/3 Part 1 – May 1915, Intelligence, HQ ANZAC, 2, 16 and 18 May.
32 AWM 3DRL/3376 11/3, Report 'Summary of events from midnight 18/19th to 6 am 20th.'
33 AWM4 1/27/3 Part 1 – May 1915, Intelligence, HQ ANZAC, 19 May.
34 AWM4 1/25/2 Part 1 – May 1915, HQ ANZAC, 20 May.
35 Diary 1915, 19 & 20 May.
36 AWM4 1/25/2 Part 1 – May 1915, HQ ANZAC, 24 May
37 AWM4 35/3/1 – May 1915, Canterbury Mounted Rifles, 20 May. Diary 1915, 20 May.
38 Diary 1915, 25 May.

> The Cove was being heavily shelled, and the troops near the beach together with the fatigue parties handling stores and ammunition, had dashed into their dug-outs like marmots at the shadow of an eagle. Birdwood came out to meet me on the very unhealthy spot; indeed, in spite of my waving him back, he walked right on to the end of the deserted pier. Just as we were getting near to his quarters, a couple of shrapnel burst … Thence I could see the enemy trenches in front of Quinn's Post, and also a very brisk bomb combat in full … Nothing was more strange than this inspection. … The spirit of the men is invincible. Only lately have we been able to give them blankets: as to square meals and soft sleeps, these are dreams of the past, they belong to another state of being. Yet I never struck a more jovial crew … overhead, the shell and rifle bullets groaned and whined … but, all the time, from that fiery crest line, which is Quinn's, there comes a slow constant trickle of wounded – some dragging themselves painfully along; others being carried along on stretchers. Bomb wounds all; a ceaseless, silent stream of bandages and blood. Yet, three out of four of "the boys" have grit left for a gay smile or a cheery little nod to their comrades waiting for their turn as they pass, pass, pass down on their way to the sea. There are poets and writers who see naught in war but carrion, filth, savagery and horror. The heroism of the rank and file makes no appeal. They refuse war the credit of being the only exercise in devotion on the large scale existing in this world. The superb moral victory over death leaves them cold. … To me, this is no valley of death - it is a valley brim full of life at its highest power. … a radiant force of camaraderie in action.[39]

The spirit of the troops, as perceived by Hamilton, was a positive reflection of Birdwood's successful leadership under fire. He commanded Anzac and he had a close affinity with his men. It was in May that a famous photograph of Birdwood swimming at Anzac Cove was taken. *The Anzac Book* suggested that this showed real affection for him. One contributor wrote that 'the morning splash has come to be indispensable. Daily at six-thirty you have been used to see the head of General Birdwood bobbing beyond the sunken barge inshore; and a host of nudes lined the beach.'[40]

Subsequently, Birdwood sent a two-and-a-half-page memorandum on the current situation and for 'an eventual advance to carry out the objective.' He detailed his current position as 'the enemy entrenched all round', with 'four and five rows of trenches,' from which they 'have the command of us.' He described the ground over which 'the big sweeping movement round' his left flank would take place as: 'most difficult – far more so than any we have occupied so far'; 'broken up with many and deep ravines'; 'large number of precipices'; and 'thick scrub everywhere.' As he believed at the Landing, 'a certain element of surprise' was necessary, because the enemy held 'interior lines and could well reinforce the crest line before we could reach it.' He acknowledged the difficulties of a night attack and realised that this could mean 'troops losing their way.' This he did not think was 'a matter of consequence,' as they would know that all they had to do was 'to press upwards,' and matters would be 'rectified in this respect in the morning.' His reconnaissance by ship, on 25 May, had shown him that Point 971 was 'entirely cut off from the

39 General Sir Ian Hamilton, *Gallipoli Diary*, vol. I & II (London: Edward Arnold, 1920), 255-58.
40 C E W Bean (ed.), *The Anzac Book*, 3rd ed (Sydney: University of New South Wales, 2010, 30 and 32.

Birdwood swimming at Anzac Cove, May 1915, Ernest Brooks, Admiralty photographer. (Australian War Memorial G000401).

main ridge by precipices.' He focused, therefore, on the ridgeline running up to the South West of 971 and stated a requirement for 'three brigades of a total of about 8,000 men' to occupy that position. He emphasised that 'digging in would therefore be absolutely essential immediately.' He required a further brigade for this and again pushed for the Indian Brigade to operate in 'ideal country for the Gurkhas.' 'When secured' he would then 'move down the ridge with at least one brigade in the hope of taking the enemy's trenches facing my present position in the rear. As this brigade approached the North-East corner of my present position, the brigade at present occupying that position would move forward to meet it.' Subsequently he planned to move down the Second Ridge and take Gaba Tepe. 'Having secured the position from the 971 ridge downwards to Kaba [sic] Tepe,' the next move within two days would be – with a further division – to take the Third (Gun) Ridge and intervening Legge Valley. The plan was to achieve the original 25 April objectives but this time it would provide the foundation for the main thrust of Hamilton's forces. Birdwood summarised his requirements as 'one Brigade for the first sweeping enveloping attack and one Division for the further advance.'[41] This plan, very much Birdwood's, would be honed over the next three months. Some things like 'to press upwards' never deviated.

41 AWM4 1/25/2 Part 4 – May 1915, HQ ANZAC, Appendix 41(b).

Whenever a plan or enterprise becomes delayed or diverted, it is easy to lose sight of the original objective. In the case of the Dardanelles venture, the strategic objective was to reach Constantinople. Any thrust from the Anzac sector would have been a tactical phase in an operational objective to meet the strategic aim of reaching Constantinople. There is nothing to suggest that Birdwood saw any attack on Sari Bair as other than a tactical phase towards meeting an overall operational objective, but certainly he appeared to have moved beyond just extending his own perimeter and gaining vital ground close-by. The use of the term 'August Offensive' can mean either just the effort from Anzac, or the Suvla landings, or both, or indeed the sum of all the efforts - as used by Crawley.[42] The plans now developed from those of just Birdwood and his staff to become the basis for the general attack by Hamilton's forces, with the addition of the Suvla Bay landings and the addition of a number of new divisions. As the overall concept grew, the detail of the first stage remained relatively unchanged. This first stage was Birdwood's command responsibility.

Meantime, Hunter-Weston, GOC VIII Corps, since its formation at Helles on 24 May, had received the go-ahead for a major attack on 4 June (Third Krithia), and Birdwood supported this with attacks at Quinn's Post and near the German Officers' Trench.[43] Meanwhile Birdwood continued his reconnaissance at the three forward outposts on the 'shore above & beyond Fisherman's Hut where Otago MR' were located.

On 9 June Hamilton took Birdwood 'down to Cape Helles for a conference with Hunter-Weston and the new French General Gouraud to show' them 'the telegram from Lord K to announce that large reinforcements were being sent out.'[44] These were three divisions of Kitchener's New Army with 'the latest to arrive no later than first fortnight in July.'[45] The assault on Sari Bair would await their arrival, not happening until late July at the earliest. This provided a longer planning period than for the Landing itself and for Birdwood to apply any lessons from then and subsequent operations.

For the Anzac area, 10-30 June was comparatively quiet and Birdwood used the word 'quiet' in eleven of those days in his diary. Everything is relative though and the War Diary of his Headquarters recorded a daily stream of approximately 5-10 killed, 30-60 wounded and 60-100 sick evacuated from Anzac – a constant drain. Convalescents and reinforcements came into Anzac in a similar steady stream. Mining and countermining went on continuously and both the Anzacs and Turks made local attacks. Birdwood recorded daily visits to all sectors of the line and reconnaissance continued. On 20 June, a party landed north of Suvla Point, returning on 22

42 Crawley details this issue very clearly and is one of the few to emphasise the August Offensive as having 'the strategic objective: Constantinople.' See Crawley, *Climax at Gallipoli*, 40-44. Crawley takes a fresh approach by allocating a major aspect of the operational level of war to each chapter, the first of which examines planning and features the development of Birdwood's ideas.

43 AWM4 1/25/3 Part 1 – June 1915, HQ ANZAC, Appendix 4. Diary 1915, 4 June.

44 Diary 1915, 7 and 9 June.

45 AWM4 1/4/4 Part 1 – June 1915, General Headquarters, Mediterranean Expeditionary Force, 8 June. These Divisions were to be 10th (Irish), 11th (Northern) and 13th (Western) divisions. Already on 6 May 42nd (East Lancashire) Division had reinforced Cape Helles and similarly 52nd (Lowland) Division on 6 June.

June.[46] It was then learnt that the three new divisions would not arrive until 10, 18 and 28 July.[47] Hamilton's staff had now been working on the plan 'for over a fortnight.' Though Hamilton saw himself as 'entirely' fathering the plan, he did not see himself as the originator, rather 'the idea was born at Anzac.' In Hamilton's view, the plan was 'based on Birdwood's confidence that, if only he can be strengthened by another division, he can seize and hold the high crest line which dominates his own left.' Hamilton concurred with that confidence.[48] On 25 June Birdwood was instructed that 'as little attention as possible should be directed to that [northern] flank.' The 'vital importance of preventing suspicion being aroused in the enemy's mind' was stressed.[49] After a fourth division, a fifth was, on 28 June, proposed by Kitchener, the same afternoon on which the last major battle at Cape Helles was fought – Gully Ravine, in which the 29th Indian Brigade participated.[50]

By the beginning of July, Birdwood's staff had prepared a lengthy thirteen page 'Proposals for using Reinforcements' – a formal justification of the number of 'rifles' required for each task, with allocation of specific troops to task where appropriate. The 'main object' was stated as 'the occupation of the 971 Ridge, as a first step in operations for clearing the Sari Bair Hill and advancing across the Boghali neck.' As well as this and holding the current Anzac position, four other 'necessary' tasks or 'operations of less importance' were identified. First was an attack on Lone Pine with the proviso that the 'attack on the 971 Ridge should not be undertaken without this operation, which should precede it.' This would 'tend to draw off the enemy's attention towards our right, and would almost certainly take off part of his general reserve and prevent reinforcements from local reserves being sent up to Baby 700 or beyond.' Secondly, the trenches on the rise of Baby 700 and on the ridge to its North East' needed to be 'occupied to complete possession of the 971 Ridge.' This was the assault across The Nek. Assessed as a 'narrow neck' it made an 'unaided assault almost hopeless, but if combined with the attack on 971, a force of 3,000 rifles should suffice for the assaulting force and for a reserve.' The other tasks related to securing the approaches towards 971, including the enemy on 'the "W" and "Chocolate" Hills' to the north of the flanking move. It was suggested that to do this too early would draw attention and that perhaps the force to undertake this could be landed in Suvla Bay to 'lessen the numbers moved out along the beach.' As it was 'new ground and does not present the difficulties of the Sari Bair Hill, troops employed would be drawn from the reinforcing troops [the new divisions].' For the 971 Ridge, the 'extent of the front on which troops' could attack was seen as 'about 2000 yards.' The NZ Infantry Brigade and the 4th Australian Infantry Brigade were identified for this but 'a further 2500 rifles are required.' Unsurprisingly from previous correspondence, this 'could best be found from the 29th (Indian) Brigade, well suited to operating in this broken and mountainous country.' It was expected that the attackers, 'certain to be disorganised and weakened' on arrival on the ridge, with a 'strong counter-attack' imminent, would need 'further

46 AWM4 1/25/3 Part 1 – June 1915, HQ ANZAC, 20 & 22 June. Suvla and Nibrunesi Points are the northern and southern promontories of Suvla Bay.
47 AWM4 1/4/3 Part 1 – June 1915, General Headquarters, Mediterranean Expeditionary Force, Memo 484, Hamilton to Kitchener, 22 June.
48 Hamilton, *Gallipoli Diary*, I & II, 328-30.
49 AWM4 1/25/3 Part 4 – June 1915, HQ ANZAC, Appendix 16.
50 AWM4 1/4/3 Part 1 – June 1915, General Headquarters, Mediterranean Expeditionary Force, 28 June. 53rd (Welsh) and 54th (East Anglia) divisions would be added.

shared the challenge of hanging on during those first tumultuous days. Pugsley has observed that Godley did not have the personal powers of leadership that Birdwood displayed.[59] With his regular visits forward it was to be expected that how Godley was planning to command the operation in detail was a reasonable concern for Birdwood. Likewise, the two key Brigadiers, Monash and Johnston, both received adverse reviews at that time.[60] As for troops, however, Birdwood had confidence in the New Zealanders and for months he had pushed for the Indian Brigade to take part. He planned to gather all the commanders, not just Godley, Monash and Johnston, in order to impress on them strongly his personal views, which included the imperative to continue upwards towards the ridge on the first night and to keep going whatever befell a column. All the men were, however, weak physically as the continual daily despatch of sick men demonstrated. The motivation of the unit and sub-unit commanders was vital. Birdwood knew the physical state of the Anzacs but perhaps expected too much of the Indian Brigade who had just come from the fighting in Gully Ravine. Birdwood recognised the power of personal leadership from his past experiences and had seen it on Gallipoli demonstrated by Malone at Quinn's Post. The desire for surprise during the Landings had led to an assault before first light but disorder had ensued. Once again, the understandable need for surprise drove the decision for a night march. Control would be paramount to deliver some or all the troops in time for the dawn assault on the Ridge. The diversionary and linking assaults by the 1st Australian Division, once they had been decided upon, could be left largely to their commander. The assault on the Ridge marked the key first stage to the launching of five new divisions on the Peninsula and demanded Birdwood's relentless attention.

On 2 August, Major General 'Cox & COs' of the 29th Indian Brigade arrived, and Major General 'Shaw Comd'g 13th Div & several of his officers' arrived.[61] The next day Birdwood took Cox and his officers 'up to left flank to look around.' On 4 August Birdwood spoke personally with 'all Australian Brigadiers & COs' and then he did the same with 'all Godley's & Shaw's Brigadiers & COs.'[62] The assault on the Ridge was to deliver three brigades to make the initial important surprise attack. Night time, the terrain, men or even leaders might contribute to delays and mishaps, but Birdwood knew he was relying on the leaders to drive forward and take the Ridge. Prior has made it very clear that everything had been reduced to taking the ridge and establishing a base at Suvla. 'What was to happen after that was not specified in any documents written at the time.'[63]

The written formal orders confirming all the briefings were issued on 7 August.[64] A few hours later Hamilton wrote in his diary 'Chunuk Bair will do: with that we win.'[65] It was not to be.

59 Pugsley, *Gallipoli The New Zealand Story*, 352.
60 For Monash, see Crawley, *Climax at Gallipoli,* 205; Ashley Ekins (ed.), *Gallipoli: A Ridge Too Far* (Wollombi, NSW: Exisle Publishing, 2013), 126-39; Robert Rhodes James, *Gallipoli* (London: Papermac, 1989), 271-73; Tim Travers, *Gallipoli 1915* (Stroud: Tempus Publishing, 2001), 176. For Johnston, see Ekins, *Gallipoli*, 145; Rhodes James, *Gallipoli*, 288; Travers, *Gallipoli 1915*, 176. Peter Pedersen confirms these criticisms in his contribution in Ekins, *Gallipoli.*
61 Cox had found Anzac wonderful '& most refreshing' due 'entirely to you living in the middle of them.' AWM 3DRL/3376 11/1, Letter, Cox to Birdwood, 19 July 1915.
62 Diary 1915, 2, 3 & 4 August.
63 Robin Prior, *Gallipoli: The End of the Myth* (New Haven and London: Yale University Press, 2009), 168.
64 AWM4 1/25/5 Part 3 – August 1915, HQ ANZAC, Appendix 11.
65 Hamilton, *Gallipoli Diary*, I & II, II-55.

7

Failure and evacuation

On 4 August 1915 Birdwood wrote to Jenny:

> My own darling girl,
> We are just about to make another big advance about which I have been busy for a long time & I do hope & think I have done all that can be done to ensure success. It is going to be a real big business … extraordinary [*sic*] difficult. I have to take an extremely difficult hill held by the Turks in great numbers, and I feel my only chance is by attacking them at the most difficult part where they will least expect us. It is a lot covered with deep ravines and precipices everywhere over which we must attack at night, so it will be a very high trial. Lots of men will lose themselves but will have to keep pressing on & will I hope find themselves again in the morning, and with real determination they will I hope succeed.[1]

Two days later, Second Lieutenant William Slim of the 9th Royal Warwickshire Regiment was waiting to go forward into action.[2] Forty years later, Slim, then the Governor General of Australia, wrote in his masterpiece, *Defeat into Victory*, words that possibly describe best what was in Birdwood's mind that final afternoon 6 August 1915, awaiting that 'big advance':

> There comes a moment in every battle against a stubborn enemy when the result hangs in the balance. Then the general, however skilful and far-sighted he may have been, must hand over to his soldiers, to the men in the ranks and to their regimental officers, and leave them to complete what he has begun. The issue then rests with them, on their courage, their hardihood, their refusal to be beaten either by the cruel hazards of nature or by the fierce strength of their human enemy.[3]

1 AWM 3DRL/3376 8/1.
2 C L Kingsford, *The Story of The Royal Warwickshire Regiment* (London: Country Life, 1921), 198.
3 FM Sir William Slim, *Defeat into Victory* (London: Cassell, 1956), 551.

The first assault was at 5:30 p.m. following an hour of 'continuous and heavy bombardment' from the supporting naval ships.[4] Major King, Brigade Major of 1st Australian Brigade, gave 'three short whistle blasts' to signal the assault on the 400 Plateau at Lone Pine.[5] Thus in Birdwood's words 'began the big attack on Turkish positions.'[6] Colonel Smyth, the Brigade commander, was directly in charge of this assault with his reserve battalion commanding officer positioned beside Brigade headquarters. This clear chain of command was unchanged from previous weeks.

As well as this diversionary attack at Anzac, VIII Corps made an even more substantial effort – the battle of Krithia Vineyard.[7] After a preliminary heavy artillery and naval gunfire bombardment, 29th Division attacked at 3:50 p.m. suffering heavy casualties. This and subsequent attacks by 42nd Division on 7 August neither distracted the enemy nor deterred the move of Turkish reserves to the north.[8]

The planned assault on Sari Bair called for two Left and Right Covering Forces to secure the flanks of the gullies and slopes, through and up which the two, Left and Right, Assaulting Columns would advance and attack.[9] The Right Covering Force, commanded by Brigadier General Russell, that consisted of his NZMR Brigade and the Maori Contingent, with objectives nearest to the existing Anzac front lines, made the first move.[10] The day 'was spent quietly resting & in a final reconnaissance from Nos 1, 2 and 3 Outposts of the ground over which the Bde is to attack that night. These reconnaissances & discussions of plans were attended by the Brigadier & staff & each Regtl Commander.' They were to attack from these Outposts and seize the flanking features – Bauchops Hill, Table Top – of Chailak Dere. For a number of the past nights Birdwood had 'arranged with our guardian-angel destroyer on that flank that she should turn her searchlight on at the same time and bombard.' This took place as usual at 9:00 p.m. as the Right Covering Force moved forward to their assault and attack with 'bomb & bayonet only.' Magazines were not charged.[11] At 9:30 p.m. the searchlight lifted and the first assaults commenced. All these operations were completed by 0:30 a.m. and the flanks of Chailak Dere, together with the southern flank of Aghyl Dere, were secure.[12] At 9:00 p.m. the Left Covering Force departed from its bivouac area, the Reserve Gully at the southern side of the Sphinx and started to move northwards along the coast. This Force contained 40 Brigade, less two battalions in reserve. Its move was 'hampered by the Chailak Dere which was crossed by a sunken road in which were troops belonging to the Right Covering Force.' After crossing the Chailak Dere, the Left Force 'marched [still northwards] without interruption to the mouth

4 AWM4 1/25/5 Part 1 – August 1915, HQ ANZAC, 6 August.
5 AWM4 1/4/3 Part 1 – June 1915, 1st Infantry Brigade, No 3 Operation Order. Major King's whistle is preserved in the AWM, Heraldry Collection REL/07579.
6 Diary 1915, 6 August.
7 AWM4 1/4/4 Part 2 – July - August 1915, General Headquarters, Mediterranean Expeditionary Force, Directive GSR Z 18/2, 29 July to GOC 8th Corps.
8 Aspinall-Oglander, *Military Operations: Gallipoli Volume II*, 171-77.
9 Ibid., Appendix 7 "Orders for the Night Advance from Anzac and the Capture of Sar Bair,' 5 August 1915.
10 Each Force had Engineers attached and Mountain Batteries were attached to each Assaulting Force. They have not been listed here.
11 FM Lord Birdwood, *Khaki and Gown* (London: Ward Lock, 1941), 274. AWM4 35/1/4 Part 1, Headquarters New Zealand Mounted Rifle Brigade, Para 2, Operation Order No 2, 5 August 1915.
12 AWM4 35/1/4 Part 1, Headquarters New Zealand Mounted Rifle Brigade, 6/7 August.

of the Aghyl Dere … and attacked the Damakjelik Bair. … The hill was occupied by 1:30 am.'[13] The northern flank of Aghyl Dere was secured.

The actions of the Covering Forces had been estimated to be completed by 11:00 p.m.[14] Therefore despite writing in retrospect that 'the start was excellent,' Birdwood's plans were running late.[15] He had emphasised to Godley that he 'should impress on the Commanders … that the objective to be reached is to be aimed at whatever the progress of columns in other parts as the success of one move will go far to ensure the success of the whole.'[16] The Right Assaulting Column was to advance to the Sari Bair objective via Chailak Dere, and the Left Assaulting Column via Aghyl Dere. They were to make the assault on their summit objectives at 4:30 a.m.[17] The Right Assaulting Column had two routes. The Canterbury Battalion advanced up the Sazli Beit Dere, which ran East to West, from South of No 2 and Old No 3 Outposts, and then Table Top, to their intermediate objective of Rhododendron Spur.[18] The remainder of Johnston's NZ Brigade advanced up Chailak Dere. Both set off as planned but were delayed in actions around Destroyer Hill and Bauchop's Hill. The Otagos, leading on the left at this point, were further delayed with actions on Big Table Top. It was only by 4:30 a.m. that the Otagos and Canterburys met as planned on Rhododendron Spur.

The Left Assaulting Column consisted of 4th Australian Infantry Brigade leading, under Brigadier General J Monash, and 29th Indian Infantry Brigade, under Brigadier General H V Cox, in overall command of the Column. These command arrangements grated with Monash, as he felt he should have commanded.[19] This Column was the largest of the four groupings and the one that had the furthest to advance. It was similarly delayed as it moved along the coast but rather than follow its planned route to the mouth of the Aghyl Dere, Major Overton was persuaded by a local guide accompanying him to cut across between Walden's Point and the western edge of Bauchop's Hill. This was via a short-cut known as Taylor's Gap. It was a narrow path suitable only for single file and it negated all the careful distance and compass bearing planning. Monash had even produced a detailed Longitudinal Section drawing showing the gradients from the seashore to the summit of Abdel [*sic*] Rahman Bair, the spur from which he was to launch his assault on Hill 971.[20] After further actions against the enemy, the now broken up Column exited slowly into Aghyl Dere, still in the dark of night. They knew neither exactly where they were in the gully, nor where they were in relation to key forks in that gully. By dawn two battalions of 4th Brigade were deployed east of the Left Covering Force on Damakjelik Bair, providing further flank protection as planned. Two Gurkha battalions had drifted further south than planned and some of these companies were soon to link up with the New Zealanders.

13 AWM4 1/53/5 Part 2 - August 1915, Headquarters New Zealand and Australian Division, Report on the Operations against the Sari Bair Position by Maj Gen Godley, 16 August 1915
14 C E W Bean, *The Official History of Australia in the War of 1914-1918, Volume II* (Sydney: Halstead Press, 1924), 459.
15 Birdwood, *Khaki and Gown*, 274.
16 AWM4 1/25/5 Part 3 – August 1915, HQ_ANZAC, Appendix 11 Instructions for Maj Gen Godley.
17 Aspinall-Oglander, *Military Operations: Gallipoli Volume II*, Para 3 (f) (2) in Appendix 7 'Orders for Sari Bair'
18 Major Overton of the Canterburys, who had named this spur back in late April, was at this time guiding the left assaulting force.
19 This is well described by Pedersen in Ekins (ed.), *Gallipoli*, 128-9.
20 AWM 3 DRL/2316 3/21, Papers of General Sir John Monash, Longitudinal Section map.

The remainder of the Left Assaulting Column were between these two groups, not knowing precisely where they were.[21] Birdwood's encouragement to keep going uphill at all costs and seize the heights was of limited value if the correct upward slope could not be identified.

Two thirds of the force that Birdwood had planned to arrive on the objective around dawn was instead at that time dispersed and not positioned to assault. As on the day of the landings there was much heroic action. Then the Anzacs never advanced further than the Second Ridge line and now they were about to fail to win Sari Bair. Many would strive mightily to grasp and hold the target summits. Delays abounded but not to the attack scheduled for 4.30 a.m. at The Nek. First the 8th Light Horse Regiment was mown down in two waves and then the 10th Light Horse Regiment. The simultaneous New Zealand assault down the slope towards Baby 700 never took place and the Chunuk Bair toehold never developed to allow such attacks.

Major Arthur Temperley, the Brigade Major of the NZ Brigade, later described the situation at 8.00 a.m. as 'Wellington and Auckland battalions being two-thirds of the way up the Rhododendron Ridge, with the two remaining battalions [Canterbury and Otago] in reserve a few hundred yards below.' He 'wondered how the Australian Light Horse Brigade had fared.' On the top of Chunuk Bair, trenches were 'bristling with rifles and a certain amount of rifle fire was coming from that direction. On "Q" all was quiet, there was no sign whatever of the Indian Brigade, which should have been well up the slopes by now. Still further north there was no sign whatever of the 4th Australian Brigade … assaulting Pt 971.' The Assaulting Columns were 'finding themselves' as Birdwood had written but the physical energy 'to keep pressing on' had been sapped by weeks of ill health and a demanding night's climbing and fighting. It was at this point that Slim's observation was so apt. The Right Assaulting Column tried again to attack after 'a heavy but inaccurate bombardment of Chunuk Bair by Ships guns and Field Artillery.' The Auckland Battalion exited the Apex though 'a tiny gap about 10 yards across.' Hundreds of Turkish rifles and many machine guns 'were trained upon the Gap and leading Auckland platoons were simply devastated.' Colonel Johnston and Major Temperley were standing at one side of the gap and 'the sight of these brave men being mown down in scores a few yards from us was sickening.' Other Companies surged forward and 'eventually the battalion reached the shelter of the Turkish trench about one hundred yards up the slope after losing between 200 and 300 men in ten minutes.'[22] '6th Gurkhas got near top [Hill Q], but could not reach it. Aus Bde failed to reach big spur of Abdel R [ahman] Bair by about ½ mile.'[23] Birdwood described the rest of 7 August as 'fighting continued all day, Lone Pine being held but Godley not making progress.' Birdwood had to decide on deploying reserves and instigating further attacks. For Godley, 'three battalions of 38th Brigade were sent up at 11am to be ready for use when needed,' but these Kitchener's Army battalions had to find their way through the same ground that had taxed Indian Army regulars and experienced Anzacs. Lone Pine received a reserve battalion and two more were moved into Monash Gully in case of further threats to Pope's and

21 AWM4 1/25/5 Part 1 – August 1915, HQ ANZAC, 6/7 & 7 August; AWM4 1/53/5 Part 2 – August 1915, Headquarters New Zealand and Australian Division, Appendix 79; AWM 1DRL/0221, Papers of General Sir Herbert Vaughan Cox, Diary, 33; Kevin Fewster (ed.), *Bean's Gallipoli: The Diaries of Australia's Official War Correspondent* (Crowsnest: Allen & Unwin, 1983), 184-6.

22 Colonel A C Temperley, 'A Personal Narrative of The Battle of Chunuk Bair,' ed National Army Museum (NZ) KMA (1994.3315, 1915), 7-9.

23 AWM 1DRL/0221, Papers of General Sir Herbert Vaughan Cox, Diary, 33-34.

General Key for All Maps

Formation/Unit National Designators

Red	German/Ottoman	**Col**	Colonial
Blue	Allied	**FR**	French
ANZAC	Australian & New Zealand Army Corps	**Gds**	Guards (British or German)
AUS	Australian	**NZ**	New Zealand
BE	Belgian	**Res**	Reserve
BR	British		

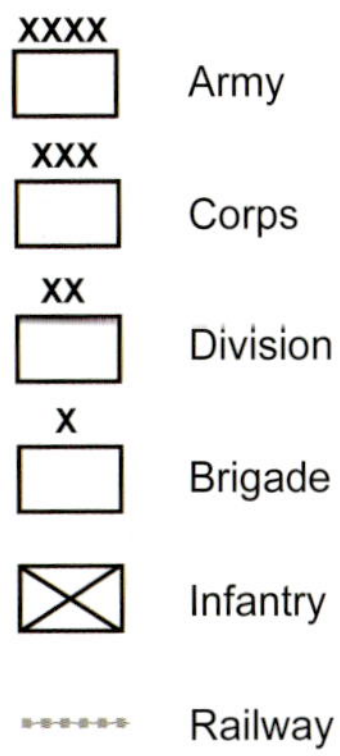

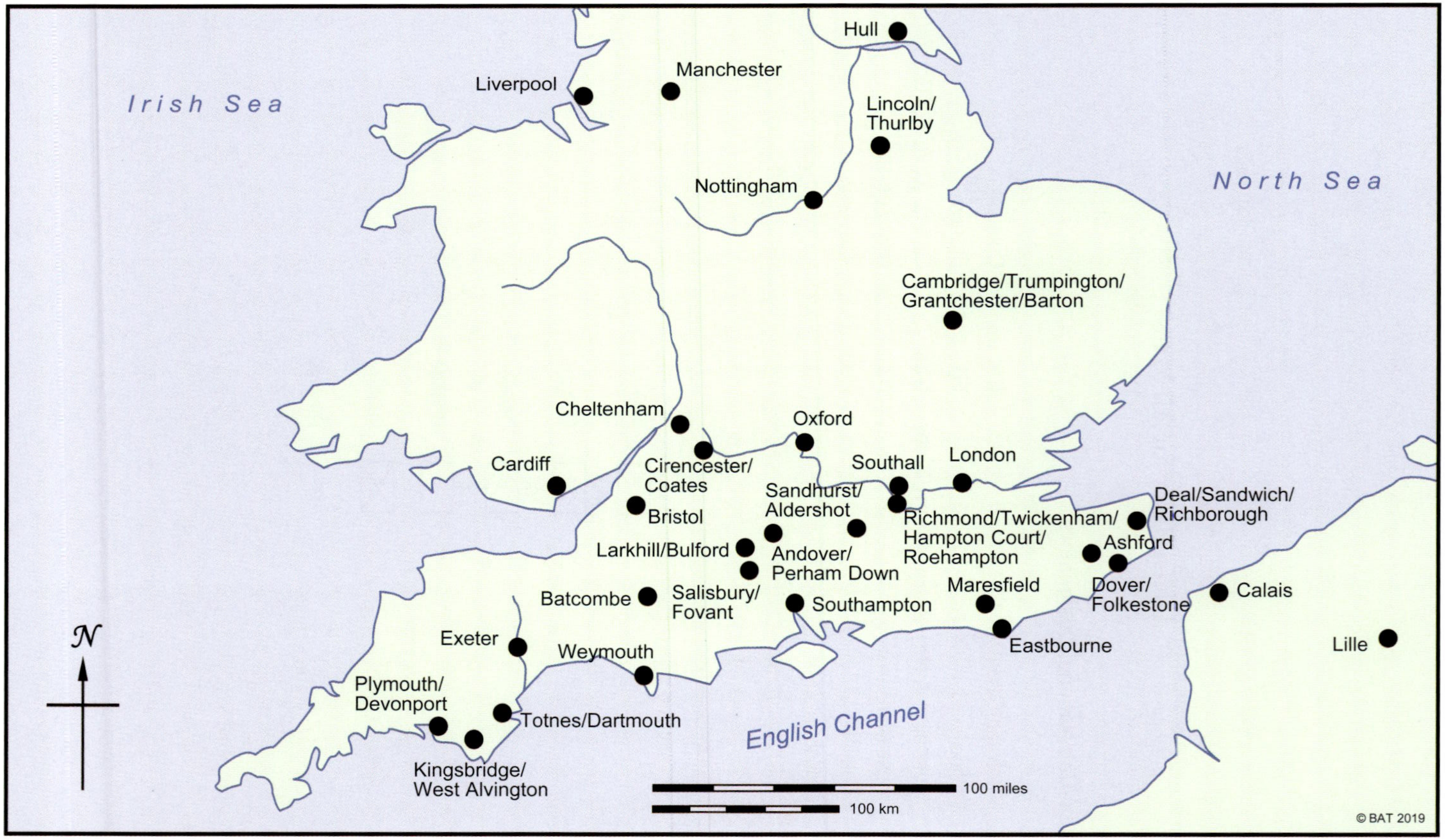

Map 1: British locations featured in Birdwood's life

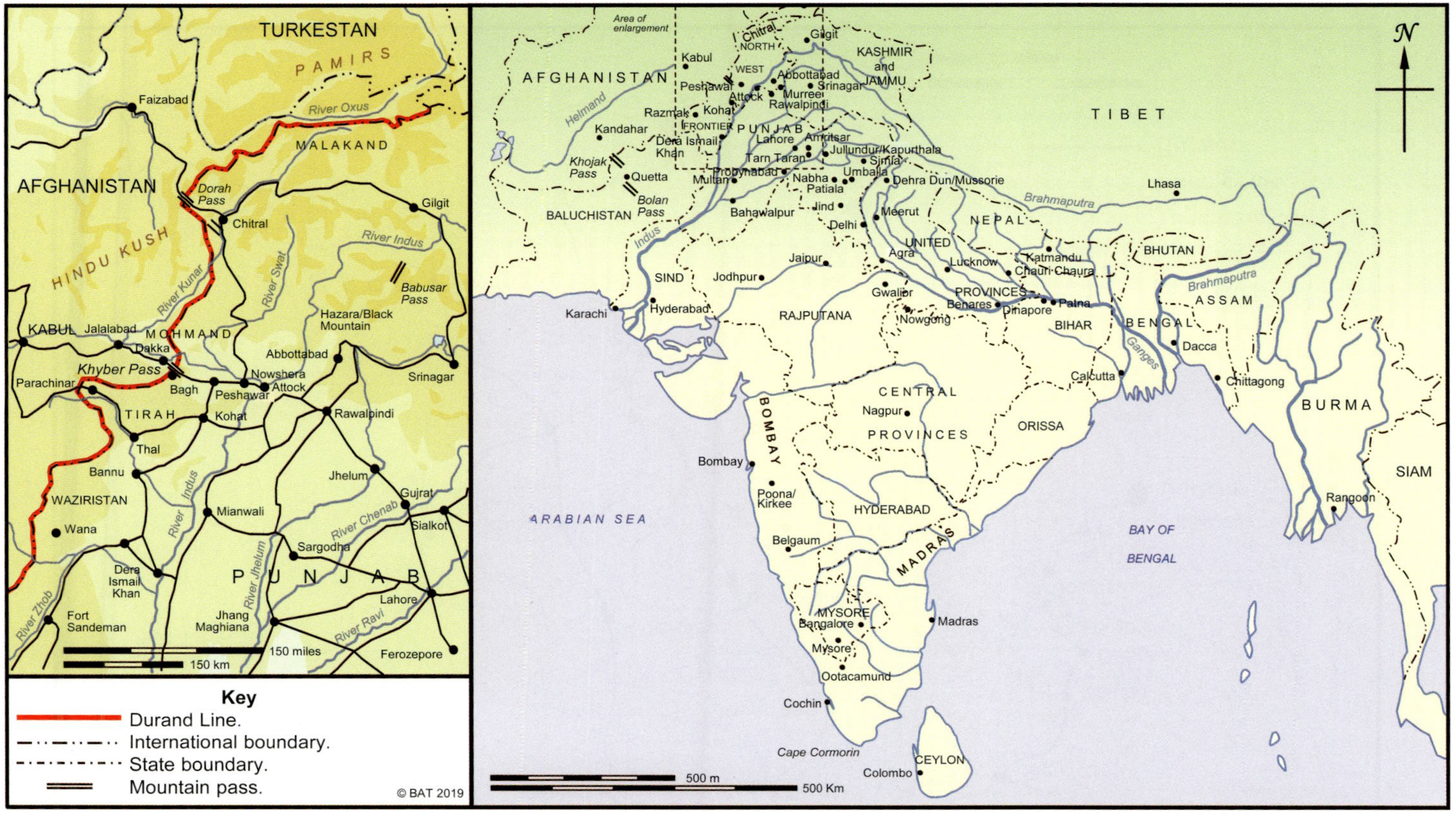

Map 2: Indian locations featured in Birdwood's life

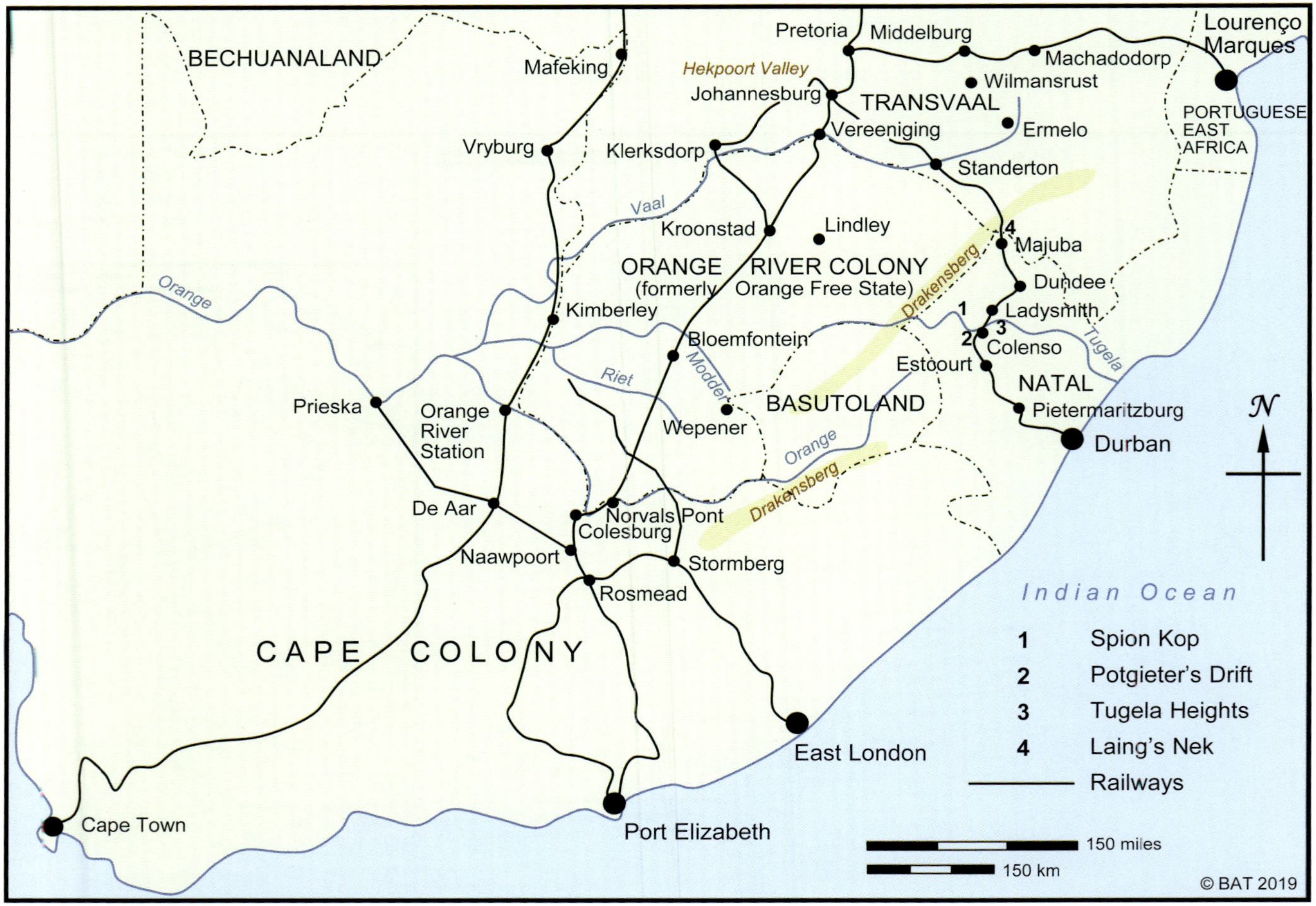

Map 3: Second Boer War

Map 4: Eastern Mediterranean, 1914-1916

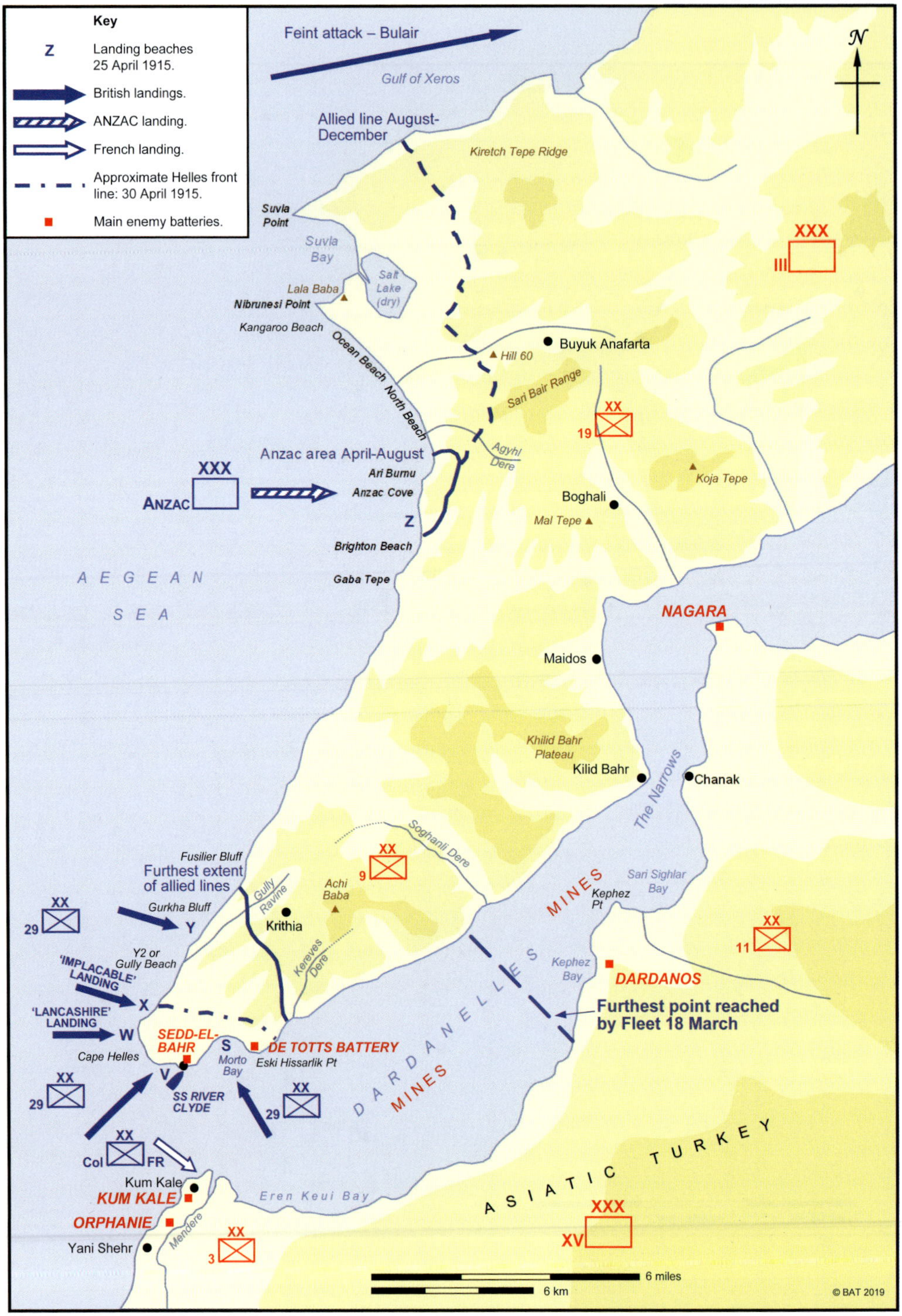

Map 5: The Gallipoli Peninsula, 1915-16

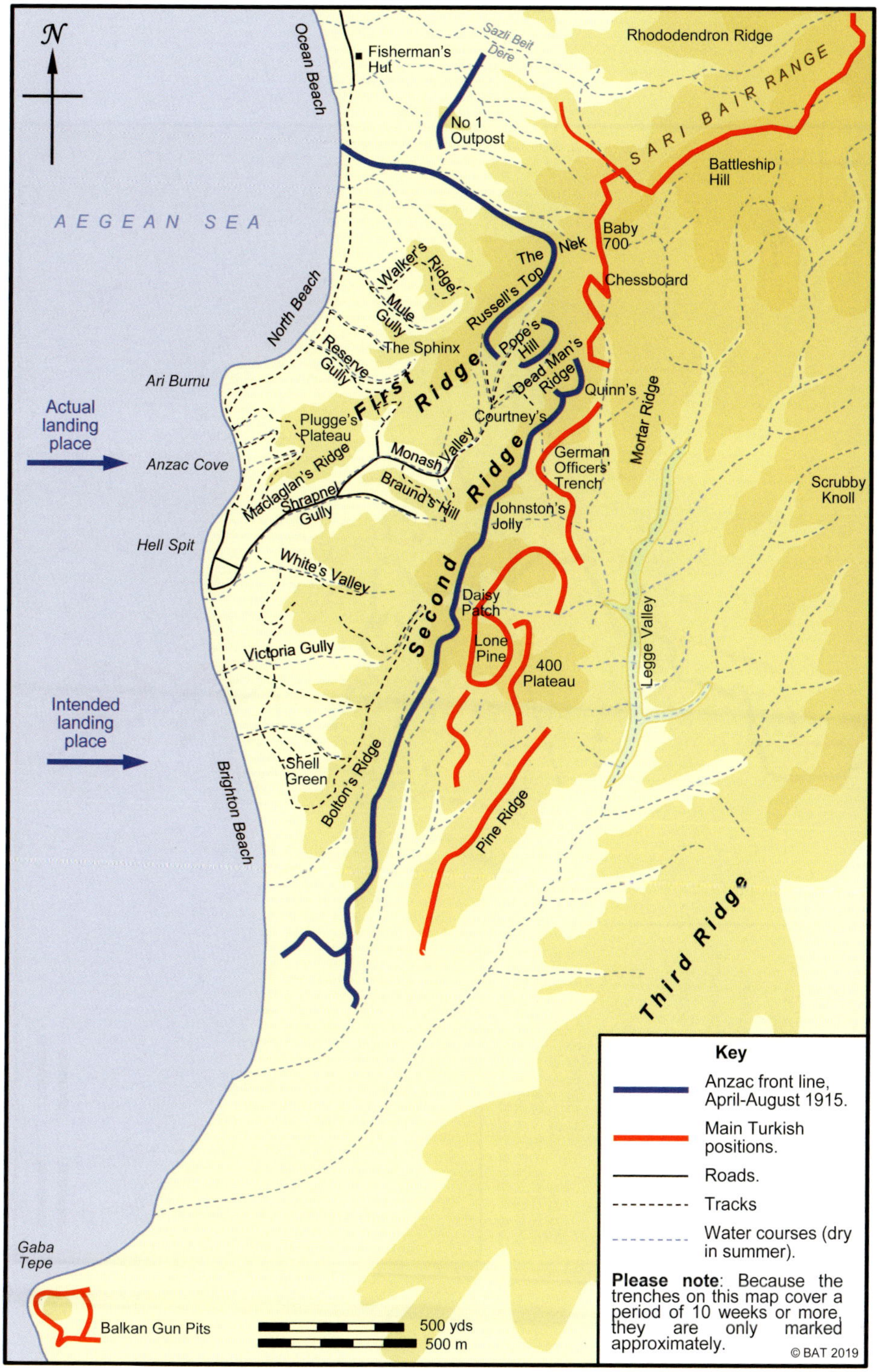

Map 6: ANZAC area, 1915

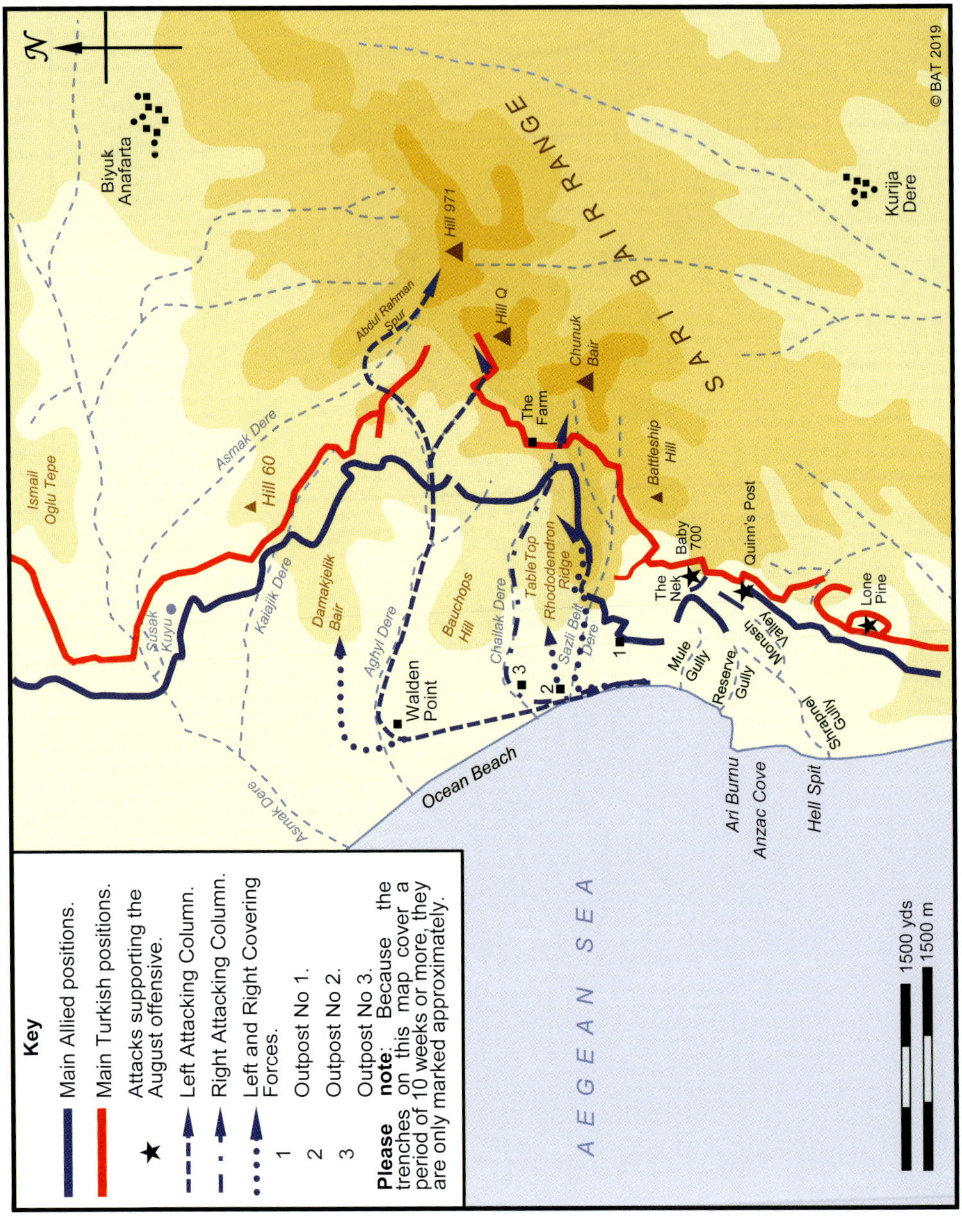

Map 7: The August Offensive

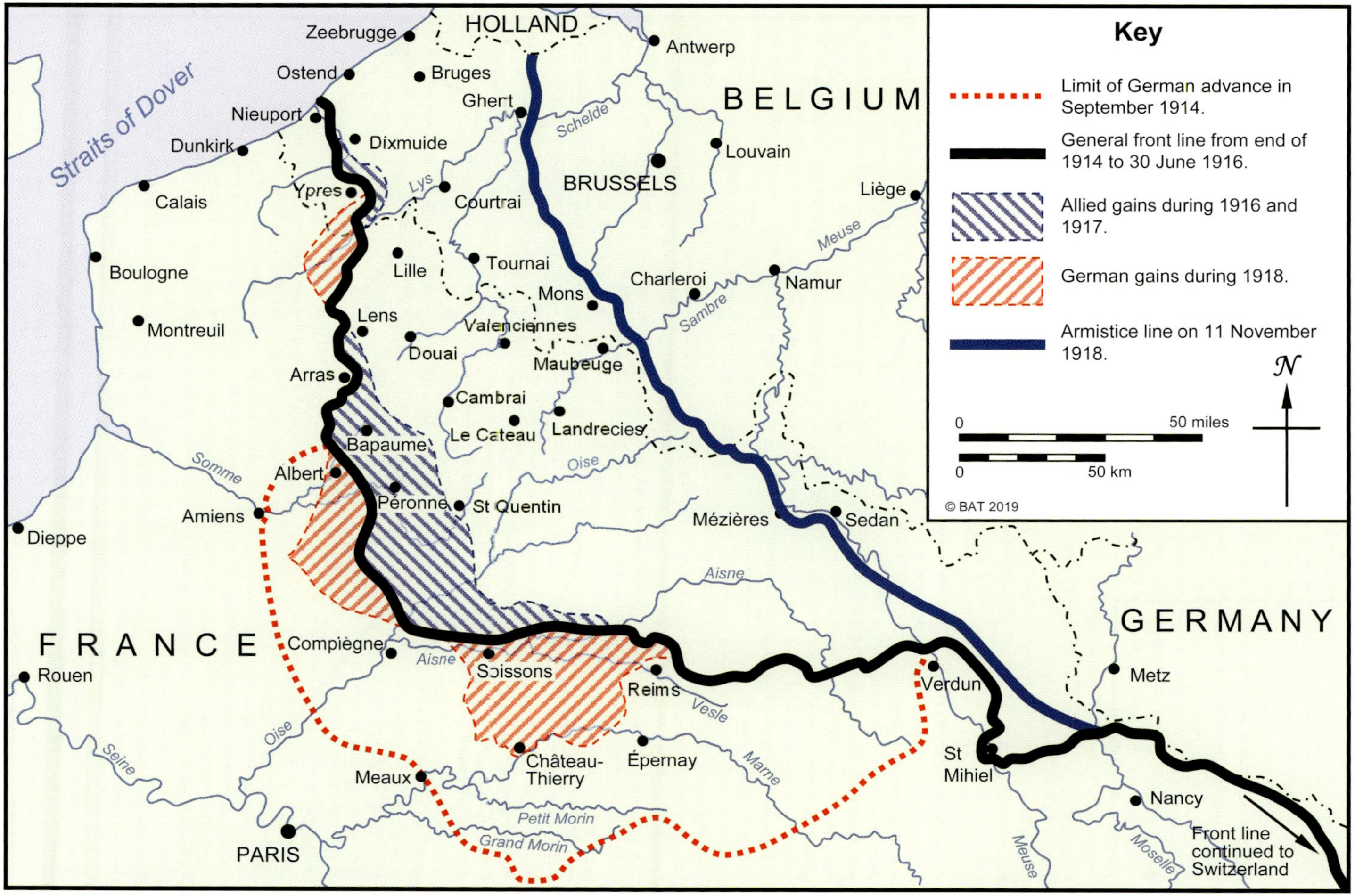

Map 8: Western Front, 1914-1918

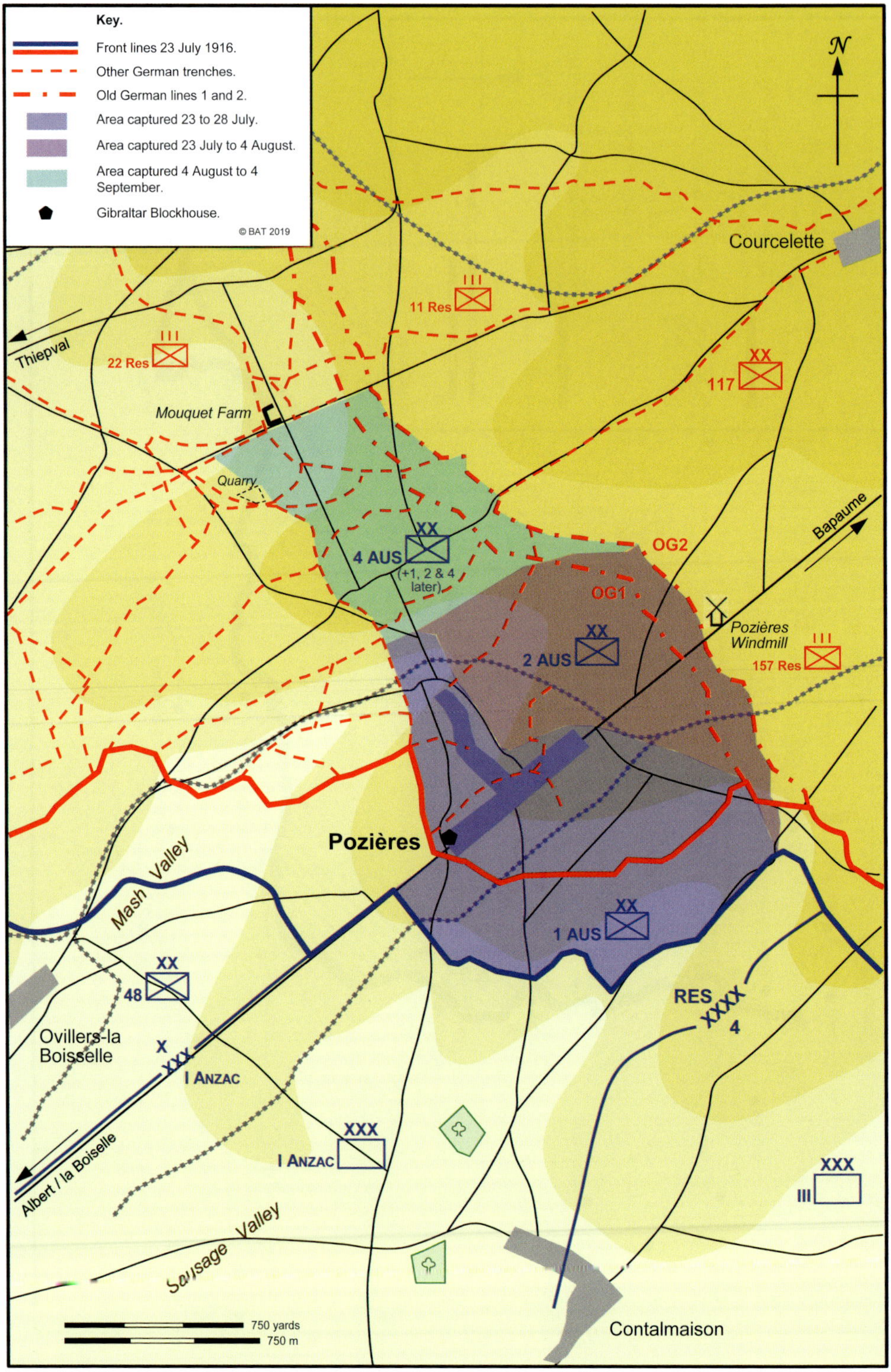

Map 9: Pozières to Mouquet Farm, 23 July – 4 September 1916

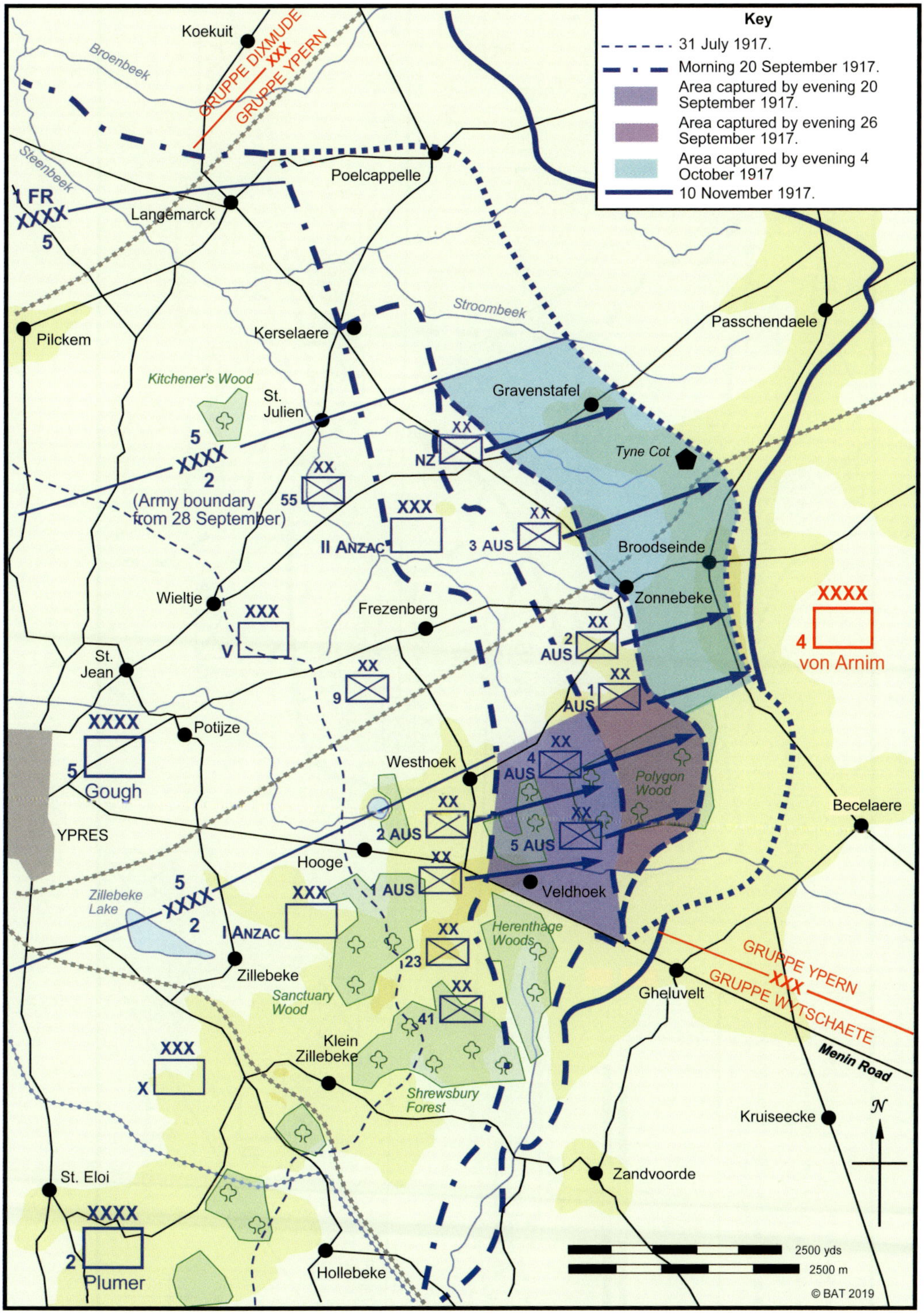

Map 10: Third Ypres, 20 September – 4 October 1917

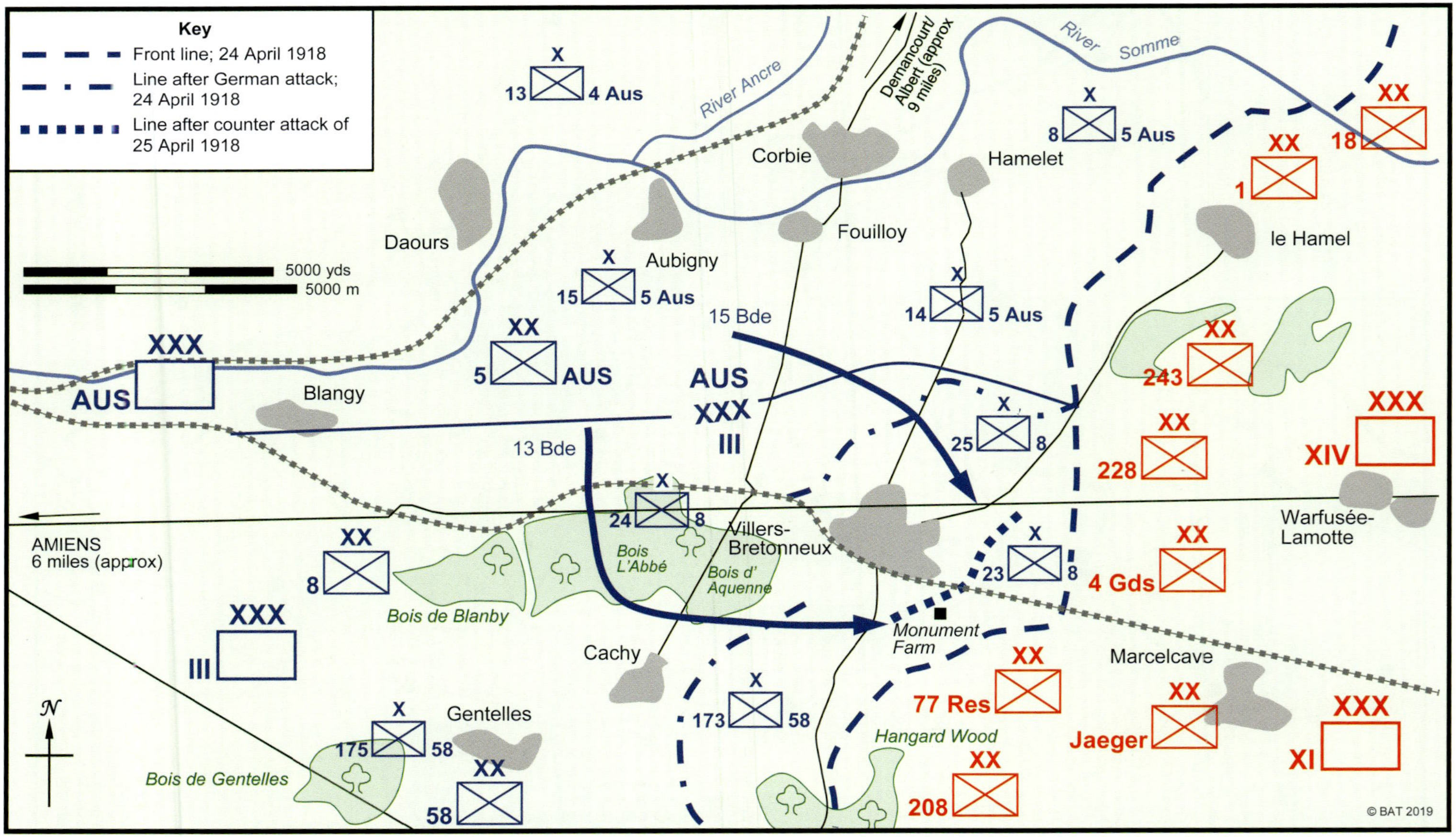

Map 11: Villers-Bretoneux, 1918

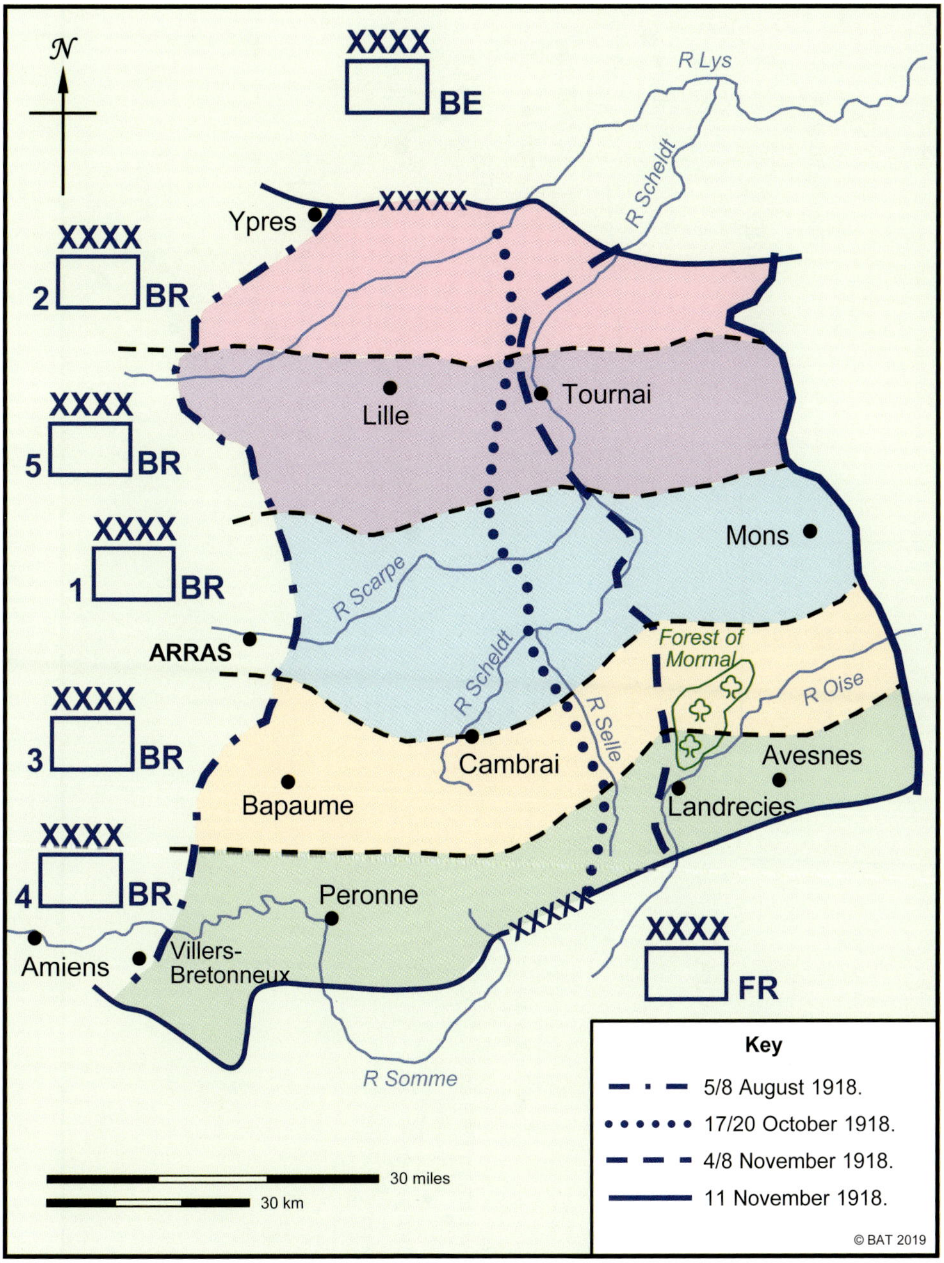

Map 12: Fifth Army, August – November 1918

Map 13: Some Australian locations visited by Birdwood 1919-20

Quinn's. Birdwood 'went out to see Godley in the afternoon,' and as a result 'arrangements were completed for a dawn assault on the 8th, preceded by a heavy bombardment from 3.30 to 4.50 am.'[24] Then another disaster occurred. Colonel Hughes of the Canterburys was tasked to move forward to the Apex and for some inexplicable reason, he formed 'up his whole battalion in close order in full view of Chunuk Bair on the broad and exposed western end of the Rhododendron Spur. Within a few minutes his battalion was simply annihilated by a hurricane bombardment from every available Turkish gun.'[25]

By the early hours of 8 August 'the troops in the new area on the left' [the area gained by all the fighting during the night of 6 and all-day 7 August] totalled '21 battalions, 4 Regiments of Light Horse, 4 Companies of Engineers, and 2 Mountain batteries of 4 guns each.'[26] This was challenging enough for Godley but he remained responsible for his original sector of the Anzac front. Birdwood's decision not to relieve Godley of his former responsibilities now appeared flawed given the number of units and the congested terrain. The dawn attack brought partial success. 'Johnston with NZ Inf Bde attacked Chunuk Bair crest & captured about 400 yards of it & hung on all day in spite of many attacks.'[27] The Wellington Battalion achieved this feat of arms, epitomised by the determination of its commander Malone. 'Chunuk Bair was occupied with little resistance. A German machine gun and crew was captured. Two platoons occupied the crest and the Battalion commenced to dig in on the reverse slope.'[28] But 'the Turks counterattacked very strongly at 06:00,' and then 'the enemy shelled the position heavily around 07:00 and attacked again.' Accurate rifle fire and bayonet charges drove them back. By this time the Wellingtons had lost half their officers. 'A company of Gloucester Regiment (Kitchener's Army) took up a position on the left flank. The Welch [*sic*] Pioneers came in on the right flank but vacated the position again leaving the flank open.'[29] This resulted in heavy enfilade fire. 'Throughout the day the enemy continued to launch attack after attack, each preceded by bombing parties, but they were invariably driven back with great slaughter.' About 17:30 Malone 'was killed by a piece of shell.' The second-in-command 'was wounded a few minutes afterwards, leaving the Battalion with only three junior officers.' The Otago Battalion arrived to relieve the Wellingtons at about 20:00. 'A party of two officers and 47 men moved down to the Apex.'[30] Malone and his Wellingtons had achieved all that Birdwood had wished for, displaying the truth of Slim's words.

24 AWM4 1/25/5 Part 1 – August 1915, HQ ANZAC, 7 August. Diary 1915, 7 August.

25 Temperley, 'A Personal Narrative of The Battle of Chunuk Bair,' 10.

26 AWM4 1/25/5 Part 1 – August 1915, HQ ANZAC, 7 August.

27 Diary 1915, 8 August on February Cash Account page at back.

28 Temperley was concerned that Malone would select a reverse slope defence rather than a forward slope, gaining observation and a good field of fire. He visited the position that evening and found 'it was a hopeless situation.' Temperley, 'A Personal Narrative of The Battle of Chunuk Bair,' 11-14.

29 7th (Service) Battalion Gloucestershire Regiment and 8th (Service) Battalion (Pioneers) Welsh Regiment – 'Welch' was reintroduced into the title in 1920. The Gloucesters lost every officer and 350 men and the Welsh Pioneers seventeen officers and 400 men. See Tim Travers, *Gallipoli 1915* (Stroud: Tempus Publishing, 2001), 167.

30 AWM 35/20/5 – August 1915, Wellington Battalion, Report on Fighting on Chunuk Bair, 2-4. Malone's wartime life and thoughts are sensitively recounted in John Crawford and Peter Cooke (eds.), *No Better Death: The Great War Diaries and Letters of William G Malone* (Auckland: Exisle Publishing, 2014).

'Cox & the other Bdes did not make much progress. Monash tried to attack up Abdul Rahman spur on 971 but was repulsed with severe loss.' Major Allanson, now commanding 1/6th Gurkhas, had progressed towards Hill Q and by the end of the day was poised under the crest, but 'reinforcement was essential.'[31] By the end of 8 August Birdwood had a small hold on Chunuk Bair, with potential for exploitation. His forces were within reach of Hill Q but not threatening 971. Further attempts would be required on 9 August. Birdwood 'went out again to No 2 Post to see Godley & Shaw & made plans for another attack on ridge at dawn tomorrow.'[32] Godley 'made the following plan for the night of 8th. The attempt on Hill 971 was to be abandoned, in view of the difficulties of the ground, and heavy casualties of the Australians. Cox was to renew his attack on Hill Q.' Brigadier Baldwin with 38th Brigade, part of 13th (Western) Division, was to occupy the crest between Chunuk Bair and Hill Q.[33] A conference was called for at Johnston's Headquarters, with Godley and Baldwin. Temperley described the failure of direction at this as: 'General Godley was unable to come... No staff officer arrived. Indeed, no Divisional or Corps Staff Officer of any kind ever came to see the situation at our Headquarters throughout the battle.' Temperley then recorded how Johnston guided Baldwin into taking an inadvisable route to Hill Q.[34] Plans for the next morning – consolidation by Johnston and assaults by two columns under Brigadiers Cox and Baldwin – were then disseminated.[35]

Forty-eight hours after the initial assault on the Ridge should have been made, the third assault on the Ridge commenced. Birdwood's diary reads sadly: 'had tremendous bombardment. Chunuk Bair all guns & ships 4.30 - 5.15 when Cox's & Baldwin's Bdes stormed crest on left of NZ Inf Bde but failed. Apparently one of Cox's Regts got up but was driven off. Baldwin apparently never got near till long after & looks as if no serious attempt was made.'[36] Allanson and his Gurkhas, supported by men of 6th South Lancashires, stormed Hill Q and carried the position. 'It was a wonderful view: below were the Straits, ... we commanded Kilid Bahr, and the rear of Achi-Baba and the communications to all their army there.'[37] This toehold of success was very short-lived. A ship landed 'a series of big shells amongst our men & inflicting heavy losses, as a result of which they retired & the Turks at once attacked them, making the whole attack a failure,' wrote Birdwood to his wife that day.[38] Realising the desperate nature of the situation, Birdwood added that 'it will not convey the great anxiety in which I now am about the final assault.'[39] The lack of a thorough meeting by commanders at Johnston's Headquarters had delivered no weight of men on the Ridge. Birdwood went 'out to see Godley & Sir Ian arrived about 1.30,' with Shaw joining them, 'on a high spur over the whole Suvla area, and across to Chunuk Bair.' Birdwood declined the reserve division offered, as it would place too big a burden on his water supplies, that had been carefully calculated by his staff. Hamilton left

31 Imperial War Museum [hereafter IWM] 107596, Papers of Colonel Allanson, Diary, 23.
32 Diary 1915, 8 August on February cash account page at back.
33 General Sir Alexander Godley, *Life of an Irish Soldier* (London: John Murray, 1939), 184.
34 Temperley, 'A Personal Narrative of The Battle of Chunuk Bair,' 17-19.
35 AWM4 1/53/5 Part 2 - August 1915, Headquarters New Zealand and Australian Division, Appendix 79.
36 Diary 1915, 9 August.
37 IWM 107596, Papers Allanson, Diary, 27.
38 The debate about whether the gunfire was naval or land is well covered in Travers, *Gallipoli 1915*, 171.
39 AWM 3DRL/3376 8/1, Letter, Birdwood to his wife, 9 August 1915.

with a sense of hope.[40] 'No change in the situation occurred throughout the day though fighting continued on the left flank [the 'new area'] and towards the evening heavy attacks developed there. By evening the line ran along Rhododendron Ridge up to Chunuk Bair where about 200 yards were occupied and entrenched and held by some 800 men. From there it ran down to the Farm and almost due North to the Asma Dere southern watershed down which it continued westward to the sea.'[41] Meanwhile the right flank, particularly Lone Pine, was subjected to bomb and counter attacks.

That night on Chunuk Bair the New Zealanders were relieved in line by the 6th Loyal North Lancashires, supported by the 5th Wiltshires but Temperley observed: they 'had tempted fate far too long. The Turkish Commander had by now been able to concentrate sufficient reserves.'[42] He was Mustafa Kemal who had taken 'command of the Anafarta Group effective 9.45 pm, 8 August.' Before 4.30 a.m. 10 August, he 'crept forward with his scouting screen' and as the initial bombardment ceased, 'he raised himself and pointed to the enemy with his riding crop.' This signalled a sixteen-battalion assault, 'a massive blow' that 'amounted to a human wave attack.'[43] Chunuk Bair could not be held. The Turks swept down onto the Farm. The New Zealanders, British, Indian and Australian troops fought determinedly, supported by naval and field gunnery. One brigadier was killed and one severely wounded. Two commanding officers were killed during the day and two declared missing presumed killed. 'By 10 am the main attack of the Turks had expended itself.' The First Phase of the August Offensive, taking the Sari Bair Ridge, had come to an end. The initial assessment was that 'the casualties were severe, amounting to 375 officers and 10,158 Other Ranks, Killed, Wounded, and Missing.'[44] Birdwood described that 'my casualties are terribly sickening – it is one of the most horrible & painful sights you can imagine to meet a constant stream of returning wounded men from the front.'[45] Godley concluded his report six days later:

> Though the Australian, New Zealand and Indian units have been confined to trench duty in a cramped space for some four months, and though the troops of the New Armies have only just landed from a sea voyage and many of them have not previously been under fire, I do not believe that any troops in the world could have accomplished more. All ranks – from the Old Country, Australians, New Zealanders, Maoris, Sikhs and Gurkhas vied with one another in the performance of gallant deeds, and more than worthily upheld the best traditions of the British Army.

The 'last four days fighting' made it 'necessary to reorganize the line.' Two new Sections 5 and 6 were added to the original four Sections of the Anzac front line. General Shaw, with six British battalions and all the New Zealand forces, held 5 Section from Walker's Ridge round

40 Diary 1915, 9 August. General Sir Ian Hamilton, *Gallipoli Diary*, vol. I & II (London: Edward Arnold, 1920), II - 79-81.

41 AWM4 1/25/5 Part 1 – August 1915, HQ ANZAC, 9 August.

42 Temperley, 'A Personal Narrative of The Battle of Chunuk Bair,' 24.

43 Edward J Erickson, *Gallipoli: The Ottoman Campaign* (Barnsley: Pen & Sword, 2010), 156-7 and 163-4; Erickson, *Gallipoli: Command Under Fire* (Oxford: Osprey, 2015), 205-7.

44 AWM4 1/53/5 Part 2 - August 1915, Headquarters New Zealand and Australian Division, Report on the Operations against the Sari Bair Position 6-10 August 1915, paras 9 and 14.

45 AWM 3DRL/3376 8/1, Letter, Birdwood to his wife, 9 August 1915.

to the new section boundary that ran through a knoll north of Rhododendron Ridge. Cox, with ten British battalions, his own Indian Brigade and Monash's Brigade, had the 6 Section front, round to the new boundary with IX Corps, established in Suvla Bay.[46] The four northern Sections were under Godley's command. Birdwood 'went over to see Godley & Shaw. Both said counter attack impossible as men were so beat & disorganised.'[47]

There were few 'best traditions' about Suvla Bay. The initial landings were generally successful during the night of 6 August and the following morning, but forward movement was minimal that day. There was more activity on 7 August and Chocolate Hill was taken. The following day was used for consolidation. Hearing a report of inactivity Hamilton went himself to see Stopford. Hamilton learned of a dawn attack by 11th Division but had little confidence.[48] Subsequently he telegrammed: 'Today there was nothing to stop determined commanders leading such fine men as yours,' and 'you must get a move on or the whole plan of operations is in danger of failing, for if you don't secure the Aja Liman Anafarta ridge without delay the enemy will.'[49] The inertia continued and Stopford had to go. Kitchener had suggested 'Birdie to take over the control of the whole of the Northern Theatre, i.e., Anzac and Suvla,' but then he offered Generals Byng, Horne and Kavanagh.[50] Hamilton was delighted – "I could wish for no better men.'[51] General de Lisle, Commander 29th Division, took temporary command of IX Corps before Byng arrived, with instructions 'to complete the reorganization of the Corps and to prepare as large a force as possible for the offensive against Ismail Oglu Tepe and Anafarta Spur, bearing in mind that time is of vital importance.'[52]

Birdwood cannot have expected such a setback on Sari Bair Ridge. Everything suggested he and his staff did their utmost to plan in detail for success. He was aware of the difficulty of the terrain and the physical state of his men. His diary entries and the two letters to his wife suggested cautious confidence. His two Covering Forces were successfully deployed. His Right Assaulting Column was late for the first dawn attack but gained its objective and twice carried out reliefs in line. His Left Assaulting Column, comprising two thirds of the assaulting brigades, did not follow its Commander's planned route and got lost. Pedersen, in his masterly overview of Monash and the failed assault on Hill 971, noted that 'once issued, Monash insisted from August 1915 onwards, orders must not be modified unless success depended on it.'[53] By the morning of 10 August, Monash's Brigade had not made a meaningful contribution to the assault of the Ridge. Cox's Brigade had by then achieved a toehold but been blown off by friendly fire. Men and ground had blended together into a confusion that was never resolved and prevented the proper application of Birdwood's instructions to drive on up the slopes, whatever the cost.

46 AWM4 1/53/5 Part 2 – August 1915, Headquarters New Zealand and Australian Division, Report on the Operations against the Sari Bair Position 6-10 August 1915, para 15.
47 Diary 1915, 10 August.
48 Hamilton, *Gallipoli Diary*, I & II, II - 63-9.
49 AWM4 1/4/5 Part 2 – August 1915, General Headquarters, Mediterranean Expeditionary Force, Hamilton to Stopford telegram, 9 August 1915.
50 Horne – First, Byng – Third and Birdwood – Fifth finished the War as three of the five Army Commanders under Haig.
51 Hamilton, *Gallipoli Diary*, I & II, II - 106.
52 AWM4 1/4/5 Part 3 – August 1915, General Headquarters, Mediterranean Expeditionary Force, Instructions to Major General H de Lisle.
53 Peter Pedersen, 'I thought I could command men' in Ekins, *Gallipoli*, 139 and fn. 66.

The total congestion of troops must have brought despair. If the Left Assaulting Column had stuck to its planned route, it might have achieved the same delayed timetable as that of the Right. Even if the assaulting brigades had each gained a foothold, linked up and established a sound forward slope defence, the command of this front alone would have been an enormous burden on Godley and his headquarters. In the confusion, it proved too much and Birdwood must take responsibility for this. He had had time to reassign command arrangements across the Anzac front and for planning the use of 13th Division Headquarters once it was allocated to him.

Some did gain the heights and their heroism is rightly revered. The subsequent studies of Gallipoli by the Senior Division of the Staff College identified 'Misfortune on 9th of ANZAC detachments on Chunuk Bair being shelled by our guns – and of, L. Column losing its way' as the main reasons for failure, and closed with the comment: 'Plan perhaps too complex for difficult terrain.'[54] The Directing Staff for these studies was Lieutenant Colonel W V Nugent, appointed DSO for Topographical Work on Gallipoli.[55] Birdwood and his staff had certainly planned but the plans had not delivered the assaulting forces in numbers at the right places, let alone the right times. The orders of the Left Assaulting Column are clear on paper but standing half way up Aghyl Dere in daylight, it is difficult to imagine two rather lost brigades trying to manoeuvre successfully against the clock at night. Just relying on striving upwards proved inadequate to overcome the unforeseen – choosing an unplanned route. It is easy to appreciate, however, how the close-run story of the August Offensive grew and continues to the present day. Those that believe the assault on the ridge could have made it, if the planned route had been stuck to, have thin grounds for this viewpoint but certainly Birdwood's men showed over many months that if they gained a piece of ground in sufficient numbers, they hung onto it.[56] In this case they never gained the ground.

On 11 August 'there was constant fighting all day and though marked attacks or counter attacks took place the day's casualties amounted to a little over a thousand.' The boundary with IX Corps was firmly established. Water was an acute anxiety. Despite all this the war diary recorded that 'preparations were made for a fresh attack.'[57] Ashmead-Bartlett came to see Birdwood on Monday 16 August after visiting Suvla and then Godley. Ashmead-Bartlett wrote:

> The whole thing is too horrible for words or details. The Anzac Corps has in fact been fought to a standstill and practically all this splendid Colonial material is gone. ... I then went round and saw Gen Birdwood who ... explained to me in detail his plan of the operations what was intended and what was actually achieved. ... He was bitterly disappointed over the failure of the 9th Corps to make good the positions in there [*sic*] front. He said that without the capture of the W Hills it would have been impossible for him to have remained on the crest of Chunuk Bair. ... The total casualties therefore

54 Lecture 3 – The August Operations, Camberley Staff College, vol. 14-3, The Dardanelles Campaign (1923), 4-5.

55 *London Gazette,* 3 June 1916, 5566 and 5569. For particulars of Nugent's work at Gallipoli, see Chasseaud and Doyle, *Grasping Gallipoli: Terrains.*

56 Hamilton, *Gallipoli Diary*, I & II, II - 89.

57 AWM4 1/25/5 Part 1 – August 1915, HQ ANZAC, 11-15 August. Diary 1915, 11-15 August.

> cannot be much under 28,000 an appalling total for the gains which as General Godley expressed it amounted to some 500 acres of bad grazing ground.[58]

General de Lisle was told on 15 August that Birdwood considered the new Anzac position to be 'a favourable one from which to launch the final assault on the ridge,' but that reorganisation would 'involve a delay of some days before the attack on the main ridge can be made.'[59] Just two days later he was told that Birdwood, 'after 48 hours for rest and reorganization,' hoped 'to be strong enough to capture Chunuk Bair without further reinforcements,' stating that his troops were 'in good heart' and that they had 'inflicted severe casualties on the enemy.'[60] This further and very unlikely attempt on the Ridge never transpired. 29th Division was brought up from Helles and troops came from Egypt to both Suvla and Anzac. General de Lisle launched his attack on 21 August against W Hills and Scimitar Hill without success. The concurrent Anzac assault against Hill 60 was also a failure. 27 August saw yet another attempt on Hill 60, and although the 'NZMR and Connaughts advanced most gallantly & took half Turkish position,' the Hill was not secured.[61]

These were the last large-scale offensive actions by the allies on the peninsula but the future of the campaign was already being closely debated before then. On 14 August General Davies, commanding VIII Corps at Helles, raised the potential problems of winter weather. Before the last attacks of 27 August appreciations were under consideration as to whether to continue to hold both Anzac Cove and Suvla Bay. When proposing to give up 'all our footholds on the Sari Bair' it was noted that 'it would probably have a bad effect on the moral[e] of the ANZAC Corps, and on popular feeling in Australia and New Zealand.' Birdwood was against any such move 'while we still hold hills.'[62] Meanwhile other problems emerged. Between 17 and 31 August Birdwood saw over 300 'sick evacuated' each day, with the highest figure of 472 on 20 August and a total approaching 5,000.[63] The 2nd Australian Division arrived and Birdwood noted 'very fine lot of men' and 'alert & keen.' This allowed the 1st Division to rest on Mudros. On 13 September Birdwood celebrated his 50th birthday and on 17th he left Anzac for a night for the first time since the landings. Hamilton noted that 'Birdie had at last worn off the fine edge of his keenness: he looks a little tired.'[64] On 27 September, he and Byng were summoned by Hamilton to discuss the possibility of having to send two divisions to Salonika to help in the event of Bulgaria attacking Serbia.[65] Eventually only 10th (Irish) Division left for Salonika.

58 Ellis Ashmead-Bartlett, *Ashmead-Bartlett's Despatches from the Dardanelles* (London: Newnes, 1923), 159-60.
59 AWM4 1/4/5 Part 3 – August 1915, General Headquarters, Mediterranean Expeditionary Force, Instructions to Major General H de Lisle.
60 AWM4 1/4/5 Part 3 – August 1915, memo to GOC IX Corps 17 August 1915
61 Diary 1915, 16-27 August. AWM4 1/25/5 Part 4 – August 1915, HQ ANZAC, Appendix 39 - Short Account of Operations on the Left Flank.
62 AWM4 1/4/5 Part 3 – August 1915, General Headquarters, Mediterranean Expeditionary Force, Letter, Davies to Braithwaite, 14 August 1915 and Lt Col Aspinall to CGS, 20 August 1915. Diary 1915, 22 August.
63 AWM4 1/25/5 Part 1 – August 1915, HQ ANZAC, 17-31 August.
64 AWM4 1/25/5 Part 1 – August 1915, 3-17 September. Hamilton, *Gallipoli Diary*, I & II, II - 194.
65 Diary 1915, 29 September.

At the end of August Hamilton completed his despatch for the period for May and June. In it he wrote, aware of Birdwood's performance in July and August as well:

> Lieutenant-General Sir W R Birdwood has been the soul of Anzac. Not for one single day has he ever quitted his post. Cheery and, full of human sympathy, he has spent many hours of each twenty-four inspiring the defenders of the front trenches, and if he does not know every soldier in his force, at least every soldier in the force believes he is known to his Chief.[66]

Thus, the title 'Soul of Anzac' was coined and it stuck to Birdwood. It was an expression both of his commitment to the Anzacs and the bond and affection between them. Birdwood's leadership had focused on the morale and mind-set of his men. He had continuously seen the frontline situation for himself, visiting forward as he had with Kitchener on the Frontier. As will be seen this tribute 'Soul of Anzac' was not tarnished even at the end of the Gallipoli campaign.

'It was about this time' that Birdwood 'lost his faithful BGGS, Andrew Skeen, who contracted a very severe attack of enteric.' He was evacuated to Malta. In his place Birdwood 'took Brudenell White from the 1st Australian Division, to which he was GSO1.'[67] This partnership of Birdwood and White once forged was to last, except for the few months in which Birdwood commanded the Dardanelles Army, until final victory in November 1918, when together they were at the head of Fifth Army. 'When asked to write an appreciation of the service of my old friend & comrade Brudenell White' after his death in August 1940, Birdwood wrote:

> During my very long years of service – now 55 years – & during which I have had the pleasure & privilege of knowing the large majority of officers of the British & many of the Dominion services, I have felt there is not one whom I would place higher than Brudenell White in almost any category in which one thinks of men of action.[68]

For the next week Birdwood took White round with him on his regular daily tours of the front line. The first warning signs of winter struck on 9 October with 'a beastly storm last night which wrecked a lot of craft – drove everything ashore & broke both Anzac piers.'[69] In the meantime a cable from Kitchener to Hamilton gave, in Hamilton's words, 'a different and a very ominous complexion to the future.' Kitchener enquired: 'What is your estimate of the probable losses which would be entailed to your force if the evacuation of the Gallipoli Peninsula was decided on and carried out in the most careful manner?' Hamilton was not to 'consider the possible danger to the Empire that might thus be caused.' Hamilton replied that one should not reckon on getting out 'with less loss than that of half the total force,' but on the other hand, there might be 'a veritable catastrophe.'[70]

66 *London Gazette*, 29303, 17 Sept 1915, 9320.
67 Birdwood, *Khaki and Gown*, 277.
68 AWM 3DRL/1400, White, Sir Cyril Brudenell Bingham, (General, b.1876 - d.1940, Appreciation of General Brudenell White by FM Lord Birdwood, 30 September 1940.
69 Diary 1915, 1-9 October.
70 Hamilton, *Gallipoli Diary*, I & II, II - 249 & 53.

Four days later and having just got into bed, Hamilton was told that there was a cable coming in that he was to decipher himself. On the morning of 16 October, he read that although the Government appreciated his work and his gallant manner, they considered 'it advisable to make a change in the command.' General Monro, with his own Chief of Staff, was to replace Hamilton.[71] Birdwood was to replace Hamilton 'pending the arrival of Monro.'[72] With very bad timing and in spite of his robust health so far, Birdwood had on 15 October 'suddenly started an attack of dysentery & had to sit very tight all day.' The next day Birdwood, still in bed, received a wire asking him to see Hamilton, with a destroyer picking him up. Birdwood learnt the news and commented in his diary that it was 'very hard lines on Sir Ian & Monro could do no more without more men & ammunition.' Hamilton left the next day.

Birdwood was now acting C-in-C Mediterranean Expeditionary Force. He was still not fully recovered so Admiral de Robeck carried 'him off to HMS *Cornwallis*' for three days to recuperate. After which he was well enough to send a lengthy cable to London giving his view of the situation. He saw 'in front a continuous line of Turkish trenches, the flanks of which cannot be turned and which therefore can only be taken by assault.' This precluded surprise. The Turks, he believed, had 125,000 infantry with 85,000 within close call. His forces were '85,000 rifles on the Peninsula and resting on islands, with 5,000 drafts on the way' but sickness and wastage was 20 per cent per month. Lack of experienced officers was critical. He saw no opportunity for advance at Helles. At Anzac, mining, 'a very lengthy process' seemed to be the only option and mine galleries had been started. At Suvla he thought 'that it should be possible to work our left forward … as far as Ejlemer Bay.' The 'move to occupy heights north of Anafarta' was 'essential to ensure to some extent safety of Suvla Bay, especially in view of possible arrival of further heavy Turkish guns and ammunition.' In order to progress, considerable ammunition supplies and 'two further complete divisions of really good troops' were necessary.[73] As ever Birdwood displayed a fighting spirit.

General Sir Charles Monro arrived on the evening of 27 October. Birdwood introduced him to the GHQ staff and then returned to Anzac, which Monro visited on 30 October to discuss the position.[74] On 31 October Monro reported back to Kitchener: 'After an inspection of the Gallipoli Peninsula I have arrived at the following conclusions. The troops on the Peninsula with the exception of the Australian & New Zealand Corps are not equal to a sustained effort owing to the inexperience of the officers, the want of training of the men and the depleted condition of many of the units.' This was a clear accolade to the Anzacs and their commander. Significantly, Monro recommended evacuation.[75] Kitchener asked Monro whether 'Birdwood and other Corps Commanders' agreed with his opinion. Byng and Davies did but Birdwood did not. Although accepting the 'grave disadvantage of our position and the extreme difficulty of making any progress,' Birdwood considered that:

71 Monro was then commanding Third Army in France.
72 LHCMA, Hamilton 7/4/8, Cable No 8853 cipher, Kitchener to Hamilton, 15 October 1915.
73 AWM4 1/4/7 Part 4 – October 1915, General Headquarters, Mediterranean Expeditionary Force, Cable MF 775, Birdwood to London, 21 October 1915.
74 Diary 1915, 28 and 30 October.
75 AWM4 1/4/7 Part 5 – October 1915, General Headquarters, Mediterranean Expeditionary Force, Cable MF 800, Monro to Kitchener, 31 October 1915.

> Evacuation [of the] Peninsula would be regarded by Turks as complete victory. From Indian experience fear result on Mohammedan world, India, Egypt, Persia. I, therefore, am opposed to evacuation. Consider if we leave Peninsula essential whole force must immediately be launched against Turkey elsewhere and fail to see where this can be done with confident hope of success … Season being so late and bad weather at hand think actual withdrawal fraught with difficulty and danger as ample time and continuous fine weather essential … The advent of any continuous bad weather after partial withdrawal might result in heavy losses.[76]

That same day Monro left for Egypt to see Maxwell. On 4 November Birdwood went over to Imbros as temporary C-in-C and 'found secret wire from Lord K waiting for me, telling me that he was coming out to make all preparations for an expedition & landing at head of Gulf of Xeros – that he refused the idea of evacuation & that I was to Command the Med Exped Force vice Monro transferred to Salonika. I at once wired protesting against such expedition as disaster & saying that I hoped Monro would continue to command force.' The proposed expedition was scuppered by the Navy's refusal to 'risk a dash up straits.' Birdwood was told to 'make plans for evacuation.' He 'replied suggesting hanging on, but that if evacuation was carried out, all the more necessary for Monro to remain on, as I must be with my own men.' Birdwood received further wires confirming his appointment and then one 'saying we would hold on here – much relieved.' He was becoming sure of being promoted to command the Force and on 6 November recorded: 'Went over to my beloved Anzac … up to Russell's Top – had tea with Godley. Very sad indeed at prospect of leaving my Army Corps & Australians even for higher command.' But then Lord Kitchener decided to visit.

On 10 November 'Dear old Lord K arrived' and Birdwood was 'delighted to see him again & he was absolutely charming.' Three days later Kitchener visited Anzac.[77] At one of the high posts, he put his hand on Birdwood's arm and said, "Thank God, Birdie, I came to see this for myself. You were quite right. I had no idea of the difficulties you were up against. I think you have all done wonders."[78] By 23 November command arrangements had been clarified. Monro was to remain C-in-C Mediterranean Expeditionary Force including Salonika but under him Birdwood was to assume responsibility for all of Gallipoli as GOC Dardanelles Army. He was now an Army Commander of three corps.[79] Kitchener left that day. Birdwood was 'feeling very down all day at the very thought of it [evacuation] & giving up Anzac.'[80]

Debate persisted as to whether there should be a complete or partial evacuation of Gallipoli.[81] Meanwhile a planning team was assembled and initial plans formulated. The totals for

76 AWM4 1/4/8 Part 2 – October 1915, General Headquarters, Mediterranean Expeditionary Force, Cable MF 805, Monro to Kitchener, 31 October 1915.

77 Diary 1915, 4-13 November.

78 Birdwood, *Khaki and Gown*, 280.

79 Generals Haig, Smith-Dorrien and Allenby were the commanders of First, Second and Third Armies respectively at this time.

80 Diary 1915, 23 November. For an overall study of the evacuation see Peter Hart, *The Gallipoli Evacuation* (Manly: Living History, 2020).

81 AWM4 1/4/8 Part 2 – November 1915, General Headquarters, Mediterranean Expeditionary Force, Paper on the Arguments for and against the complete or partial evacuation of Gallipoli, 22 November 1915.

evacuation were calculated as 134,720 men, 14,587 animals and 393 guns.[82] Three stages were proposed: the preliminary to allow withdrawal of men and equipment that could be evacuated before the evacuation order was received; the intermediate and final stages. The forces of nature, however, were about to strike. On 26 November, Birdwood recorded 'Very heavy storm came on in evening – heavy rain & wind.' Then for three days there were severe blizzards.[83] This weather was 'at least a month earlier' than usual and before 'preparations for winter were complete.'[84] The casualties were 205 deaths and 10,500 evacuated, including 4211 from frostbite.[85] In a Special Order Birdwood expressed his admiration for 'the strenuous and self-sacrificing devotion' shown by all ranks during the severe weather.[86] The 'Turks apparently had a far worse time of it.'[87] By 1 December Birdwood was ready to receive the evacuation order of Suvla and Anzac. Naval resources and storm damage precluded concurrent evacuation of Helles.[88] Finally on 8 December Birdwood 'had wire saying evacuation Anzac & Suvla decided upon – Helles to stay.' He warned Godley and Byng and noted 'holding on however to Helles means a good deal as regards prestige.'[89] Birdwood issued his instructions on 10 December and informed Monro that he had decided not to await the full moon but instead 'the wisest plan is to go straight ahead and carry out the final stage as soon as the Navy can provide the necessary ships, more especially as there is a good prospect of cloudy nights at this time of year.'[90]

Birdwood visited his three corps areas constantly.[91] By 12 December the final stage dates of 18 and 19 December were decided upon and detailed orders issued.[92] Meanwhile Birdwood was 'carefully considering the requirements of the Helles garrison in the event of the Government deciding to maintain our position there throughout the winter.'[93] He had to ensure his Army was alert and ready to fight. Birdwood issued a Special Army Order:

82 AWM4 1/17/1 Part 1 - November 1915, General Headquarters, Dardanelles Army, Outline Scheme for Evacuation of the Peninsula, 25 November 1915.
83 Diary 1915, 26-30 November.
84 AWM4 1/4/9 Part 1 – December 1915, General Headquarters, Mediterranean Expeditionary Force, Birdwood to Monro, Report on Effects of Storm, 3 December 1915.
85 AWM4 1/4/9 Part 1 – December 1915, Cable CM 46, Monro to London, 4 December 1915.
86 AWM4 1/17/1 Part 2 – November - December 1915, General Headquarters, Dardanelles Army, Special Army Order, 2 December 1915.
87 Diary 1915, 1 December.
88 AWM4 1/17/1 Part 2 – November - December 1915, General Headquarters, Dardanelles Army, Letter, Birdwood to CGS GHQ, 1 December 1915.
89 Diary 1915, 8 December.
90 AWM4 1/17/1 Part 2 – November - December 1915, General Headquarters, Dardanelles Army, Letter, GSR Z/48/1, Birdwood to CGS MEF, covering Instructions to GOCs 9 Corps and ANZAC, 10 December 1915.
91 Diary 1915, 11 December.
92 AWM4 1/17/2 Part 3 – December 1915, General Headquarters, Dardanelles Army, Army Order No 1, 12 December 1915; AWM4 1/53/9 – December 1915, General Headquarters, Dardanelles Army, Special Army Order 2 December 1915; AWM4 1/53/9 – December 1915, Headquarters New Zealand and Australian Division, Army Corps Order 21 and Divisional Operational Order 22. National Army Museum (NZ) KMA, 1990.1030 and 1039, Papers of Brigadier-General Sir Herbert E Hart, NZ Inf Bde and Wellington Batt Special Operation Orders, December 1915.
93 AWM4 1/4/9 Part 1 – December 1915, General Headquarters, Mediterranean Expeditionary Force, Letter, Birdwood to CGS MEF, 14 December 1915.

> On the final night of the retirement, those to be withdrawn from the front trenches will quietly withdraw and take up covering positions in silence which have been previously arranged for. Those left in the front trenches to the last will in their turn quietly and silently leave their trenches, passing through their comrades in covering positions and to their places of embarkation in the same soldierly manner, in which the troops have effected their magnificent landings on the shores of this peninsula during the last eight months. To withdraw in the face of the enemy in good order, and with hearts full of courage and confidence for the future, provides a test of which any soldier in the world may be justly proud, and that the 9th and "Anzac" Corps will prove themselves second to none as soldiers of this Empire, I have not the slightest doubt.[94]

Hart – the replacement Wellingtons commanding officer for Malone – recorded, however, that 'the men view very unkindly the thought of clearing out. It jars very very heavily upon them. Hundreds have volunteered to stay & fight it out or to stay & fight as a covering force to sacrifice their lives if required to get even with the enemy & save their pals. We do not like admitting it as a failure. One man said to me "Hell sir I hope our poor pals who lie all around us sleep soundly, & do not stir in discontent – as we go filing away from them for ever."[95]

During the nights of 18 and 19 December Birdwood was on board HMS *Chatham* with Rear Admiral Wemyss, commanding the naval forces vice De Robeck, and cruised slowly and quietly up and down the Anzac and Suvla positions. On the first night 'all went off capitally & we have to thank God for a perfect night for it.' On 19th he visited Anzac for the last time and 'went for a final tour round my old 1st Aust Div trenches.'[96] Russell was in command as the Corps staff had left. Hart, commanding the remaining Wellingtons manning the line at the Apex, recorded that

> … there were no troops in Anzac except those actually in the firing line, but this was as strong as ever … the day was perfect and everyone was confident of complete success now … At midday the enemy shelled our position very heavily … The first party moved away at 5:40 pm & the second at 9:15. I then went down to the beach to see that all was clear & in order. They embarked most rapidly … At 2:15, in the bright moonlight, the first of the 'C' [final] parties could be seen hurrying towards the pier & during the next minutes they came puffing in just as quickly as we could check them aboard … The whole stupendous movement was a magnificent success, & there was not a single casualty.[97]

94 LHCMA, Hamilton 7/4/39, Special Army Order, 17 December 1915.
95 National Army Museum (NZ) KMA, 1990.1014, Papers of Brigadier-General Hart, Diary 3, 15 December.
96 Diary 1915, 17-19 December.
97 Brig H Hart, 'Papers of Brigadier-General Sir Herbert E Hart', National Army Museum (NZ) KMA (1990.1014, Diary 3: 15 August 1915 - 19 February 1916, 1916), 19 December.

At the end of the night Birdwood stayed on board watching the ships bombard the camps and dumps of supplies left behind.[98] He was 'feeling very low & sad at leaving the place to which we had got much attached & where my men had made trenches which I don't suppose could be beaten in the world. But truly thankful & grateful to Almighty God for the wonderful weather given us which alone made it possible.'[99] Monro reported to London that 'about 65,000 men and 140 guns have been got away without the Turks being aware of movement. Entire credit due to Birdwood, his Corps Commanders and Admiral Wemyss.'[100]

Two days later Birdwood 'got Thatcher the doctor to open up the old bullet wound in my head & he extracted a long strip of the case of a bullet.'[101] On Christmas Day instructions were received at the Dardanelles Army 'to make all preparations necessary for rapid evacuation of position at Helles.' Birdwood crossed to Helles and later responded to Monro with an urge 'that if this operation is to take place, it should not be delayed beyond 14th January, after which date it seems almost hopeless to expect suitable weather.' He offered to be ready for evacuation on 12 January. He laid detailed plans for how the French would leave first and finally begged 'that the importance of coming to an early decision should be impressed on the Home Authorities,' so that the staffs would not have to continue planning for evacuation as well as a winter campaign.[102] This correspondence with Monro occurred while he was returning to France to take over First Army vice Haig, who was to command the BEF. On 28 December, Murray, then CIGS, cabled Birdwood to say that 'the position at Cape Helles may now be evacuated. The withdrawal should be carried out as soon as possible and at your complete discretion.'[103] Detailed prior planning allowed for the issue of evacuation orders as quickly as New Year's Day 1916. The Intermediate Stage had already commenced and the Final Stage was to be 'carried out on the nights of the 6th and 7th January.'[104]

The continually variable weather, the number of troops that the Navy could embark in one night and the numbers needed to ensure defence if prolonged weather delays occurred were factors that kept changing. Night by night men and guns were withdrawn as opportunity presented. The Navy were willing to commit to getting 17,000 men off in one night and Davies was prepared to hang on with this number.[105] Birdwood visited Helles and the final evacuation was set. As before Birdwood watched and waited off shore, this time with de Robeck. The wind 'got worse … Rising sea made evacuation very hard. One pier swept away. 1400 men got onto one destroyer … Gully Beach embarkation had to be abandoned … All guns got off but 1 good

98 Throughout, the first edition of Pugsley, *Gallipoli: The New Zealand Story* has been cited, but a revised 6th edition has recently been published (2022). In this he notes that new research has 'concluded that some 16,000-17,000 New Zealanders served on the Peninsula in the campaign, doubling the previously used official figures', 11.

99 Diary 1915, 20 December.

100 AWM4 1/4/9 Part 2 – December 1915, General Headquarters, Mediterranean Expeditionary Force, Cable CM 94, Monro to London, 20 December 1915.

101 Diary 1915, 22 December.

102 AWM4 1/4/9 Part 2 – December 1915, General Headquarters, Mediterranean Expeditionary Force, Cable G649, London to GHQ, and letter, GSR Z 56, Birdwood to Monro, 25 December 1915.

103 AWM4 1/4/9 Part 2 – December 1915, Cable 1490, CIGS to Birdwood, 28 December 1915.

104 AWM4 1/17/3 – January 1916, General Headquarters, Dardanelles Army, Dardanelles Army Order No 2, 1 January 1916.

105 Birdwood, *Khaki and Gown*, 292-93.

6" and … 3500 mules got off, but alas! 500 were destroyed … One man only wounded – no French. About 50,000 men evacuated from here.'[106] Birdwood signalled GHQ in Egypt that 'successful result entirely due to complete Naval arrangements of Admiral de Robeck and all staff officers who have done excellently.'[107]

On Monro's last day of command GHQ wired that

> By the successful execution of this operation, the first phase of the Mediterranean Force comes to an end, and, unimpaired in moral[e] by heavy losses incurred in withdrawing from before the enemy, though the contrary might well have been expected, it is set free to reorganize and become a powerful factor in other theatres of war. If the first landing on April 25th 1915 may be regarded as a tactical victory that was strategical defeat, the evacuation was both a strategical and tactical victory, when regarded in the light of its effect on the future of the war. To assess the military and political profit & loss of the Dardanelles Expedition will be a matter for the historian, but it cannot be doubted that in this undertaking many valuable lessons have been learned, especially in the domain of combined action between the Army & the Navy.[108]

For over eight months Birdwood had first engaged his Corps in battle and then an Army. The landings had not been sufficiently successful in area gained to allow his Corps to manoeuvre and develop its position. Birdwood could have landed earlier to influence his commanders. Despite reaching the summit, his attempt at breakout had failed. The first lesson of the campaign taught at Staff College after the war was the 'vital necessity of exhaustive examination of all the factors, and of evolving a comprehensive plan of operations beforehand.'[109] Birdwood's plan did not allow adequately for the health of his troops or the command and control challenges. In spite of these criticisms his reputation was high, and this was notwithstanding failures and disasters in this theatre. Similar would occur on the Western Front. His standing had been enhanced by Monro's assessment of Birdwood and his Anzacs. This had been further reinforced by Kitchener. The final evacuations were successes. The Anzac legend and the 'Soul of Anzac' mutually benefitted each other.

106 Diary 1915, 8 January.
107 AWM4 1/4/10 Part 2 – January 1916, General Headquarters, Mediterranean Expeditionary Force, Cable OBC 45, Birdwood to GHQ, 9 January 1916.
108 AWM4 1/4/10 Part 1 – January 1916, General Headquarters, Mediterranean Expeditionary Force, 9 January 1916, the last day of MEF.
109 Para. IX in Lecture 4 – The end of the Campaign, Camberley Staff College, Vol 14-4, The Dardanelles Campaign (1923).

8

A harder challenge yet

Birdwood arrived back in Alexandria on 19 January 1916, having commanded for nearly three months an army comprising three British corps and a French division, and having achieved two successful withdrawals. In France Haig had become C-in-C BEF and his four army commanders were Monro, Plumer, Allenby and Rawlinson. Birdwood had faced all the same trials of army command, but in addition he had the unique challenges of dealing with the leading political figures of two Dominions. His dutiful approach to this task and his skilful letter writing contributed to the overall harmonious relationship between the Home Government and two of its Dominions, despite the never-ending toll of casualties.

In New Zealand's case, Birdwood largely communicated with James Allen, the Minister of Defence, a conservative politician who represented a rural Otago seat. Allen was a stalwart politician who weathered early storms to receive public recognition at the War's end. Sadly, his son, John, was killed at Gallipoli with the NZEF. Later in their correspondence Birdwood and Allen would learn that they were both Old Cliftonians.[1] Allen's letter of 15 January 1915 initiated an exchange of at least fourteen letters over the following year.[2] Less than a month after arriving, Birdwood replied assuring Allen of his pride in commanding New Zealand troops. In case Allen got to hear of 'complaints about the behaviour of some of our men in the town,' Birdwood decided to explain the background and sent a copy of his directive given to Bridges and Godley. Right from the start Birdwood did not hide sensitive issues or events. Using 'our' and closing with 'you may count on our giving the very best account of ourselves when our time comes, as it will do,' showed a sense of togetherness. [3] It struck the right chord with Allen who replied that 'we are equally proud that so distinguished an officer commands our men and we have every confidence that a good record will be put up for our country and that some traditions will be created to help us along the path of nation making in the future.' He sought to hear if there was 'any falling off in quality or training' of the drafts coming out to Egypt and was very frank about outstanding issues concerning howitzers, hospitals and Maoris.[4] Only two letters during

1 Ian McGibbon, Allen, James, *Dictionary of New Zealand Biography*, 2015, <https://teara.govt.nz/en/biographgies/3a12/allen-james> (accessed 25 May 2021).

2 Archives New Zealand [hereafter ANZ] C 361 202 Allen1-9, Sir James Allen Papers, letter, Allen to Birdwood 15 January 1916.

3 ANZ C 361 202 Allen1-9, Letter, Birdwood to Allen, 21 January 1915.

4 ANZ C 361 202 Allen1-9, Letter, Allen to Birdwood, 31 March 1915.

the Gallipoli campaign are extant between the Governor of New Zealand and Birdwood, both referring to earlier correspondence.[5] Birdwood's letter of 13 December is a detailed exposition on how certain officers were performing in command.[6] His priorities were leadership in battle and command experience. In May Birdwood had written to the Governor-General of Australia, Sir Ronald Munro Ferguson, preparing him for the worst regarding the injured Bridges.[7] He stated that 'in a previous letter' he had 'mentioned how fond I was of him [Bridges] and how much I liked working with him'.[8] Twenty-three letters survive from then until the end of the Gallipoli campaign.[9] Again Birdwood's approach was factual and open, demonstrating trust and confidentiality, to a man he may have met before albeit very briefly. His letter of 6 June included: the performance of the Australian brigadiers; the Mounted Brigades in the trenches; honours for Australians; standard of training in Australia before despatch; personal views on Sir Ian Hamilton ('a most charming chief') and Winston Churchill ('personally responsible (though I may be absolutely wrong in doing so) for what has happened…'); and the future – 'I think we shall have to get still further heavy reinforcements before we can begin to win through'.[10] His letter of 3 October concentrated on which Commanding Officers had been injured and unfit for Brigade command at present, others showing potential, and some just too old for the task. He showed he knew what was needed to face the challenge of command.

Finally, Birdwood corresponded with Sir George Pearce, the Defence Minister of Australia and Labor party senator.[11] Although they had an extensive correspondence throughout the war, it appears only to have commenced with a non-extant letter from Pearce to Birdwood on 11 September 1915. Birdwood was aware that the Governor-General shared his correspondence with both the Prime Minister and the Defence Minister. During his time at Gallipoli Birdwood, probably, wrote in excess of twenty-five letters, each usually over eight typed pages, to these Dominion personalities. By the end of the Gallipoli campaign Birdwood had established trusted and warm written communications with these key individuals. It was an achievement of inestimable value to the relationship between Great Britain and its Antipodean Dominions. Written from a dugout at the side of a valley running up from Anzac Cove itself, these letters produced immediate benefits in Egypt.

There he found three divisions of the Anzac Corps and 8th Australian Brigade; three Light Horse brigades and the NZMR; plus 30,000 Australian and 6,000 NZ troops in the Anzac

5 AWM 3DRL/3376 3/1a, Letters to Birdwood by Lord Liverpool. AWM 3DRL/3376 3/1b, Letters written to Lord Liverpool by Birdwood. The position of Governor of NZ was raised to Governor-General in 1917.

6 AWM 3DRL/3376 3/1a, 13 December 1915.

7 From the establishment of the Commonwealth of Australia in 1901 until the Statute of Westminster in 1931, the Governor-General represented the British Government and had a supervisory role over the Australian Government. A similar status existed in New Zealand.

8 AWM 3DRL/3376 6/3a, Letters and cablegrams by Birdwood to Sir Ronald Munro Ferguson, letter, Birdwood to Ferguson, 17 May 1915.

9 AWM 3DRL/3376 6/3a, and AWM 3DRL/3376 6/1, Letters to Birdwood by Sir Ronald Munro Ferguson and other correspondents.

10 AWM 3DRL/3376 6/3a, Letter Birdwood to Ferguson, 6 June 1915

11 B Beddie, Pearce, Sir George Foster (1870-1952), *Australian Dictionary of Biography*, <https://adb.anu.edu.au/bipographypearce-sir-george-foster-7996/text13931> (accessed 25 May 2021); AWM 3DRL/3376 7/1 Parts 1 & 2, Letters by Birdwood to Sir George Pearce; AWM 3DRL/3376 7/2 Letters by Sir George Pearce to Birdwood.

Training Depot at Cairo. Godley had written to General Sir Archibald Murray, recently arrived to command the Mediterranean Expeditionary Force defending the Suez Canal, proposing that the unallotted troops could form two new Australian divisions and a New Zealand one. Bean recorded that 'Birdwood, returning to Egypt after the breaking up of his Dardanelles Army, seized with enthusiasm upon the proposal to create not merely a new army corps, but an Australian and New Zealand army.' Bean noted that it would be as big as the original British Army in France.[12] The next day Birdwood 'went to see Sir A Murray in morning at GHQ who suggested formation of A&NZ Army & asked me to formulate proposals from my Corps & the 30,000 odd reinforcements now here. My idea is to make the first 16 Aust & 4 NZ Bns each provide itself with a 2nd Bn. Each Div to give an Artillery Bde to 3rd and 4th Divs.' On 22 January Birdwood wrote that he had 'worked out all my details for formation of the A&NZ Army and took them to Murray who entirely approved & wire was sent to WO [War Office] asking for sanction in general & all details to be settled by me in direct communication with A&NZ Govts.'[13] Bean later wrote that Murray 'understood that Birdwood had the confidence of the Australian and New Zealand Governments' and that if the scheme was agreed to, 'he proposed to let Birdwood arrange all the details by direct communication with them'.[14]

Birdwood's scheme was to increase the force to five divisions. For the Australians, he planned to build two new divisions around 4th Infantry Brigade, released from the NZ&A Division, and 8th Infantry Brigade recently arrived from Australia. Each of the original sixteen battalions of the original four brigades, Birdwood then planned to split in half. This would provide the necessary sixteen battalions for a further four brigades. These four new brigades together with the original 4th and 8th Brigades would form the new 4th and 5th Australian Divisions.[15] A new New Zealand division would be created with their current brigade, together with the Rifle Brigade that was then arriving in Egypt, and a new brigade built, as with the Australians, on splitting the original battalions.[16] The Indian Army used this splitting of units as a means of mobilisation. Birdwood was familiar with the concept and confident of its efficacy. White did not have the same confidence and neither did the Divisional commanders nor other commanders, 'when the news was broken to them. But Birdwood held to his decision.'[17] By 4 February, just sixteen days after tabling his initial ideas, Birdwood received assent from Australia and by 7 February all decisions as to method and personnel had been made. White took four days leave before returning to execute the creation of the new formations.[18] Birdwood, however, had news from Murray that Robertson, the CIGS, was against the formation of an Australian

12 C E W Bean, *The Official History of Australia in the War of 1914-1918, Volume III* (Sydney: Halstead Press, 1929), 34.
13 Diary 1915, 20 and 21 January.
14 Bean, *The Official History of Australia in the War of 1914-1918, Volume III*, 35-36.
15 Birdwood suggested that a further division – 3rd – be raised in Australia before it proceeded overseas. Jeffrey Grey, *A Military History of Australia* (Cambridge: Cambridge University Press, 1999), 96.
16 Lt Col W S Austin, *The Official History of the New Zealand Rifle Brigade* (Wellington: L T Watkins, 1924), 18-21.
17 Bean, *The Official History of Australia in the War of 1914-1918, Volume III*, 37.
18 Bean, *The Official History of Australia in the War of 1914-1918, Volume III*, 48. Diary 1916, 4 & 12 February.

army of such a limited number of divisions and that instead two corps would be created.[19] These would be: I and II ANZAC corps.[20] With Brigadier Gwynn moving from 6th Brigade to be Godley's Chief of Staff, five brigade commanders were selected, as were sixteen new battalion commanders. All these were to be Australians but Birdwood did not regard any Australians under his command as being suitable yet to command a division, which was too much for Pearce and his advisor Lieutenant Colonel Thomas Dodds, the Adjutant-General. So McCay, the commander of 2nd Brigade at the landings and subsequently injured at Krithia, was sent from Australia to command 5th Division. Major General Cox (Indian Army) was appointed to 4th Division. Birdwood wrote to Pearce on 24 March explaining all these appointments and their background. It is an eighteen-page letter demonstrating a comprehensive knowledge of the officers under him and an appreciation of what is required for an individual to take the next step up in command.[21] Tested leadership and command experience were key for Birdwood. The conscientious effort and diplomacy of all the letters written by Birdwood from Gallipoli had established sound and confident relationships and paid a valuable dividend in the speedy acceptance of his plans for this reorganisation.

There was already a sense of urgency. The 1st and 2nd Divisions had, on their return started 'vigorously with a 21-day programme of training'. On moving into positions east of the Canal, the training continued, as 'there is little enough time in which to fit ourselves to take the field against the Germans, which may be our next move and every moment is precious'.[22] Cox was placed in charge of forming up the new divisions at Tel el Kebir and on 15 February Birdwood visited him to see the new brigades.[23] The reorganisation meant that half of each of all of the original battalions were departing to Tel el Kebir and the other halves were staying in their defensive positions. Reinforcements were moved to both locations to bring the individual units up to strength. Bean cited the example of the 56th Battalion. 'Some 450 men under fifteen young officers separated from the 4th Battalion on February 14th. On the evening of the 16th 508 men and three reinforcement officers arrived from Cairo to complete the unit.'[24] That same day as the second batch of battalions split, the Germans commenced their attack on Verdun. Murray had been warned previously of the need to provide six divisions for France. The demand was now urgent. Murray sent 31st Division immediately and 29th Division commenced embarkation on 6 March. Simultaneously the 1st and 2nd Australian Divisions both moved in from East of the Canal. Legge's 2nd Division, whose battalions had not been split, was the first to embark on 13 March.[25] It was less than two months since Birdwood had arrived back in Egypt. He had planned and then steered the task of creating new divisions. Others, particularly White, had made immense contributions in planning and constructing accommodation, moving the necessary troops, and organising the training. It was a gargantuan achievement.

19 AWM 3DRL/3376 11/5b, Correspondence between Birdwood and Colonel Fitzgerald, *PS* to letter Birdwood to Fitgerald, 7 February 1916.
20 AWM4 1/29/1 - February 1916, I ANZAC Corps, Circular Memorandum No 3, 14 February 1916.
21 AWM 3DRL/3376 7/1 Part 1, Letters by Birdwood to Sir George Pearce, letter 24 March 1916.
22 AWM4 1/29/1 - February 1916, I ANZAC Corps, Notes on Training, February 1916.
23 Diary 1916, 15 February.
24 Bean, *The Official History of Australia in the War of 1914-1918, Volume III*, 50.
25 Ibid., 49 and 62; Diary 1916, 5, 12 & 13 March.

It must be stressed, however, that not a single division was presently either finely honed or operationally experienced. As Bean clearly states: 'Nearly three-quarters of the men in both "veteran" and new battalions were now reinforcements'.[26] Both Birdwood and his Anzacs were about to be tested beyond their experiences to date. In his last letter from Egypt to Fitzgerald, Kitchener's Military Secretary, Birdwood detailed his intentions for the administration of the AIF, which he hoped to finalise in London. He also commented on General Murray: 'I am not saying a word against Murray, who is a most charming man, and always very nice to me; but, if I may do so, I do not think he possesses the same human touch [as Maxwell], and strikes one as rather inclined to look upon life from the Aldershot and General Staff point of view.'[27] That was an interesting comment knowing that Birdwood was about to depart for France, the main focus of the war effort and where the 'Aldershot and General Staff point of view' had established itself from August 1914.

On 30 March Birdwood left Alexandria. At Marseilles, he was summoned to GHQ and told not to proceed to London as expected. He and White lunched with Sir Douglas Haig on 6 April.[28] The historian Gary Sheffield and some others, who have probably followed his lead, suggest that Haig had little time for Birdwood, without ever explaining quite why Haig subsequently made Birdwood an army commander.[29] It will be shown that this verdict of distrust or lack of regard is based on very few diary entries and these do not provide the full picture of the relationship. Sheffield makes the point that Haig 'had just emerged from the pack', that is from the other Army commanders with the same rank. Birdwood had also been an Army commander. This meeting was Haig's first opportunity to see how Birdwood would take his return to corps command. Haig had recently inspected 7th Australian Brigade and 'expressed himself as very pleased with the appearance, smartness and physique of the men', and so could comment personally on the troops, allowing Birdwood to express his deep pride in those he commanded.[30] Birdwood was pleased to hear that his Corps would join Second Army under Sir Herbert Plumer and gain experience in a 'nursery section' of the front line.

Birdwood may also have learnt that I ANZAC had been intended for the forthcoming Somme offensive but the status and unpreparedness of its artillery prevented this. Birdwood and Plumer met that afternoon and the next day Birdwood saw his new HQ location at Chateau de la Motte au Bois, south-east of Hazebrouck.[31] He then visited HQ II Corps, 'who are looking after my 1st & 2nd Australian Divs pending our taking over'. On 8 April the first Australians, 7th Brigade, entered the line. Two days later Birdwood visited them and the rest of Legge's Division, and that afternoon Plumer visited HQ I ANZAC now complete with staff. 2nd

26 Bean, *The Official History of Australia in the War of 1914-1918, Volume III*, 54.
27 AWM 3DRL/3376 11/5b, Correspondence between Birdwood and Colonel Fitzgerald, letter, Birdwood to Fitzgerald, 17 March 1916.
28 Diary 1916, 30 March & 6 April.
29 Gary Sheffield, *The Chief: Douglas Haig and the British Army* (London: Aurum Press, 2011), 138; Gary Sheffield in foreword to Meleah Hampton, *Attack on the Somme* (Solihull: Helion & Company, 2016), xiv.
30 AWM4 23/7/7 – March 1916, 7th Infantry Brigade, 27 March 1916.
31 Birdwood and a previous tenant, General Allenby, both liked the chateau and its chatelaine, who wrote of her experiences in Baroness Ernest de la Grange, *Open house in Flanders, 1914-1918* (London: John Murray, 1929), 180. On first meeting him, the Baroness described Birdwood as 'most agreeable. Short, thin, active, quick, and energetic, with grey-blue eyes, full of frank gaiety'.

Division as a whole entered the line on 11 April. 1st Division was still training and 'Russell with leading part NZ Division arrived' on 14 April. Birdwood, however, was still keen to go to London.[32] Having heard nothing from Fitzgerald, Birdwood wrote again on 14 April, stressing his desire to get to London. [33] This had effect. On 18 April he was 'wakened up with wire at midnight to say that Lord K wanted to see me at War Office next day'. [34]

At Victoria Station Birdwood was met by Jenny. They had not seen each other since saying farewell in Egypt at the end of 1914. With her was the Australian High Commissioner Andrew Fisher and 'several Australian officers who 'welcomed me most kindly'. [35] Birdwood then met Lord Kitchener. The next day he saw the King at Buckingham Palace. 'He rec'd me most kindly upstairs – knighted me & gave me KCSI & KCMG. We then sat down & he talked to me for an hour and a half about the war & many things & most nice thanking me for Gallipoli & what I had done with Australians'.[36] Birdwood must have told the King about his injury as a few days later His Majesty related the story to the NZ Sapper Horace Moore-Jones when he was presenting his Gallipoli sketches.[37] Then over a private lunch, he had his first meeting with Billy Hughes, the Australian Prime Minister, at which Hughes insisted that Birdwood should retain command of the AIF. The next day's meetings at the War Office 'settled fairly satisfactorily questions about AIF sick, depots, etc.' – the administration of the AIF in principle.[38] Birdwood, as Commandant of the AIF, would retain in France the small number of staff who had achieved the whole of the recent reorganisation.[39] Temporary arrangements had been created by the Australian High Commissioner's office to handle Gallipoli casualties evacuated to England. A London HQ was proposed, eventually to be in Horseferry Road, together with a Base Depot organisation. The Administrative HQ in Egypt would move to England in May.[40] Birdwood now had a clear command responsibility for all aspects of the administration of the AIF. This arrangement would continue to the end of the war.

After further meetings, Birdwood saw family, old friends, such as Sir Ian Hamilton, and Anzacs in hospitals. His daughter Nancy was working as a Volunteer Aid Detachment nurse at Harefield Hospital for the Australians and had been given a pet kangaroo. One Aussie told her that it needed a mate – a jackaroo. Asking about how to find a jackaroo, she learnt that it was young gentleman on a pastoral station! On Tuesday 25 April the first anniversary of the Landings was commemorated. Before the memorial service at Westminster Abbey 'the A&NZ troops [2,000 had set off from the Aldwych] marched past me at the end of Whitehall before

32 Diary 1916, 7-14 April.

33 AWM 3DRL/3376 11/5b, Correspondence between Birdwood and Colonel Fitzgerald, letters Birdwood to Fitgerald, 4 and 14 April 1916.

34 Diary 1916, 18 April.

35 Diary 1916, 19 April. These could have been officers, injured at Gallipoli and then working for the AIF in London. See Birdwood, *Khaki and Gown*, 302.

36 *Taunton Courier and Western Advertiser*, 26 April 1916. Diary 1916, 20 April.

37 The Birdwood collection in the AWM includes eight paintings by Moore-Jones – one which is of Birdwood outside his dugout. AWM 3DRL/3376 14/4, Paintings by Sapper Moore-Jones.

38 Diary 1916, 21 April.

39 AWM 3DRL/3376 11/5b, Correspondence between Birdwood and Colonel Fitzgerald, letter, Birdwood to Fitgerald, 17 March 1916.

40 AWM 1/66/1 – May 1915 - October 1917, General Officer Commanding AIF Depots in UK, Report on AIF Depots in the UK and extracts from Sixth Annual Report of the High Commissioner of the Commonwealth, January 1916.

filing into the Abbey. King & Queen present. Jenny & I were in the choir.' At the end of the service Birdwood went over to see the Australians who 'cheered, standing, for minutes on end of uncontrollable admiration.'[41] Birdwood went to a lunch for the Australians, including two or three hundred wounded men from various hospitals and then went on to the New Zealand depots for a parade and presentation of medals.[42] Later Birdwood met Major General Sir Newton Moore who was to take charge of the Australian depots and reinforcements, lunched with the British Prime Minister and Mrs Asquith, and bade goodbye to Kitchener, which was to be his last farewell.[43] Birdwood arrived back at his HQ on Sunday 30 April. Two-and-half years of fighting still lay ahead.

Birdwood taking salute at corner of Whitehall prior to First Anzac Day Service, 1916, (Museums Victoria Collections 390933)

41 *The Times*, 26 April 1916, 2 and 7; *Daily Express*, 26 April 1916, 8.
42 Diary 1916, 25 April.
43 Moore had been Premier and then Agent-General for Western Australia. Birdwood, *Khaki and Gown*, 304.

Instead of being in their own separate area in a distant theatre, Birdwood and his Anzacs were now in the main theatre of war, where by the end of 1916 the two ANZAC corps would be just two among eighteen infantry corps and the Australian and New Zealand divisions would be only five among fifty-nine British infantry divisions (with 3rd Australian Division still in England).[44] Their dress made them distinctive and they were largely kept together as divisions within their own ANZAC corps, not quite to the same extent as the Canadians but far more so than British divisions. The Anzacs had arrived as the costly fighting at Verdun continued, resulting in nearly 200,000 French and German casualties by the end of March, and as the planning for a British offensive on the Somme was developing.

Unlike in the wider historiography of the AIF and Gallipoli, Birdwood's operational command of AIF formations must be precise – both when and where.[45] During the following eighteen months Birdwood commanded I ANZAC but not all the Australian divisions available in theatre. From November 1917 he commanded the Australian Corps after its creation but again divisions were at times detached. He handed over this Corps to Monash on 1 June 1918. In Western Front historiography, few, apart from Bean, have addressed the AIF service on the Western Front as a whole, from 1916 through to the end in 1918.[46] The most well known to have done so was the journalist Les Carlyon, who described the Australian soldiers as having an aura at Gallipoli and finishing with an element of success despite the evacuation. In *The Great War* Carlyon described a long costly struggle, which ended simply in a job finally done. He saw this as not quite ranking in Australian eyes as much as Gallipoli.[47] The historians who have contributed a more studied approach have focused on key episodes of AIF Western Front fighting – Fromelles 1916; Somme 1916-17, Passchendaele 1917 and Somme 1918.[48] A common trait is positive stories of individual bravery contrasted with criticism of British generals. None show the bitter criticism undermined by its own viciousness which characterises John Laffin's work.[49] Those, however, with both operational understanding and a systematic approach, such as Lee and Stevenson, are more balanced in this regard. Birdwood is dealt with fully in Pozières coverage but the focus on him declines in works on later battles. Andy Simpson's major work concentrated on British corps commanders. He believed the BEF structure only allowed such commanders to operate as individuals when asserting their personalities and 'it was here, as a

44 Paddy Griffith, *Battle Tactics of the Western Front* (New Haven: Yale University Press, 1994), 214-19.

45 *As a well as in Bean this is detailed in Sir Charles Lucas, The Empire at War, Vol III, Australia, New Zealand, The Pacific Islands* (London: Humphrey Milford, Oxford University Press 1924).

46 Robert Stevenson, *To Win the Battle: The 1st Australian Division in the Great War, 1914-1918* (Melbourne: Cambridge University Press, 2013) provides masterly coverage of the 1st Div which generally served under Birdwood.

47 Les Carlyon, *The Great War* (Sydney: Pan Macmillan Australia, 2006).

48 Roger Lee, *British Battle Planning in 1916 and the Battle of Fromelles* (Farnham: Ashgate, 2015); Robin Prior and Trevor Wilson, *The Somme* (Sydney: University of New South Wales Press, 2006); Christopher Wray, *Pozieres: Echoes of a Distant Battle* (Cambridge: Cambridge University Press, 2015); Hampton, *Attack on the Somme*; Jonathan Walker, *The Blood Tub: General Gough and the Battle of Bullecourt, 1917* (Staplehurst: Spellmount, 1998); Peter Edgar, *To Villers-Bretonneux with Brigadier-General William Glasgow DSO and the 13th Australian Infantry Brigade* (Loftus, NSW 2006); Peter Fitzsimons, *Victory at Villers-Bretonneux* (Sydney: William Heinemann, 2016).

49 John Laffin, *Digger* (London1959).

leader of men, that Birdwood excelled.'[50] His uniqueness in commanding a national entity for so long is ignored and his inspiring ability to pick his men up to go again and again are not recognised. It is intended to rectify these absences.

When Birdwood returned to France, both his 1st and 2nd Divisions were in the line south of Armentieres. The New Zealand Division was training in the rear. On the first morning Plumer came over to see Birdwood about taking over more of the line. On 6 May, he received the report that '20th Bn of 5th Bde was attacked last night & apparently – though it was reported at the time all had passed off quietly – 20 were killed & about 60 wounded while Germans got into the trenches & got away with 5 prisoners & 2 Stokes guns [mortars] – a real bad thing to have allowed to happen'.[51] A bland report had already made its way up the chain from 2nd Division and been reflected in GHQ's report to London. Plumer's HQ had subsequently picked up by wireless that the Germans had captured prisoners, machine guns and mine throwers. Plumer tasked Birdwood for the details. GHQ had laid down that the Stokes mortars were only for use under restricted conditions and were not to be captured by the enemy. The plan had been to unveil their full effectiveness during the forthcoming major offensive. The Australians on receiving their first German trench raid had lost sensitive weapons, failed to keep the enemy out of their lines and, with no Germans killed, had apparently not vigorously expelled the raiders.[52] It was an inauspicious start and Haig noted in his diary: 'It is difficult to get these Colonials to give a true report on first arrival!'[53] Perhaps Birdwood's front line had missed his regular trench tours during his nearly two weeks in London. On 16 May, the NZ Division took over the stretch of the front line to the left of 2nd Australian Division and I ANZAC assumed responsibility for the extended front. Birdwood spent the day in 1st NZ Brigade front line trenches. The month closed with a second fierce German trench raid that was handled with more success but similar casualties. On this occasion the reporting was timely and accurate.[54] By the end of May all of Birdwood's brigades had served in front-line trenches.

June commenced with a visit by the Australian Prime Minister and the High Commissioner, who both stayed overnight at Birdwood's HQ. Then on 6 June he received 'a wire from Creedy, PS to Lord K:

> Giving me the awful news that my beloved old Chief who was on "*Hampshire*" with Fitz en route to Russia had been lost. It is too dreadful even to think of it from the national point of view & my own personal affection. All the 9 years I was with him, I was hardly ever away from him & I think he was fonder of me than almost anyone. It is just a real blank. He cannot be replaced.

50 Andy Simpson, *Directing Operations: British Corps Command on the Western Front 1914-1918* (Stroud: Spellmount, 2006), xx-xxi.
51 Diary 1916, 1-6 May.
52 Bean, *The Official History of Australia in the War of 1914-1918, Volume III*, 195-6, 200-1, 06-7; AWM4 23/5/11 – May 1916, 5th Infantry Brigade, 5-7; AWM4 1/29/4 Part 1 – May 1916, I ANZAC Corps, 6-7.
53 LHMCA GB0099 KCLMA MF 856-865, FM Earl Haig: Autograph diaries and letters home to wife, 1914-1919, 6 May 1916.
54 AWM4 1/29/4 Part 2 – May 1916, I ANZAC Corps, 46. Diary 1916, 16-31 May.

Plumer came understandingly to see Birdwood that afternoon and he 'went for a quiet walk along canal after'.[55] Years later he wrote that 'the news of the tragedy overwhelmed me'.[56] Among many letters, Hamilton wrote: 'I must write to you whilst we are both under the shadow of this public calamity.'[57] Birdwood had been a substantive captain in 1900 when he first met Kitchener in South Africa. He was now a substantive lieutenant general and had commanded an Army for a period. Kitchener had called him to Egypt and Birdwood had not failed him. Now his powerful patron was gone. Among a crowd of Aldershot-experienced British Army Camberley graduates, Birdwood was a non-*psc* Indian Army officer. Now he could only call on his own ability to maintain his position or even advance his career.

His diary suggests Birdwood returned the next day to work with determination. The previous evening had seen the first Australian trench raid by a combined team from 27th and 28th battalions, assisted in their training by two Canadian officers. It drew praise from Birdwood in a Special Order: 'The great success attained was entirely the result of very careful preparation and great forethought and attention to every possible detail'. He wanted every battalion and then every company to develop the ability to raid, every Brigadier to look to carrying out a weekly raid, and divisional commanders to consider simultaneous raids. He proposed ideas and looked for 'the ingenuity and dash of officers' to seek 'alternative methods'.[58] A week later another raid took place and again it was a success. Birdwood held a memorial service for Kitchener on 13 June at the same time as the national service at St Pauls. The next day Godley came to see Birdwood. II ANZAC was now arriving in France.[59] There was a desire to get 4th and 5th Divisions into line and gain experience and it was decided to move the New Zealand Division to II ANZAC under Godley, the NZEF commander. At this time Plumer was considering an operation further north against the Messines Ridge.

On 22 June Haig came to inspect 12 Brigade and visited I ANZAC HQ. Birdwood recorded he 'had a talk with Kiggell [Haig's CGS] about administration of AIF'.[60] As noted recently to Pearce: 'Nothing has yet been definitely settled regarding my administration of the force which is a nuisance – though, as a matter of fact I continue to carry on, and trust difficulties will not be put in my way'. In September 1915 powers had been vested in 'the Anzac Corps Commander,' Birdwood's position at that time, but now there were two ANZAC Corps.[61] Clear confirmation of Birdwood's overall administrative command of the AIF was still outstanding but he maintained his administrative command, particularly regarding men under training in

55 Diary 1916, 6 June.

56 Birdwood, *Khaki and Gown*, 305.

57 AWM 3DRL/3376 2/10, Letters to Birdwood about the death of Lord Kitchener, letter from Sir Ian Hamilton, 11 June 1916. The file also includes notification that Kitchener had left Birdwood £200 in his will.

58 AWM 3DRL/3376 2/8, Wartime correspondence and papers, Special Order, 7 June 1916.

59 The desert marches of 4th and 5th divisions, the absorption of rejects left behind by 1st and 2nd divisions, and the establishment and training of divisional artillery are not covered here. See Bean, *The Official History of Australia in the War of 1914-1918, Volume III*, 288-92 and 95-97.

60 Diary 1916, 22 June.

61 AWM 3DRL/3376 7/1 Part 1, Letters by Birdwood to Sir George Pearce, Letter 6 June 1916.

England, until formal notification dated 17 August 1916.[62] Following Haig's visit, Birdwood wrote 'a friendly letter' to him and on 26 June had a reply: 'My dear Birdie':

> I have the greatest confidence in your judgement as a Commander, and I feel sure that you will very soon get the Australian Divns thoroughly fit for the struggle which is in front of us. They know what we are fighting for, and mean to play their part like men. So I feel sure that with a little more knowledge of the game, they will prove themselves more than a match for the enemy – But it means hard work, thoroughness, & self sacrifice ... Need scarcely add that if I can help you in any way at any time you have only to let me know & will do my best. Meantime I wish you & your gallant fellows everything that is good.[63]

Two days later in a letter to the King, Haig wrote regarding a discussion with Hughes: 'But if an opportunity arose of using the 2 Australian Corps under Birdwood for any operation I would try to do so, and then call the force the 'Australian Army'. I understand that the Australian Prime Minister is as keen about the name as anything else ...'[64] Haig had therefore twice expressed confidence in Birdwood and in what he was achieving, while acknowledging that more was to be done.

By this time Birdwood had been back with his Corps for nearly two months. Brigades had been effectively rotated through the front line. Raids had been successfully carried out and German raids repulsed.[65] Since I ANZAC had taken over a 'nursery' sector on 14 April its Corps War Diary had recorded the loss of 436 killed and 1,823 wounded in 1st and 2nd Divisions. There had not been a day without casualties. Two Brigades, 7th and 2nd, were currently detached further north to V Corps. II ANZAC was in France. 4th Division was starting to gain front line experience with 2nd Division. HQ 5th Division was still in Marseilles with its Brigades moving to billets in the rear Anzac area. Birdwood had only second-hand views from Godley on the operational effectiveness of these two new Divisions, both needing to gain experience of fighting in France and carrying out raids. Events, however, would overwhelm the overall steady development of the two ANZAC corps.

The Somme offensive commenced on 1 July and the urgent need for more divisions was immediately clear. The next day I ANZAC and 1st and 2nd Divisions were put on 24 hours' notice to move. II ANZAC with the New Zealand and 4th Divisions was to take over by midnight, 3/4 July, with all six brigades in the front line. They were in place within twenty-four hours. That same day 2nd Division took over responsibility for the part of the line that lay further

62 AWM 3DRL/3376 2/9, Appointment of GOC AIF, Extract from *Commonwealth of Australia Gazette* No 105.

63 AWM 3DRL/3376 2/3, Letters received by Birdwood, 1 June-25 December 1916, Letter Haig to Birdwood, 26 June 1916.

64 Letter to King George V, 28 June, in Gary Sheffield and John Bourne (eds.), *Douglas Haig: War diaries and Letters, 1914-1918* (London: Weidenfeld & Nicolson, 2005), 193.

65 Haig viewed such experience as important. He added to the typewritten version of his diary for 29 June that 'the only doubt I have is regarding the VIII Corps which has no experience of fighting in France and has not carried out one successful raid.' See Sheffield and Bourne, *Douglas Haig*, 195.

north and was held by 2nd and 7th Brigades.[66] Birdwood still had his other responsibilities and wrote a detailed fourteen-page letter to Senator Pearce on 3 July, mentioning Monash leaving 4th Brigade on 12 July to command 3rd Division on Salisbury Plain, together with associated changes at other levels.[67] On 7 July orders were received for I ANZAC with two divisions to move south and for 4th Division to move into GHQ Reserve – both moves to be completed by 12 July. McCay's 5th Division took over from Cox's 4th Division. Birdwood 'held that the infantry of the new Divisions would prove as well trained as that of their predecessors.'[68] 5th Division, however, had none of the step-by-step 'nursery' introduction previously undertaken by 1st and 2nd and partially by 4th Divisions. It was about to become the first Australian division to fight in France.

On 5 July, the day after Godley's II ANZAC had taken over, it was discovered that the 13th Jäger Battalion had been sent south from that front to the Somme battlefield. The II ANZAC Corps southern boundary, at the southernmost point in Plumer's Second Army, was with General Haking's XI Corps of General Monro's First Army, and opposite Fromelles. Birdwood had recorded three earlier meetings with Haking.[69] The various possible operations being considered and how they developed are well covered by Bean, Roger Lee and Senior, and furthermore Lee describes clearly the operational planning behind 'pinning operations.'[70] The subsequent 5th Division orders were to prevent 'the enemy withdrawing troops from our front,' and attacking together with 61st Division under the command of GOC XI Corps to 'capture and hold the German front line trenches on the front opposite.'[71] The general view was that the attack was a disaster.[72] This opinion is so entrenched, particularly among Australian writers, that the better-informed and more recent assessment of modern scholarship, including very convincingly by Roger Lee, Australian Army History Unit, has struggled to dispel this view of Fromelles. The attack resulted in 5,500 Australian casualties including 1,700 killed, 1,550 British and fewer than 2,000 German.[73] Birdwood must have known of the intentions of Plumer and Monro and knew the state of 5th Division. But its use did release 4th Division and after the Fromelles attack, no further German units moved south to the Somme.[74]

66 Diary 1916, 1-4 July. AWM4 1/29/6 - July 1916, Headquarters I ANZAC Corps, 1-4 July. AWM4 1/32/5 - July 1916, Headquarters II ANZAC Corps, 4&5 July.

67 AWM 3DRL/3376 7/1 Part 1, Letters by Birdwood to Sir George Pearce, letter 14 July 1916.

68 Bean, *The Official History of Australia in the War of 1914-1918, Volume III*, 334.

69 Diary 1916, 12 May, 3 and 20 June.

70 Bean, *The Official History of Australia in the War of 1914-1918, Volume III*, 328-35; Lee, *British Battle Planning in 1916 and the Battle of Fromelles*, 61-2 and 66-7; Michael Senior, *Haking: A Dutiful Soldier* (Barnsley: Pen & Sword, 2012), 114-5.

71 AWM4 1/50/5 Part 2 – July 1916, Headquarters 5th Australian Division, Order 31, 16 July 1916.

72 Bean, *The Official History of Australia in the War of 1914-1918, Volume III*, 444-5; B H Liddell Hart, *The Real War* (London: Faber and Faber, 1930), 261-2; Denis Winter, *Haig's Command* (Barnsley: Pen & Sword, 2004), 279; Simon Robbins, *British Generalship on the Western Front 1914-18: defeat into victory* (Abingdon: Frank Cass, 2005), 20.

73 Lee, *British Battle Planning in 1916 and the Battle of Fromelles*, 3; Senior, *Haking*, 108.

74 Lee argues that 'criticism of the actions or decisions of individuals or groups is easy' for those with all the time to sift through all the available information but who have 'never commanded or led troops in battle'. See Lee, *British Battle Planning in 1916 and the Battle of Fromelles*, 204.

Birdwood was now on the Somme, where the Franco-British offensive had commenced on 1 July.[75] The first day failures had necessitated the summons to I ANZAC.[76] These also resulted in General Gough's Reserve Army taking over the two left flanking corps of Fourth Army, both of which were in no fit state to continue with attacks. Joffre, the French C-in-C, met Haig on 3 July. It was an argumentative meeting but over the coming days the resulting decisions became clear. Fourth Army would continue its advance north-eastwards between Fricourt and Montauban, while Reserve Army would be tasked with outflanking the key German strong point of Thiepval by taking Pozières and working westwards along the ridge that had held the original German second line.[77] The inter-army boundary now ran south of the Albert–Bapaume road. While Gough mounted small operations, Rawlinson planned for a further offensive.

On 13 July, 4th Australian Division arrived to join I ANZAC and that same day 1st and 2nd Divisions were put on six hours' notice to move. For the first time Birdwood and Australia had a Corps of three Australian divisions. Time was spent in hurried training. A 1st Divisional training conference held on 13 July laid down priorities as: 'semi-open warfare probably in the nature of a struggle for localities (a wood or a village)'; the necessity for control of units in depth attacking over a limited frontage, and 'consolidation must be commenced as soon as ground is won'. The next day lessons were issued from other 'divisions that have taken part in recent fighting'.[78] Birdwood spent the majority of his time with 2nd and 4th Divisions, the latter being the least experienced.

Rawlinson's offensive commenced on 14 July and Fourth Army pushed forward to the edges of High and Delville Woods. Birdwood was asked to go over and see Gough that evening. They had both progressed far in their careers since South Africa where they had served together under Dundonald and then later Birdwood had signed Kitchener's letter admonishing Gough's impetuosity. Birdwood displayed nothing but loyalty to his immediate commander. 1st Australian Division was ordered to move to Contay, west of Albert. That move was completed on 16 July, the same day that Reserve Army finally took Ovillers. Haig's orders to Gough were now to take Pozières and I ANZAC was transferred from GHQ to Reserve Army with effect midnight 17/18 July. The next day 1st Division was 'placed on two hours' notice to move' and 'to be under Reserve Army direct for special operations'.[79] Instructions were still being circulated within the Division: 'It has been established in recent operations that troops should not assault a hostile prepared position from a distance of more than 200 yards'. If further apart then either 'a jumping off place' would have to be established or 'cover of darkness' used to achieve the required distance.[80] In a few days the Division would apply such teaching. Orders were issued that on 19 July 'the Division will relieve the 34th Division in the front line and will take over a

75 For detailed descriptions of all levels of the campaign, including to the German withdrawal to the Hindenburg Line, see William Philpott, *Bloody Victory: The Sacrifice on the Somme* (London: Little, Brown, 2009). for the impact of later memorialisations, see Hugh Sebag-Montefiore, *Somme: Into the Breach* (London: Viking, 2016) and its accompanying twenty-one informative maps. For a sobering alternative perspective, see Prior and Wilson, *The Somme*.

76 For the causes behind such a huge casualty toll see Philpott, *Bloody Victory*, 189-92; Prior and Wilson, *The Somme*, 112-8.

77 Philpott, *Bloody Victory*, 216.

78 AWM4 1/42/18 Part 1 – July 1916, Headquarters 1st Australian Division, Appendices 7 and 8.

79 AWM4 1/29/6 – July 1916, Headquarters I ANZAC Corps, 17 July.

80 AWM4 1/42/18 Part 1 – July 1916, Headquarters 1st Australian Division, Appendix 9.

portion of the line held by 1st Division (Imperial) tonight'.[81] Birdwood saw Walker just before he moved his HQ and afterwards Gough came to see Birdwood, their first meeting since 14 July. The relief was 'completed by 3 am'. The frontage was about 1200 yards, the distance for which the Division had been training. That morning Birdwood 'went over to Albert where I met with Gough at Walker's HQ & we discussed plans'. After that Birdwood 'motored on up the Bapaume road to Smyth's HQ [1st Bde and the left of the two forward Bdes] & walked from there past La Boiselle to head of Sausage Valley & saw Maclagan at HQ of 3rd Bde'.[82]

It may be assumed that the plans discussed were those when Haig 'saw General Gough at Toutencourt (HQ Reserve Army). The Australians went in last night opposite Pozières … He proposes to attack Pozières with them. I told him to go into all the details carefully, as 1st Australian Division had not engaged before, and possibly overlooked the difficulties of this kind of fighting'.[83] Meanwhile 48th (South Midland) Division on the left of the Australians still continued its attacks up Mash Valley towards Pozières.[84] The next day, 21 July, Birdwood went to see Walker again, while the two forward brigades strengthened the line, constructed trenches 'in advance to facilitate the attack' to meet the two hundred yard requirement, and made 'a complete reconnaissance of the enemy's position.'[85] Haig saw Rawlinson and it was decided that the forthcoming attacks, including Pozières, would 'take place as simultaneously as possible'. Haig went on to see Gough and arranged 'to attack Pozières at the same time as Fourth Army attacked on their right. The hour of attack is still under discussion. It depends to some extent on the time taken to get the troops into position'.[86] The same day 1st Division issued its orders for the attack on Pozières.[87] The objectives were very clear; the method of attack and consolidation paragraphs reflect earlier training notes with the barrages detailed in an attached map. Later that same day 'The Zero time' was 'fixed for the attack by this Division on 22/23rd' at '12.30 am', together with a revised barrage map.[88] Birdwood visited Walker once more on 22 July and then accompanied him to see his divisional batteries.[89] Haig came to see Gough 'after lunch to make sure that the Australians have only been given a simple task. This is the first time that they will be taking part in a serious offensive on a big scale'.[90]

81 AWM4 1/42/18 Part 1 – July 1916, Appendix 11.
82 Diary 1916, 20 July.
83 LHCMA, Haig Diaries MF 858, 20 July 1916.
84 The author's grandfather, 2 Lieutenant Joseph Farrimond, was declared missing believed killed that night, together with 112 other casualties, in an attempt by two companies to bomb up a trench and capture two points in the valley. See TNA WO 95/2763: 1/5th Battalion Gloucestershire Regiment, 20/21 July 1916. 1/5 Gloucesters were part of 145th Brigade of 48th (South Midland) Division. Joseph Farrimond is commemorated on the Thiepval Memorial.
85 AWM4 1/29/6 – July 1916, Headquarters I ANZAC Corps, 22 July.
86 LHCMA, Haig Diaries MF 858, 21 July 1916.
87 Also on 21 July Bean had returned from 5th Division, having rushed there by car early on the previous day. 'He was appalled at what he learned, and saw, and at once began to piece together'. To him, 'the scene in the Australian trenches, packed with wounded and dying, was unexampled in the history of the AIF'. See Dudley McCarthy, *Gallipoli to the Somme: The Story of C E W Bean* (London: Leo Cooper, 1983), 232.
88 AWM4 1/42/18 Part 1 – July 1916, Headquarters 1st Australian Division, Division Orders 31 & 33 at Appendices 13 and 15
89 Diary 1916, 22 July.
90 LHCMA, Haig Diaries MF 858, 22 July 1916.

In a little over six weeks at Pozières Australia would suffer 23,000 casualties, a figure close to that of 28,150 for the nine months at Gallipoli. As well as the casualties themselves, the interactions between the commanders leading into the battle are a subject of criticism by historians. Gough was an acknowledged 'thruster' and keen for his formations constantly to 'push on'.[91] The 1st Division was sent into attack under Reserve Army rather than under I ANZAC. There is no record of disharmony between Gough and Birdwood over this and so Gough's more experienced HQ took 1st Division into its first Western Front assault. Bean described well Gough's initial urging of Walker but also showed that both Birdwood and White, and not just Walker, prevented any excessive haste.[92] Haig was himself concerned with this Australian attack and involved himself regularly with Gough. Walker took three days to prepare and issue his orders. Throughout this period, he had regular meetings with both Gough and Birdwood, who was quite capable of handling Gough. In his comprehensive study of 1st Australian Division throughout the First World War, Stevenson, who – as did Lee on Fromelles – brings to bear his military professional understanding, stressed that Walker drew on his involvement on Gallipoli for the formulation of his plan.[93] Stevenson emphasised Walker's orders: 'Prior to the preliminary bombardment the infantry will move out to the selected position in front of the enemy's trenches. As soon as the bombardment begins the infantry will move forward as near as possible to the hostile trenches. As soon as the bombardment lifts, the trenches will be rushed.'[94] The Division did so with success and prior to the assault the men were within 50 yards of the barrage.[95] Bean described the ferocity of the supporting barrage, the like of which was never quite replicated over the coming six weeks. He went on to detail the advances, from 12:30 a.m. onwards, on the left and in the centre. The right flank of the assault included the old German second line, with two trenches, OG1 and 2. Hampton is critical that more was not ascribed to the challenge of these trenches but I note that Bean did detail the extra steps that were taken – a special two-hour barrage and a different disposition of the attacking infantry. The struggles in OG 1 and 2 gained two VCs, lost three company commanders of the right-hand battalion and at dawn saw a concerted counterattack by over 500 of the enemy, which was repulsed. One of two buttresses on the northern flank of the German position had fallen but Thiepval remained.[96] A little over a week later Haig was to write that 'the capture of Pozières by the Australians would live in history!'[97]

Certainly, Fourth Army had little success on the right that night.[98] At midday 1st Division reverted to command of I ANZAC. Decisions were taken elsewhere that day which would affect the remainder of the I ANZAC time on the Pozières ridge. Haig had met Rawlinson in

91 Philpott, *Bloody Victory*, 244-5; Gary Sheffield and Dan Todman, eds., *Command and Control on the Western Front* (Stroud: Spellmount, 2004), 72-3.
92 C E W Bean, *Two Men I Knew* (Sydney: Angus & Robertson, 1957), 134.
93 Stevenson, *To Win the Battle: The 1st Australian Division in the Great War, 1914–1918*, 149-52.
94 Ibid., 153.
95 AWM4 1/42/18 Part 1 - July 1916, Headquarters 1st Australian Division, Appendix 19, Report of the Operations of 1st Australian Division at Pozieres.
96 Bean, *The Official History of Australia in the War of 1914-1918, Volume III*, 497, 99-500, 15-6 and 26; Hampton, *Attack on the Somme*, 45-9.
97 LHCMA, Haig Diaries MF 858, 29 July 1916.
98 Bean, *The Official History of Australia in the War of 1914-1918, Volume III*, 525; Philpott, *Bloody Victory*, 264.

the morning and instead of 'renewing the general attack', local assaults were to be made on 'such points as each corps required for the favourable launching of the next wide offensive'. In the afternoon at a meeting at III Corps, Kiggell – Haig's CGS, Gough, Pulteney – commander of III Corps, and White agreed to coordinate the next attack on the OG lines.[99] Birdwood's first orders directed 1st Division to advance, on the night 24/25 July, to a point on OG 2 midway between the railway and the Bapaume road. The Division further ordered that 'in addition to the operations on the right flank the division will occupy the whole of Pozières as far north as the cemetery [the northernmost point of the village on the road to Mouquet Farm].'[100] Preparations for the two attacks were severely hampered by intense German shelling throughout the day. On the right and south of the railway OG 2 was gained but north of the railway only one platoon made the start line. Those who had gained OG 2 then had to fall back due to the developing threat from their northern flank. In the event about a quarter of the objectives were gained. On the left flank, an incorrect date had caused confusion and everything was rushed at the last minute. Both 48th Division on the left and 1st Brigade, however, fought through until the northern edge of the village was secure. At 7.15 a.m. the German shelling of Pozières recommenced and continued all day, by the end of which relief had to take place. By 09:00 on 27 July Legge and his 2nd Division were in line, facing north-westwards.[101]

But what of Birdwood? When his HQ had taken over at midday, Birdwood visited Walker, meeting up with Gough and later 'saw our wounded … some looking bad.' Orders for the following night had been issued. The next day Birdwood and White visited Walker together. On 25 July Gough came to see Birdwood first thing and again he and White went to see Walker. Birdwood went on to HQ 3rd Brigade which was attempting to advance along the OG lines and witnessed for himself the heavy shelling. When Haig saw Birdwood that afternoon, he recorded that 'the situation seems all very new to Australian HQ. The fighting here and shell fire is much more severe than anything experienced at Gallipoli! The German too, is a different enemy to the Turk!' Haig had known Birdwood's CRA [BGRA] before he left for Gallipoli and realising that he had 'no experience of our present artillery or methods', he offered Birdwood a new CRA. Birdwood 'thanked me and said he would take anyone I selected'.[102] Gough came to see Birdwood again the next day and later Birdwood met Walker and Legge 'to fix up the latter taking over command of troops at Pozières' with his 2nd Division. Birdwood met Gough once more that evening and the first orders to 2nd Division were issued: 'to make an attack on the German positions north and north-east of Pozières on a night and at a time to be determined by GOC 2nd Aust Div'. [103] On 27 July Birdwood saw Legge, whose division was in line, and that afternoon Haig called on Birdwood.[104]

The 2nd Division objective was the OG lines running northwest from the Bapaume road. The highest point, the Windmill, lay just behind OG 2 on the north side of the road. This crest

99 Bean, *The Official History of Australia in the War of 1914-1918, Volume III*, 529-30.
100 AWM 1/29/6 – July 1916, Headquarters I ANZAC Corps, Order No 14. AWM 1/42/18 Part 2 – July 1916, Headquarters 1st Australian Division, Order No 37.
101 Bean, *The Official History of Australia in the War of 1914-1918, Volume III*, 558-67 and 70-74; Hampton, *Attack on the Somme*, 52-5. AWM4 1/42/18 Part 2 – July 1916, Headquarters 1st Australian Division, Sketch 6: Position at 9 am 27 July.
102 LHCMA, Haig Diaries MF 858, 25 July 1916.
103 AWM4 1/29/6 – July 1916, Headquarters I ANZAC Corps, Order No 16.
104 1916 Diary, 24-27 July.

line had to be secured before any further movement towards Thiepval could be attempted. The orders emphasised the need for reconnaissance, to dig trenches and make other preparations necessary to form up for the attack. In the early morning of 28 July three advance posts had been secured and further trenches dug in front of the Australian lines. For the main assault 7th Brigade would be inserted between the two forward brigades which would advance on either flank. The 7th Brigade commanders spent the morning going forward to reconnoitre, the afternoon in preparation and then at 6 p.m. the Brigade moved from east of Albert towards their assembly positions. German shelling had continued all day delaying further preparatory works.[105] Birdwood's diary for the day neither showed adverse concern nor frequent and reassuring supervision. He visited Legge at his HQ at Albert. Some criticise Gough for his persistent pushing, some Legge's enthusiasm to attack and others, White for not holding Legge back, but Birdwood could have directed more, in my opinion.

Birdwood's orders had set the prerequisites for the attack; he knew that his new BGRA had only just arrived; he himself had been forward. At 6 p.m., zero hour was set for 12.15 a.m. At 7.40 p.m. the GSO 1 of 2nd Division sent a written message to 7th Brigade: 'Do you think you will have time to reach OG 1 by 12.15 if you only start to advance from the tramway at midnight. It looks rather as if we're cutting it too fine. It will be rough walking and very dark. I suggest starting from the tramline at 11.45 pm at least. Still I do not want to interfere and I know you will have thought it all out.'[106] This is not ruthless pushing. 7th Brigade did reach their starting positions on time but then everything went wrong. The Australians were seen as they moved forward to striking distance of their objective by zero hour and were fired on. The dislocated attack then met uncut barbed wire entanglements. Despite a small advance on the left by 6th Brigade the attack was a failure. The casualties were 2,002, in addition to 1,500 caused by enemy shelling in the first two days. In comparison 1st Division had lost 5,285 in taking Pozières village.

The next morning there was a conference between Birdwood, White, Legge and his GSO 1 Bridges at which it was 'decided to repeat the attempt … after more thorough preparation had been made and all details worked out'.[107] Birdwood 'twice went out … with the intention of going to see the Brigadiers of 5th, 6th & 7th Bdes at the front but was sent for the first time to come back & see Gough & second time to see Haig about our attack & future plans'.[108] Haig's diary recorded his assessment of the attack as 'not successful last night. From several reports I think the cause was due to want of thorough preparation.' He listed four reasons: the attack not being formed up squarely opposite the objective; the advance being over 700 yards when 150 yards was 'the limit for a successful charge'; the challenge for one of the Brigades of having to move such a distance with little opportunity to understand their objective; and finally, only one minute of bombardment before the attack.

Haig went on to see Gough to impress that he must supervise more closely the plans of the Anzac Corps. Haig wrote: 'some of their Divisional Generals are so ignorant and (like many Colonials) so conceited, that they cannot be trusted to work out unaided the plans of attack.' Haig might have heard frequent mentions of Gallipoli. In his *Letters from France*, 'written

105 AWM4 1/44/12 Part 1 – July 1916, Headquarters 2nd Australian Division, 27&28 July.
106 AWM4 1/44/12 Part 1 – July 1916, Appendix 108.
107 AWM4 1/44/12 Part 1 – July 1916, 30 July.
108 Diary 1916, 29 July.

at the time and within close range of the events', Bean often mentioned Gallipoli before 26 July but seldom, if at all, after that. Perhaps such harsh words about Gallipoli needed to be said. Haig went on to Birdwood at his HQ and famously said: 'you are not fighting Bashi-Bazouks [irregular Ottoman soldiers] now. This is serious scientific war, and you are up against the most scientific and most military nation in Europe'. Haig further recorded that he found White 'a very sound capable fellow, and assured me that they had learnt a lesson, and would be more thorough in future.' He emphasised artillery to Birdwood, stressed making use of Napier, the new BGRA, and recorded that the 'capture of Pozières ... [will] live in history.' His diary closed with 'Birdwood was very grateful for my visit and remarks.'[109] Haig's assessment appeared to be correct and his direction to his subordinates most reasonable.[110] This did not point to any breakdown between him and Birdwood but rather to a senior commander instilling thoroughness in a commander facing new and far more extensive challenges than in his previous theatre. Birdwood, as will be seen, successfully overcame these challenges.

Birdwood visited his forward Brigadiers and 'was nearly had by a 5.9 bombardment' and then 'very nearly caught there first by burst of shrapnel & then by 5.9s'. The next two days were 'spent in consolidating the defences of Pozières with a view to future offensive operations.'[111] On 1 August Birdwood visited Legge; then Gough, meeting Haig there as well; and finally, Haig came to see him.[112] 2nd Division's preparations for the attack were detailed in thorough worktables and maps. All was far from quiet during the preparations, as the Germans continued shelling – 'There has been no diminution of the enemy's shelling which has been continuous, causing severe casualties'.[113] As zero hour was going to be set at around dusk the attacking troops would have to move forward to their assault positions in daylight, so the forming-up trenches needed to be deep. Preparations were not complete on 2 August. The next day Birdwood recorded he 'sat rather tight all day', which meant he was unwell. White's input that day in restraining Legge's enthusiasm and delaying the attack was well documented by Bean. The Divisional orders went out instead at 8 p.m. for the attack to take place at 9.15 p.m. the following day. The ten pages of orders were comprehensive and Haig's admonishments had taken effect.[114] After three hours all objectives were reported as gained and by mid-morning 7th Brigade had taken the Windmill. Throughout the whole day, 'fierce and accurate bombardment' fell but 'in spite of this our troops held on with the greatest gallantry in spite of heavy casualties'. Birdwood had directed more during this second attempt.

Birdwood visited Legge that day taking Cox with him, in readiness for relief in place between the divisions. Birdwood noted that 'Haig came to see me that afternoon to thank us for last night,' and Haig wrote: 'The Australians gained all their objectives north of Pozières and beat off

109 LHCMA, Haig Diaries MF 858, 29 July 1916. C E W Bean, *Letters from France* (London: Cassell, 1917), 102; *The Official History of Australia in the War of 1914-1918, Volume III*, 643-44; *Two Men I Knew* 137-8. AWM 3DRL/3376 7/1 Part 1, Letters by Birdwood to Sir George Pearce, letter 1 August.

110 Wray also saw the criticism as justified. See Wray, *Pozieres: Echoes of a Distant Battle*, 53.

111 AWM4 1/29/6 – July 1916, Headquarters I ANZAC Corps, 30 & 31 July.

112 LHCMA, Haig Diaries MF 858, 1 August 1916.

113 AWM4 1/29/6 - July 1916, Headquarters I ANZAC Corps, 2 August. Bean described the incredible intensity of the bombardments in Bean, *The Official History of Australia in the War of 1914-1918, Volume III*, 658-62.

114 AWM4 1/44/12 Part 2 - July 1916, Headquarters 2nd Australian Division, Order No 37.

3 counter-attacks. A fine piece of work'.[115] I ANZAC noted that: 'Further offensive operations on the N of Pozières were contemplated but were cancelled to allow of a more complete preparation.'[116] 2nd Division was exhausted but the benefits of taking a thorough approach had been learnt. 4th Division commenced a series of advances along the summit of the ridge towards Mouquet Farm. Birdwood later wrote about Legge '… no doubt a very able officer with powers of administration and organization, but I am afraid I am never able to feel anything like [the] same confidence in him as a divisional commander as I do in both Generals Cox and Walker when their divisions are engaged.' He added that Legge had an excellent staff officer in Colonel Bridges and that all his brigadiers had done well.[117]

GHQ had already started planning for I ANZAC to vacate the sector, with 1st Division probably departing on 25 August, 2nd on 2 September, and 4th on 6 September. The front on which Australian divisions were now attacking was centred on the ridge itself, with the right of the position resting on a line of old German gun positions, running back via the OG lines to the Bapaume road. 4th Division repulsed two strong counter attacks during their first morning. Their first attack was set for the night 8/9 August. The Australians were successful but on their left 12 (Eastern) Division was not, so 15th Battalion had to pull back to conform. The inter-divisional boundary was extended and the next night 16th Battalion gained the whole objective. It should be recalled that unlike 1st and 2nd divisions, 4th had carried out no raids.[118] Birdwood was seeing Cox daily and was himself regularly seen by Gough. Birdwood visited the Brigades in line and met those that had come out. He liaised with his flanking corps and divisional commanders about attacks.

On 10 August King George V visited Birdwood's HQ and saw three Brigades formed up at the roadside. On 11 August, Haig noted that Gough 'is to carry on his operations against Thiepval' and to be congratulated on 'the daily progress made'. Seeing White at the Anzac HQ, Haig 'congratulated the Corps on the splendid way it was operating'. He also expressed satisfaction with Cox and noted that Napier was 'fully appreciated'. Haig also recorded options for the replacement of Monro who was leaving First Army to be C-in-C India, stating: 'No other Corps Commander, who is fit for it, is available, e.g. Byng, Horne, Cavan. The MS [Military Secretary] sends me four names to select from, Birdwood, H Wilson, Horne and Cavan.' Sheffield notes that Haig 'selected his protégé, Horne'. From this diary entry, it appears Haig had no difficulty in seeing Birdwood on a short list of prospective army commanders.[119]

Birdwood wrote to Senator Pearce: 'in my more recent attacks, I have made the infantry go in as weak as I possibly dare send them. In this way I find we can minimise losses tremendously … I find that the same very much applies in defence and am doing all I can to hold our own trenches with a minimised garrison.' This was in line with Haig's direction. Birdwood then turned to the problem of reinforcements. He expected 'that in our recent phase of fighting, each division will be said to have some five thousand casualties.' He anticipated that he would get 'a very large proportion back' but, with normal reinforcements of 'about 2,400 per month

115 Diary 1916, 5 August. LHCMA, Haig Diaries MF 858, 5 August 1916.
116 AWM4 1/29/7 – August 1916, Headquarters I ANZAC Corps, 7 August.
117 AWM 3DRL/3376 7/1 Part 1, Letters by Birdwood to Sir George Pearce, letter, 14 August 1916.
118 Bean, *The Official History of Australia in the War of 1914-1918, Volume III*, 726-28; AWM4 1/29/7 Part 1 – August 1916, Headquarters I ANZAC Corps, Summary of Operations 4-11 August.
119 Sheffield and Bourne, *Douglas Haig*, 11 August , 217-18.

per division', he expected 'to go a bit short.' He, however, hoped 'that after another fortnight or so our turn will come for a bit quieter time'. Haig had also recently raised the idea of breaking up 3rd Division for reinforcements but Birdwood strongly represented the expected views of Australia against such a proposal, writing a personal letter to the Deputy Adjutant General, who came and visited him.[120] 4th Division came out of the line on 16 August, replaced by Walker's 1st Division.

Bean wrote about this change over:

> Some, it is true, thought that the extent of the casualties in the first tour would save the division from a second; but Birdwood, who knew, and in all probability approved, the army commander's intention, never allowed these false hopes to grow. His speeches to the resting troops always adopted an invigorating tone – they had drubbed the Germans and he was sure they were all anxious to get back and kill some more. Some caught his spirit; many more listened grimly to his praises, and called them by a harsh Australian name for flattery; a certain number suspected the desire to furnish a success had caused him to pledge them to an impossible task. These – with many fine men among them – returned to the line to do their "job" but with deep bitterness in their hearts.[121]

Stevenson observed that 'In comparison with the plans and conduct of the operation at Pozières, Mouquet Farm was a disaster.' Commentators from Bean to Hampton agree. The 1st Division had been reinforced for its losses but was still only at two-thirds strength with a mixture of inexperienced and those 'recovering from their first tour'. The second tour cost 92 officers and 2,558 soldiers by 22 August when 2nd Division again relieved it.[122]

Birdwood saw Gough at least every other day and visited the divisional commander in line nearly every day. He went forward to see his brigadiers once or twice each divisional tour. He had ample opportunity to grasp the situation for himself. From his diary and the I ANZAC summaries of operations, it is clear that he was satisfied with the actions of his divisions and brigades in line. He wrote to the Governor-General: 'We have simply gradually been making ground, and eating up German trenches, and I trust killing a considerable number of Germans'.[123] Having seen 1st Division undertake its second tour, Birdwood did not change the orders to subsequent divisions. He stuck with not risking severe casualties. As tired and under-strength divisions they could hardly have done much more than they did – brigade by brigade for a few days each. Haig was clearly aware of this state of affairs and that of all the other British divisions that came into line. It was a command judgement to use the formations in this way and the Australians undoubtedly gave their all in doing their part. As Birdwood later wrote: 'The

120 AWM 3DRL/3376 7/1 Part 1, Letters by Birdwood to Sir George Pearce, Letter, 14 August 1916.

121 Bean, *The Official History of Australia in the War of 1914-1918, Volume III*, 771.

122 Stevenson, *To Win the Battle*, 154-55.

123 Diary 1916, 16 August – 3 September. AWM4 1/29/7 - August 1916, Headquarters I ANZAC Corps, Summary of Operations weeks ending 11, 19 & 26 August. AWM 3DRL/3376 6/3b, Letters by Birdwood to Sir Ronald Munro-Ferguson, Letter, Birdwood to Ferguson, 29 August 1916.

men fought hard and with unflinching courage, taking their punishment without complaint and constantly pushing the Germans back'.[124]

On 2 September Birdwood and White went to lunch with Haig, who recorded White as 'a sound capable soldier,' and Birdwood as 'useful too, though at present he is not much use for directing operations. His taste lies in making speeches to the Australian rank and file and so keeps them contented. He is wonderfully popular with them, but seems to do work which his subordinate generals should perform'. This diary entry is often quoted to demonstrate how Haig disliked Birdwood, but never with any cogent reason why Haig ultimately selected him to become an army commander. Apart from remonstrating with Birdwood, and thereby his staff and subordinates, about the poor first attempt on the OG lines, the records suggest Haig was satisfied with Birdwood, considering him as a potential army commander. In this diary entry he identified two failings: Birdwood's need to be more active in the directing of operations, and to be less involved in the work of his subordinates.

At Anzac Cove Birdwood had had a smaller force and by his constant and frequent visiting he was able to affect even tactical decisions. Operating this way, Birdwood did more than advise and thereby strayed into the tasks of juniors. When 2nd Division moved into Pozières, Birdwood should have directed more on that its own first full Western Front attack. Haig wanted such attention to detail, particularly to support new formations making their first attacks and as well as generally for complex starts to operations. The nature of such close supervision means that it has to be balanced with encouraging responsibility in one's junior commanders, as Birdwood had done at Gallipoli and would do again. Furthermore, Haig may have thought that Birdwood was not influencing operational approaches over the forty-eight-hour timespan. This is not to say that Haig could identify what changes should have been made but rather that he did not see Birdwood making such regular forward considerations. It is likely that Haig did not yet fully appreciate the wider role that Birdwood was fulfilling. Other corps commanders did not have the depth of involvement in their divisions that Birdwood had. As an example of his AIF responsibilities, he interviewed all the 'excellent lot of non-commissioned officers' replacing 'the losses of young officers.'[125] Haig's diary finished on a positive note: 'I told Birdwood how satisfied I was with what the Australians had done, and though they were going to Ypres, I had no intention of leaving them there all winter'.[126]

124 Birdwood, *Khaki and Gown*, 308.
125 AWM 3DRL/3376 7/1 Part 1, Letters by Birdwood to Sir George Pearce, letter, 14 August 1916.
126 LHCMA, Haig Diaries MF 858, 2 September 1916.

9

A long struggle on the Western Front

Before 1914 Birdwood's operational experience had been with formations of two divisions, as had landed at Anzac Cove with him. The Western Front was to be completely different. For the remainder of 1916 and of the war, Birdwood progressed and matured as a commander with an array of responsibilities far beyond his corps. He ensured appointments, promotions and further training so as to advance the most experienced individuals under his command. His relationship with his soldiers remained personal, and vital to both himself and to the morale of the whole force. Over the coming months the Australians grew into the formidable and confident force that Monash would inherit from Birdwood in June 1918, while he retained all his wider AIF responsibilities. When the final victory came, both Birdwood and the Australian Corps were at the forefront.

During the evening of 3 September 1916 Birdwood arrived back in the Ypres area where I ANZAC was taking over from the Canadian Corps and returning to Plumer's command. Next day, he saw Plumer and Walker, then Godley and McCay of 5th Division – an opportunity to discuss Fromelles. That same day he wrote to Ferguson saying 'we have come North to defend the Ypres salient – a horrible part of the line I am sorry to say during bad weather, as it is all so low-lying and badly drained. Life will of course be much quieter here than what we have been having, and I hope we shall have a chance of fully replacing our casualties, and getting ourselves together again.'[1] On 13 September he issued a corps-training circular, focusing on officer and specialist training, and detailing a 'manoeuvre area' for unit training.[2] Work on defences was also emphasised.[3] To address the requirement for junior officers he established – with the assistance of the War Office – four-month courses at Balliol College, Oxford; and Trinity College, Cambridge, to which thirty cadets were to be sent each month. He wrote to Clive Wigram, the King's assistant private secretary and an old Indian cavalry colleague of Birdwood's, that 'with the very free hand that the Australian Government have so kindly given me in all matters concerning their troops, I have arranged this on my own responsibility'

1 AWM 3DRL/3376 6/3b, Letters by Birdwood to Sir Ronald Munro-Ferguson, Letter, Birdwood to Ferguson, 5 September 1916.
2 AWM4 1/29/8 - September 1916, Headquarters 1st ANZAC Corps, GS Circular 16: Training.
3 AWM4 1/29/8 - September 1916, Appendix 5, Monthly Summary of Work on Defences, 28 September 1916.

confident of support from Mr Hughes and Pearce. He said he was 'a firm believer' in regular visits to troops:

> … seeing them as I do in this way daily, I find that the thing that affects them mostly is the shortage of numbers, … I never lose an opportunity of impressing on them and instilling the offensive spirit in them every day. I find, however, that it is really not much in doing this while numbers are still low, but directly reinforcements begin to arrive, they cheer up wonderfully, and by the time battalions are complete they are ready to believe me when I tell them that their one wish is to go and kill any amount of Germans again![4]

Bean later wrote about this period that Birdwood 'though still beloved by most of the force, incurred a marked loss of popularity in some quarters through the notion that he had too readily offered to undertake impossible tasks. His actual attitude had been to undertake in earnest what was required by those directing the British strategy.'[5] Perhaps endorsement of offensive spirit suggested to some that lessons such as thorough preparation might be forgotten in a future rush to kill Germans but as will be seen Birdwood and White did manage more responsibly the tasks placed upon their corps. Bean further recorded:

> Birdwood, straight honest little man that he is, will not tell the men that they are going to have a prolonged rest if he knows that they are not. It is unpopular to tell them that they have to go into it again, & he knows that they don't like it. But he never hides the fact from them. His attitude all through is to assume that they want to get at the Germans again & to cheer them on to do it. "Well, boys, having a good rest, eh?" Their faces drop at this but he never lets them see that he notices it & he never varies his attitude. Occasionally he says, "I wish I could tell you that you were going to have a complete rest now – but we've got the Germans on the run now & we can't afford to let them stop running. We have to hit them & hit them & hit them again" – he says in his quiet way.[6]

'Though still beloved by most of the force,' is still a fine accolade for a commander. Birdwood continuously saw the impact of his decisions at dressing stations, and hospitals, and so had to withstand and cope with such pressure.

Birdwood constantly visited all his troops in the new area by car, on horseback or on foot. Behind the divisions the AIF had its own casualty clearing stations and general hospitals. At these Birdwood would see the progress of the injured but his highest priority was the fighting units, to judge both the battalion and brigade commanders, and any officers that would take their places. He invited many of his commanders to join him over dinner. As Haig had said that Birdwood's corps would be returning to the Somme, making up the loss of 23,000 men was

4 AWM 3DRL/3376 11/2, Letters written by Birdwood to Lord Clive Wigram, Letter, 16 September 1916.
5 Bean, *The Official History of Australia in the War of 1914-1918*, 876-77.
6 AWM 3DRL606/60/1, Records of C E W Bean, Diary September-October 1916, 5-6.

an urgent task, and Birdwood produced his own Statement on Reinforcements.[7] The state of affairs continued to worsen and it was becoming clear that the steady 'normal reinforcements' of '2,400 per month per division' was not going to take place or if it did, not be sufficient to meet the shortfall. He summarised the situation to the Governor-General, suggesting that around 11,000 of the 20,000 reinforcements in England might be 'sufficiently trained' to be sent out reasonably rapidly. Birdwood stated that his next port of call had been Egypt, where he believed there were a 'large number of surplus reinforcements' but General Murray, in Birdwood's own words, '(perhaps naturally) said he could not spare them.' Birdwood had cabled Pearce to see if things might be overturned but this attempt failed as well.[8] By this time the idea, raised by Haig in mid-August, of breaking up 3rd Division into reinforcement drafts had faded. Monash, commanding 3rd Division, had argued that the division was being trained from scratch as a complete entity and it was not 'training personnel as drafts' – 'a different procedure.' His arguments held sway and consequently only a third of the troops were released for training as draftees. These steps would release 2,800 men for France by the end of September.[9] The last option considered by Birdwood was more reinforcements from Australia. All these demands were mingled with the political turmoil in Australia and the pressure for conscription.

The Governor-General had written to Birdwood on 12 July stating that: 'I am personally now in favour of conscription. Even if men could not all be sent to the front it w[oul]d have a good moral effect. The Australian slacker is very slack & is unlikely to be anything else without compulsion.'[10] On 31 July Prime Minister Hughes, arrived back in Australia from his travels and Ferguson wrote to Birdwood: 'Hughes returned in the nick of time. There is a shortage of 10,000 men for the July and August recruiting on the 11,000 a month scale of reinforcements.' Ferguson had a talk with 'Hughes before he retired into the seclusion of his Cabinet and caucus.' The Australian Government had received a demand for reinforcements on 24 August in a cablegram from the British Army Council recommending 'that in addition to the normal monthly reinforcements [15 per cent of infantry strength] a special draft of 20,000 infantry be sent as soon as possible' to make good the current deficit and restore 3rd Division. Additionally, for three months the reinforcements should be increased from 15 to 25 per cent that is to about 16,500. The Governor-General delayed posting his letter to Birdwood to await the outcome of the Prime Minister's caucus and next day added that the decision had been taken to hold a referendum on conscription in October.[11] On 23 September the Australian High Commissioner, Andrew Fisher, came to France to see Birdwood, with Colonel Robert Anderson, Commandant of the AIF Headquarters, 'regarding the taking of the referendum.' Birdwood wrote reassuringly to Pearce that all would be well. Birdwood 'had at first thought that every man would have voted blindly for universal service, but I now find that this is not likely to be the case, ... What many men tell me is something as follows: "We were three brothers. Two of us came out here, and

7 AWM 3DRL/2316, Monash, Sir John, Personal Files Book 13, 1 July-16 August 1916, Statement on Reinforcements, 15 August 1916.
8 AWM 3DRL/3376 7/1 Part 1, Letters by Birdwood to Sir George Pearce, letter, 14 August 1916. AWM 3DRL/3376 6/3a, Letters by Birdwood to Sir Ronald Munro-Ferguson, letter, 29 August 1916.
9 AWM 3DRL/2316, Monash, Sir John, Personal Files Book 13, 16 August - 30 September 1916, Correspondence: War Office 18 August; 3rd Australian Division 21, 28 & 30 August and 1 September; and AIF Depots in UK 31 August 1916.
10 AWM 3DRL/3376 6/3b, Letters by Birdwood to Sir Ronald Munro-Ferguson, Letter, 12 July 1916.
11 AWM 3DRL/3376 6/3b, 29 August 1916.

one has been killed, while the last brother is now at home looking after the family. I certainly do not want to see my remaining brother out here."' Birdwood also added that he and Anderson had agreed that it would 'be practically impossible to send out the complete Australian Act [detailing the referendum] and he therefore asked Anderson 'to prepare a small resume [*sic*] of it.'[12] For Fisher's last two days, the journalist and Hughes' confidant Keith Murdoch joined the visit. Subsequently Birdwood and Murdoch had a regular exchange of correspondence but their relationship would become rather acrimonious in early 1918.

Having spent a month ensuring his corps was settled back around Ypres and its training underway, Birdwood went back to England to see his wife and family and satisfy himself about the administrative arrangements for the AIF in the UK, that would see them through to the end of the war. In March 1915, an AIF Intermediate Base Depot had been established in Egypt.[13] Its first Commander, Colonel Sellheim, detailed its formation, organisation and function in a comprehensive memorandum. This same organisation supported the Australians ashore at Gallipoli and in January 1916 received them back in Egypt.[14] There, Birdwood reorganised the AIF with 'a special, small staff of four officers in my capacity of Commandant of the AIF, with which I have been able to work the whole of this reorganization ...'[15] Birdwood took this small team to France. From May 1915, Australian casualties 'had been 'indiscriminately mixed with British and other troops, and evacuated in several directions – to Egypt, Malta, and England. Reaching England, these casualties entered the UK-wide military medical network that would later encompass the Australian Hospitals in the UK but no administrative arrangements existed to support matters Australian, so everything devolved on the High Commissioner's office, in particular on the Military Adviser, Lieutenant Colonel Buckley. The first AIF Base Depot had been established in Weymouth, with Sir Newton Moore as its Commandant.[16] These organisations grew over subsequent months. New and larger offices needed for the London-based headquarters were found in Horseferry Road.[17] In May 1916 the Administrative Headquarters from Egypt arrived in England, followed in June by Reinforcement troops. These arrivals 'terminated the High Commissioner's organization and transferred to the AIF the responsibility for the management of the troops in the United Kingdom'.[18] Birdwood thereafter assumed individual responsibility for all aspects of the administrative command of the AIF. His senior Indian Army appointments were a preparation for this. Moore remained in command of the AIF Depots in the UK until 30 April 1917, by which time the AIF Depots in UK organisation included: five Training Depots, consisting of sixteen Training Battalions with an

12 AWM 3DRL/3376 7/1 Part 1, Letters by Birdwood to Sir George Pearce, letter, 25 September 1916.
13 AWM4 1/28/4 - March 1915, Administrative Staff, Headquarters, Australian and New Zealand Army Corps, Orders by Lieut-General W. R. Birdwood, 19 March 1915.
14 AWM 3DRL/2316, Monash, Sir John, Personal Files Book 2, 1-11 April 1915, Memorandum on the formation, organisation and functions of the AIF Intermediate Base in Egypt, 7 April 1915.
15 TNA 30/57/64: Letter from Birdwood to Lieutenant Colonel Oswald Fitzgerald, Military Secretary to Lord Kitchener, 17 March 1916.
16 AWM 1/66/1 – May 1915 - October 1917, General Officer Commanding AIF Depots in UK, Report on AIF Depots in the UK.
17 AWM 1/66/1 – May 1915 - October 1917, Extracts from Sixth Annual Report of the High Commissioner of the Commonwealth, January 1916.
18 AWM 1/66/1 – May 1915 - October 1917, General Officer Commanding AIF Depots in UK, Report on AIF Depots in the UK.

overall capacity of over 35,000; thirty-two specialised training units and sections; and four Command Depots which received discharged medical cases, 'allotted according to the probable duration of their disabilities.'[19]

Birdwood went to 'the country without appearing in London,' as he 'was particularly anxious to avoid being called at this time to give evidence before either the Dardanelles or Mesopotamian Commission.'[20] He gave his views to the Governor-General:

> What I feel is that there is nothing whatever I can say that is going to help win this war, and that is all we want keep our thoughts on at present, while one might be dragged into saying things, which would only hurt other people's feelings and cause general recriminations without doing any good.

He believed 'the Mesopotamian people' wanted to get hold of him regarding 'Indian military administration' as 'a certain number of people headed by Lord Curzon' wished to throw responsibility for any failures there onto 'the system inaugurated by Lord Kitchener.' Birdwood while acknowledging that 'there were failures' thought that these could be traced to the 'want of judgement of individuals' but 'the system was by no means to blame.'[21] For five days he was at Thurlby Hall, the home of his father-in-law, where his wife Jenny and his elder daughter Nancy were staying.[22] Birdwood then risked one full day in London, seeing AIF HQ, the High Commissioner, Sir Ian Hamilton regarding the Dardanelles Commission, Lady Plumer, Lady Godley, and a number of War Office personalities including Robertson. He arranged 'a long talk with Lloyd George [Secretary of State for War after Kitchener's death], who has certainly an interesting and fascinating personality, and I do hope things will go well, but I rather gather there is just inclined to be a little friction between him and the military staff. I trust, however, that both will have sufficient common-sense to avoid this spreading in any way.'[23] Birdwood left promptly the next day to visit the AIF Depots in the UK: Moore and his HQ at Tidworth; 1st Division training battalions at Perham Down; and Monash and 3rd Division staff at Larkhill. Then on 15 October, he and his wife motored over to Bristol to see Christopher at Clifton and to 'Mrs Bush's hospital across the Downs & saw the Australian sick there.'[24]

Back in London, Birdwood found Bean, with 'an urgent line there from Mr Hughes PM Australia asking me to do my best to help the men's vote *re* the referendum, so wired putting off the elections to be held tomorrow & made out a message from myself.' He later explained to Ferguson that he 'tried to avoid doing either the politician or the general, for I feel it would be so fatal in every way if it could be thought in Australia that the men were being told to

19 AWM 1/66/2 – July 1916 – April 1917, General Officer Commanding AIF Depots in UK, Report on the Administration of AIF Depots in the UK 1916 – 1917.

20 His attendance at the Commission is covered on pages 177-9.

21 AWM 3DRL/3376 6/3b, Letters by Birdwood to Sir Ronald Munro-Ferguson, Letter, 20 October 1916.

22 Following three centuries in the care of the Bromhead family, Thurlby Hall was sold in late 2015.

23 AWM 3DRL/3376 6/3b, Letters by Birdwood to Sir Ronald Munro-Ferguson, Letter, 20 October 1916.

24 The full story of how a beautiful house in Bristol, owned by a rich Australian, became a 100-bed hospital that ultimately treated more than 2,000 soldiers is told in Chris Stephens, *Bristol's Australian Pioneer* (Bristol: Bristol Books CIC, 2016).

vote by order of their general.'[25] Birdwood had resisted requests from Lloyd George and Keith Murdoch to intervene but he felt he could not refuse the Australian Prime Minister, who said that 'opposition to conscription in Australia was due to the formidable intrigues of the ultra-socialists & the Fenians; & that everything depended upon the lead which our force in France gave to Australia.' Hughes 'called on Birdwood, with all the earnestness he could put into the cable, to put aside precedent & to use his great influence with the troops to get them to carry conscription by a big majority.'[26] Birdwood 'at once dictated a message asking the troops to vote according to their consciences, but telling them of the considerations, perhaps better known to him than to them, which rendered urgent the need for reinforcements.'[27] He also sent a telegram to Hughes, avoiding a blatant political statement, expressing the 'need of reinforcements' … 'to finish enemy quickly, so that we may sooner return to those we voluntarily came away to shield'.[28] Birdwood travelled back to France and to 'much office work as I found many moves on referendum very trying. Mr Hughes evidently very anxious indeed about it.'[29] Murdoch also returned to France and saw Haig who 'saw no objection to civilians going round and expressing Mr Hughes' views (or any other Australian views) and getting opinions expressed in a resolution.'[30] Polling duly took place. In the end the AIF voted for conscription 'only by 72,399 against 58,894' but in Australia itself 'the anti-conscriptionists won by the narrowest of margins, some 72,476 votes in an electorate of 2.3 million.'[31] The Governor-General later wrote that 'As to the cable from our little PM, it placed you in a serious difficulty, out of which you came very well.'[32] Birdwood had astutely handled the political pressures on himself in a military post. The provision of reinforcements continued as an issue of concern between Birdwood, the Governor-General and Pearce for the remainder of 1916.

Birdwood told the Governor-General that he was 'glad to say we have gradually nearly refilled our battalions, and all are again fit and keen, though there are many changes among officers and men.'[33] I ANZAC was now preparing to move back to the Somme. This was not welcomed by the Australian soldiers and did not assist the referendum vote.[34] The Corps would now consist of the four Australian divisions then in France. Divisions started moving into line – Flers to Gueudecourt – ten kilometres south of Bapaume, on 21 October and I ANZAC took over on 30 October. The ground was appalling:

25 Diary 1916, 14-15 October. AWM 3DRL/3376 6/3b, Letters by Birdwood to Sir Ronald Munro-Ferguson, Letter, 20 October 1916. AWM 3DRL606/60/1, Records of C E W Bean, Diary, October 1916, 21-23.
26 AWM 3DRL606/60/1, Records of C E W Bean, Diary, October 1916, 15.
27 Bean, *The Official History of Australia in the War of 1914-1918, Volume III*, 890-91. Birdwood also gave assurances regarding brothers.
28 Birdwood to Hughes, cable 19 Oct 1916, WM Hughes Papers, 1538/20/197, NLA.
29 Diary 1916, 17 October.
30 Sheffield and Bourne (eds.), *Douglas Haig*, 242.
31 Bean, *The Official History of Australia in the War of 1914-1918, Volume III*, 892; Carl Bridge, *William Hughes* (London: Haus Publishing, 2011), 45.
32 AWM 3DRL/3376 6/3b, Letters by Birdwood to Sir Ronald Munro-Ferguson, Letter, 20 October 1916.
33 AWM 3DRL/3376 6/3b, Letters by Birdwood to Sir Ronald Munro-Ferguson, Letter, 20 October 1916.
34 Bean had stated that 'it will affect the vote on conscription,' AWM 3DRL606/60/1, Records of C E W Bean, Diary September - October 1916, 130-1.

> The state of the country is truly awful and the whole area forward of Fricourt Chateau is a sea of mud. … The communications trenches keep falling in for lack of revetting material, which the means of communication and the difficulties of transport make almost impossible to get up to the front line. The transport horses are suffering a good deal from overwork and most of the GS wagons require 6 to 8 horses to pull them through the mud.[35]

The weather necessitated postponements to attacks by various formations. On 8 November, Haig visited and went for a ride with White, telling White 'that when talking to the Duke of Connaught he [Haig] had told him he considered the Australians about the best disciplined troops he had & when the Duke expressed surprise, he said – Yes – as when ordered to attack they invariably did so & there were no questions about it.'[36] The final Australian attack of the year took place on 14 November.[37] Haig ended the Battle of the Somme on 18 November. Bean's history recorded the ending of the Australian attacks with: 'The morale of the AIF was never low; … but this period represented the bottom of the curve.'[38] Birdwood's challenge now was to maintain and then increase the effectiveness of his corps through the coming winter.

Birdwood now issued his directions on training. As well as GHQ and Army schools, a Corps School was established 'for the purpose of training Lewis Gunners and Stokes Mortar personnel,' and each division was to establish its own divisional school.[39] 1st Division directed that 'training of companies and battalions in the attack will occupy a prominent place. The organisation of the attack in waves, the formation and assembly of the waves and the working out of details in such a manner as will permit the development of the full strength of the unit in a single blow are to be carefully considered and practised.' It was noted that 'the experience of the 2nd Division on 14th Novr has again emphasised the necessity to train the troops to press up close under the artillery barrage.'[40] Birdwood's focus on maintaining the initiative and killing the enemy was apparent down the training chain, strongly reflecting his own thorough training as a young officer.

Senior officer casualties also challenged Birdwood, who wrote to Pearce that 'In all our fighting near Pozières we had not a single brigadier touched, and I think only one commanding officer injured.' Recently Brigadier Glasfurd had been killed and Brigadier Paton severely injured. Two commanding officers had been killed and two, having lost the confidence of their divisional commanders, removed from command by Birdwood. General Cox had been notified about moving in January to India and Brigadier Maclagan was going to England to bring his fighting experience to bear as Inspector of Infantry, as Birdwood was keen to 'send good men to do their training' in order to get good results. He instituted 'a regular turnover of officers for training battalions each month, the intention being that no individual shall stay with a training battalion

35 AWM4 1/50/8 Part 1 - October 1916, Headquarters 5th Australian Division, 27 October.

36 Diary 1916, 8 November.

37 Bean, *The Official History of Australia in the War of 1914–1918, Volume III*, 927, 28 & 31.

38 Ibid., 940.

39 AWM4 1/29/11 – December 1916, Headquarters 1st ANZAC Corps, GS Circular Training – Preliminary Instructions, 10 November.

40 AWM4 1/42/22 - November 1916, Headquarters 1st Australian Division, GS Memo 78, Appendix 14; 1st Division's school operated from November 1916 until 1 May 1917, training 802 officers and NCOs, see Robert Stevenson, *To Win the Battle*, 101-02.

for more than six months.' Birdwood was adamant that people needed the right experience and even Blamey, the successful 1st Division GSO 1, was appointed to command a battalion so that he should have 'an opportunity of proving himself a leader or commander of men.' In this respect Birdwood was still not totally convinced about Legge. He was 'doing better now,' but Birdwood wished 'he had more of the personal factor which engenders complete confidence in all those serving under him.'[41] By the end of 1916 he was informing the Governor-General that there was no let-up as the 'cold, damp and mud finds out and gets to the bottom of any man who is not really strong and young.' McCay had 'stuck it most manfully' but 'had to be evacuated to England.' Legge, 'too, was bowled over by one of those bad attacks of influenza.' Birdwood was not too distressed to lose him, as he did not carry 'the complete confidence of all those under him' and his division was not 'in a high state of efficiency.' Birdwood selected Hobbs vice McCay and Holmes vice Cox. Replacing Legge, Birdwood felt that he 'had not an Australian officer on whom I could confidently lay hands to command a division.' MacClagan was unfit. Birdwood selected Smyth who had been commanding 1st Brigade since just after the Landings. Chauvel and others had urged Birdwood to select Smyth first for promotion.[42] These appointments were generally very successful, being based on performance in a command position. In addition, Birdwood endeavoured to ensure that commanders received personal direction.

The year 1916 ended for I ANZAC back on the Somme, having faced some further hard fighting. Plans made at Chantilly in November for joint allied attacks early in 1917 were thrown into disarray somewhat by the replacement of Joffre by General Nivelle as Commander-in-Chief of the French Armies, with differing ideas based on his recent successes around Verdun. He proposed a main French attack, north across the Aisne, with two secondary attacks – one British around Arras. To allow the French to position the required weight of forces, Rawlinson's Fourth Army was to extend its front further south and consequently I ANZAC widened its frontage. Soon all four of its divisions were in the line.[43] This continued until the end of February when the line was adjusted to have three divisions forward and one in reserve.[44] The wet and increasingly cold weather remained the greatest challenge of all. At the beginning of 1917 Birdwood returned to England, visiting the AIF Administrative HQ, the tens of thousands of Australians under training, and the wounded and convalescing Australian officers and soldiers in five different hospitals.[45] At the War Office he was told 'that they were about to press Australia and New Zealand to provide a 6th and 2nd Division respectively, … to have as strong an army as possible by the early autumn.'[46] Birdwood awaited the outcome of this issue, concerned about reinforcements in general. Back in France Birdwood was 'feeling a bit chesty.' When White returned from his own leave on 16 February, Birdwood went on two weeks' convalescence to the French Riviera where a network of homes had been loaned by

41 AWM 3DRL/3376 7/1 Part 1, Letters by Birdwood to Sir George Pearce, letter, 30 November 1916.

42 AWM 3DRL/3376 6/3b, Letters by Birdwood to Sir Ronald Munro-Ferguson, letter, 31 December 1916.

43 Diary 1916, 12 December. AWM4 1/29/12 – January 1917, Headquarters 1st ANZAC Corps, Appendix A, Corps Order No 90, 17 January 1917

44 AWM4 1/29/13 – February 1917, Headquarters 1st ANZAC Corps, Appendix A, Corps Order No 100, 21 February 1917.

45 Diary 1917, 3-14 January.

46 AWM 3DRL/3376 6/4, Letters by Birdwood to Sir Ronald Munro-Ferguson, Letter, 17 January 1917.

wealthy individuals for convalescent use.[47] Birdwood soon recovered in such 'beautiful' and 'lovely' surroundings and started work on Dardanelles Commission papers. I ANZAC, now back with Gough's Fifth Army, was active in Birdwood's absence and reports included: enemy forward post was found unoccupied; no enemy were encountered; and, enemy did not appear to be occupying forward posts. Birdwood returned to his HQ, with just time to meet with Gough, and assemble his papers before leaving for London.

The Dardanelles Commission of Enquiry arose due to the pressure on the Asquith government of two major military defeats – Gallipoli and Kut-al-Amara – 'the second major reverse provoked the enquiry into the first.'[48] Asquith announced both commissions in late July 1916. In August Hamilton, preparing his position, had written to Birdwood that 'it might be well for you and I to talk over the broad line to be taken before this blessed Dardanelles Commission'. Hamilton emphasised 'there is nothing for either of us to say anything than exactly what happened. The only thing is that to do this sounds a good deal simpler that it really is with men of legal acumen cross-examining one'.[49] Birdwood replied trusting 'that I shall be able to get out of appearing in any way before either commission'. He was 'extremely sorry that Nick [Field Marshal Lord Nicholson] is on either commission. After the terrible fiasco he made of the last one over which he presided in India, I should have thought that Government would have been wise enough to refrain from ever putting him on another.'[50] While on leave in January 1917 Birdwood had seen Hamilton, who later decided 'to open up my heart to you on the subject of your coming examination.' He was particularly vexed over Monro's recommendation to evacuate and Birdwood's reluctance to take over from Monro. Hamilton encouraged Birdwood to stress 'the very slender basis of personal knowledge or experience on which Monro's advice for evacuation was based,' and to state firmly how little time Munro had spent on the Peninsula.[51] Birdwood made a measured and careful reply, adding: 'I am also most anxious not to say anything I can help against others.' On arrival in England Birdwood went 'to Sir Ian Hamilton to see Dardanelles papers.'[52] On 6 March Birdwood appeared before the Dardanelles Commission at the House of Lords 'from 12 - 4.45 pm' and afterwards 'dined with the Ian Hamiltons'.[53]

The Commission's Chairman, Sir William Pickford, a Lord Justice of Appeal, opened the questioning with enquiries about Birdwood's reconnaissance in mid-February 1915 and his views on landing options. Birdwood's answers were short and precise when that sufficed, but when a fuller explanation seemed appropriate, he gave one, with personal observations on his own judgements. Once the questioning moved on to the period after Hamilton's arrival, Birdwood kept his focus on his own Anzac responsibilities and was careful not to comment on others, for example: 'but that I should qualify again by saying that I do not for a moment criticise Sir Ian

47 TNA WO 222/213: Report on the Convalescent Homes for the Nursing Staff in France, Section 6: The Riviera.
48 John Lee, *A Soldier's Life: General Sir Ian Hamilton 1853-1947* (London: Macmillan, 2000), 231.
49 LHCMA, Hamilton papers 8/1/1, Papers relating to the Dardanelles Commission, 1916-1919, letter, Hamilton to Birdwood, 4 August 1916.
50 LHCMA, Hamilton papers 8/1/1, Letter Birdwood to Hamilton, 6 August 1916.
51 LHCMA, Hamilton papers 8/1/1, Letter, Hamilton to Birdwood, 27 January 1917.
52 Jenny Macleod, 'General Sir Ian Hamilton and the Dardanelles Commission', *War in History*, 8(4) (2001), 418-441. Although highlighting Hamilton's 'secret orchestration' of witnesses, Macleod shows that Birdwood did not fully follow advice, perhaps a reflection of Birdwood's high principles.
53 Diary 1917, 5 and 6 March.

Hamilton's position.' The commission had accepted the contents of the various dispatches and so there was no questioning on either 'the detail of the landings' or 'the behaviour of the troops.' Birdwood did state that he 'never intended to land at Gaba Tepe' and confirmed that he was 'going for the Sari Bahr Ridge.' Turning to casualty evacuation, Birdwood emphasised that then it had been an army responsibility and although 'before leaving Egypt I had asked to be given a DDMS. That was refused.' Another personal representation was for canteen stores. Again, Birdwood had only limited success. At this stage Birdwood was less than half way through his interrogation when the subject moved to the August offensive. He returned to making concise answers. Questions became more based on quotations from previous witnesses and Birdwood, who had seen these past evidential statements from Hamilton, was unfazed by this. If he knew, he was firm in his answers but circumspect if he did not. Pickford handed over to the other Commission members to lead.

Mackenzie, the New Zealand High Commissioner, led off and soon turned to the evacuation. He remarked that he had not noticed any recognition of Birdwood's feat, who less than subtly, commented that the French Government had given him two awards. Moving quickly on, Mackenzie addressed the business of Birdwood's appointment vice Monro. Birdwood stated that he 'had much hoped that this point would not come up.' He had, however, clearly done much thinking and preparation in conjunction with Hamilton's correspondence. He gave his longest answer so far. It was precise and correct and did not invite further questions of opinion. The subject turned to Suvla and suddenly Birdwood, again with lengthy answers, expressed very critical opinions of those landings. Mackenzie understandably finished with questions about Colonel Malone's death and then it was Nicholson's turn. The questions became longer and longer and Birdwood's answers became shorter and shorter. He remained totally consistent with what he had said before.

The other three Commission members present then had their turns.[54] Birdwood again strayed into statements of opinion only over the Suvla landings – once more very critical – before he finished.[55] He recorded later that 'at the conclusion of my evidence, I was told that I was one of the very few witnesses who had cast no aspersions on anyone.' He added that 'then, as ever, I had tried to realise how fatally easy it is to be wise after the event!'[56] His bout of sickness had given him an opportunity to refresh himself physically and to focus mentally on the challenge of thorough questioning. In his own eyes, he had done himself justice and the Commission did not feature further in his own writings. The remainder of Birdwood's five-day trip was focused on forming the 6th Division, starting with a new 16th Brigade, with Antill as commander, who had come from Egypt to command 2nd Brigade, fallen ill but was now available.[57]

On returning to his HQ Birdwood found that the German withdrawal had continued at a brisk pace. Aggressive patrolling had discovered that the enemy had evacuated two defence lines forward of Bapaume and now 2nd Division was to 'advance and consolidate' and push posts 'to

54 In order Walter Roch MP, Stephen Gwynn MP and Admiral of the Fleet Sir William May.

55 LHCMA, Hamilton papers 8/2/7, Papers relating to the Dardanelles Commission, 1916-1919, typed copy of Birdwood's evidence, with handwritten comments, paras 21268-70, 72, 88-99 & 212348; AWM 3DRL/3376 11/3, Dardanelles and Mesopotamia Commissions Reports, Final issued version of Birdwood's evidence.

56 Birdwood, *Khaki and Gown*, 311-2.

57 AWM 3DRL/3376 7/1 Part 1, Letters by Birdwood to Sir George Pearce, letter, 11 March 1917.

maintain contact with the enemy.' 5th Division was advance in line with 2nd. [58] Around 6:30 a.m. on Saturday 17 March Australian patrols entered Bapaume.[59] German 'troops and transports were seen slowly disappearing to the east.'[60] Birdwood then instructed each of the forward two divisions to create a brigade strength advance guard, which were not to operate further and further in advance of the main body. The two brigadiers chosen were John Gellibrand and Harold 'Pompey' Elliott of the 2nd and 5th Divisions.[61] Each had a brigade strength force with a field artillery battery and some light horse. They were to obtain and maintain contact with the enemy, while keeping links with flanking forces. Elliott showed his impetuosity when suffering a setback at Beaumetz and was restrained by Hobbs, who cancelled an imminent but rash attack.[62] Gellibrand initially outpaced Elliott and 'others on the British front.' As Gellibrand approached Lagnicourt, Gough pushed for more progress. Gellibrand's force was about to be relieved but this was delayed. In the rush to push on, Gellibrand proposed a 'daring and ingenious plan.' His troops, however, were tired, had little training for open warfare and were to attack without close reconnaissance. It was not a success but the resulting difficult withdrawal in close contact was achieved. A secure line was established short of Lagnicourt, a village forming the rear-guard in front of the Hindenburg Line. Lagnicourt was captured on 26 March.[63]

From entering Bapaume it had been an extremely successful period for I ANZAC, during which Birdwood's diaries contain more references to White than usual. Earlier, one or other of them had been away but now they were working in tandem. Haig visited HQ I ANZAC on 30 March at Bapaume and together with Birdwood and Holmes, went to see 13th Brigade and Glasgow, whom Haig noted as 'in the Australian Light Horse first of all and is a capable commander.' Haig saw Hobbs' 5th Division and 'found the Australians everywhere in the most splendid spirits, and full of confidence.' The capture of Bapaume and 'some 20 villages after some slight skirmishes had added to their keenness'. Haig made the point 'to Birdwood and the Australian officers regarding the importance of ensuring that at the end of the war our Imperial Army is homogeneous. With this object every effort must be made to train colonial commanders & staff officers so that the Dominion Forces may be self-contained in this respect.'[64] Later Haig wrote to the King that 'the change to open warfare has especially benefited the Australians: indeed, they seem 50 per cent more efficient now, than when they were in the trenches ...' Haig's accolades crowned this successful period.

Allenby's Third Army was planning an attack in the Arras-Vimy region to distract German reserves from the major French attack in Champagne. The Hindenburg Line now ran southeast

58 AWM4 1/29/14 Part 1 – March 1917, Headquarters I ANZAC Corps, Corps Order No 109, 12 March, and Corps Order No 110, 13 March 1917.
59 AWM4 1/29/14 Part 3 – March 1917, Headquarters I ANZAC Corps, I ANZAC Summary of Operations for week ending 23 March.
60 C E W Bean, *The Official History of Australia in the War of 1914-1918, Volume IV* (Sydney: Halstead Press, 1933), 124-26.
61 Peter S Sadler, *The Paladin: A Life of Major General Sir John Gellibrand* (Melbourne: OUP, 2000), 116-27; Ross McMullin, *Pompey Elliott* (Scribe: Victoria, 2008), 265-275.
62 Bean, *The Official History of Australia in the War of 1914-1918, Volume IV*, 169-70. Diary 1917, 24 March.
63 Bean, *The Official History of Australia in the War of 1914-1918, Volume II*, 176, 79-80 and 84-86; Diary 1917, 26 March.
64 LHCMA, Haig Diaries MF 860, 30 March 1917.

from the front-line east of Arras and the German withdrawal gave the opportunity for Gough's Fifth Army to assist on the right flank of Third Army's attack, at least with artillery. By 20 March Gough, as keen as ever, was considering attacking part of the Hindenburg Line and he outlined his thinking to his two corps commanders – Birdwood and Lt Gen Edward Fanshawe, V Corps, previously commander 11th (Northern) Division under Birdwood at Gallipoli. In discussion with Haig it was agreed that Gough could seize a sector of the line with two divisions and allow the passage of a cavalry division. This would then link up with the three cavalry divisions participating in the Arras-Vimy attack. Haig also approved the allocation of some tanks to support Fifth Army. Artillery support was vital. Roads had to be repaired to move this into place and provide for transportation of ammunition. Fifth Army's attack was to conform to that of Third Army on 9 April. Gough settled on two divisions bypassing either side of Bullecourt – V Corps' 62nd Division, commanded by Walter Braithwaite, previously Hamilton's Chief of Staff at Gallipoli and Holmes' 4th Division, whose secondary objective was Riencourt, a fortified village to the rear of the Hindenburg Line.[65] The assault route to this followed a re-entrant between Bullecourt, which was to be neutralised with artillery, and Quéant, a village east of Bullecourt, which was to be screened by smoke. Both Birdwood and White were concerned about the dangers of the route and the distance to the second objective. When Gough pushed for a further 'final advance eastwards on a front of 3,000 yards and to a depth, on the right, of more than a mile,' Birdwood objected and it was dropped.[66]

By 5 April, 4th Division had advanced to the railway embankment that was to serve as the start line but patrols found that the wire remained uncut. This was reported to Gough at conference on 8 April and White estimated eight days to complete the task. The delay was accepted but the next day brought news of Allenby's initial successes. Gough was even keener to participate and the commander of the tanks allocated by GHQ gave an opening, by suggesting that the tanks should line up at night in front of the infantry and provide fire instead of the normal advancing barrage. Birdwood 'objected strongly as enormous breadth of wire was uncut, line strongly held & tanks unreliable.' He also believed that Third Army's progress was not sufficiently advanced 'to justify great losses.'[67] The order stood, so 'the troops were formed up ready to attack, but the tanks lost their way in the dark.' They were not going to make the start line until broad daylight so the attack was cancelled. A snowstorm aided the infantry's withdrawal. The attack went ahead the following morning but although the tanks were initially reported to be in position, only one made it to the Hindenburg Line. Two lines of trenches were captured with 'heavy casualties,' though 'efforts to push on to Riencourt failed.' As feared resupply parties were 'mown down by machine gun fire from Riencourt and Bullecourt.' Under a heavy barrage the attackers withdrew back to their lines.[68] 4th Division was relieved by Smyth's 2nd Division. The next day Haig sent a message: 'Please convey to the 4th Australian Division my appreciation of the great gallantry shown ....'[69]

65 Sheffield and Bourne, *Douglas Haig: war diaries and letters, 1914-1918*, 278.
66 AWM4 1/48/13 Part 2 – April 1917, Headquarters 4th Australian Division, Report on Attack against Hinderburg Line.
67 Bean, *The Official History of Australia in the War of 1914-1918, Volume IV*, 264-66.
68 Diary 1917, 9 April.
69 AWM4 1/48/13 Part 2 – April 1917, Headquarters 4th Australian Division, Appendix 47.

To the right 1st Division had advanced and early on 14 April came 'to within 1,000 yards of the Hindenburg Line with the objective of threatening that line,' but at 4 a.m. the next day the enemy attacked in strength. The war diary recounted a hard battle, the commitment of reserves and finally after heavy fighting, the regaining of the line held before the last advance of 1,000 yards.[70] The major French attack, on 16 April, stumbled and faltered within forty-eight hours but was resumed on 4 May. The British had pressed again on 3 May. 4th Australian Division attacked over a wider front down to east of Bullecourt in a repeat of 2nd Division's attack, but this time with considerable preparatory bombardment. An imposed delay had not been Gough's immediate wish but it gave the advantages of greater planning and rehearsals. The actual attack started well but heavy machine gun fire disorganised it. Each setback appeared to be resolved by a commitment of reserves or a change of barrage. This included the insertion of 7th Division to take Bullecourt which Birdwood urged on Gough as essential, and the reintroduction of brigades from 1st and 5th Divisions some of whom had thought that their turn at the front was over.[71] By 17 May Bullecourt was secured and the Germans had withdrawn north of the Hindenburg Line. The Second Battle of Bullecourt was over.[72] I ANZAC was relieved on 26 May and departed from Gough and Fifth Army.

The previous seven weeks had demonstrated again that with time to prepare, success, although costly, was possible, but once again Gough's wild haste could result in failure. Birdwood and White did protest legitimately on occasions.[73] Birdwood, despite being the AIF commander, had no right to demand that matters be referred personally to the commander-in-chief. If he had had that right, he would have had to use it carefully and judiciously, and if possible not cause any untoward friction or his even own dismissal – a difficult challenge. Birdwood, with his experience of the individuals and acknowledged ability to get on with people, might just possibly have been able to achieve it. He did note in a later letter to Pearce that being 'an officer of the Indian Army, I am entirely under the India Office <u>except for the present war</u> [my emphasis], and am therefore quite independent of the War Office', which, 'I think, fully realise this.' He still had to tread carefully, respecting the chain of command, and it was also less than a year since he had lost his powerful patron.

1st, 2nd and 5th Divisions were now about to enjoy 'what was probably the longest, most complete, and most pleasant rest ever given to the British infantry in France.' This was due in part to representations by Hobbs and White to Birdwood, and then by Birdwood to Gough and thence Kiggell.[74] 4th Division, however, was moved on 12 May to II ANZAC, which participated in the attack on 7 June on Messines Ridge, where Monash's meticulous preparation ensured that 3rd Division, in its first action, acquitted itself with distinction. The following day Birdwood visited an Australian hospital full of injured from Messines and then went back to

70 AWM4 1/42/27 Part 1 – April 1917, Headquarters 1st Australian Division, Appendix 5, Report of Enemy Attack 15 April 1917.

71 AWM4 1/44/22 Part 2 – May 1917, Headquarters 2nd Australian Division, Operations against Hindenburg Line, 3-10 May 1917.

72 E M Andrews, *The Anzac Illusion* (Cambridge: CUP, 1993), 99-101 has very strong criticisms of Gough, and also Birdwood and White.

73 For further objections to Gough, and White's frustrations, see C E W Bean, *Two Men I Knew*, 151-56; Walker, *The Blood Tub*, 189-91; Robert Stevenson, *The War with Germany – The Centenary History of the Great War Vol 3* (South Melbourne: Oxford University Press, 2015), 135-37.

74 AWM 3DRL/3376 7/1 Part 2, Letters by Birdwood to Sir George Pearce, letter, 22 June 1917.

England.[75] As ever, manpower was the issue. The level of casualties meant that maintaining five divisions let alone six would be a challenge. 16th and 17th Brigades were nearing completion but it was agreed with the War Office not to proceed with an 18th. The visiting Premier of New South Wales, William Holman, told Birdwood that a further attempt at conscription might be made and so no firm decision on the use of the 6th Division brigades was taken.

Holman visited the front and was concussed when a shell exploded near his party, killing 4th Division commander Holmes. Birdwood considered Holmes to be one of the bravest of men and a great loss. When Birdwood had last said goodbye to Holmes, he commented to Holmes' staff officer, 'Mind you look after your General well, and don't let him go forward rashly and too much to the front.' Holmes had laughed and replied: 'How about yourself Sir? You must set me the example of not going about too much.'[76]

In late July, I ANZAC moved north to the Hazebrouck area as GHQ reserve and was allocated a training area suitable 'especially in wood fighting.'[77] On 29 July, Haig inspected 2nd Division, drawn up in column of brigades: 'A splendid spectacle,' and then 5th Division. Haig felt that 'the Australians have never looked better since they came to France'. He was 'greatly pleased with their bearing & evident desire of each one to do his very best to show up well at my inspection.' Haig believed that they had benefited from their training out of line for three months.[78]

On 31 July Gough's Fifth Army commenced the Third Battle of Ypres (Passchendaele). Only on Gough's left was good progress made towards the first day's third objective. Birdwood recorded the subsequent downpours, following the first day of the battle as: 'poured all day', 'still very wet' and 'pouring again all day.'[79] The battlefield was now waterlogged. On 25 August, after assaults on the key Gheluvelt Plateau and then the sub-battle of Langemarck, Haig gave command of the offensive to Plumer, with whom Birdwood and White lunched the following day. On 30 August I ANZAC joined Second Army. Plumer requested, and was granted, three weeks to prepare for his attack. His objectives were set as the Polygon Wood – Broodseinde Ridge, then facing II Corps, just transferred from Fifth Army. Its relief was essential and into its place moved I ANZAC, which would later be joined on its left flank by II ANZAC. Both corps were required to fight with two divisions in line and two in reserve, so each would require an added British division. Birdwood, knowing that the Commonwealth Government was keen that all Australians should be under one command, asked Plumer 'with Haig's consent' that I ANZAC 'be kept entirely Australian with the return to it of the 4th Division.' This was agreed and on 3 September a hard fought 4th Division, with its new commander Sinclair-Maclagan, joined three well-rested and freshly trained divisions in I ANZAC.[80]

Birdwood and White had a strong rapport with Plumer and his MGGS Harrington, who was particularly supportive of White. The two staffs also had a happy relationship, so different from

75 28 May in General Staff, Headquarters I ANZAC Corps, AWM, vol. AWM4 1/29/16 Part 1 – May 1917, Australian Imperial Force unit war diaries, 1914-18 War (1917), 31.
76 Diary 1917, 10-20 June.
77 Diary 1917, 3 & 8 July.
78 LHCMA, Haig Diaries, 29 August 1917.
79 AWM4 1/29/18 – July 1917, Headquarters 1st ANZAC Corps, 23-30 July, and GS Circular No 79 Training Areas. Bean, *The Official History of Australia in the War of 1914-1918, Volume IV*, 732.
80 Diary 1917, 1-3 August.

being in Gough's Fifth Army. I ANZAC had the chief task to attack 'the main ridge and then sidestep farther north as the ridge trended that way.' This was to be the first attack with a four-brigade frontage by I ANZAC and the largest concentration of an Australian attack in the war.[81] The orders produced by White and his team reflected thoroughness. Birdwood visited Claud Jacob, his fellow Indian Army officer and commander of II Corps, to discuss the approaches to Glencorse Wood and Polygon Wood. Plumer had issued clear 'bite and hold' instructions that each stage of the attack was to gain just 1,500 yards, built up of smaller steps, the last step to be taken by the strongest force and then dug in to face the inevitable counter-attack. These GHQ general instructions had not yet been applied in the battle. This was the opportunity for refreshed commanders and staffs to apply themselves under Birdwood's leadership and White's coordination. On 17 September Haig 'visited all Corps HQ in 2nd Army,' and at every corps he 'found officers full of confidence on the result of the forthcoming attack. Every detail had been gone into most thoroughly, and the troops most carefully trained.' Birdwood felt that Haig was 'extremely affable.' Birdwood had a 'very troubled night as the rain started at 10 pm.' Plumer called him around 11:15 to say that 'Gough wanted to postpone.' He asked for Birdwood's 'wishes.' He 'was against any postponement, as after so many dry days' he believed the ground would 'not be too bad & it would probably get worse later.' Others also wanted to postpone but Plumer decided to carry on. The rain did stop and a drying wind arose.

At 4.50 a.m. under the cover of a creeping barrage, I ANZAC attacked on a 2,000-yard front. 'The attack was completely successful. All objectives were captured, and the enemy's system was penetrated to a maximum of 1,500 yards. Posts were pushed well beyond the final objective, which was successfully consolidated', despite counter attacks.[82] Haig noted that 'very careful artillery arrangements had been made to deal with counter attacks. As the afternoon made very clear these plans worked out well.'[83] This was further credit to the Anzacs. After the successful attack on Menin Road, 4th and 5th divisions relieved 1st and 2nd Divisions by the night of 23/24 September, in readiness to take the remainder of Polygon Wood and clear the plateau on which I ANZAC was now entrenched. But on 25 September, the enemy made a serious counter-attack, particularly against 15th Brigade on the right, which continued all day. The next attack was due on 26 September and finally in the evening, the BGGS, White, told Maclagan that the attack would go ahead as planned at 05:50 and 15th Brigade would need fresh troops for the capture of the Blue line, the second of the two corps objectives. Thirty minutes after that order the Germans were counter-attacking once more. Memories of Fromelles were in the distant past and 5th Division and 15th Brigade successfully made all the necessary battalion moves. The second phase against Polygon Wood was a similar success for 4th and 5th divisions. The ridge now swung northwards, so 1st and 2nd divisions were brought in line to the left of 4th and 5th as they withdrew. In war diaries and Birdwood's own diary, all this was calmly reflected, displaying a confident professionalism in the Australian staffs. Haig visited HQ I ANZAC once more on 28 September.[84]

81 Bean, *The Official History of Australia in the War of 1914–1918, Volume IV*, 733; AWM 3DRL/3376 7/1 Part 2, Letters by Birdwood to Sir George Pearce, letter, 3 September 1917.
82 Diary 1917, 19 & 20 September.
83 LHCMA, Haig Diaries MF 860, 20 September 1917.
84 LHCMA, Haig Diaries MF 860, 28 September 1917.

As planned for the third phase, II ANZAC came in on the left with 3rd Division on the right. As a result, 3rd, 2nd and 1st Divisions were in line together.[85] With the New Zealand Division on the left of II ANZAC, four Anzac divisions were to attack together – shoulder to shoulder. Again, the orders were similar: two brigades to assault, employing one battalion to take the Red Line and two for the Blue, and for the third time the Anzac efforts were successful. 1st Division met a German attack as they advanced. The Germans 'were absolutely wiped out.' These three attacks were the high-water mark of success despite the casualty toll. Birdwood could be proud of the performance of all four divisions of his corps. The near uniform performance demonstrated the excellence of training in his corps. It was also a personal success, as every single one of the commanders at battalion level and above had been selected or approved by Birdwood. This was unique among British corps on the Western Front. Birdwood wrote to his men:

> All I think must realise that the fighting we have been through has been of an entirely satisfactory nature in that we were able to attain our objective in every one of the many attacks which we have put in, and that without a single hitch of any sort. The Army Commander has testified to this after each attack made, and we know with what appreciation the Commander-in-Chief wired to Australia regarding the results of the fighting done by her troops.[86]

Now the 'lovely weather' turned. Careful preparation transitioned to more hurried attacks.

On 9 October, the two British divisions of II ANZAC undertook the main thrust towards Passchendaele Ridge. II ANZAC's attack failed and it attacked again on 12 October with 3rd Division and the New Zealand Division. Again, it was a failure, 'owing to the bad weather and the appalling country,' and was the costliest day in New Zealand's military history. Birdwood expected the final casualty toll to be 5,000 – 6,000 per division.[87] Birdwood's letter to Pearce mentioned: 'the weather is just as bad an enemy as the Germans', and 'having to be out for hours in liquid mud is indeed a terrible trial'. On 18 October, the Canadian Corps with its four component divisions, took over from II ANZAC and finally took Passchendaele on 6 November.[88]

When winter planning commenced, Birdwood was told that his corps would consist of just three divisions, with a division going to II ANZAC. Furthermore, the two ANZAC corps would remain on the Broodseinde heights, maintaining pressure upon the enemy until a further Flanders offensive in the spring. To Birdwood the prospect of a second winter struggle against both the enemy and the mud was daunting. The Australian divisions were 18,000 men short. With the probability of 28,000 men from reinforcements and convalescents, and another 7,000 from sick and wounded still in hospital, the shortfall would be filled and 17,000 would be

85 Haig had recently inspected 3rd Division – 'a very fine body of men, parade was a great success.' The field marshal thought that 'Monash had a good head & commands his Divn well.' Monash dined with Haig that evening. See LHCMA, Haig Diaries MF 860, 22 September 1917.

86 AWM4 1/29/22 Part 2 – November 1917, Headquarters I ANZAC Corps, Appendix C, Birdwood address 12 November 1917.

87 AWM 3DRL/3376 7/1 Part 2, Letters by Birdwood to Sir George Pearce, letter, 16 October 1917. Total Australian losses among the five divisions and artillery brigades amounted to 38,000.

88 The Canadians had been allotted to Plumer rather than Gough as they 'don't work kindly under the latter.' See LHCMA, Haig Diaries MF 860, 5 October 1917.

available to face winter wastage. But the Somme winter wastage had been 25,000. If repeated, Birdwood and the Australians would face the spring offensive 8,000 men short and, as Birdwood wrote to Kiggell, 'there will be nothing behind them', until May.[89]

For some time there had been correspondence between the Australian Prime Minister and his Defence Minister with the Army Council about bringing together all the Australian Forces. On 29 October Birdwood and White met Kiggell to discuss the organisation of the AIF, and afterwards lunched with Haig.[90] Birdwood proposed that one of the divisions be withdrawn to act as a depot division and the corps itself be concentrated in a quiet sector. With renewed fighting in the spring the most depleted division could be replaced by the depot formation and so on. Haig accepted this proposal. The Australian Corps, as it would be named, would consist of 1st, 2nd, 3rd and 5th Divisions, and be transferred to the Messines sector. The 4th, welcoming a long rest, would move to near Boulogne. Birdwood confirmed all these arrangements with Pearce, noting that 'this placing of one division in reserve is only a stepping-stone to the total abolition of a division, unless reinforcements come forward much better.'[91]

On 7 November, Hughes announced the second referendum for 20 December, proposing a ballot to conscript men whenever the monthly enlistments fell below 7,000. Birdwood wanted to be confident of the vote, 'as I just dread even the possibility of having to break up divisions here.'[92] The proposal was again lost, this time by a larger majority, despite the soldiers voting in favour but by a smaller majority.[93] Birdwood felt 'humiliated' by the result.[94] To the Governor-General, he commented that 'I really felt inclined to say "*Morituri te salutamus*" [Those who are about to die salute you], for that I am afraid is what it must come to eventually.' But he went on to say that all must just do their best. He acknowledged Munro-Ferguson's congratulations on his promotion to General and his appointment as ADC General to the King, explaining that the Mesopotamia Commission report had resulted in the retirements of two senior Indian Army generals and that 'the senior Lt-General has by Royal Warrant to move up to fill a vacancy in the establishment, and no selection comes in.' 1917 ended with Birdwood's Australians spending their fourth Christmas on active service a very long way from home.[95] Six brigades were now in the front line and in the previous ten days Birdwood had walked round every single battalion and visited every artillery gun-pit.[96]

The Australian Corps came into being on New Year's Day and Birdwood's diary commenced with the usual summary of his personal military position. His Corps had 'all Australian units concentrated in it' and together with his UK organisation, he had nearly 300,000 under him as GOC AIF. The 4th Division, which had started as the depot division, had been moved south in

89 AWM 3DRL/3376 7/1 Part 2, Letters by Birdwood to Sir George Pearce, letter, 2 December with attached letter from Birdwood to Kiggell dated 27 October 1917.
90 Dairy 1917, 29 October. LHCMA, Haig Diaries MF 860, 29 October 1917.
91 AWM 3DRL/3376 7/1 Part 2, Letters by Birdwood to Sir George Pearce, letter, 5 November 1917.
92 AWM 3DRL/3376 6/4, Letters by Birdwood to Sir Ronald Munro-Ferguson, letter, 10 December 1917.
93 Jeffrey Grey, *A Military History of Australia* (Cambridge: Cambridge University Press, 1999), 111.
94 Diary 1917, 22 December.
95 Birdwood laid out his policy for the coming winter to all his commanders in a directive, 7 November 1917, attached to AWM 3DRL/3376 7/1 Part 2, Letters by Birdwood to Sir George Pearce, letter, 9 November 1917.
96 Diary 1917, 21-29 December. The weather was cold, snowy and windy.

early December, as a reserve division for Third Army, but was about to return to the Australian Corps. With Plumer's departure to Italy the Australians were now under Rawlinson's army command.[97] The performance of the four I ANZAC divisions had demonstrated the excellence of their summer training and again training was the priority. The problems of winter living remained serious, though there were far fewer sick cases than before, so the strength of the Divisions increased. On 13 January Birdwood took temporary command of Fourth Army for two weeks when Rawlinson went on leave. Birdwood stayed at his own HQ. Rawlinson was soon to move again. In mid-February Birdwood noted that 'Robertson had resigned as CIGS & Henry Wilson to succeed him' and then 'Rawly was to succeed Henry Wilson at Versailles', where a Supreme War Council had been created with a permanent British representative. Birdwood was again in acting command of Fourth Army until Plumer returned from Italy. This time Birdwood located himself at the Army HQ 'as Chief wanted me to live there.' On 1 March Haig met Birdwood at the 'boundary between 4th & 5th Armies' and after lunch, examined the defensive lines south of Messines together. Haig found them 'already very strong.' The next day Birdwood attended his first conference of army commanders.[98] There is nothing to suggest that Haig was other than pleased with Birdwood as both commander of the Australian Corps or as an acting army commander.

Haig had, however, written to his wife comparing the Canadians – 'really fine disciplined soldiers, and so smart and clean' – to the Australians – 'not nearly so efficient.' Haig added that he 'put this down to Birdwood, who, instead of facing the problem, has gone in for the easier way of saying that everything is perfect and making himself as popular as possible.'[99] A few days later, Haig responded to criticism of Godley in the New Zealand House of Representatives, correcting the positive comparison to Birdwood and his Australians regarding discipline.[100] Either of the two comments is often cited to illustrate Haig's low opinion of Birdwood but instead Haig seems to have been well satisfied with Birdwood, while frustrated by Australia's determination not to apply the death sentence.

Discipline – particularly the number of courts martial, offences of desertion and absences without leave – had been a challenging and continuous issue for Birdwood. The problem was not just one of numbers but of adverse comparison with the British Army, Canadians and New Zealanders, descending in that order.[101] Robert Stevenson rather unfortunately but perhaps aptly entitled his excellent chapter of the AIF's disciplinary record: '*Bad Boy of the Imperial Family*.' It was after Pozières 'that desertion and absence became endemic in the AIF.'[102] Under Section 98 of the Commonwealth Defence Act the death sentence, a punishment for desertion,

97 Diary 1918, 1 January.

98 Diary 1918, 13 January; 18, 20 21 and 22 February; 1 & 2 March. LHCMA, Haig Diaries MF 860, 1 & 2 March 1918.

99 LHMCA, Haig Diaries MF 860, letter to wife, 28 February 1918.

100 LHCMA, Haig Diaries MF 860, 3 March 1918.

101 For a comprehensive analysis of Canadian discipline see Kenneth Radley, *Get Tough, Stay Tough: Shaping The Canadian Corps, 1914-1918* (Solihull: Helion & Company, 2014), 89-173 and 372. For New Zealand see Christopher Pugsley, *The ANZAC Experience* (Auckland: Reed Publishing, 2004), 148-64.

102 Stevenson, *The War with Germany, Vol 3*, 104-27. For a comprehensive overview of Australian discipline in UK, see R T Beckett, 'An imperial force? : the AIF in the United Kingdom, 1914-1918'(PhD thesis, King's College London, 2008), 291-331.

could not be carried out until confirmed by the Governor-General.[103] In effect the sentence was unavailable and furthermore politically difficult when trying to win conscription referendums. Birdwood first wrote to the Governor-General about these issues in March 1917, regretting 'the loafers' who having 'discovered that imprisonment is the only punishment that can be inflicted' deliberately desert when their battalion is ordered to the front.[104] They were also confident that imprisonment 'would be remitted as soon as the war was over'. Birdwood also raised absenteeism, which he wondered perhaps was 'due to the national character.' He had some sympathy with those who had fought hard, been relieved, got drunk in the nearest French town and then absented themselves, believing that it was hard to lose 'the customs of a lifetime during two years' soldiering.'[105]

General Holmes and Brigadier-General Glasgow both wrote to Birdwood stating that 'if in one or two cases the penalty of death were actually inflicted, the effect throughout' the AIF would be immediate. '90% of these cases of desertion would immediately cease.' Both were concerned that some stronger characters were influencing 'men of weak will,' and Holmes feared 'the fair name of Australia is likely to be seriously besmirched.' Birdwood passed both these letters to the Governor-General and Pearce. Although Birdwood agreed with such a sentence for one or two cases, he 'should be extremely sorry to see the death sentence inflicted on any of our men' and reported back 'that after full consideration your Government have been unable to agree to altering the existing law.' He recounted to Pearce that he had stood before 'the whole 4th Division' to point out 'that they had come willingly to fight for their country and freedom,' and that 'only 1%' would ever 'think of deserting.' He had 'implored the other 99% to do what they could to save us from such men'.[106] By November Birdwood could report no improvement but rather that desertions 'still continue prevalent in a way none of us can regard except with dismay.' He then proposed that the names and sentences of convicted men be published in Australian newspapers.[107] This took effect in January 1918. Although in late February Birdwood reported that 'our desertion and crime returns have shewn a decided improvement' he feared 'that, when we come in for heavy fighting, we may again be faced with something like the same troubles.'[108] 'Cumulatively throughout the war roughly a brigade's worth of Australian troops was court-martialled for desertion'.[109]

Discipline was but one of many issues addressed by Birdwood in his extensive correspondence with the Governor-General and the Defence Minister, in which he invited both addressees to

103 Dianne Kaye De Bellis, 'Stories of Australian Deserters in World War 1' (Univesity of South Australia, 2014), 86-87 and Appendix B; Interestingly, Stevenson suggests that the incorporation of precedents from the States was due not to the Morant affair but rather the Wilmansrust incident, in which Birdwood was, as has been shown, involved in the administrative follow-up. See Stevenson, *The War with Germany – The Centenary History of the Great War Vol 3*, 121-22.
104 AWM 3DRL/3376 6/4, Letters by Birdwood to Sir Ronald Munro-Ferguson, letter, 31 March 1917.
105 AWM 3DRL/3376 6/4, letter 4 April 1917.
106 AWM 3DRL/3376 6/4, letter 22 May 1917, with letters from Holmes and Glasgow of 19 May 1917. AWM 3DRL/3376 7/1 Part 2, Letters by Birdwood to Sir George Pearce, letter, 22 May 1917.
107 AWM 3DRL/3376 7/1 Part 2, letter 5 November 1917..
108 AWM 3DRL/3376 6/4, Letters by Birdwood to Sir Ronald Munro-Ferguson, letter, 25 February 1918.
109 Stevenson, *The War with Germany, Vol 3*, 112-13 and 117.

share elements with the Prime Minister.[110] In 1917 Birdwood wrote twenty letters to Pearce and sixteen to Munro-Ferguson. Letters could be up to twenty typed pages in length. Birdwood wrote about battles and their impacts; whether or not Australian divisions were being asked to do more than the British: the performance of commanders and associated changes; promotions and the drive to have Australians in every position; honours and awards for which Birdwood was personally responsible; the reinforcements and divisional strengths; health; training battalions and hospitals in England; and even boots. To both men he showed a friendly and confident approach.

Birdwood was more intimate with the Governor-General, sharing some burdens and expressing quizzical views about Australia that he could not have done with an Australian politician. For example, he wrote about 'a great deal of jealousy against me at the War Office on account of the position I hold with the Australian troops – also, they never look very favourably upon the Indian Army officer, and especially nowadays upon one who was one of Lord Kitchener's closest friends.'[111] When Birdwood had been acting army commander for the second time, he wrote that 'Everyone seems to have jumped to the conclusion that I should have been appointed to the permanent command of the army,' which he would have liked as it contained the Australian Corps. He acknowledged that he could not have remained as a corps commander 'but I could have continued as GOC AIF, and, as such, looked after the destiny and interests of the men, to whom I am so devoted.'[112]

Towards Pearce, Birdwood was constantly respectful of the Defence Minister's political and elected position and addressed wider topics: the referendums; the dockers strike; federal elections; the Australian Comforts Fund; a proposed Gallipoli Star; pensions; and leave back in Australia. In the case of leave, Birdwood appreciated that neither transport ship space was available nor could he really spare the large number of man-days involved in sending men home on leave, but he sent 'home on every returning ship some fifty of most deserving cases of originally enlisted men.' He was 'not calling this leave,' and proposed to employ the men 'on submarine guard duty, etc.' He asked Pearce not to publish anything about this 'as neither your life nor mine would be worth living'. Birdwood was also considering the future employment of the AIF, as 'the whole aspect of operations here may change', and there might be value in transferring the Force to Egypt at the turn of year – saving on transport journeys and with an eye on both demobilisation and the health of his men. Birdwood acknowledged it was neither a matter for GHQ nor one that he should initiate, but rather for the Commonwealth Government. He said that he was writing to Sir James Allen to inform 'him of the gist of it and what my ideas are on the subject.'[113]

Birdwood had kept up his earlier correspondence with New Zealand's Defence Minister, despite the New Zealand Division moving away from Birdwood's direct command. This correspondence was not as extensive as with the Australian dignitaries – just seven letters in 1917 – but again equally as friendly. Understanding that Godley did 'not seem to be able to command the affection of officers and men' Birdwood tried to encourage the thought that

110 The depth of this correspondence was introduced at the start of Chapter 8.

111 AWM 3DRL/3376 6/4, Letters by Birdwood to Sir Ronald Munro-Ferguson, letter, 14 February 1917.

112 AWM 3DRL/3376 6/4, letter, 25 February 1917.

113 AWM 3DRL/3376 7/1 Part 2, Letters by Birdwood to Sir George Pearce, letter, 1 February 1918

as he was 'a good soldier', this 'feeling must and will I hope disappear.' Allen often sent the letters on to both the Governor-General and the Prime Minister, the latter annotating sections to be read out in the House of Representatives.[114] With these continuing letters Birdwood successfully contributed to the overall good relations between the British Government and the two antipodean Dominions and his years of dealing with correspondence at viceregal level paid dividends in his tactful handling of key Dominion figures. This was an important strand of Birdwood's method of command.

On 13 March Plumer returned from Italy and Birdwood handed over command of Second Army. Unbeknown to him, Sunday 17 March was probably Birdwood's pinnacle with his Australians. He attended a 'Church Parade with Walker & 1st Division,' gave medals, 'saw successful raiding teams of 5th Div with Hobbs & Elliott' and then rode home. He was accompanied by his son who had just joined as an ADC. Four divisions were very nearly up to strength and the numbers in 4th Division were increasing. For these reasons, the Australian Corps had not instigated the reorganisation from a twelve- to a nine-battalion divisional establishment but Birdwood did not expect the casualties from any future fighting to be fully replaced. The next day Birdwood left his now homogeneous Corps and went on leave. Five days later he wrote: "Still lovely weather. We did some weeding in the garden [at Thurlby] in the morning', and then 'heard of big German offensive between the Scarpe & St Quentin as expected.'

A car came from AIF HQ to take Birdwood to London and on Monday 25 March he was flying back in a Bristol Fighter to his Corps. On arrival, he found that 3rd and 4th Divisions had already left, and that 2nd and 5th were under orders.[115] He issued the following Corps Order:

> The time has now come when we must be prepared to 'take the strain.' I need hardly say more. You all know what this means, and I know I can confidently appeal to every single individual in the AIF to realise that this is up to him, personally, to 'take the strain' for the sake of his country and all he holds dear. Remember that personal determination to attain victory at whatever self-sacrifice by every individual is what counts, and it may well be that spirit on the part of even a few men may be the deciding factor of the great battle in which we are now engaged. Remember that they are thinking of us all in Australia now and remember the lasting traditions our Force has made for itself.[116]

The 4th Brigade was the first to face the enemy as the Operation Michael advance had pushed both Third and Fifth Armies rearwards. It arrived west of Hébuterne as Birdwood was flying over to France. It occupied the village itself, fought off German attacks over the coming week and stayed there until 25 April. Maclagan's remaining brigades were deployed on 27 March at Dernancourt, southwest of Albert and north of the River Ancre. They fought a stout defensive action for the coming ten days.[117] Both divisions had been allocated to Congreve's VII Corps,

114 ANZ C 361 202 Allen1-9, Sir James Allen Papers, letters, Birdwood to Allen, 6 May 1916, 21 January 1918 and 24 July 1917.

115 Diary 1918, 13-25 March.

116 Birdwood, *Khaki and Gown*, 321.

117 'About 50 officers and 281 other ranks' were 'awarded decorations' in these actions. AWM 3DRL/3376 7/1 Part 2, Letters by Birdwood to Sir George Pearce, letter, 7 May 1918.

then falling back to the Ancre. The 3rd Division had been tasked with plugging the line of the triangle formed by the confluence of the Ancre and Somme. Monash, who also had rushed back from leave on the Riviera, deployed his brigades and established his defence with a fighting advance. The Australian Corps had lost both its reserve divisions and now the front-line divisions were to be released, with other British divisions relieving them. The first to go was 5th Division on 27 March.

The German advance had already caused the appointment of General Foch as overall commander of both French and British forces and the removal of Gough, replaced by Rawlinson and his own staff on 28 March.[118] 5th Division arrived northwest of Albert and joined X Corps. On 3 April, 2nd Division departed to VII Corps, and finally the Australian Corps HQ itself moved. Birdwood visited both Byng's Third Army HQ and Congreve's VII Corps HQ while his own HQ established a temporary base west of Doullens. The next day, 4 April, he saw Rawlinson of Fourth Army – as Fifth had been renamed – that was on the right flank of VII Corps. Birdwood's HQ moved forward on 5 April to its new location just north of Amiens. That day Birdwood spent time with Maclagan whose 'Brigades were being attacked near Dernancourt where we lost the high railway embankment. He counterattacked later but did not get back all he had lost.' At midday on 6 April the Australian Corps took over from VII Corps in Third Army. The next day the Corps passed to Fourth Army. Birdwood now had 2nd, 3rd and 4th Australian divisions under his command, but each had brigades detached to other formations. He gained 8th (Regular) Division which had fought in the March offensive. The 2nd and 3rd divisions were in line and 4th withdrawn into reserve after its very hard fighting. Hobbs and 5th Division, again with a brigade detached, were on the Australian Corps' right flank under III Corps, the Somme being the boundary.[119]

South of 5th Division and all under III Corps and 18th Division was: 9th Brigade, detached earlier from 3rd Division to protect Villers-Bretonneux; then 5th Brigade just detached from 2nd Division to hold a reserve line; and finally, 8th Brigade detached from 5th Division to take over from a tired 24th Division. 8th Brigade was Rawlinson's southernmost formation and adjoining the French forces.[120] Fourth Army consisted of two corps, III and Australian, but the Army's front was now entirely held by Australians. 1st Division had been on its way to relieve 3rd Division when it was recalled to Second Army to defend Hazebrouck against the German advance, Operation Georgette. Birdwood managed to see Walker and his commanders as they headed northwards.[121] Haig visited the next day seeing White, 'a fine cheery fellow,' who assured Haig that 'the Australians would do their best for' him.

Further German offensives seemed imminent but Rawlinson had had time to reconfigure his two corps. The Australian Corps was to defend the Somme and therefore be astride it. III Corps would defend Villers-Bretonneux. On 17 April, 8th Division was transferred to III Corps and took over Villers-Bretonneux, although Elliott's 15th Brigade, which up until then had had a

118 Peter Pedersen, *The Anzacs: Gallipoli to the Western Front* (Melbourne: Penquin, 2007), 317-22; Jean Bou (ed.), *The AIF in Battle* (Melbourne: Melbourne University Press, 2016), 254-62.

119 Diary 1918, 3-6 April.

120 C E W Bean, *The Official History of Australia in the War of 1914-1918, Volume V* (Sydney: Halstead Press, 1941), 499-500.

121 Diary 1918, 11 April. AWM4 1/35/1 Part 1 – April 1918, Headquarters Australian Corps, Corps Order No 64.

responsibility to recapture the town if lost, kept a battalion ready to counter attack just in case. On 21 April 5th Division re-joined the Australian Corps, with 14th Brigade south of the river and 8th north of it. 15th was in reserve.[122] 2nd Division widened its frontage by taking over a portion of Third Army's front. Birdwood continued to visit his commanders and those on his flanks. By 22 April all the readjustments were complete.

In the early morning of 24 April enemy bombardments intensified and an attack towards Villers-Bretonneux, including tanks, commenced around six o'clock. Brigadier Elliott immediately sent out two strong patrols so as to confirm his own plans. These patrols were soon fighting alongside 8th Division, whose commander, General W.C.G. Heneker (GOC Southern Command India ten years later under Birdwood), rejected offers of help from Hobbs and his 5th Division, and attempted two counter attacks, assisted by British tanks. Meanwhile at 09:30 a.m. Rawlinson ordered Glasgow's 13th Brigade, in reserve north of the Somme, to move southwards to III Corps and when Rawlinson was still concerned at 11:30 a.m., he ordered Heneker to contact Hobbs about a counter attack. 5th Division was tactically transferred to III Corps at 4 pm. Elliott and his 15th Brigade grabbed their opportunity. The resulting feat of arms by which Glasgow's 13th Brigade to the south and Elliott's 15th Brigade to the north encircled Villers-Bretonneux and drove back the Germans is one of the most distinguished in Australian military annals. Understandably it further raised the reputation of the Australians among the British forces.[123]

Fortuitously this feat took place on the third anniversary of the original landings and notably some men had been serving since then.[124] Unlike the mad rush forward from the beach at Anzac, there was now control.[125] Over the weekend 27 and 28 April, command of the III Corps sector passed to Birdwood's Corps. 4th Division joined its 13th Brigade on the right flank of the Corps on a line in front of Villers-Bretonneux. This was Haig's southernmost formation. 4th Brigade had just come back from Hébuterne and it took over from 15th. Birdwood took time to visit both Glasgow and Elliott to offer his congratulations. He now had all four divisions in line and all were once more complete with their three brigades. The flow of reinforcements was not sufficient now to replace the casualties, so the three brigades – 9th, 12th and 13th, that had borne the brunt – each lost a battalion. Battalion numbers were retained and transferred to training establishments in England.

The Corps advanced during the following weeks. This was a successful period for Birdwood although he himself had not directly led his formations during the major events of the past weeks. Only 2nd Division had not fought away from the Australian Corps and furthermore six brigades – 4th, 5th, 8th, 9th 13th and 15th – can be considered to have fought independently. Haig had noted on 18 April that the Canadian Corps wished to fight only as a 'Canadian Corps,' whereas he wrote personally to Birdwood two days earlier that:

122 AWM4 1/35/1 Part 2 – April 1918, Headquarters Australian Corps, Corps Order No 69. Bean, *The Official History of Australia in the War of 1914-1918, Volume V*, 535-6 and 40-1.

123 Pedersen, *The Anzacs: Gallipoli to the Western Front*, 336-44. For the two commanders, see McMullin, Pompey Elliott, and Peter Edgar, *To Villers-Bretonneux with Brigadier-General William Glasgow DSO and the 13th Australian Infantry Brigade* (Loftus, NSW: Australian Military History Publications, 2006).

124 Men who had fought at Anzac wore an embroidered gold 'A' on their regimental patches. Bean, *The Official History of Australia in the War of 1914-1918, Volume VI*, 5.

125 Bean, *The Official History of Australia in the War of 1914-1918, Volume V*, 603.

> The right of our line in close connection with the French is so vital to me, that I must keep reliable troops there, and I cannot tell you with what confidence I contemplate the situation in that part of my front as long as the Australian Corps are holding it … Thanking you for all you and your gallant troops are doing for me.[126]

Birdwood had supported Haig in facing an extreme situation and had shown confidence in his subordinates to lead their formations. That they all succeeded cannot be a coincidence. All were from the same stable – Birdwood's. All the commanders were confident, flexible and decisive. All ranks displayed exactly what Birdwood had called for – 'personal determination to attain victory at whatever self-sacrifice.' Haig may have been irritated by Australian discipline but he had high regard for the performance of the Australian Corps. On 12 May Birdwood was summoned to GHQ and 'saw Lawrence CGS about taking up Army Comd. Told him I was most reluctant to give up Corps but he held out by stating I blocked Aus. Officer getting it.' A few days later Haig came to see Birdwood '& was very nice about my becoming Army Commander & specially about retaining GOC AIF.'[127]

There were two clear candidates for command of the Australian Corps – White and Monash. The former had had responsibility while Birdwood was away at times but he had commanded neither a brigade nor a division. His performance as a formation chief of staff had been outstanding and confirmed all the promise that he had displayed in his monthly reports from Staff College in 1906.[128] The latter had grown in stature from the brigadier who struggled on the northern slopes of Sari Bair and Haig admired him. Birdwood chose Monash as his replacement. He wrote later that 'Brigadier-General Frederick Maurice was to have been' my MGGS but was not available due to difficulties with the Prime Minister. Maurice had written to *The Times* accusing the Prime Minister of lying about manpower figures. White was ideally suited to accompany Birdwood as his MGGS and this was agreed. These apparently simple and logical selections, however, did not have the support of those who believed White should have been the corps commander or that Birdwood, as an army commander, should relinquish his AIF appointment.

Bean and Murdoch both saw Australia better served with White as corps commander and Monash, with his organising powers, in administrative command. Prime Minister Hughes was due to come to England. Lobbying resulted in the appointments standing but not being confirmed. In early July, Hughes came to France and found that all the senior Australian officers endorsed the selections that had been made. Hughes offered Birdwood 'the option of remaining as administrative head of the AIF provided that he relinquished his army command.' Haig advised Birdwood to accept the administrative command but ask to be allowed to continue in his army command until 'after autumn operations.' The *status quo* stood and Bean later wrote: 'So much for our high-intentioned but ill-judged intervention.'[129] The comments that endorsed Birdwood included:

126 LHCMA, Haig Diaries MF 860, 18 April 1918.

127 Diary 1918, 17 April.

128 White's potential shines through in these reports, sent monthly to DAAG Military Forces of the Commonwealth. See AWM 3DRL/1400/23, Papers of Gen White.

129 Birdwood, *Khaki and Gown*, 324-5; LHCMA, Haig Diaries MF 860, 7 May 1918; Bean, *The Official History of Australia in the War of 1914-1918, Volume V*, 169-71. Diary 1918, 23 August.

> Monash: 'General Birdwood's personality counts for everything in the AIF. He possesses the complete confidence of the whole force. … He has been the chief factor in creating and maintaining its prestige and its spirit of unity.'
>
> Hobbs: 'No man could have more devotedly studied the interests of Australia and her soldiers than General Birdwood has done, and I am confident that nothing would induce him to sacrifice Australia's interests, either for his own or any other person's or persons' advantage.'[130]

On 31 May Birdwood 'handed over command after 3½ years of my beloved Australian Corps to Sir J Monash.[131] I leave them all with the very greatest respect for no lot of officers & men c[oul]d have done better – never failing me.'[132]

By the end of the war Birdwood's time as a corps commander on the Western Front would be the ninth longest of over fifty such commanders.[133] Simpson examined a sample of corps commanders' diaries identifying 'six main categories (here given in no particular order): (1) attending inspections, parades … (2) meetings … (3) fighting battles … (4) meals… and entertaining; (5) exercise … and (6) being on leave …' All had strongly featured in Birdwood's approach to corps command. Interestingly Simpson quotes a post-war staff system study that found that 'the best method of testing the efficacy of the work of a Commander's Staff is by paying constant visits to the lower formations, where the results of the Staff work of the higher formations are most readily apparent.'[134] In doing this so extensively, Birdwood also was able to encourage his commanders and their men both to discuss and influence future plans. When fighting battles, Birdwood did go forward to find out for himself and where necessary instil urgency. Throughout his corps command, Birdwood had the great advantage of continuity with his Australian divisions. Despite the demands of communicating with other governments and the responsibilities of AIF command, this advantage allowed him to develop the Australian Corps into the powerful entity that he handed over to Monash.

Birdwood moved to his Fifth Army HQ at Crecy, noting 'No orders yet.' For some weeks his daughter, Nancy, had been at Abbeville with 3 Australian General Hospital, so he was able to have time with her together with his son Chris. He went over to England for a week and called on Prime Minister Hughes. They talked 'about present situation' and Birdwood's position as GOC of AIF. Two days later he 'went into Thurlby Church.' It is a small peaceful church set beside the Thurlby estate. For quiet contemplation Birdwood had an ideal place. It is the only time during the War that he wrote about going into that church. Perhaps he just wished to give thanks for the three and a half years with his beloved Australian Corps, including remembering all those lost under his personal command.

130 BL AAS, Mss Eur D 686 folio 77, letter, from Monash to Pearce, 21 June 1918, letter from J Talbot Hobbs, 27 June 1918, and letter from Arthur M Ross, 7 June 1918.

131 At this HQ, Château de Bertangles, King George V knighted Monash, the first occurrence of a sovereign knighting a commander in the field for two hundred years.

132 Diary 1918, 31 May.

133 Simpson, *Directing Operations*, Appendix 1. Birdwood's command lasted for 786 days.

134 Simpson, *Directing Operations,* 184-6.

General Sir William Birdwood, Walter Urwick, November 1919. (Reproduced by permission of the Cavalry and Guards Club).

Birdwood returned to France and on 1 July Fifth Army took over a section of the front – from Merville to Bethune – between First and Second Armies. Birdwood's army consisted of Haking's XI Corps and Morland's XIII Corps.[135] Haking is forever associated by Australians with Fromelles. He had, however, just successfully completed an identical operation – two divisions from separate corps, astride an army boundary. Success was attributed by Senior to greater preparation time, secrecy and clearly defined objectives.[136] Like Haking, Morland was a vastly experienced corps commander.[137] As to be expected no hint of difficulties between two senior officers and Birdwood arose. The Portuguese Corps, 'decimated in the big German attack in March,' was added and Birdwood used his tact in assisting their reorganisation.[138]

135 TNA WO 95/522/1: War Diary Fifth Army, July 1918, 1 July.
136 Senior, *Haking*, 222-24 & 33-36.
137 Only Pulteney, Haking and Morland served more than 1,000 days as corps commanders. See Simpson, *Directing Operations*, 229-30.
138 Birdwood, *Khaki and Gown*, 326.

In July Monash achieved success at Hamel, while Fifth Army saw shelling by both sides, active patrolling, and improving existing defences and plans.[139] Birdwood visited his new corps, divisions and brigades, but all was 'absolutely new and strange,' knowing 'only one or two of the generals and practically none of lower rank,' with little knowledge of individual units.[140] By the end of July Fifth Army was planning for limited advances using its own resources.[141] Birdwood continued to write to Pearce, who in mid-June while acknowledging 'a partial severance' of Birdwood's 'more direct connection', observed:

> Although we have never met, your letters have such a personal touch in them, that I feel I have been dealing with an Officer who understands Australia and Australians and sympathises alike with our ideals and our peculiarities. I can further assure you that your name is a household word in Australia, and that particularly among the relatives of the soldiers, is held in high esteem. The many kindly letters that you have sent to those relatives in their hour of sorrow, or of success, have endeared you to them.[142]

August saw Birdwood visiting London for the opening of Australia House by the King.[143] He returned in time to find that the enemy had made local evacuations of some outposts. Birdwood instructed his two corps commanders to establish distinct small forces of all arms to maintain contact with the enemy rear guards, similar to the advance to the Hindenburg Line. As the enemy withdrew further Birdwood ordered his main forces to make limited advances keeping contact with the advance guards. All this coincided with the start of the Battle of Amiens and the success of the Australian Corps. On Saturday 10 August, the King visited Fifth Army meeting all Birdwood's commanders. As the German withdrawal continued, Birdwood issued more aggressive orders for maintaining contact. On 23 August, he passed on Haig's new instructions: 'the changed conditions under which operations are now being carried out' called for 'boldness and resolution' from all ranks; recognised the part played by Second and Fifth Armies in 'gaining considerable ground' in the Lys sector; and spoke of a new Allied attack across the whole front. Limited objectives were 'no longer suited' and instead 'the most resolute offensive is everywhere desirable. Risks which a month ago would have been criminal to incur ought now to be incurred as a duty.' Divisions should now have individual and distant objectives.[144] Birdwood set out such objectives, noting that 'to effect this policy a return to conditions as nearly as possible approximate to mobile warfare is necessary.' He held a conference with his corps commanders, discussing objectives, cooperation with First Army, and as ever including concern about looking after 'the condition of the men and keeping them fit.'[145] Birdwood also

139 TNA WO 95/522/1: War Diary Fifth Army for July 1918, Weekly Summaries of Operations, Apendices 10, 16 and 19.
140 AWM 3DRL/3376 7/1 Part 2, Letters by Birdwood to Sir George Pearce, letter, 7 July 1918.
141 TNA WO 95/522/1: War Diary Fifth Army for July 1918, Preliminary Instructions No 2, 31 July 1918.
142 AWM 3DRL/3376 7/1 Part 2, Letters by Birdwood to Sir George Pearce, letter, 20 June 1918.
143 Diary 1918, 3 August; Eileen Chanin, *Capital Designs* (Melbourne: Australian Scholarly, 2018), 269-77.
144 TNA WO 95/522/2: War Diary Fifth Army for August 1918, Appendices 11, 13, 17 and 25.
145 TNA WO 95/522/3: War Diary Fifth Army for September 1918, Appendices 2 and 4, order SG436/31 dated 1 September 1918.

visited Monash, approximately every three weeks. His visit on 9 September occurred after the Corps had distinguished itself at Mont St Quentin, north of Péronne. He managed to see the eight hundred men from 1914 who were about to return on furlough as a result of Mr Hughes' efforts. He was, of course, surrounded and pressed by 1915 men asking when their turn would come. His response was that 'the 1914 men had cleared out so as to give them their chance of killing many more Germans.' If they did this 'in really large numbers' then everyone might be able to go home.[146] Birdwood's army continued to harass the withdrawing Germans and a line running west of Estaires to south of La Bassée was held, with detailed artillery plans to harass and inflict loss on the enemy if a larger withdrawal developed.[147]

Having spearheaded the attack on the Hindenburg Line, Monash's corps was now withdrawn, having been in near constant combat since March.[148] Its losses necessitated the reduction of more battalions within brigades. Birdwood was still going down to say good-bye to the departing 1914 men, all of whom, after carrying him around, sought a handshake and signature.[149] Meanwhile Fifth Army continued to push eastwards.[150] On 17 October, Lille was completely surrounded and then entered. Birdwood was 'very glad that 5th Army had the honour of doing this.' Just two days later and amid much acclamation, Birdwood 'met Clemenceau the very fine 78-year-old French Prime Minister' and together drove through the city, which had been in German hands since October 1914.[151]

With his HQ in Lille, Birdwood then urged that 'the advance will be continued and the present policy adhered to,' setting objectives for his corps and proposing steps 'upon reaching the [River] Scheldt.'[152] This was reached on 25 October. At the end of the month he wrote in his diary: 'News of Turkey's surrender came in. It looks like the beginning of the end,' but still he pressed on. He had now been given the Cavalry Corps – General Kavanagh – of two cavalry divisions. On 7 November Haig visited him and held a conference with Plumer, Kavanagh and Birdwood. The next day the bridgeheads west of the Scheldt withdrew and Fifth Army pushed over the river. In expectation of such an enemy move, Birdwood had already stated his intentions 'to press forward to the [River] Dendre, drive in the enemy's advance troops and force the line of the Dendre without delay,' in the expectation of an opportunity to employ the Cavalry Corps as a whole. This did not transpire as the enemy withdrew further.[153] Then he 'heard that Germany had accepted our armistice terms thus acknowledging complete defeat & bringing this 4-year war to an end. … We can none of us ever be grateful enough to providence for seeing this through for us with success & victory.'[154]

146 AWM 3DRL/3376 7/1 Part 2, Letters by Birdwood to Sir George Pearce,letter, 18 September 1918.
147 TNA WO 95/522/3: War Diary Fifth Army for September 1918, Appendix 23, Special Instruction 5, and Summary of Operations, Appendix 26.
148 It is sometimes portrayed that Monash commanded the Corps for the entire period. This is inaccurate inasmuch as Birdwood commanded for the first third.
149 AWM 3DRL/3376 7/1 Part 2, Letters by Birdwood to Sir George Pearce, letter, 18 October 1918.
150 Peter Hart, *The Last Battle* (London: Profile Books, 2018), 144-7.
151 Diary 1918, 17 & 19 October. TNA WO 95/522/4: War Diary Fifth Army for October 1918, Summary of Operations 18 October 1918.
152 TNA WO 95/522/4: Appendix 33, Special Instruction 12.
153 Diary 1918, 7 November. TNA WO 95/522/6: War Diary Fifth Army for November 1918 Part 1, Appendix 10, Special Instruction 10.
154 Diary 1918, 11 November.

Thus, encouraging his men to go and kill Germans was no longer necessary. His troops, and particularly his Anzacs, would be going home. Birdwood was present at the finish, as one of just five army commanders, a fact that declared his war service a success. He had experienced failures, lesser performances and near-successes but even after four years he displayed a desire to take the fight to the enemy, a willingness to visit constantly his men and their commanders, an ability to get on with people and to stay fit. For the overwhelming majority of this time he had kept by his side his chosen key staff officer White, now a Major General. They had made a most successful team and like White, the various commanders in the Australian Corps who reached the end of war that day were personally selected by Birdwood. His mark on the corps and his personality had in this and many other senses counted for everything in the AIF.

10

A Man of Empire

In March 1919 at the wedding of Birdwood's elder daughter Nancy to an Australian, Royal Flying Corps officer, some Australian officers commented that the event was a fine ending to his career. He noted later: 'the proverbial intolerance of youth for old age!'[1] It certainly was not the end of his military career. He would go on to become the first C-in-C India as a Field Marshal, a combination which neither Roberts nor Kitchener achieved. Subsequently, Birdwood did not attain his desired pinnacle as Governor-General of Australia but rather received distinction in a totally different field before his country faced another war, which thankfully he saw won before his own days were over. After his Great War successes, Birdwood progressed to becoming a prominent man of the British Empire.

On the day of victory Haig summoned his army commanders to a meeting. Second and Fourth Armies were to continue 'to advance in 30 days to Rhine' and the remainder 'to stand fast.' For Birdwood, his Australians needed to be repatriated. He sent White to London to preside over the formation of a branch for demobilisation and repatriation, and later Birdwood went briefly to London for a conference with Hughes to fix up AIF administration. It was decided that Birdwood would remain as GOC AIF but Hughes chose Monash for the demobilisation of the AIF. Bean believed that Hughes wanted Monash and White to work in tandem but Monash had no need of White who returned to France.[2] Birdwood went to the Australian Corps to brief 'all the Div & Brig Genls …about future demobilisation arrangements.' It was his last meeting together with this group.[3] Then major celebrations began for Birdwood with the State entry by the King and Queen of the Belgians into Brussels. His own monarch stayed two nights with him in Lille, after which he returned to England for the State procession through large crowds to Buckingham Palace. After lunch, the King was photographed with his Commander-in-Chief and the Army Commanders. As Haig's original invitation suggested, this gave Birdwood the opportunity to stay in London for Christmas. On Christmas Day he visited the limbless soldiers at the Australian hospital at Southall and on Boxing Day he went to the Australian hospital at Maresfield.[4] Birdwood travelled back and forth to Fifth Army, which continued

1 Birdwood, *Khaki and Gown*, 337.
2 Diary 1918, 11-21 November; Bean, *Two Men I Knew*, 180-82.
3 Diary 1918, 26 November.
4 Diary 1918, 7, 8, 19, 25 and 26 December. The Prince of Wales spent Christmas Day with the Australian Corps HQ, see AWM4 1/35/12 Part 2 – December 1918, Headquarters Australian Corps, Appendix

to exist until 24 March when it was reduced to an administrative area.[5] On 3 March, there was 'little Nancy's wedding day,' taken by Bishop Long of Bathurst. 'Dear old Sir Dighton Probyn [of Probyn's Horse], Ian Hamilton & Mr Fisher, HC of Australia, signed the register.'[6] In July he participated in the Victory Parades in Paris and London, with Jack Churchill as his staff officer who had been with him since Gallipoli.[7] Then he took Jenny on a trip around his Western Front locations. He returned to receive the Freedom of Totnes, that he had been invited to accept in 1918 but had then replied: 'I should take it as the greatest honour … but we have to finish the war first.' At a grand civic event, he was 'sworn in as a Freeman of Totnes,' the sixth of his family – the last having been his great grandfather.[8] Two weeks earlier he had heard from Lloyd George that he had been granted a Baronetcy and a grant of £10,000. He chose as his title 'of Anzac and of Totnes, in the County of Devon.' He later 'found that the other 4 Army Commanders had each rec'd Baronies & grant of £30,000, which seems to me most unjust.'[9]

In early April and after years of correspondence, Birdwood had the pleasure at last of meeting Senator Pearce, who came to London with his family to oversee repatriation and financial arrangements with Britain. A few days later Birdwood made the first of many trips to Devonport to see off 'a shipload of men for Australia.' Next it was to Portsmouth but this time the ship was HMAS *Australia* carrying the Prince of Wales and Brudenell White to Australia. Birdwood had known White since December 1914 and they had served together as commander and senior staff officer from August 1915. Birdwood was a leader of men and White had complemented him as a superlative staff officer. They had been a team and their success was a joint one. Later on White's untimely death, Birdwood wrote to Mr Menzies that he had regarded Brudenell White 'not only as the finest officer in the AIF, but I can say there was none better than him in the whole forces of the Empire.'[10] Farewells continued throughout the summer, including to his daughter Nancy and her now RAF husband in June.[11] After the signing of the Treaty of Versailles, Hughes met Birdwood in London and 'formally asked me to visit Australia in the autumn & I consented.'[12]

3. The event was recorded in water colour, see Anne Gray, *Henry Fullwood War Paintings* (Canberra: Australian War Memorial, 1983), 74 and 90.

5 TNA WO 95/522/8: War Diary Fifth Army for December 1918 - March 1919, Appendix 1 dated 21 March 1919.

6 Diary 1919, 3 March.

7 Diary 1919, 14 and 19 July. Celia Lee and John Lee, *Winston & Jack* (London: Celia Lee, 2007), 280-95.

8 Val Price, *The Honorary Freedom of the Borough of Totnes 1888 to 1975* (Totnes: Totnes Image Bank Publications, 2008), 1919; Diary 1919, 21 August; *The Exeter and Plymouth Gazette,* 25 August 1919, 4.

9 Diary 1919, 5 and 6 August.

10 *The Age*, 16 August 1940, 8.

11 'It took 176 voyages to bring all the Anzacs home, the last ship departing on 23 December 1919.' Stephen Garton and Peter Stanley, 'The Great War and its aftermath, 1914-22' in *The Commonwealth of Australia.* The Cambridge History of Australia (Port Melbourne: Cambridge University Press, 2013), 55.

12 L F Fitzhardinge, 'W M Hughes and the Treaty of Versailles', *Journal of Commonwealth Political Studies* 5, No 2 (1967), 139. Birdwood arranged his arrival to be after the December Federal Elections, which were won by Hughes.

On 22 July Birdwood dined with Sir Edwin Montagu, Secretary of State for India and another Old Cliftonian.[13] Any discussion about the violence at Jallianwala Bagh in Amritsar was not recorded. Montagu asked Birdwood to consider going 'to India en route to Australia as President of Committee' regarding towns in Punjab but nothing came of this. In October Birdwood appeared before the Esher Committee enquiring into the administration and organisation of the army in India.[14] His views were sought on the relative merits of a Viceroy's Council supply member or an Army director of supply.[15] Before leaving for Australia Birdwood met Montagu again who said 'he was determined to do everything he could to ensure' that Birdwood succeeded Monro as C-in-C India but the 'WO were dead opposed to any IA man.' Montagu was going 'to stick to it' but Birdwood's appointment as GOC Northern Army was settled.[16]

Birdwood, his wife Jenny, daughter Judith and her governess, landed at Fremantle on 18 December, five days before the final Australian repatriation ship left England. Lady Birdwood wrote in her privately published journal of their trip: 'It was a great day in Will's life and one that we shall never forget.' The ship swung alongside Victoria Quay, packed with returned servicemen as well as dignitaries, as the photos of the day show.[17] Before Birdwood's tour Admiral Jellicoe had visited Australia, May to August 1919, as part of his review of the naval defences of the Dominions. Birdwood was immediately followed by the Prince of Wales who toured Australia during May to August 1920.[18] The details surrounding Birdwood's tour are slight. Some major works on the post-war years do not mention any of these visits.[19] Birdwood's visit was not a national tour like the Prince's. It was, rather, a multitude of individual calls on the local branches of the Returned Sailors' and Soldiers' Imperial League of Australia. Birdwood met his old diggers. The only discordant note seemed to have occurred in Brisbane. The Labour Premier was Ted Theodore but he was away in London for both Birdwood's and the Prince's visits. The acting Premier John Fihelly, a supporter of Irish views, welcomed Birdwood at the state banquet but closed his speech pointedly welcoming neutrality. Birdwood did not rise to this. On the same occasion for the Prince, worse was expected but Fihelly surprised everyone with an exceedingly generous welcome. When the time came for consideration of Birdwood as Governor-General, poor health had taken Fihelly out of frontline politics and Theodore's star was waning due to allegations of fraud. Birdwood had continued to build on the relationship with his diggers with his annual Anzac Day broadcasts, talking to an Australia he had visited, he knew and he loved.

13 Diary 1919, 22 July.

14 NAM 6707-19-594 & 595, Letter from Brig Wagstaff, with Esher Commitee terms of reference, 6 August 1919, Letter, Wagstaff with note by Esher to Secretary of State India, 8 August 1919.

15 BL IOR/L/MIL/5/840, Army in India (Esher) Committee, 1919-1920: report of the committee to enquire into the administration and organisation of the army in India, (London, 1920).

16 Diary 1919, 5 November.

17 Lady Birdwood, *A Visit to Australia and New Zealand* (London: Printing Craft, 1922), 9.

18 Kevin Fewster, 'Politics, Pageantry and Purpose: The 1920 Tour of Australia by the Prince of Wales'. *Labour History*, 38 (1980), 59-66. Accessed 21 June 2021.

19 Andrews, *The Anzac Illusion*; John Lack, K S Inglis, and Jay Winter, *ANZAC Remembered: Selected Writings by K. S. Inglis* (Melbourne: University of Melbourne, 1998); Joan Beaumont, *Broken Nation* (Crowsnest: Allen & Unwin, 2013); Alison Bashford and Stuart Macintyre (eds.), *The Cambridge History of Australia, Volume 2* (Port Melbourne: CUP, 2013).

The Fremantle quayside was packed with returned servicemen and dignitaries and one poster had a very big hand and a small general, with the words "Put it there, Birdie."[20] Senator Pearce, himself a Western Australian, welcomed Birdwood who addressed the crowd from the gangway. 'The 'diggers' gave him a most tumultuous reception; on his part, General Birdwood was obviously moved by deep sentiment on setting foot on the land which he had never seen before.' His brief speech was typical of the many speeches to follow: sincere expression of thanks; some recognition of the place or state he was in; acknowledgement of the sacrifice made by the people and mentioning the names of those who had given distinguished service; closing with a view to the times ahead and the application of standards of military service to the new challenges of building the future country. Four nights later, at a returned servicemen's reception, Birdwood gave a twenty-one-page address covering every Western Australian unit, their commanders, their distinguished officers and the winners of VCs, all interwoven with anecdotes of operational incidents. It was the result of deep personal knowledge of and affection for those who served under him.[21] He would do the same in all the other States. He frequently mentioned the wives and mothers, and the women of Australia for the Comforts Fund. He delighted in telling of the loss of his daughter to Australia. Between Christmas and New Year, he was busy with events, parties and speeches in and around Perth, but on Sunday 4 January his tour began in earnest with an overnight train to Bunbury. After a swim at 6:30 a.m. he officially arrived at 9 a.m. for: five speeches; a reception; laying the foundation of a memorial; visiting a soldiers' agricultural resettlement; and finally, a *levée* 'at the Town Hall with all returned soldiers & their families with whom I shook hands.' Then it was *via* Busselton, Nannup, Bridgetown, Pemberton, Katanning and Mount Barker to Albany, where he met a group of widows and mothers: 'some very sad women but all so nice – a very trying duty.' On his journey back to Perth, 'returned soldiers insisted on meeting the train at half a dozen stations & seeing me during the night.'[22] Jenny had stayed in Perth with Nancy for the birth of her child and Birdwood saw his grandson, Robin, that morning.

The next day Birdwood was off to Coolgardie and his schedule for the next nineteen weeks matched the previous week. In Melbourne he met Lady Bridges and Lady White, and the Lord Mayor gave a dinner for 2,000. The venue had an outline of Australia on one wall, with a central heart and inside that 'BIRDWOOD' in lights. At Ballarat he went to the town hall 'where some 200 widows & mothers of killed men came & shook hands.' In Hobart there were 100 soldiers in the hospital, still recovering. He visited an artificial limb factory in Adelaide. In the town of Birdwood – renamed in 1917 from its German name Blumberg – he laid a stone for a memorial arch: 'This stone was laid by the soldiers [*sic*] beloved General Sir William Birdwood…' In Randwick, Sydney, there were still 1,000 soldiers recovering in the Fourth Australian Repatriation Hospital. Lady Birdwood recalled having met many of them previously at Roehampton and Southall. Later, together, they attended a reception 'given for him by the mothers, widows, wives and relations of soldiers … Will shook hands with all those who had

20 Birdwood, *A Visit to Australia and New Zealand*, 9-10.

21 Diary 1919, 19 – 23 December. AWM 3DRL/3376 10, Speeches and addresses 1919-1920, 1-2 and 16-38; *Western Mail*, 24 December 1919, 20 & 29.

22 Diary 1920, 4-11 January.

lost husbands and sons in the war. Some of the poor women had lost no less than three sons. It was very touching to see them, and nothing that one can say seems adequate.'[23]

Having inspected and addressed the cadets at Duntroon, he unveiled a 'memorial stone to Genl Sir William Bridges on a small hill above College – lovely site with a fine solid granite tomb with sword on it.' The next day at Tuggeranong he visited Bean, who was 'now installed writing the official history of the war.' On horseback he led the Anzac Day parade of five thousand men through Sydney.[24] In Newcastle he returned to the ladies of Newcastle what is now entitled the Birdwood Flag. In September 1917 'the Australian Comforts Fund Commissioners presented me with a magnificent Australian flag from the ladies of NSW.' It flew over his and the Australian Corps HQ until the end of the war.[25] In Brisbane, the returned soldiers had organised a special lorry, onto which he had to climb, and brought to a halt he gave a spontaneous speech listing every one of the old battalions founded from Queensland. On 12 May, at Rockhampton, he was 'spared all speeches!! The first time!' His last function was at Glenhurst, NSW, on 24 May and from there he left for Sydney.[26]

Birdwood sailed for New Zealand on 29 May – 'going down through the lovely Sydney harbour & out through the Heads, with old AIF artillery there as a guard of honour.' Birdwood recalled:

> The last 5 ½ months have been wonderful for I have been treated almost like a Royal Prince – met everywhere with the very greatest kindness & affection – every house & every village turning out & having decorated, in fact an honoured guest anywhere & the Commonwealth Govt has been hospitality itself paying every expense … everywhere. Returned soldiers have been more than warm in their welcome & seem to think I have done more for them than I can myself take credit. … I wonder if I'll ever come back. They all seem to say they would like me to do so as Governor General – But.[27]

And of course, he did not do so but that story was then a decade away. This tour was his last act as GOC AIF. Nearly twenty years later Birdwood looked back on his five years as GOC AIF as 'years which I shall always regard as among the happiest and most eventful of my life' and 'the best and most loyal of comrades' who made them so.[28] He had encouraged the men and women of the AIF to be proud of their individual and joint achievements far away from home. Now as ex-service people, this pride was openly displayed beside their loved ones and in their own towns and villages. Such pride was rightly tinged with sadness and acknowledged sacrifices but returned soldiers pulling Birdwood round their towns were joyous events. He expressed hope for the future wherever he went and stressed the value in applying the standards learnt in the AIF. The subsequent reality is well described by Garton and Stanley.[29] Return was

23 Birdwood, *A visit to Australia and New Zealand*, 22-23.
24 Diary 1920, 20, 23 and 29 January; 7, 14, & 20 February; 15 March; 4, 15, 16 and 25 April.
25 Diary 1917, 28 April. *Newcastle Morning Herald and Miners' Advocate*, 29 April 1920, 5. *The Birdwood Flag Conservation Project* <https://uoncc.wordpress.com/2017/08/01/birdwood-2017/> (accessed 29 November 2017).
26 Diary 1920, 29 and 30 April; 2, 5, 9, 12 and 24 May.
27 Diary 1920, 29 May.
28 Birdwood, *Khaki and Gown*, 353.
29 Stephen Garton and Peter Stanley, 'Return and its discontents', *The Commonwealth of Australia*, 55-61.

neither easy nor smooth, despite the support of traditional social structures. Land settlement was an attractive option but of the 40,000 settled, half failed at a cost to individuals and the government. Birdwood's tour, however, provided an uplift to fuse national sentiment and an agent to cultivate the Anzac legend, to be most importantly shaped by Bean's monumental official history.[30] The final Western Front volume, VI, of that history was not published until 1942. For twenty years the regular publication of volumes built up another legend, that of Birdwood himself, already created by his renowned title: Soul of Anzac. Furthermore from 1920 onwards until shortly before his death, Birdwood annually broadcast an Anzac Day address. He also occasionally visited his daughter and her family in Western Australia. The name of Birdwood spread geographically across Australia.[31] When he was promoted to Field Marshal in 1925, he was also given the corresponding Australian rank and therefore on Australia's active list until his death. As Bean observed in 1942, all this was built on 'the prestige of Birdwood's leadership in the field combined with his integrity and his good judgement of character.'[32]

Birdwood visited New Zealand during June and July 1920.[33] His travels there were more leisurely than those in Australia, with stops at sheep stations and country residences. He travelled the length and breadth of the country, welcomed everywhere by the old soldiers. On disembarking at Wellington, he found Prime Minister Massey and his wife most hospitable and he met his old comrade, General Russell. As in Australia there were sad moments – lunching with Mrs Johnston, the mother of Earl, brigade commander at Gallipoli and later killed in France, and having tea with Mrs Bauchop whose husband, commanding the Otago Mounted Rifles, was killed in the August offensive at Gallipoli.[34] Throughout both tours he had taken every opportunity to ride, swim or walk, to stay fit. The long cruise across the Pacific was an added benefit.

In Washington, Birdwood learnt of 'Rawlinson's appt as C-in-C India … the first I had heard of it & naturally disappointed as know how very hard Montagu & the IO had been urging my appt. I had hoped – but never mind!'[35] Having landed at Tilbury on 10 September his first call was to the India Office, where he learnt that 'Lloyd George had been undecided for months as to whether appt me or Rawlinson as C-in-C India, but Wilson finally won for the WO.' Later Birdwood heard more background from India Office associates. The King had apparently been keen on Birdwood's appointment but 'Montagu had made a bargain with Churchill – if Army Council would back him (Montagu) up over the "Dyer" [Amritsar massacre] case – he wd withdraw his backing of me!!' When they did meet, Montagu assured him that he had done all he could but 'it was a WO appt & Churchill though personally "very sweet on me" [Birdwood] said Wilson strongly supported Rawlinson.' Montagu offered 'Mil Sec India Office' but Birdwood said he was 'too active to take up London office life.' Furthermore, he believed that having been away from India for six years, another four would make a useful return impossible. Birdwood said that he still hoped he 'might succeed Rawly if the latter

30 Beaumont, *Broken Nation*, 552.
31 Birdwood's name is honoured by the naming of the town of Birdwood, South Australia, and numerous Birdwood Streets and Avenues. There are over seventy Birdwood geographical references in Australia.
32 Bean, *The Official History of Australia in the War of 1914–1918, Volume VI*, 192.
33 Archives New Zealand, R10623386, Visit Sir William Birdwood, 1-3.
34 Diary 1920, 6 June and 13 July.
35 Diary 1920, 27 August.

did not complete his time.'[36] Birdwood was now set for Northern Command, India. The two antipodean High Commissioners hosted a large welcome home luncheon, at which Birdwood gave a forty-minute speech, covering the Repatriation Departments of both Dominions, and in regard to Australia: vocational training schemes, housing, and business loans. It was a very comprehensive overview, displaying an in-depth appreciation, good and bad, of the situation surrounding returned soldiers. His speech displayed perhaps too much knowledge and opinion for a prospective governor-general but time would pass before that opportunity arose.[37] He sailed for India on 8 October, with the good wishes of Winston Churchill, then Secretary of State for War.[38] His final ten years in India were to be dominated by both military and political changes.

On his way to Marseilles he drove through all his wartime locations, stopping to see Australian War Graves detachments at work and viewing Australian divisional memorials. He arrived in Bombay on 30 October 1920, just a few weeks short of six years since leaving for Egypt.[39] Then the number of Indian personnel under arms was 155,423. By the end of the war it had risen to 573,484. Furthermore, approximately 700,000 to 800,000 had passed through the army during the war, excluding a further 400,000 non-fighting men. Sixty-two thousand had been killed.[40] Birdwood arrived at his headquarters in Rawalpindi as the reduction of the Indian army to peacetime strength was still ongoing.

As well as impacts on the Army, the war had brought much political change in India, including an emphasis on nationalism. When the current Viceroy, Lord Chelmsford, was appointed in early 1916, he found demands for Home Rule that could not be ignored. Within his Executive Council he sought to define the goal of British rule in India and sent his ideas to the India Office before the end of 1916. The publication of the heavily critical report of the Commission on Mesopotamia had led to the appointment of a new India Secretary – Sir Edwin Montagu. He picked up the on-going debate and announced to the House of Commons in August 1917 that the Government's policy should be 'the gradual development of self-governing institutions with a view to the progressive realisation of responsible government in India,' and that he would shortly visit India. The result was a joint report, July 1918, and subsequently the Government of India Act, 1919, was passed in December of that year. The overall result was the Montagu-Chelmsford reforms. A dual form of government – dyarchy – was to be introduced, with particular changes in the major provinces. Certain reserved subjects were kept back for the Governors and their executive councils: half British officials and half Indian. Other unreserved subjects were transferred to Indian Ministers, drawn from Provincial Legislative Councils,

36 Diary 1920, 10,13 and 15 September.
37 AWM 3DRL/3376 10, Speeches and addresses 1919-1920,142-152.
38 NAM 6707-19-597, Letter, W S Churchill to Birdwood, 25 September 1920.
39 Diary 1920, 7-10 October.
40 Jon Wilson, *India Conquered* (London: Simon & Schuster, 2016), 398-99; T A Heathcote, *The Military in British India: The Development of British Land Forces in South Asia, 1600-1947* (Manchester: Manchester University Press, 1995), 224-25. The Indian contribution on the Western Front is chronicled in Gordon Corrigan, *Sepoys in the Trenches: The Indian Corps on the Western Front 1914-15* (Stroud: Spellmount, 1999). Issues surrounding Indian war graves are fascinatingly covered in Santanu Das (ed.), *Race, Empires and First World War Writing* (New York: Cambridge University Press, 2011), 308 12. More recently, inequalities in commemoration have been investigated by the CWGC. See *Report of the Special Committee to review historical inequalities in commemoration*, CWGC (2021).

which were enlarged with a higher proportion elected. The Princely states were to be linked directly to the Government of India and a Chamber of Princes established.[41] While Birdwood's first years saw the initial operation of dyarchy and the lead up to the second elections under the Montagu-Chelmsford reforms, Birdwood concentrated on his command. The Congress Party boycotted the first elections in 1920. Then after the Chauri-Chaura incident, February 1922, where twenty-one policemen were horribly murdered, Gandhi had been jailed. A new Swaraj party under C R Das and Motilal Nehru did participate in the second elections of November 1923.[42] During this time the British were reluctant either to use the army to suppress nationalist agitation or impose widespread martial law. The police were to the fore.[43] Low well explained how more than once 'unfulfilled expectations' led to an 'agitational campaign.' The first of these was the Non-Cooperation movement of 1920-2 and then the 'renewed Civil Disobedience movement of 1931-2. Birdwood's final ten years fell neatly for him between these two. The Montagu-Chelmsford Reforms called for a review after ten years – in 1929 but the political pressure built up such that a review was announced in November 1927. This, the Simon Commission, dominated Birdwood's last years in India.[44]

Birdwood was in a new post, as the four commands that had previously existed in India until 1908, prior to their merging into two armies, had been reinstituted. Birdwood was GOC-in-C Northern Command, the largest of the four, which included the Punjab and the Frontier, and he had selected Brigadier Cyril Wagstaff as his BGGS. Captain Wagstaff had sailed with him to Egypt, been on his staff at Gallipoli and progressed to GSO 1 of 5th Australian Division. In Cairo, it was Wagstaff who, according to Bean, proposed the term Anzac to Birdwood.[45] Latterly he had been Secretary to Lord Esher's committee. Birdwood took off immediately to inspect his four districts – Peshawar, Kohat, Rawalpindi and Lahore – and their various stations.[46] Generally he visited four units a day and well into his second year was still visiting units for the first time. In his diary, he listed each unit with the name of the commanding officer together with a short comment: 'Regt does not look of great value'; 'much better than I expected to find them after the strain of war'; and 'evidently a good Regt & all looking smart'.[47] He spent two weeks visiting local units, then on to Peshawar for a week and next to Kohat, which he was delighted to see again: 'old home where we were so happy', and see 'all the trees I had put down.' He knew two regiments there well: 'still looking capital with very fine spirit' and 'very good indeed in all respects'.[48] He wrote letters of encouragement after his visits and for some of these he received personal letters in return saying how uplifting they were.[49] Lord Rawlinson passed

41 Sir Penderel Moon, *The British Conquest and Dominion of India* (New Delhi: India Research Press, 1999), 973-84.
42 Wilson, *India Conquered*, 417-21; Moon, *The British Conquest and Dominion of India*, 1015-20; Edward Thompson and G T Garrat, *Rise and Fulfilment of British Rule in India* (London: Macmillan, 1934), 613-18.
43 D A Low, ed. *Congress and the Raj* (New Delhi: OUP, 2004), 7-8, 166.
44 Wilson, *India Conquered*, 423-4. Chaired by Sir John Simon, a Liberal politician and barrister, members included Clement Attlee.
45 Bean, *The Official History of Australia in the War of 1914-1918, Volume 1*, 124-25.
46 NAM 6707-19-601, Northern Command Orders, paragraph 302, 2 November 1920.
47 Diary 1920, 12, 16, 17, 26 and 30 November.
48 Diary 1920, 9-12 December.
49 NAM 6707-19-605, Letter from CO Connaught Rangers, 25 November 1920.

through Rawalpindi after Christmas and they had their first face-to-face meeting in their new appointments.

In the New Year, Birdwood held a 'Garden Party for 70 native officers.' He spoke with Indian Officers but noted with sadness that far fewer regimental officers spoke the necessary languages. He identified issues with soldiers' rations and wrote firmly to GHQ to sort this out.[50] He had been back in India for only two months and already his diary reflected a certain contentment, though different from the expressions of affection for the Australian soldiers. He next visited Lahore, noting that he 'first passed over this road when Adjt of XI BL & marched up it *en route* from Nowgong to Pindi in 1887-88 !!' In Lahore Christopher briefly joined him as ADC, wearing some of his father's old uniform.[51] Birdwood also started a lengthy correspondence with his friend Clive Wigram, Assistant Private Secretary and Equerry to the King, that continued over the next ten years, mentioning that regiments had 'no longer a dozen good officers,' and could 'hardly find more than one, or two, who really know their men and speak their language.'[52]

It was for political developments that Birdwood was visiting Lahore. He first attended the 'very last Punjab Provincial Durbar as all the old Punjab States are to be handed over to the Govt of India,' and then the 'First Punjab Legislative Council.' After visiting Lahore-based units he made a brief visit to Amritsar. He wrote no comments on the Jallianwala Bagh Amritsar massacre of 13 April 1919 or the Hunter Committee that had reported on such events in May 1920.[53] In Delhi Birdwood met the Viceroy for the first time. In February for the introduction of the new Central Government arrangements, Birdwood watched as the Duke of Connaught opened both the Council of State and the Legislative Assembly.[54] Despite these momentous changes Birdwood's initial months were focused on his own command. He visited continuously up until late April but by then he still had not seen every unit or location in his command. His visit to the XI BL at Jullundur was a highlight and at dinner, he was 'delighted to see all the old mess plate, etc, with its tradition.' At the Regimental Sports he 'ran in the officers' race with all others but sprung a tendon in my leg.' Perhaps others aged fifty-four would have just watched. Birdwood was 'really sad to think of the possibility of the old regt being broken up.' He had arrived as reviews of the regimental structures of the cavalry and infantry were coming to a climax. At the end of the war there were thirty-nine regiments of cavalry. Only twenty-one were to be retained and the debate in early 1921 was how this reduction was to be achieved. As with the infantry, the single regiment system had not provided an effective supply of wartime reinforcements. Birdwood entered into heartfelt correspondence with the Adjutant-General. It was decided to retain the regiments in pairs, but to renumber them rather than retain both numbers as with the British cavalry. The *Sillidar* system, beloved by Birdwood, was now finally ceased. XI BL was amalgamated with XII Cavalry and renumbered as 5 King Edward's Own

50 NAM 6707-19-608, Paper on rations to QMG, 20 January 1921.

51 Diary 1921, 4 and 7 January.

52 Royal Archives [hereafter RA] PS/PSO/GV/C/N/2556/1, letter, Birdwood to Wigram, 23 January 1921.

53 A comprehensive study of the incident and period, without assumption of traditional viewpoints, can be found in Nick Lloyd, *The Amritsar Massacre* (London: I B Tauris, 2011). The lasting nature of the controversy is emphasised in Vanessa Holburn, *The Amritsar Massacre. The British Empire's Worst Atrocity* (Barnsley: Pen & Sword, 2019).

54 Diary 1921, 31 January and 9 February.

Probyn's Horse.[55] The new regiments were grouped into seven geographic groups with each regiment having a similar class composition and each group to generate a depot on mobilisation.

Likewise, infantry battalions were reorganised into twenty groups, with the 10th battalion of each group becoming a training battalion. The class composition of each regiment was reviewed and further rationalised. Birdwood was again concerned with the class composition of the regiments: 'Hard fought all day in conference … trying to retain the old classes in Ind Inf Regts – a very uphill fight as others don't seem to realize how much political confidence & contentment really rule the question, so much more than normal efficiency & training at present in India.' Birdwood 'pressed hard' but 'I failed as I failed to keep our cavalry Regts & I am sure I am right.'[56] Thus, all the numbering and names established by Kitchener in 1903, staffed by Birdwood himself, were now completely altered.[57] It was a time of turmoil for British units as well. 3rd and 4th battalions of regiments were being disbanded and southern Irish regiments were leaving India to disband.[58] Again like Amritsar, he must have been circumspect as there are no records of Birdwood's views on Irish independence.

In April, the Australian Senate had resumed after its summer break and 'Pompey' Elliot, now a Senator, embarked on a series of allegations about wartime events, including being passed over for promotion in favour of Gellibrand and Glasgow, after Villers-Bretonneux. This sorry saga was managed over a number of weeks as best it could be by Senator Pearce and Elliott 'attracted little sympathy and some sharp criticism.' In India Birdwood only observed remotely.[59] At the end of April – with his family, his personal staff and the majority of his headquarters – Birdwood moved to Murree. Walking now took the place of riding in the mornings and he regularly played tennis. Long walks brought him into contact with local Mussalmans, all with an interest in the army. He took a long summer leave each year, trekking and having three or four weeks at Srinagar in Kashmir, using houseboats loaned to him by the Maharajah of Patiala. His 1921 trekking trip started from Simla. He stopped at Snowdon, the C-in-C's residence, which he had not seen for seven years and found 'several of dear old K's servants still here.'[60] Returning to Rawalpindi in October, his frequent unit visits – both British and Indian – restarted. It was a particularly happy time for the Birdwoods as a family. Christopher visited regularly and performed some duties for his father. Nancy and her son, Robin, came to stay from Australia and Judith was still with her parents. Birdwood had completed a year in his new command, readapted to India and established his routine. In February 1922, the Prince of Wales spent a

55 NAM 6707-19-591A, Letter from Gen Delamain, AG, 3 December 1920; Orders for reduction of Cavalry, A-1209-1-AG-5, 18 December 1920; Birdwood to Delamain, 22 & 29 December 1920. This is a different Delamain from Birdwood's friend in XI BL.

56 Diary 1921, 4 and 8 February.

57 John Gaylor, *Sons of John Company: The Indian and Pakistan Armies 1903-91* (Tunbridge Wells: Spellmount, 1992), 11-13 and 18-20; Heathcote, *The Military in British India: The Development of British Land Forces in South Asia, 1600-1947*, 241-2. For a specific example of the changes, see Major General Rafiuddin Ahmed, *History of the Baloch Regiment 1820-1939* (Abbottabad: The Baloch Regimental Centre, 1998), 226-28.

58 Diary 1921, 27 February and 21 March, Visits to 1st Battalion, Connaught Rangers and 4th Batttalion, Royal Fusiliers.

59 McMullin, *Pompey Elliott*, 544-64. A J Hill, Elliott, Harold Edward (Pompey) (1878-1931), *Australian Dictionary of Biography* <http://adb.anu.edu.au/biography/elliott-harold-edward-pompey-6140> (accessed 20 August 2018).

60 Diary 1921, 31 July.

few days with the Birdwoods at Rawalpindi, including a garden party for all the serving Indian Officers in the garrison.[61] Just before Birdwood left for his summer in Murree, a commanding officer wrote: 'Thank goodness, the Northern, and the most important Army [sic], in times to come has a commander who knows human nature in the shape of the *sowar* and *sepoy* – and is their friend.'[62]

In September two issues arose that would be of significance for Birdwood over the coming two years. On 7 September, he had a meeting with the CGS, Jacob, about Waziristan and two days later Birdwood was in Amritsar noting that the Akali Sikh situation was 'interesting & not at all good.' The Sikh state of affairs would continue to develop, but Waziristan called for prompt military operations. The Third Anglo-Afghan War of 1919 had stirred up the Waziris and Waziristan was nominally under the direct control of GHQ. It was now decided to occupy Waziristan and establish a headquarters at Razmak. Two columns, south and north, would enter Waziristan, converge on Razmak and drive roads through the mountainous countryside. Birdwood and Northern Command were to be responsible for the northern column. The final conference, with military, RAF and political representatives, to confirm plans was held at Kohat, 22-24 November,.[63] Birdwood paid visits to his force as it pressed forward, including the old fort at Datta Khel, last visited in 1911.[64] At the end of the year Birdwood learnt that he had been created GCB and received a warm letter from Jacob, saying that he 'should have had it long before and during the War.'[65] Birdwood also received a letter from Rudyard Kipling, to whom he had written after the latter's operation. Addressed to 'Dear General Sahib' Kipling wrote that he 'didn't like what he was hearing about India & the border. But if we will take more trouble to wreck India than we took to win it, I suppose we are bound to reap the rewards of our labours.' Kipling closed by saying he would 'give a good deal to be able to have a look at the Northern Command once more.'[66] On a visit to his column again, Birdwood was delighted to find his tent marked *Snow'd On,* a delightful play on *Snowdon,* the residence he knew so well with Kitchener.[67]

Later the same month Birdwood was in Delhi for Rawlinson's annual meeting with his commanders, which included discussion about which Indian Army regiments were to be Indianised. One afternoon Birdwood accompanied Lord Reading, Viceroy since April 1922, in his carriage to polo and was told that 'he hoped that I would succeed Rawly as Chief when Chief left.' The next day 'Rawly sent for me – told me he wd probably go in March 24 – that he thought I was sure to succeed him & asked who I wanted as a CGS – I plumped for White – then Tim Harrington.'[68] Birdwood obtained neither but instead Andrew Skeen, White's predecessor as Birdwood's chief of staff at Anzac, then commanding at Peshawar. After two-and-a-half years the ultimate position of C-in-C was within his grasp but not yet assured.

61 Diary 1922, 9-11 March.
62 NAM 6707-19-621, letter from CO 54 FF, 24 April 1922.
63 Birdwood, *Khaki and Gown*, 370-71. Diary 1921, 22 and 23 November.
64 Waziristan, Razmak and Dardoni have come to prominence once more as the Pakistan Army has seen action in the area, and Datta Khel was the site of a CIA drone strike in March 2011, killing 44.
65 NAM 6707-19-646, Letter from Jacob, 2 January 1923.
66 NAM 6707-19-646, Letter from Rudyard Kipling, 28 December 1922.
67 Diary 1923, 1 and 2 February.
68 Diary 1923, 20-22 February.

From September 1923, political issues surfaced more often in Birdwood's diaries, particularly regarding Sikhs. Since the War the Sikhs had established two new organisations: the Shiromani Gurdwara Parbandak Committee, who sought to transfer control of Sikh temples – *gurdwaras* – to elected bodies, and the Akali Dal, a more aggressive offshoot that subsequently developed into a political party.[69] In September Birdwood visited the units at Amritsar when plans for the 'arrest of the Prabandak committee leader at Amritsar' were discussed but put off. In early October, he had a 'long talk about the Akali situation' with the Maharajah of Patiala, a leading Sikh. The unrest continued as the Akalis continued to press for full control of the gurdwaras.[70] At the end of March 1924, the Akali issue was still unresolved and Birdwood received a most unusual request from the Viceroy, seeking Birdwood's service 'as President of a Committee on the Sikh situation in the Punjab.' Birdwood would be appointed by the Governor of the Punjab to avoid the appearance of an inquisition being held into the actions of that administration. The Viceroy saw this as an all-India question impacting on opinions in England, the rest of India and non-Sikh communities. He believed the Punjab Government to be 'naturally unyielding' due to being 'defied', and the other party as 'sulky & wholly unreasonable & obstinate.' He believed the position was getting 'worse instead of better.' He wrote to Birdwood: 'Your personality and your qualities of knowledge, persuasion and patience will be invaluable; and in addition, you will stand for the Army and in what it means to the Sikhs.'[71] This was a notable accolade reflecting Birdwood's known personal qualities, his language abilities and his knowledge of and love for Sikh soldiers. It confirmed his current success and he gave up the opportunity for home leave to apply himself to framing a measure to address 'the administration and management of the Sikh gurdwaras and shrines.'[72]

Henry Craik, then Chief Secretary and a future Governor of the Punjab, assisted Birdwood, who spent April and May meeting with Sikh leaders in Amritsar, Lahore and Tarn Taran, including a 'long talk with Mehtah Singh & others in jail.' If there was cooperation in drawing up a measure, Birdwood had the Viceroy's permission to promise release of any Akali followers in prison for purely gurdwara offences but more extremist Akalis demanded release for all detained before cooperating. These demands proved to be too much despite worthwhile discussions. On 1 June, the committee ceased and Henry Craik wrote to Birdwood: '... I am glad to have been of assistance to you in a task in which your sympathy with a knowledge of the Sikhs has been the principal asset. Your influence on them has been a revelation to me, and your infinite patience & courtesy to them throughout the whole business have been, if I may say so, our most positive chance of success.' He believed that it was no fault of Birdwood that they had not succeeded but rather believed that he had laid foundations for future moves by the Sikhs 'at no very distant date.'[73]

69 Harjot Oberoi, 'Sikh fundamentalism,' in Aakash Singh and Silika Mohapatra (eds.), *Indian Political Thought* (Abingdon, 2010), 151-2.

70 Diary 1923, 6 October; Moon, *The British Conquest and Dominion of India*, 1022; Birdwood, *Khaki and Gown*, 371.

71 NAM 6707-19-665, Letter from Viceroy, 23 March 1924.

72 *The Times of India*, 14 April 1924, 10.

73 Diary 1924, 17 and 25 April. 3, 7, 18, 24 and 28 May; NAM 6707-19-678 & 9, Letters from Craik, 4 & 5 June 1924; *The Times of India*, 7 June 1924, 12; Birdwood, *Khaki and Gown*, 372.

Throughout this period Birdwood had been corresponding with Rawlinson about deputising for him when he went on home leave. Rawlinson kept changing his dates and, as his wife was staying in India, it was not immediately clear that Birdwood would be able to use Snowdon. Finally, Rawlinson decided to leave on 4 August and Birdwood was to use the upper ADC's house. He left Northern Command for the last time and arrived in Simla to be sworn in as a member of the Viceroy's Executive Council. The Viceroy told him that 'it was practically decided I'd be next Chief.' Birdwood's first Executive Council meetings addressed the findings of the Lee Commission on the racial composition of the Indian Civil Service and other all-India services, including addressing the current problems with remuneration. Birdwood obtained the same extensions for officers of the Indian Army as had been made for the Indian Civil Service. At his first Council of State meeting, he 'made a speech on the Sikh question,' which was well received.[74] In addition he enjoyed 'my box at the theatre,' (as the C-in-C's box is still marked at the Gaiety Theatre to this day). In mid-October, he left Simla on tour. At Kohat, he unveiled a memorial to the officers of Frontier Force who had been killed in the War.[75] During a visit to Delhi, he 'drove out to Raisina and saw C-in-C's new house in course of construction,' which he later refused to occupy. After a farewell in Delhi, he left for Bombay, met Rawlinson and handed over. Birdwood sailed for England on 22 November, after a militarily and politically successful four years.[76]

Birdwood landed at Tilbury on 12 December. He called on both the India Office and War Office, where Lord Cavan, CIGS, told him he was 'certain for India.' After an audience with the King for his appointment as GCB, he left for Thurlby, now on the temporarily unemployed list.[77] Unlike preceding ones, his 1925 diary commenced with no commands or military appointments. Rather the start of the year featured log cutting at Thurlby with occasional trips to London. He spoke at both the Secretary of State's Council at the India Office and at the Committee of Imperial Defence in support of artillery for Indian States. 'Eventually all decided for – except Winston.' Churchill was then Chancellor of the Exchequer.[78] He spoke at the Overseas League 'of the need of the British people spreading themselves over the Dominions, and suggested an appeal should be made to the Public schools to send out boys to form group settlements.'[79] On his way to a holiday in the West Country, he stopped at Tidworth to visit the XIIth Lancers, of which had just been appointed Regimental Colonel. This had been his very first regiment and he was to be their Colonel for the next thirty-one years. On arrival in Exmouth on 16 March, he 'found wire & letters telling me the King had approved of my promotion to Field Marshal & appt Commander-in-Chief in India. I have indeed much to be thankful for & have far more than I have deserved.'

He and Jenny were at Exmouth to visit Judith at school and attend her confirmation. Two days later the *London Gazette* published the appointments and consequently: 'enormous number

74 Birdwood, *Khaki and Gown,* 373; Diary 1924, 4, 8, 22, 24 and 29 August, 8 and 9 September; *The Pioneer,* 11 September 1924, 6.

75 NAM 6707-19-705A, Service sheet for Kohat Memorial, 23 October 1924.

76 Diary 1924, 17 and 23 October, 6, 21 and 22 November.FM Sir W R Birdwood, *Reminiscences of the Residencies of the Commanders-in-Chief in India* (Pagoda Tree Press: Bath, 2006 reprint of 1930 privately published edition), 25.

77 Diary 1924, 12, 13, 17 and 19 December.

78 Diary 1925, 1, 6, 20, 21, 27 and 28 January, 6 February.

79 *The Times*, 24 January 1925, 7.

of letters & telegrams pouring in.'[80] His personal pleasure was short-lived as on 28 March he wrote: 'Very sorry to hear Rawlinson very ill indeed & fear sounds as if he might not recover. Later wire received of his death which I deeply regret.' Responding to an urgent wire Birdwood went up to London to see Lord Birkenhead, India Secretary, to learn that the Viceroy 'wanted Birdwood out at once.' Birdwood explained that 'things were quiet & Jacob was there & up to the ropes.' It was agreed that Birdwood did not need to leave until September. He returned to the West Country and then went back to Thurlby. He came down to London for Rawlinson's funeral and then went to tea with the Viceroy who was back on leave and who 'evidently wanted me to go out in July.' Two weeks later at the India Office, Birkenhead said that 'to ensure harmony with Viceroy … I'd best go end of July – a great loss.' Three weeks later, Birdwood saw Reading 'who told me I must go out at least with him in July – a nonsense.'[81] Thus before undertaking five years as C-in-C his leave was shortened. The two significant events before departure were an invitation for a weekend in Cambridge by the Master of Peterhouse, reflecting the long association of the Birdwood family with the College and an audience with the King for the presentation of his 'FM's baton – quite beautiful thing.'[82] He left England on 22 July for France, where he unveiled memorials in both Orleans and Marseilles cathedrals 'To the Glory of God and to the memory of one million dead of the British Empire who fell in the Great War 1914 – 1918 and of whom the greater part rest in France'. He then met up with Jenny, and the Viceroy and his party at Marseilles, and sailed for India.[83]

On 6 August 1925 and forty years after commission as a second lieutenant, he was greeted by Sir Claud and Lady Jacob, and assumed the appointment of C-in-C. He was the first person to hold the position as a Field Marshal. Even illustrious predecessors such as Roberts and Kitchener had only been full generals in the post. He went without delay to Simla and his residence, Snowdon – now his for five years.[84] For his first two months Birdwood concentrated on his legislative responsibilities. He became one of the seven members of the Viceroy's Executive Council, whose members took it in turns to entertain one another once a week to dinner in their homes. Birdwood appreciated and enjoyed this custom. He was also a member of the Council of State, the upper house of legislature consisting of sixty appointed and elected members. Furthermore, he often attended the Central Legislative Assembly that contained 145 members, either nominated or elected from the Provinces. Later he wrote warmly about making new and renewing old friendships among Indian members of all legislatures.[85]

The new session of the Legislative Assembly was opened by the Viceroy in late August and in early September, Birdwood 'made a speech on proposed bill to alter law *re* use of troops in aid of Civil Powers.' Birdwood spoke against suggested amendments which in his view tended 'strongly to safeguard' the 'law-breaking and unruly mob … at the expense of' both innocent and law-abiding citizens and soldiers.' He obviously felt for 'the man on the spot' and although

80 NAM 6707-19-721, 723 and 728, Letters Hankey, Robert and Franks.
81 Diary 1925, 6-17, 22-25, 28 and 31 March; 24 & 25 April: 6 & 20 May.
82 Diary 1925, 26-9 April, 25 May. His baton is now on display in the First World War Gallery of the AWM, REL/04253.001.
83 Diary 1925, 22-4 July.
84 E J Buck, *Simla Past and Present* (Shimla: Minerva, 1925), 71-88; Birdwood, *Reminiscences of the Residencies of the Commanders-in-Chief in India*, 1-19.
85 Birdwood, *Khaki and Gown*, 377-9.

wishing to provide clear instructions, Birdwood did not want hands tied by 'hard and fast regulations by law.' The suggested amendments were, however, carried.[86] Later at the Council of State, Birdwood spoke again and this time the amendments were 'negatived.'[87] At the end of the session he held a 'big garden party at Snowdon for all members of the Council of State & Legislative assembly.'[88]

Before leaving on his first visits as C-in-C, he 'saw Indian cadets fm Sandhurst – only 2 out of 16 passed.' Officer training for Indians would become an issue for him. The Skeen or Indian Sandhurst Committee – Birdwood's CGS and ten Indian members, including both Pandit Motilal Nehru and Jinnah – had started their investigations in June.[89] Passing through Delhi, Birdwood went 'to see the C-in-C's new house.' He attended the opening of the Khyber Railway and visited Kohat once more. With his interest in soldiers' wellbeing he visited married quarters and the new King George's Military Schools, at Jhelum and Jullundur. Both of which subjects would appear in his next Assembly speech. After ten days viewing manoeuvres at Attock, he went to the stud farms at Coleyana and Probynabad, places that held his affection as did Kohat. Back at Delhi he was delighted to meet his daughter Nancy, visiting from Western Australia with son, Robin, and Birdwood's new granddaughter, Judith Mary. The family group together with friends departed for Gwalior as guest of the Maharajah for ten days. It was to be his regular Christmas and New Year retreat. Tiger shoots were a big feature of these stays.

Birdwood clearly treasured his 1926 diary and pasted inside the cover a piece of wrapping paper, which read: 'To Birdie with every good wish for the New Year. H – Haig, Bemersyde.' The 1927 diary was also from Haig. In March, Birdwood spoke for the first time in a budget debate at the Legislative Assembly. He opened cautiously by acknowledging 'that having been brought up among soldiers and having never been fed on figures' he could not 'hope to intervene in a budget discussion with any real advantage.' He emphasised the 'current of military affairs has run smoothly' and highlighted the success of the Waziristan operations. The latter comment drew applause. He talked about efforts to reduce the budget but emphasised, as Rawlinson had done, that the target figure of Rs 50 crores [50 million rupees] had entered popular belief but was 'a pious aspiration.' He underlined his regular talks with Indian Officers but avoided the thorny issue of the Skeen Committee, as it had not yet reported. He closed by encouraging members to visit military establishments. He knew, however, that he was in a rather false Assembly environment as the 'Swarajist had conspiracy of non-cooperation,' and consequently the expected two-day debate closed after the first morning.

A few days later Birdwood undertook what was to be one of his most satisfying tasks as C-in-C – the presentation of Colours. His first were to the 2nd Bn Wiltshire Regiment in Kamptee, near Nagpur.[90] On 1 April he bade farewell to Lord Reading and his wife at Bombay and welcomed the new Viceroy, Lord Irwin and his wife. Birdwood had a 'long talk with Lord Irwin, 6' 3", very quiet & unimpressive, but nice, very anxious to hear about everything – so evidently a gentleman – 20 years younger than me – She a very nice woman with two small

86 NAM 6707-19-1205, Legislative Assembly Debates, Vol VI - No 13, 9 September 1925.
87 NAM 6707-19-1215, Council of State Debates, Vol VI - No 15, 15 September 1925.
88 Diary 1926, 15 September.
89 Pradeep Barua, *Gentlemen of the Raj: the Indian Army Officer Corps, 1817-1949* (Westport, CT. Praeger, 2003), 29-30.
90 Diary 1926, 4 and 8 March. They now hang in Salisbury Cathedral.

boys!' Birdwood was to establish a very warm relationship with Irwin, writing to the Prime Minister, Stanley Baldwin: 'If I may thank you specially for … your selection of Lord Irwin as Viceroy ... to me it has been the greatest delight to be intimately associated from day to day with such a real fine character.'[91] In the coming weeks, they discussed Private Secretaries, Secretaries of Departments, etc.[92] Before leaving, the King had impressed on Birdwood 'the necessity of constant touring and seeing all I could of the troops.' Birdwood had requested Wigram that 'when the King sees the new Viceroy impress on him the necessity of Chief's touring.' Wigram reported that the 'King expressed his views with some vigour to Lord Irwin.'[93] The summer months at Simla followed their normal routine and the various Legislatures were uneventful for Birdwood. On his 61st birthday' he recorded: 'Thank God, I do not feel so old & have indeed much to be thankful for – especially good health for us both & a very happy life.'[94] In October, he left for a two-month tour of Assam and Burma, including a 'strategical survey' of the Burma-China frontier for the Secretary of State India, on which he fully reported to the King.[95]

In 1927, the Executive Council considered 'possible sending tps to China.' and a brigade was sent to 'safeguard Br & Ind interests in Shanghai.'[96] The annual budget debates in both the Assembly and Council of State were more contentious than in his first year, as the Swarajists fully participated. In the first Assembly debate, Birdwood announced the disposal of Aden to the Home Government, continued to argue against the pious target of Rs 50 crores and acknowledged that troops had been 'called out on many parts of India as wide apart as Burma to Quetta in aid of the civil power,' with very few casualties. The Skeen Committee report was not yet available but Birdwood did say, in respect of British officers, that they had 'not been getting boys from Sandhurst in the number we want.' In the Council Birdwood displayed the value of his thorough personal visits.

The military budget was discussed for a second time a week later. In the interim a number of issues had arisen. Jinnah felt that military policy had not been adequately addressed. Birdwood explained how he had looked into the use of troops over the past twelve months. He suggested that Jinnah was really concerned that nothing had been said about Indianisation but 'had been told, I think privately, and certainly been told in answer to a question' that the Sandhurst Committee report was as yet unavailable and that Indian officers were only a part of Indianisation. Ultimately the desire of the Assembly was for Indian civilian control of the military, and for an Indian Army in the fullest sense. Jinnah had an enthusiasm for establishing a Territorial Force and thereby reducing both its full-time strength and the budget. Birdwood explained all the reductions to date and that 'a skeleton army' would produce 'skeletons of an innumerable number of civilians' in time of conflict. A subsequent questioner picked Birdwood up on the phrase 'English boys.' Europeanisation of the Indian Army had been interpreted by this phrase and the questioner outlined the greater emphasis Rawlinson had laid on Indianisation

91 G M Young, *Stanley Baldwin* (London: Rupert Hart-Davis, 1952), 135.
92 Diary 1926, 1 April; 7 and 9 May.
93 RA PS/PSO/GV/C/N/2556/40 & 43 letters, Birdwood and Wigram, 7 November 1925 and 6 April 1926.
94 Diary 1926, 13 September.
95 NAM 6707-19-772, HE FM Sir William Birdwood, Tour in Assam & Burma, 23 October-18 December 1926.
96 Diary 1927, 8 and 15 January, 4 February, 3 March.

Field Marshal Sir William Birdwood, C-in-C India, with the officers of the Governor-General's Body Guard, 1927. (Governor-General's Body Guard Digest of Service 1889-1947, National Army Museum 1954-05-10-1)

in his last speech before his death. He, of course, had the advantage of instigating the Sandhurst Committee, whereas Birdwood was, in effect, marking time while the report made its way through the corridors of Whitehall. As ever Birdwood was polite. The debate closed but the issue did not go away.[97]

On 21 March, *The Times* announced that Birdwood had been elected to an honorary fellowship at Peterhouse; this would later lead to a more significant appointment.[98] At the end of the month he said goodbye to his two grandchildren – 'very sad losing them,' and only a fortnight later Jenny and Chris left for England. Birdwood then spent some weeks of Frontier inspections at Quetta.[99] He added air travel – Bristol fighter – to his means of transport. A joke was reported that Birdwood was flying to Razmak and a sergeant commented: 'Well I suppose he'll fly here

97 NAM 6707-19-1207, -1216, -1208, Legislative Assembly Debates, Vol IX - No 28, 3 March 1927; Council of State Debates Vol IX - No 15, 5 March 1927, Legislative Assembly Debates, Vol IX - No 37, 15 March 1927.

98 *The Times*, 21 March 1927, 16.

99 Diary 1927, 29 March, 10 and 13 April. The author's father's first battalion '4/10th late 129th Baluchis' were noted as 'a fine smart Regt.'

the same as any other "Bird would!"[100] He returned to Simla in mid-April. One of his guests, at the frequent lunches and dinners that dominated his diaries, was Srinivasa Sastri, founder of the Indian Liberal party but previously a Congress party member. He was off to South Africa as the first Agent for the Government of India. He wrote:

> Few things have happened in my life so fine and so tender. I now understand why the simple hearts of soldiers are drawn to you. One should be lucky indeed to be thrown into contact with a person in whom the purely human element remains in its essence through a long life and leaps forward to its kindred in spite of the distractions of office, rank and colour. Honour & glory to you![101]

Birdwood's 'human element' was reflected in a directive from the Adjutant-General, based on the C-in-C's inspections to cavalry regiments. He had noticed 'a tendency to overlook some of the many old traditions and customs,' that had enhanced the family of the regiment and that he sought to retain, particularly 'the holding of weekly durbar ... at which the presence of all ranks is made welcome.'[102]

The Sandhurst Committee 'Skeen' report was published before the next round of legislative debates. Resolutions were tabled to Indianise half the cadre of officers in the Indian Army within fifteen years, and to establish an Indian Sandhurst.[103] Before the first debate, Birdwood received a delegation of Indians holding King's or Viceroy's Commissions and representing the martial races. They pressed that soldiers of their classes should not be called upon to serve under officers of non-martial classes.[104] Birdwood listened but deferred matters to his forthcoming speech. The Government had been able to make only 'provisional proposals' to the Home Government and 'a considered judgement' would be sent as 'a result of this debate.' *The Times* reported his as 'a tactful speech.[105] At the end of October, Birdwood went to Bombay to meet Jenny, Chris and also Judith, who had finished school. He took them all on his lengthy Royal Indian Marine inspection tour round to Madras.[106] After Christmas in Gwalior, the New Year delivered a blow. On 31 January, he received a 'telegram from home announcing Haig had died suddenly – a great loss, especially to the old soldiers. I had recently heard from & written to him.' He telegraphed Lady Haig immediately on behalf of the Indian Army.[107]

While on his naval tour the Simon Commission had been announced.[108] The Simon Commission was now underway. The Montagu-Chelmsford Reforms had called for a review after ten years, i.e. in 1929. The announcement of an earlier review had satisfied Indian

100 NAM 6707-19-781, unreferenced cutting.
101 NAM 6707-19-779, Letter from Sastri, 1 June 1927.
102 NAM 6707-19-782, AG Directive, 14 July 1927.
103 *Report of the Indian Sandhurst Committee* (London: HMSO, 1927).
104 Daniel Marston, *The Indian Army and the End of the Raj* (New York: CUP, 2014), 10-12, 15-17. This explains the martial race theory where some groups, Sikhs and Dogras for example, were considered martial and others were not. Both world wars introduced changes to this approach and to the composition of the army.
105 *The Times*, 26 August 1927, 11.
106 Diary 1927, 28 October - 21 November.
107 Diary 1928, 31 January. *The Times*, 1 February 1928, 16.
108 Sir John Simon, Liberal politician and barrister. Members included Clement Attlee.

opinion, but not a single Indian was announced among its members. Skeen had sat with a totally Indian committee. The Viceroy's Executive Council included Indians. Lord Irwin subsequently proposed a committee of the Indian Legislature and the Commission to consider the Commission's report, but the Congress Party led the way with a complete boycott. Later in the year it produced the Nehru Report, that 'framed a constitution for self-governing India.'[109] On 5 February 1928, the Viceroy's Council met the Commission and subsequently Birdwood briefed three members, including Attlee, on the Army in India.

A happy interlude then occurred. Birdwood's senior ADC married Jenny's niece. Captain Dawson was an Australian who had enlisted in 1915, served at Gallipoli and in France, was wounded at Bullecourt and had successfully applied to join the Indian Army. He had been posted to Kohat before joining Birdwood's staff. The reception was at Flagstaff House with the Viceroy proposing the toast to the bride and groom.[110] Birdwood was still in his old residence, having refused to move into the proposed new one, but when he heard that the Maharajah of Kashmir was looking for a new home, the sale of his proposed residence was successfully negotiated! He then found an attractive and available site, and embarked on his own new plans for a residence.

In early March, Birdwood was back at the Assembly for the budget debate and in a very lengthy speech he first explained a reduction in expenditure despite certain costs being added. He dispelled suggestions that the budget contributed to a 'drain of money from India to the United Kingdom' by showing that seventy-seven per cent was spent in India and explained at length how he saw expenditure benefitting India and Indians more widely. He then turned to the Sandhurst Committee Report, starting with three considerations: that 'a further measure of Indianization [*sic*] is necessary; there be no decline in efficiency of the Army; and 'no breakdown in the supply of British recruits [officers] to the extent required.' He announced a doubling of Sandhurst vacancies to twenty with an additional five for Viceroy's Commissioned officers. Eight places were to be available at the Royal Military Academy Woolwich and two at Royal Air Force College Cranwell, with a view to forming Indian artillery, engineer and air units. The entry examinations for Indian candidates would be changed to reflect the different background but not made easier. The eight-unit Indianisation scheme proposed under Rawlinson was to be kept but, as it was not possible to predict the future candidate numbers, the establishment of an Indian Sandhurst by 1933 – as proposed by the Committee – was not supported by the Government.

Both Motilal Nehru and Jinnah made, in Birdwood's words, 'violent political "anti" speeches.' Nehru included a suggestion that remittances from Indian troops in China were partially due to looting. Adjournment for lunch thankfully restricted further debate.[111] On 10 March Birdwood attended a special Neuve Chapelle parade of the 59th Rifles but that same day Jinnah introduced a motion for adjournment. The Assembly President, Mr Patel, allowed the motion and after some speeches announced that, having given a lengthy speech it was discourteous of the C-in-C not to be present for replies. The Viceroy called on Birdwood the next day to discuss this serious accusation of discourtesy. Political bitterness was diffused by Patel and Birdwood meeting for an arranged lunch 'to talk over all the trouble with former re his accusations to me

109 Moon, *The British Conquest and Dominion of India*, 1027-31; Wilson, *India Conquered*, 123-4.
110 Diary 1928, 20 February.
111 NAM 6707-19-1210, *Legislative Assembly Debates* Vol I - No 23, 8 March 1928.

in Assembly on 10th, since when I have not been near it! Poor old rascal – quite hopeless!' The next day Birdwood spoke about clearing up the misunderstanding and that he was 'glad to be addressing you again on the floor of this House.' Mr Patel was equally gracious.[112] Birdwood, however, wrote to Wigram that 'I do not propose again attending or speaking in the Assembly except when it is essential for me to do so.'[113]

C-in-C India's staff polo team with Birdwood's son, Christopher (right), Simla 1928. (Author's collection)

After visits to the Punjab and the Frontier and a break in Kashmir, Birdwood was back in Simla, where the polo had started. He himself played in some warm-up games and his own Snowdon team won the competition in May. His diary was now full of Executive Council meetings on the Simon Commission. The Simla session of the Assembly brought questions about a presentation given at the four Army commands regarding finance and economy, with a view to achieving savings that was seen as a means of funding mechanisation and thereby modernisation. The year concluded with a notable change of CGS. Skeen left on retirement and

112 Diary 1928, 9, 10, 11, 20 & 21 March; *The Times*, 22 March 1928, 16.
113 RA PS/PSO/GV/C/N/2556/70, letter, Birdwood to Wigram, 24 March 1928.

was replaced by Sir Philip Chetwode, a British Army cavalry general.[114] Birdwood's last two years in India were dominated by the Simon Commission and the issue of Indianisation of the army. But problems also arose in Afghanistan, where King Amanullah appeared to be becoming too progressive, provoking a possible rising. It was decided to evacuate British, French, Italian and other legations by air. As Birdwood later reported, the Royal Air Force 'made 86 journeys from Peshawar to Kabul and back, and flew a distance of 28,000 miles.' Birdwood was full of admiration and his diary entry for the last day of flying expressed his relief.[115] The Simon Commission now had returned to England. Life in Simla continued, now with Judith heavily involved in acting.[116] Birdwood later announced changes to the military budget, based on his agreement with the Finance Secretary that the budget would be Rs 55 crores annually for the coming three years and out of the total sum the army would find 10 crores for modernisation. The Executive Council began to consider the 'future constitution' and the Simon report, and the strong probability that it would be 'far from satisfying Congress's aspirations.' At the end of June, the Viceroy and his wife left on a short home leave and Birdwood was 'very sorry indeed to be losing them.' The Viceroy was able to meet with the new government of Ramsay MacDonald and at the end of September the acting Viceroy showed Birdwood 'wires recently passed between him & SofS re account to be made by Irwin on his return.'

Just before Irwin returned, Birdwood's successor was announced as Chetwode, thus maintaining the interchange of British and Indian Army officers. At the same time, it was published that Birdwood was to receive a three-month extension up until the end of November 1930.[117] Once his successor and his own extension were announced, there was a flurry of speculation in the press about the possibility of Birdwood becoming the next Governor General of Australia. His personal archives have eleven press cuttings about the rumours, his own rejection of them and that Mr Scullin, the Australian Prime Minister, apparently knew nothing of it.[118] In 1920, Lord Irwin had experienced similar turbulence. He had accepted the Governor-Generalship of South Africa and then had it withdrawn.[119] He would have known of Birdwood's strong desire to go to Australia. The rumour appeared to have started in London, not India, and Irwin was there in London. It is pure conjecture whether he tried to initiate such consideration for his colleague. On Irwin's return they lunched together and the next day Irwin made his key announcements. The first was that once the Simon Commission had reported, a Round Table Conference would be held between the British Government and representatives of both British India and the Indian States to discuss the constitutional process, and the second was that the outcome would be dominion status.

The Congress party had, meanwhile, declared *Purna Swaraj*, complete independence for India, and announced 26 January 1930 as a day for all Indians to demonstrate opposition to British rule. The Viceroy had narrowly escaped being blown up on 23 December as his train

114 Skeen subsequently wrote a small guide for young officers fighting on the Frontier. Still relevant, it remains in print. See General Sir Andrew Skeen, *Passing It On* (Aldershot: Gale & Polden, 1943).

115 Birdwood, *Khaki and Gown*, 394; NAM 6707-19-1219, Council of State Debates, Vol I - No 6, 25 February 1929. Diary 1929, 25 February.

116 M M Kaye, *Golden Afternoon* (London: Viking, 1997), 243-45.

117 *The Times*, 23 October 1929, 16.

118 NAM 6707-19-840 to -850, Various cuttings.

119 D J Dutton, 'Wood, Edward Frederick Lindley, first Earl of Halifax (1881–1959),' *Oxford Dictionary of National Biography*, 2004 <https://doi.org/10.1093/ref:odnb/36998> (accessed 25 September 2018).

approached New Delhi.[120] This was an early introduction to what was to become a much more tumultuous year.[121] On 25 January, the Viceroy addressed the Assembly and stressed dominion status as the ultimate aim but the civil disobedience campaign started the next day. In March Birdwood spoke about the budget debate in the Council of State. He had still not spoken in the Assembly since the outbursts of March 1928. He challenged a point made in the Assembly that the Skeen Committee's recommendations had been unanimously turned down. He explained that only two had not been supported – the creation of an Indian Sandhurst and the abolition of the eight-unit scheme.[122] Later in the Assembly Jinnah, using a newspaper report rather than the proceedings, suggested that Birdwood's statement was 'a tissue of lies.' This calumny was refuted later in the Council of State with a statement of confidence in the C-in-C.[123] The creation of an Indian Sandhurst had made no progress despite the production by the Skeen Committee of a table that clearly showed the evolution of Indianisation if one was created.[124] This was a major issue for Indian politicians and would not be resolved in Birdwood's time. By April Gandhi had completed his salt march and Jawaharlal Nehru had been arrested. These and other events triggered violent demonstrations in Peshawar, during which the 2/18 Garhwalis were deployed on riot duty. The next day two platoons refused to go back on duty. The resulting imprisonment and discharge could not take away the shock of the word 'mutiny.' Control in Peshawar was not regained until 4 May.[125]

At the beginning of June, the Simon Commission report was published and Birdwood spent two whole days reading it. It recommended the development from dyarchy into full provincial responsibility but failed to mention Dominion status. In its survey of defence, it was an even-handed understanding of Indian aspirations, agreeing that this must be a slow process, and not accepting Indian legislative control over British forces. It suggested an Imperial constitutional treatment for defence, removing the C-in-C from his portfolio in the Government of India.[126] For the next month, the Executive Council met nearly every day – often morning and afternoon. The Viceroy addressed both Houses on 9 July setting out his clear focus on a Round Table Conference. 'Simon Commission' was the constant entry in Birdwood's diary up until late September, with the last being: 'Defence taking some time as I insisted on my point, in saying that rapid Indianisation might cause inefficiencies & can only be carried out for political reasons.' The lack of an Indian Sandhurst and the continuation of the eight-unit scheme, as highlighted by the Commission, appeared to show a slow and illiberal approach to Indianisation. Birdwood, however, feared the danger of any loss of efficiency in the army and in his eyes, such could be caused by rapid change. On 11 September invitations to attend the Round Table Conference

120 *The Times of India*, 24 December 1929, 11.

121 Percival Spear, *India: A Modern History* (Ann Arbor, MI: University of Michigan Press, 1961), 374-81; Stanely Wolpert, *A New History of India* (Oxford: Oxford University Press, 1982), 314-17; Burton Stein, *A History of India* (Oxford: Blackwell, 1998), 324-27.

122 *The Times of India*, 8 March 1930, 18.

123 *The Times of India*,10 March 1930, 11; NAM 6707-19-1221, Council of State Debates Vol I - No 16, 27 March 1930.

124 *Report of the Indian Sandhurst Committee*, 56.

125 Philip Mason, *A Matter of Honour* (London: Jonathan Cape, 1974), 451-53. Diary 1930, 30 April; 1, 12, 13, 14 & 16 May.

126 *Report of the Indian Statutory Commission Vol I - Survey*, Cmd 3568 (London, 1930), 92-107; *Report of the Indian Statutory Commission Vol II – Recommendations*, Cmd 3569 (London, 1930), 167-80.

in London were issued to representatives of both the Indian States and British India, Congress having boycotted the event.[127] Shortly after this date, farewells started to dominate Birdwood's diary, whether dinners or more poignantly last walks over Simla hills and leaving Snowdon. He spent a month travelling round familiar stations and cantonments on his way to New Delhi, including farewell to Probyn's Horse – a two-day affair which included many old pensioners.[128] A week of farewells in Delhi followed, including 'my last good ride for a long time to come,' before all of the Viceroy's Body Guard paraded to see him off to Bombay to greet his successor and on 29 November, sail away from India.

Birdwood had been born in India sixty-five years earlier and had given forty-five years of his life in the service of her Army. He had reached the highest pinnacles of both rank and appointment. From his first days as a junior officer he had learnt to get alongside soldiers – *sowars* or *sepoys* – and talk to them in their own languages. He had continued this approach throughout his service up to and including as C-in-C, whether on parade, during informal meetings or on walking visits to villages. He had improved accommodation for both single and married soldiers, as well as education for sons of soldiers. He had imaginatively negotiated a fixed budget for defence from which the expenses for a modernisation programme were being drawn. General Tim Harington, Commander Western Command and previously Plumer's Chief of Staff for two years, wrote earlier to Birdwood that 'I do feel you are laying down a very solid foundation at the moment which must result in greater efficiency both in the field for war and in a well housed, well administered & contented Army.' In saying farewell to 'My Dear Chief', Harington observed:

> I like also to think that you & Lady Birdie will pull down the flag knowing that you have both played a most splendid innings for India: that you have both won the hearts of everyone and that every Indian village, from which the Indian soldier comes, re-echoes your praises … I like also to think of all the progress which has taken place in the last 5 years. I have been privileged to see all the improvements in equipment, MT, roads, barracks, etc. It is quite wonderful & all done in your time. Those who have served under you realize it and are most grateful … It must be a source of great satisfaction to you that through the past very trying year, the Army has stood so loyally against all attempts at tampering and to know that this has been accomplished mainly by your own great personality & thoughtfulness for all who serve under you. It is your example of the art of command by leading instead of driving which many of us try in a humble way to copy. Many, who act differently, criticize us but they have never known what the love & affection of a soldier means and we can afford to be sorry for them. They have missed what is best in life.[129]

This was a truly fine accolade from a highly successful wartime general. Before Birdwood had departed India the first Round Table Conference had started in London. A defence sub-committee was appointed which gave its report, 'centred around Indianisation,' to the

127 *The Times*, 11 September 1930, 9.
128 The Regimental Christmas card for 1930 contained a picture of Birdwood surrounded by the pensioners.
129 NAM 6707-19-621 & -903, Letters from Harington, 28 January 1929 & 1 November 1930.

whole conference on 16 January.[130] As a result, the eight-unit scheme was doubled and in May 1931, a committee was formed under Chetwode to implement the Indian Sandhurst. The Indian Military Academy opened at Dehra Dun in October 1932. Chetwode addressed the cadets that December:

> First, the safety, honour and welfare of your country come first, always and every time. Second, the honour, welfare and comfort of the men you command come next. Third, your own ease, comfort and safety come last, always and every time.[131]

This address was given just two years after Birdwood had left India. Despite all the successes enunciated by Harington, Birdwood was not a progressive and his firm emphasis on efficiency could have been interpreted by some Indian nationalists as shielding a blind spot.[132]

Birdwood sailed from Bombay with instructions from Lord Stamfordham, the King's Private Secretary, to take a cipher book with him, 'as the King will have an important message for you.'[133] A draft telegram offering Birdwood the 'Governor Generalship of Australia on the recommendation of Australian Prime Minister' had been prepared.[134] Earlier on 22 January 1930, Lord Stonehaven, the then Governor-General of Australia, had responded to letters from Birdwood acknowledging his admirable qualifications for the post and giving advice on the financial burden of it. Later he provided the breakdown of expenses showing that the deficiency in expenditure to be met by the incumbent was £5,000 *p.a.* His two further letters in February and April discussed the apparent preference among Labor party members for an Australian Governor-General.[135] An undated – but probably from the same period – letter from General Harry Chauvel reported that he had spoken with a Minister but not the Prime Minister and the message was that the present Cabinet would not ask for a soldier.[136] Stonehaven was being unforthcoming with Birdwood for already Scullin, the Prime Minister, had sought advice from his Liaison Officer in the Cabinet Secretariat in Whitehall, Richard Casey, as to the procedure followed in selecting governors-general. In late March Scullin advised the Secretary of State for the Colonies that his Cabinet favoured Sir Isaac Isaacs, the Chief Justice. The King was astonished at this but as Scullin would be in London for the Imperial Conference during 1 October - 14 November, the topic was left for personal discussion then.[137]

130 'Indian Round Table Conference 12th November 1930-19th January 1931,' Government of India, (Calcutta, 1931), 373-6.
131 Heathcote, *The Military in British India: The Development of British Land Forces in South Asia, 1600-1947*, 221; Mason, *A Matter of Honour*, 465. These words are carved on the walls of Chetwode Hall at the Academy.
132 From N G Jog, *Churchill's Blind Spot: India* (Bombay: New book Company, 1944).
133 Birdwood, *Khaki and Gown*, 408.
134 RA PS/PSO/GV/C/L/2293/329, draft telegram, undated but filed with correspondence 21-29 November 1930.
135 BL AAS, Mss Eur D 686 folio 80, Letters from Lord Stonehaven, 22 and 24 January, 13 February and 15 April 1930. Although Fehilly had left parliament by 1930 and Theodore was absent due to financial charges, their views from the days of Birdwood's Brisbane would not have changed.
136 BL AAS, Mss Eur D 686 folio 80, Letter from Chauvel, n.d .
137 Christopher Cunneen, *King's Men* (Sydney: George Allen & Unwin, 1983), 173-5; Christopher Cunneen, *King's Men, 173-181.*

At the Conference, it was resolved that on the matter of appointments of governors-general, the King should act on the advice of Dominion ministers and any formal submission should take place after informal consultation with the King. On 20 November, Lord Stamfordham passed the King's views to Casey who on 21 November wrote to Scullin, then visiting Ireland. The letter strongly urged Birdwood's appointment and stated the 'King's objections to Isaacs.' It was now 'hoped that finance would not be an objection to Birdwood's acceptance.' It was also felt that the precedent of an Australian governor-general would cause difficulties in both Canada and South Africa, both of which had two races to consider. The meeting between the King and Scullin took place on 29 November. Scullin insisted on Isaacs and with great reluctance the King, having found Scullin 'obstinate and unmoveable,' finally accepted his advice. On 2 December, the announcement was made. This was not from the Palace as usual but instead from Australia House. The London press drew attention to the snub.[138]

In Cairo Birdwood received a letter saying that matters had not materialised and the King would explain in the future. The Viceroy wrote to Birdwood, while he was still travelling, adding a handwritten *postscript* saying that 'I deplore Australia but I suppose HM cd not help himself. I fear it will be a very bad precedent.'[139]. Birdwood arrived In England on Christmas Eve and went straight to Thurlby. He was invited to stay at Sandringham at the end of January but before then he had learnt from members of the Royal Household: 'How very keen the King was to appt me & very angry with Scullin for having committed himself to Isaacs,' and that Scullin had refused to give way. Birdwood's descriptions of both his and his wife's enjoyment of their time at Sandringham do not include any reference to the Governor-Generalship.[140] He had been available but he did not fit the new criteria for the position, to which he had long aspired.

In the middle of February, Birdwood went down to stay for a weekend at Peterhouse and while there, the then Master astounded Birdwood by asking if he should succeed him as Master. Two weeks later there came a formal letter seeking Birdwood's permission for his name to be put forward for election. On 9 March, he received a telegram saying that the Fellows had unanimously elected him as Master of the oldest, founded in 1284, and then the smallest college in Cambridge. He and his wife moved at the end of July into the Master's Lodge, an attractive Queen Anne residence across the road from the College.[141] Before moving to Cambridge, Ramsay MacDonald had planned to submit Birdwood's name to the King for a peerage. 'His own party were so angry at Peers made during his time already voting against the Govt in the Lords, that he had to make it a condition … I wd undertake to sit on the Govt benches. I refused.'[142] As Master, he was to serve seven years. The appointment was a genuine surprise to Birdwood, whose approach to the post was typical of him. He soon established: walking routes round the Botanical Gardens, the Wranglers' walk, or out to Trumpington and Grantchester; swimming in the river from the University Sheds at Grantchester meadows; and riding from

138 RA PS/PSO/GV/C/L/2293/331, 332 & 340, letters, Stamfordham to Hardinge [APS], 21 November 1930, Casey to Scullin, 21 November 1930 & Stamfordham to Prime Minister [Ramsay MacDonald], 29 November 1930; Christopher Cunneen, *King's Men,* 173-181; Harold Nicolson, *King George the Fifth His Life and Reign* (London: Constable & Co, 1952), 480-2.

139 NAM 6707-19-965, Letter from Lord Irwin, 9 December 1930.

140 Diary 1931, 1, 10, 21, 21 and 31 January, 1 and 2 February.

141 Diary 1931, 14-15 and 28 February, 9 March, 29 July.

142 Diary 1931, 22 April.

stables near Barton. In College, he set about meeting individually all the Freshmen – about sixty in number – then the third-year undergraduates and so on. He breakfasted with each crew in turn before the Lent and May Bumps and interviewed all scholarship candidates. He dined regularly in his own Hall with Fellows and guests, at the annual college feasts, and as a guest himself in other Colleges. At the end of his first academic year he had established his routine for the years to come and his diary showed him as entirely at ease with his new role and circumstances.[143]

In the long vacation of 1932, he, Jenny and their younger daughter, Judith, travelled to see Nancy and her family in Western Australia. Sadly, Birdwood developed a very painful foot which restricted his walking or even wearing a shoe but he did meet old soldiers on a number of occasions. His foot problem was diagnosed as periostitis and it recurred in later years.[144] Age had caught up with his health. Back home, Jenny was also in hospital off and on for a number of months and this encouraged another summer journey in the Long Vacation of 1933 – this time to South America. Long summer breaks were becoming their routine, with Australia again in 1934, still seeing and broadcasting to retired servicemen.[145] The next holiday was around the Mediterranean, including a day at Constantinople. To his regret, they passed up and back down the Dardanelles in the dark, seeing nothing.[146]

Perhaps this encouraged his subsequent trip in 1936 to Gallipoli and Salonika. This was a three-week springtime voyage from Liverpool, organised by two ex-servicemen who approached both Birdwood and Lord Keyes to be sponsors[147] The party was an amazing six hundred strong. All paid for their berth on the SS *Lancastria*. They sailed up to Constantinople for a day and on the way back anchored in Kilia Bay, north of Maidos, that was part of the stretch of water viewed by the most forward advancing Anzacs on 25 April and by those who reached the summit of Chanuk Bair. The party was welcomed by an Australian, Tasman Millington, of the Imperial War Graves Commission, who had been on the Gallipoli Peninsula for fifteen years. They visited all Birdwood's 'old Anzac haunts.' Able to see 'the enemy's point of view' he 'marvelled 'that the Anzacs had hung on for 'all those long months.' He saw and laid wreaths at the memorials: Australian on Lone Pine, New Zealand at Chanuk Bair and Turkish near the Nek. He found it 'a more emotional experience than … foreseen.' The next day they visited Cape Helles and then sailed on to Salonika.[148] Approaching Gibraltar, they were passed by the SS *River Clyde* (now SS *Maruja y Aurora*) of V Beach fame. On his return to the College Birdwood gave a presentation on the Gallipoli campaign to the history society. The talk was comprehensive, reflecting that it was given to many 'who were not born when the war started.' It still has a freshness and honesty about it.[149] Sadly just after their 1935 trip, Jenny's father passed

143 Diary 1931, 29 July, 11 and 29 August, 9 & 12 October, 8 November, 7 December. Diary 1932, 4 January, 10 & 11 February.
144 Diary 1932, 30 May-7 October.
145 Diary 1934, 29 June-5 October.
146 Diary 1935, 26 and 27 August.
147 I am grateful to Emma Dolman, granddaughter of one of the two organisers, Mr C D Clark, for access to her grandfather's suitcase full of memorabilia of the cruise – passenger lists, berth allocations with ship layout, programmes and menus, photographs of landing sites and cemeteries, etc., and newspaper cuttings.
148 Diary 1936, 11-14 May. Birdwood, *Khaki and Gown*, 420-1.
149 Birdwood, *Gallipoli*.

away, aged ninety-seven, at Thurlby. Birdwood had a deep and strong affection for his father-in-law, culminating in many later references to 'dear old Dadoo.'[150]

Birdwood had arrived at Peterhouse as a figure of great distinction and his status grew during his Mastership. In March 1933, he was invited to become Colonel of the Royal Horse Guards – The Blues, thereby becoming one of the two Gold Sticks of the Royal Household. To Birdwood this was a 'very great compliment & never before held by an I.A. officer.'[151] He attended Royal Courts, the State Openings of Parliament and the King's Birthday Parades, the latter with a cuirass for the first time in his service. Birdwood later chose the dress of his Colonelcy of The Blues for his official portrait at Peterhouse – rather different from all the others. The next honour to be bestowed on him by the King was Captain of Deal Castle. He and Jenny went down in January 1935 to see if they could afford to live there. In May 1935, he had a meeting with the Australian Prime Minister Lyons who asked him 'if I wd accept apt Governor of Australia. I told him it was very much a matter of means & he said he wd look into this – a very nice fellow.' A few days later Birdwood talked with the Earl of Athlone, the King's uncle, 'about possibilities of Australia.' Nothing came of it and in August, Hore-Ruthven, later Lord Gowrie, was appointed.[152]

Birdwood began to spend more time at Deal and in 1936 the family spent their whole summer there. That year was an eventful one for anyone in the Royal Household. King George V died and Birdwood attended King Edward VIII on his taking the oath before the Privy Council. As the senior non-royal Field Marshal, he assisted the Duke of Connaught in presenting the new King with his baton.[153] On 3 December, he recorded nastiness in the papers about the King's affairs. He kept a number of cuttings about utterances by bishops regarding the King. Birdwood marked them: 'Who are we to judge or throw stones.'[154] The next mention was that he had 'heard King Edward VIII had definitely abdicated. The most awful disaster that I can ever remember & I cannot get over it at all – he who showed so much promise & was so beloved by all in the whole Empire has thrown away everything. It is too awful.' On New Year's Day Birdwood wrote: 'Let us hope that our new King George VI may have a happy year & reign. He will, I am sure, follow in his father's footsteps but I personally much regret all that happened in connection with his brother Edward VIII of whom I am very fond & I think he of me.'[155] Birdwood, in May, had great delight in seeing both the Indian and Australian contingents for the coronation. In the absence of the Duke of Connaught he presented the new King with his Field Marshal's baton.[156] That year he returned to Australia and as always met retired servicemen. He particularly enjoyed opening Birdwood House, the Returned and Services League Hall at Geraldton. 'Twenty years had passed by' since the end of the War but he was still 'their great commander and steadfast friend.' He assured all those present of the 'excellent way the old war graves were being kept.[157] He would have had many memories of his trip to share at a time when

150 Diary 1935, 1 and 3 August.
151 Diary 1933, 1 March.
152 Diary 1935, 2 and 6 May. Lyons was conservative.
153 Diary 1936, 21 and 22 January, 26 May.
154 NAM 6707-19-1100 -1103, Select cuttings..
155 Diary 1936, 10-12 December. Diary 1937, 1 January.
156 Diary 1937, 4, 6 and 10 May.
157 *Geraldton Guardian and Express*, 28 August 1937, 3, and 31 August 1937, 4. Diary 1937, 27 August.

Turkey had just closed the battlefield to visitors and would not reopen them until the fiftieth anniversary in 1965.[158]

When Birdwood returned to Peterhouse for his last academic year, Neville Chamberlain asked whether he would accept a peerage. He did, but noted 'had it come after the war when the other 4 army commanders in France rec'd theirs it wd have been more welcome.' Bean wrote in the NSW veterans' journal that: 'Among all soldiers of the Great War on the British side, Birdwood was one of those with the greatest capacity for personal leadership of men. He was exceptional in that he could combine this quality with a simplicity and friendliness which made him approachable by all ranks from the highest to the lowest. He did away with caste distinction which so often attaches itself to the gradations of the military command.'[159] Birdwood took the title of Baron Birdwood, of Anzac and of Totnes in the County of Devon. On his escutcheon, he added the stars of the Southern Cross to the five martlets of his family crest and the supporters were a sergeant of the XIIth Lancers and a Sikh *daffadur* of the XI BL, both mounted.[160] In June 1938 he dined in Peterhouse for the last time as Master. *The Times* commented that he had 'passed from the routine of military and political life to that of a high academic position with apparently no difficulty.' He 'endeared himself to dons and undergraduates,' showing 'a rare versatility, which has been reflected in his unfailing geniality and his youthful habit of mind and body.' One of his dons, an old ICS man, Sir Hubert Sams, wrote that Birdwood was a scholar in his own military line, knowing as much about Urdu and Punjabi and of the peoples who spoke them as the classical dons do of Latin or Greek. He knew all the undergraduates 'by name and everything about them.' He was 'so human' with the servants, some of whom he had led 'into battle.' Of the military attitude, Peterhouse 'never caught even a glimpse of it in the wise and benign rule of our beloved Master.'[161]

Birdwood then settled into life at Deal Castle – gardening, walking, swimming and enjoying visitors. He had become a director of Norwich Union Fire Insurance and a trustee of the Imperial War Museum. Meetings and various dinners took him regularly to London. He accompanied the King and Queen on their State visit to France, including to Villers-Bretonneux for the unveiling of the Australian War Memorial. A considerable number of old Diggers were present and after the round of cheers for the King, a cry of 'We want Birdie' went up. Birdwood was made to walk between the King and Queen to the cheers of the Diggers.[162] That royal tour indicated that the *entente cordiale* was restored. In November Mustafa Kemal Ataturk, the President of Turkey, died and Birdwood was directed to represent the King at the funeral in Angora (Ankara). His foot became inflamed once more and so with mobility severely restricted, Birdwood was given a prominent position on a gallery above where the body was to rest. Birdwood's presence signified that Turkey and Britain had re-established their pre-war relationship – an important message

158 Antonio Sagona, et al (eds.), *Anzac Battlefield* (Port Melbourne: Cambridge University Press, 2016), 217.
159 NAM 6707-19-1146, *Reveille* cutting, 1 January 1938.
160 His coat of arms may be seen on the staircase to the House of Lords with those of other military peers and on a plaque in his old stall as a GCB in the Henry VII Lady Chapel in Westminster Abbey. His GCMG banner now hangs in Clifton College chapel.
161 *The Times*, 25 June 1938, 14; *Illustrated Weekly of India*, 21 August 1938.
162 Diary 1938, 22 July.

Birdwood as Gold Stick when Master of Peterhouse by Francis Dodd, 1935. (Reproduced by permission of the Master and Fellows of Peterhouse, Cambridge).

to Germany and Italy. These two occasions showed that Birdwood now strongly epitomized the man of empire. He was trusted to represent his King and embody the Empire.

When Birdwood disembarked at Deal, both feet were in great pain and later both bronchitis and pleurisy developed. It was not until 9 February, 1939 that he went outside for a walk. In 1936 Birdwood had become President of Clifton College. A crisis at the school had occurred in late 1938 and the headmaster had resigned. A new Head was required for the start of the summer term. It was over these months that Birdwood strongly recommended one of the Peterhouse dons, Bertrand Hallward, who was appointed in late March.[163] Together in June, they chaired the annual Commemoration event, which Birdwood always conscientiously attended. At the beginning of 1939 Birdwood was confirmed as Honorary Colonel of 7 (Home Counties) (Cinque Ports) Anti-Aircraft Regiment, R.A. (T.A.). As the year proceeded, he visited the House of Lords more often, saw his commissioned grandson leave for India – as he himself had

163 C S Knighton (ed.), *Clifton College: Foundation to Evacuation*, Bristol Record Society's Publication Vol 65 (Bristol: Bristol Record Office with Clifton College, 2012), 94-96; Derek Winterbottom, *Bertrand Hallward. First Vice-Chancellor of the University of Nottingham 1948-1965: A Biography* (Nottingham: University of Nottingham, 1995), 63-64 & 68.

done fifty-four years earlier – and visited the War Office concerning his two regiments. In late August, he wrote: 'War news very bad – looks like Germany determined on war more than ever,' and then 'Anxious day wondering if we are for peace or war.' The declaration of war caused his daughter, Judith, to bring her wedding forward. Birdwood wrote that year for his birthday: 'But for those beastly Germans life wd be all right.' He saw the XIIth off to France and visited all the gun positions of his artillery regiment. He was appointed chair of a 'Committee to provide broadcast for the troops in France' and finished the year by commencing his memoirs.[164] He composed a number of inspirational letters to the commanders of the 2ndAIF. Brigadier Leslie Morshead, commanding 18th Brigade, wrote that he felt 'flattered that you still remember me and appreciate your congratulations and good wishes.' Brigadier A S 'Tubby' Allen wrote that: 'I well remember the encouragement and inspiration, you were to me when, at the age of 23, you patted me on the back on the occasion of my taking the 45 Bn into action for the first time as a Bn Commander … and you were also the first to greet me on my return from that tour of duty in the line.'[165]

In February, together with Field Marshals Deverell, Jacob and Montgomery-Massingberd, he flew to Gort's BEF HQ and spent a day with each of I and II Corps. Then 'Germany invaded the poor unfortunate Danes & Norway who are absolutely innocent & defenceless.' Soon news came that the 'Germans had invaded Holland & Belgium,' and the same day there was 'heavy gun & bomb fire off the coast.' A week later two 6" guns were moved to Deal Castle and just as the troops were disembarking from Dunkirk, Birdwood and his wife took a little cottage in Batcombe, Somerset, initially for three months.[166] Having written earlier about the potential value of a 'Local Defence' force, he was meeting such volunteers in Bruton.[167] His last trip outside the UK was, as the commander of Portuguese forces at the end of the last war, on a diplomatic mission to Portugal with the Duke of Kent. On return he settled into visiting and encouraging Local Defence Volunteers, shortly to become the Home Guard, all over the West Country. Regular forces were coming into the area and Birdwood was soon being invited to speak about Gallipoli to messes and courses. These visits pleasingly included seeing Morshead's 18th Australian Brigade at Tidworth and Bulford, and General Wynter's – one of his old AIF staff officers Australian HQ at Amesbury.[168] Birdwood finished writing his memoirs in time sadly to include the death of his 'good friend Brudenell White' in an air crash. 'He was not only a great man, but a God-fearing man: indeed he was great because he trusted in God.'[169] A few weeks later 'half a dozen bombs fell in our little village in the night, some damage but no casualties.' On 5 October, he 'heard of a direct hit on our Castle at Deal & all the 1720 part – our bedrooms, my nice office, drawing & dining & 2 small sitting rooms with much of our furniture, clothes, etc. – great nuisance – once more up to Hitler.' He visited the Castle to see the damage and his regiment at work. In December, another place dear to him was bombed

164 Diary 1939, 1 January, 24 May, 3 and 4 July, 3, 16, 23 and 26 August, 7 and 13 September, 12 & 16 October, 2 and 23 November.
165 NAM 6707-19-1159 – 1163, Five letters.
166 Diary 1940, 9 and 10 April, 10, 28 and 31 May.
167 *The Times*, 23 May 1940, 9.
168 Diary 1940, 24 June-1 July; 12 July; 8 August.
169 Birdwood, *Khaki and Gown*, 437.

– Clifton College. He found Bristol 'horribly damaged,' and presided at the College Council meeting that decided to evacuate the school.[170]

In the New Year of 1941 Birdwood became very busy as President of the Selection Board for officers in the Home Guard throughout the West Country.[171] At the beginning of April he and Jenny left Batcombe to rent the country home of a cousin of hers at Coates just outside Cirencester. On his walks Birdwood came across some New Zealand wood cutters working in the nearby forest and made great friends with them. He was now called upon to visit towns and cities for War Weapons weeks and subsequently Salute the Soldier weeks. Talks to factory workers in the West Country were later added to his portfolio of encouragement. For all these he travelled as far afield as the Scottish Borders. In May, he commenced writing regular military commentaries for *The Tablet*. He wrote nearly thirty articles, each of around eighteen-hundred-words, reflecting his military and Indian knowledge, and coloured also by a depth of history that he may have gained from his regular attendance at history lectures given by one of his Peterhouse dons.[172] He broadcast to the 'mothers, wives & widows of all Indian soldiers,' in addition to his now regular Anzac Day broadcasts to Australia. After Christmas, he and his wife lunched at Badminton House, during which he had a long discussion with Queen Mary.[173] Whether or not this initiated the offer to Birdwood of a grace-and-favour apartment at Hampton Court is not known. Certainly, it was unusual to accommodate a married couple rather than a widow or spinster. Viscount Wolseley and his wife had lived at Hampton Court and this was the precedent for the Birdwoods. In May, they went to look at Apartment Number 39, with its fascinating decorations from the Wolseley years and comprising three floors in the East Wing of the main entrance. They moved there in April 1943. It was to be their last home.[174]

Birdwood started 1943 with an address to the Senior Officers Course at Brasenose College. This became a permanent commitment for the rest of the war and soon he was giving corresponding talks to Canadian and American officers at Oxford.[175] In April, he gave his longest speech in the House of Lords in a debate on India, 'in the position I hold as father of the Indian Army'. It was now more than a decade since he had left India. He expressed gratitude to the Government for the thanks it conveyed for the one and a half million men now in the Indian Army, with recruits flowing in at a rate of 60,000 a month. After a quite lengthy review of Indian history, he cited the examples of Mahomedans and the Depressed Classes both of which were unwilling to accept Congress domination. He believed it would be cowardice to abandon holding together very divergent peoples and suggested 'what the state of the country will be if we withdraw – absolute anarchy and chaos, and the most appalling and bloody fighting ever known, with tremendous casualties on every side.' It was a very prescient speech.[176]

170 Diary 1940, 4 September, 5 and 7 October, 7 December. Knighton, *Clifton College: Foundation to Evacuation*, 402.
171 Diary 1941, 5 February; *The Times*, 10 February 1941, 2.
172 *The Tablet*, 31 May 1941-23 September 1944.
173 Diary 1941, 2 April, 8 July, 12 and 28 November, 28 December.
174 Sarah E Parker, *Grace & Favour* (Hampton Court Palace: Historic Royal Palaces, 2005). Apartment 39 is occasionally opened for public view. Beside one window overlooking the river, there is a watercolour by Jane Birdwood depicting the same view of Hampton Court bridge with East Molesley church spire in the distance.
175 Diary 1943, 6 January, 22 February.
176 *HL Deb*, 6 April 1943, vol 127, cols 32-42.

Birdwood's wife was very ill in May but he retained his health. He closed the year in his diary with a Japanese proverb: 'Death is lighter than a feather: Duty heavier than a mountain.'[177] In April 1944, Birdwood and his wife celebrated their Golden Wedding – fifty years 'since Jenny stood beside me in Lahore Cathedral as such a beautiful very young-looking girl.' June saw the Normandy landings – 'We started our great landing on NW coast of France,' and flying bombs: 'Lots of glider bombs' and 'Quite a lot German flying bombs falling all around day & night.' By now he was helping out in the Palace gardens. Hope of victory grew and grew. In October, he went down to Eastbourne to see the quarters 'to be occupied by Aust prisoner of war when they return.'[178] At the end of November, the Home Guard were stood down. Before the victories of 1945, his son, Chris, was invalided home and was seriously ill for the next three years. When his last remaining brother died in April 1945, Birdwood was the last survivor of five brothers and one sister.

On 8 May, he wrote: 'Germany utterly beaten & surrendered! Put in vegetable seedlings. Sir Claude & Lady Auchinleck – C-in-C India – came to tea.' Thanksgiving services followed and then on 10 August, 'Heard the real good news that Japan had surrendered.' In September, he celebrated his '80th birthday. I am indeed fortunate to be so fit & strong as I still am though I may not be able to do all I cd years ago.'[179] That fitness had enabled him to be an industrious and enthusiastic encourager and energiser of military and non-military organisations.

In 1946 he had a brief Indian summer. Although he was no longer walking as far or as often, both he and Jenny were well. On Anzac Day, he 'met Mr Chifley PM Australia.' In June, he enjoyed visiting all the Indian troops who had come over for the VE Day parade. At this time his granddaughter, Judith Mary, was spending a year with them, and the two Judiths – granddaughter and daughter – had become very close. In December Birdwood gave what was to be his last speech in the House of Lords, concerning the Cabinet Mission to India in the first half of the year.[180] Having made no discernible progress on the formation and operation of a Constituent Assembly, the Viceroy, Wavell, was in London attempting still to gain agreement and support for his Breakdown Plan.[181] The Lords debated the current situation in light of ongoing communal violence and intransigence by the two leading parties. Birdwood reflected on his family's long association with India and strongly decried an earlier statement in the Commons that the British had 'stirred up communal strife.' He acknowledged the decision to vacate India had been taken, but prayed 'that for many years to come prosperity, good health and happiness may be with India and her people.'[182]

In the New Year his wife was ill and then after her recovery Birdwood himself became 'seedy & shaky, resulting in a month's incapacity. He travelled to London far less frequently and usually had a car sent for him, such as for his attendance at the Anzac Day events. He did not ride in the King's Birthday Parade. After her further severe bout of illness in July, Jane managed to accompany him to Deal and then down to the West Country to see Judith, who was very happy at her new partner's home. Birdwood managed a talk in Twickenham as the local vicar

177 Diary 1943, 10 and 14 May, end page.
178 Diary 1944, 5 April, 6,18 and 21 June,14 October.
179 Diary 1945, 8 May, 10 August and 13 September.
180 Diary 1946, 25 April, 6 June and 16 December.
181 Penderel Moon (ed.), *Wavell: The Viceroy's Journal* (Oxford: Oxford University Press, 1973), 383-96.
182 *HL Deb,* 16 December 1946, Vol 144, cols 948-54.

wrote to him to say: 'Thank you for shewing us how to be brave, and how to do our duty, even when we are not very well, and thank you too, for making such a positive witness to the truth of God's revelation in Christ.' On 30 September, he wrote: 'Jane's 75th birthday & thank God she is still wonderfully well – better than a few years ago – may she long remain so.'

On 3 November, Birdwood went into hospital for a long-scheduled eye operation. While recovering he was told that "Jane had a nasty heart attack in the night.' Birdwood managed to get home three days later but within two days at 5 am, their housekeeper 'came in to say my darling had had a collapse – I was just able to see her & then collapsed. Mabel & night nurse got me to bed.' The next day his diary read: 'Just – a blank.' Birdwood was too unwell for her funeral in the Chapel Royal of the Palace and he did not get up for just over a month.[183] He stayed with Judith in North Devon until the end of February. Instead of past entries listing his commands and the whereabouts of his family, he wrote on 1 January: 'The world seems to me a complete blank & I can feel & hope that I may join her in the not far distant future – if I am worthy – for I know that she who was such a real saint is now at complete rest & peace.'[184]

Nancy arrived from Australia in February and was his constant companion for the next eight months. In April in a letter to *The Times*, he initiated a drive for a separate 'Indian Army room' where arrangements could be made for the various artefacts, papers and memorials in the India Office to be kept. He was later joined in this by Auchinleck and the Commandant of Sandhurst offered to provide suitable accommodation. The two Field Marshals then sought funds and historical objects. [185] In July, he went up to Thurlby 'to dedicate the memorial I have put [up] to my dear darling beloved Jenny.' He added: 'Feel very broken.' A month later his 'oldest friend Arthur Christie Crawfurd' died. They had enjoyed together the adventurous ride to 'Ooty' in 1886. He said farewell to Nancy in October on her departure home for Australia.[186]

With bouts of ill health his first major trip was to the 1949 Anzac Day events and then he only managed regimental reunion lunches and viewing the future Indian Army memorial site at Sandhurst. In the autumn, his diary entries became very spasmodic and the last was to record receiving the 'sacrament in bed' on Christmas Day. That 1949 diary was his last and on the end page he wrote: 'Forgive always the ills that others do – But to forget them – this is nobler still.'[187] Birdwood had received a letter from General Cariappa, the C-in-C of the Indian Army, and Field Marshal Slim, then CIGS, learnt of this when he met Cariappa in summer 1950.[188] Slim wrote to Birdwood and organised the publicity of that letter, in which Cariappa had written: 'I write this to you, as the senior most serving officer of the Indian Army, on behalf of myself and all Indian officers of our Army to thank you and all officers of the Commonwealth who were responsible for building our army in the manner it has been built, and also for all the help, advice, and guidance you gave us … We know that the foundations of our army were truly and well laid by the blood and sweat of you all … it stood up to the "buffetings" of the many military problems which came after partition.' Cariappa went on to assure Birdwood that the traditions

183 Diary 1947, 22 February, 19 and 30 September, 3,14,15 and 18 November.
184 Diary 1948, 1 January.
185 *The Times*, 6 April 1948, 5, 27 October 1948, 5, 4 December 1948, 5.
186 Diary 1948, 17 and 24 July, 25 November, end page.
187 Diary 1949, end page. The ancient Tamil text, *Thirukkal,* couplet 16.1.
188 Major General V K Singh, *Leadership in the Indian Army: Biogrpahies of Twelve Soldiers* (New Delhi: Sage, 2005), 19-50.

and customs were being kept up, that morale was high, that the Gurkhas were as grand as ever, and that old officers were most welcome to come and visit.[189] This described the fine state of his army as Birdwood slipped away. He died in his apartment at Hampton Court on Thursday 17 May 1951, aged eighty-five.

Birdwood's body lay in the Chapel Royal of Hampton Court Palace. Both the Royal Horse Guards and XIIth Lancers mounted guard. On 23 May three Australian and three New Zealand officers were pall-bearers. The King, Queen Mary, the Prime Minister and Winston Churchill were represented. A nineteen-gun salute was fired from Hampton Green as his coffin travelled to Twickenham Cemetery, where he was buried alongside his father and mother.[190] Memorial services were held at Peterhouse, Clifton and at St Martins-in-the-Fields. On 21 May in Australia, flags were flown at half-mast on Commonwealth buildings and later, services were held across the country. Field Marshal Blamey, before his death just ten days after Birdwood, said: 'There have been few commanders who gave more of themselves to men in the ranks under them and few who received a more adequate return of their affection.'[191]

189 NAM 6707-19-1185, letter from FM Slim, 3 August 1950; *The Times*, 24 August 1950, 2.

190 *The Times*, 24 May 1951, 6. In 2013, the Australian Department of Veterans Affairs paid for the refurbishment of the grave.

191 *The Times*, 29 May 1951, 6; 30 May 1951, 8; 1 June 1951, 8; *The Argus*, 18 May 1951, 1; *The Canberra Times*, 19 May 1951, 4; *The Mercury*, 21 May 1951, 1.

Conclusion

More than 'Soul of Anzac'

When in June 1922 Lord Haig unveiled the War Memorial Gateway at Clifton College through which future generations would pass daily, he extolled:

> Courage, manliness and truth, clean living and honest dealing are the qualities that have made our nation great and must be preserved if that greatness is to last. Nothing can take their place.[1]

Haig had seen these qualities exemplified in Birdwood, who would continue to personify them during the remainder of his life. Such qualities may be desired and applied in any walk of life and under most creeds. Birdwood did so in peace and war, in junior and very senior ranks, in military and civilian life and in the expression of his personal Christian faith. He was consistent in his approach to his Indian soldiers in XI BL, then to the GGBG, later to his Kohat Brigade, notably to the Anzacs and to Peterhouse. He acknowledged before leaving India for the last time how heritage, family and school – Clifton and Newbolt – had set him on his life's course. His 1886 diary recorded his arrival with the XI BL at Nowgong but sadly those of 1887 and 1888 are missing. By 1889, however, Birdwood's entries have a purposeful air and reflected a determination as to how he would apply himself in his chosen profession. By then he had gained a genuine affection for the *sowars* of that *Silladar* regiment. Such regard became a way of life for him. Although there is no record of him saying so, we can be certain he would not have treated Victorians the way Beatson did. Birdwood was an Indian Army officer during much more of his service than his war years but it was with the Australians that his greatest bond was established. Put simply, this was because he had demonstrated a willingness to die beside them at Anzac Cove. Generals were killed visiting fronts but as the ANZAC commander at Gallipoli, Birdwood lived there. He maintained this honest approach throughout the long, hard months on the Western Front. This rare relationship between leader and men is worthy of special emphasis and it became the bedrock of his approach to his professional and personal life.

On 26 April 1915 Birdwood went about his enclave encouraging his men. He would do the same after the Turkish attack on 19 May, to troops returning from Krithia, and subsequently

1 Sarah Wearne and James Kerr, *To Our Brothers: Memorials to a Lost Generation in British Schools* (Warwick: Helion, 2018), 63.

to all who had fought in the August offensives. By then it was no longer just encouragement but rallying both commanders and men to persist and fight again … and then again, and again. In 1918, the Australian divisions and brigades that performed individually, uniformly and so admirably on the Somme and at Villers-Bretonneux – not forgetting 1 Division away with Second Army – must have lost count of the number of times that they had been urged to go and kill more Germans, but they did go and do so, time and again. By then, they were fighting together in their fourth year of operations. Birdwood was the common link in their performance and they responded to him. His letters to the key officials in both Australia and New Zealand reflected his affection for the men and women of those Dominions, and the consequent harmonious relationships in correspondence benefitted the overall effort of the Allies. Even with New Zealand it was Birdwood's letters that carried weight, rather than those of Godley or Russell. His relationship with Australian dignitaries meant that they retained Birdwood as the Commander of the AIF, producing a continuity of administrative oversight and approach, and a format which finally even the Canadians followed. Of course, Birdwood wished to retain that appointment for himself but in light of the acknowledged benefits, criticism does seem rather miserly. As victory had been won, the Australians did not have to be picked up again after the One Hundred Days. Whether Monash could have managed to achieve what Birdwood had done time and time again, is an interesting question.

With his reformed Fifth Army, Birdwood's harmonious dealings with corps commanders as they passed through his command were consistently evident. Haig's choice of Birdwood for army command illustrated Haig's genuine feelings about him. Haig's frustrations with another colonial army learning the ropes and then showing ill-discipline were but exasperations when set against the performance of a commander who delivered an effective fighting force time and again. Birdwood's promotion showed that Haig's oft-cited dislike of Birdwood is incorrect. Birdwood is also criticised for his lack of staff work and reliance on Brudenell White but Birdwood had shown from the Boer War onwards that he was an able and effective staff officer. On this basis he had been recommended to Kitchener with whom Birdwood's proven performance earned his subsequent advantageous selection to Kitchener's staff in India. Birdwood's tactful handling of the challenging reorganisation of the regiments of the Indian Army to the satisfaction of generals and the colonels of regiments was a noteworthy success. With an intimate appreciation of the demands of staff work, Birdwood personally chose White, together with others at a divisional level and below, ensuring that the ever-increasing challenges of intricate staff work were mastered as the Western Front increased in technical complexity and breadth. Birdwood displayed the same understanding as he steered the reorganisation of the defence budget in India to encompass modernisation and mechanisation.

Birdwood's poor choice not to proceed with an Indian Military Academy – a judgement overturned after his departure – was made at the same time as those budget decisions. Slim referred to 'the moment in every battle' when things were decided and occasionally in Birdwood's career there did seem to be moments when things might have been different. Should he have landed earlier on the first day at Gallipoli and given himself the chance to influence the battle? For the August Offensive, he clearly was aware of the health of the troops and made his own decision regarding their capabilities. For some of them he was proved right but for the majority it was too much. Command and control of the left hook towards Sari Bair was not addressed with the same rigour as other factors. The ground defeated him. The attack of 2nd Division at Pozières was Birdwood's first as corps commander on the Western Front. When it failed, he had to bear responsibility. He immediately supervised more closely and Legge and his Division were successful on their second attempt. Birdwood had learnt his lesson and it was only at Second Bullecourt that he became entrapped by Gough's enthusiasm once more. Overall, Haig would have observed a man learning from his mistakes and Slim himself acknowledged the necessity of mistakes.[2]

Despite all the things Birdwood did well, there is, however, no noteworthy victorious military event that may be ascribed to him. Withdrawals at Gallipoli cannot satisfy that definition, although in the overall campaign he was a significant commander. If the opportunity for him to resolve the Sikh problems had produced a positive resolution, that would have been noteworthy, but an impasse not of his making stalled progress. The one appointment – Governor-General of Australia – in which he might well have triumphed, had been denied him but he might not have been a winner. His speeches after his tour in Australia were rather political but ten years passed before selection and by then his diplomatic experience was even more advanced. He subsequently became a distinguished 'Man of Empire.' In truth his consistent success was due to his personality and the way he treated others. He made 'valuable friendships.' The present to 'Bungo from Birdie' is a delightful touch. Jenny had bought that and she was a constant support in his life. The way he cared for her after the miscarriage of their first pregnancy spelt out his devoted affection. He was decent, upright and honest. Both his Diggers and his superiors could see that. He maintained his personal standards relentlessly – both in his behaviour and his physical fitness. Perhaps only soldiers who have been encouraged time and again to return to the front can really judge the immense pressure on the commander. By their response and the reputation that they won for Australia, Birdwood did not fail.

It may be that the lack of a distinct success or achievement that has led to there being a dearth of studies of Birdwood. He is either a British general disregarded by Australian historians or a commander of Australians unheeded by British historians. Rather than judging the man alone, if the achievements of those who served under him are considered, Birdwood can worthily be judged a success as a commander of men, not only during the war years of 1914-18 but in the decades before and after. The performances of his divisions and brigades operating independently to stem the German onslaught in late March and April 1918, and when Fourth Army's front was held by Australians, are a testimony to and a highlight of this success. Birdwood had challenged his men 'to 'take the strain' for the sake of his country and all he holds dear,' and they did not let him or their country down. Yet again he instilled aggression. Their performance then was greater than at the landing at Anzac Cove, and it deserves far more public praise.

To sum up, Birdwood may be admired, above all, for his relationships with people, in which he displayed both emotional intelligence and a common touch – valuable characteristics especially in one so senior. When appointed to be Secretary to Government in the Army Department, he was noted as 'an able and most tactful officer ... under whose regime all will go well.' His reputation still lives on at both Peterhouse and with the Blues and Royals, more than sixty years after his death.[3] The letters such as Birdwood wrote to Brigadiers Allen and Morshead at the start of the Second World War must have had an inspirational effect on them. But it was Birdwood's impact on the thousands of Australians whom he commanded that had counted

2 Slim, *Defeat into Victory*, 14.
3 Author's personal discussions with current members.

most of all and the gift of a handwritten scroll during his Australian tour perfectly expressed that devotion:

> The Diggers of Burnie (Tasmania) salute you as their commanding officer, the General of the Australian Armies in Gallipoli and France, and pay respectful homage to your inspirational leadership of the AIF. They welcome you most heartily to their homeland. They greet you as a comrade and as a friend and are glad beyond measure that you have been able to look up your old comrades – the men with whom you fought in Gallipoli and France – and who remember with gratitude your manly comradeship, your ready sympathy, your anxiety at all times to smooth out their difficulties and lighten their load. Your name is cherished by those who were privileged to serve under you, and with whom the blood brotherhood of the battlefield will ever remain a sacred memory.
>
> We thank you, Sir, for what you did for us in camp and trench and assure you amongst all the magnificent tributes which have been paid you in this Commonwealth, none is more earnest and sincere than this little token of thanks and good wishes of the Diggers of Burnie.[4]

Significantly Birdwood chose the Southern Cross to be the centre of his personal coat of arms. The final judgement on Birdwood should be made by those that came from the furthest reaches of Australia to fight with him and under him. They loved him.

4 AWM 3DRL/3376 14/3 Scroll; *The Mercury*, 3 March 1920, 6, Birdwood's visit and 18 February 1924, Unveiling of Burnie War Memorial with 94 names from Burnie and municipality.

Bibliography

Archival Sources

Australia

Australian War Memorial, Canberra

AWM 4 Unit War Diaries, 1914-18

- 1/4 General Staff, General Headquarters, Mediterranean Expeditionary Force
- 1/17 General Staff, General Headquarters, Dardanelles Army
- 1/25 General Staff, Headquarters Australian and New Zealand Army Corps
- 1/27 Intelligence, Headquarters Australian and New Zealand Army Corps
- 1/28 Administrative Staff, Headquarters Australian and New Zealand Army Corps
- 1/29 General Staff, Headquarters 1 ANZAC Corps
- 1/32 General Staff, Headquarters 2 ANZAC Corps
- 1/35 General Staff, Headquarters Australian Corps
- 1/42 General Staff, Headquarters New Zealand and Australian Division
- 1/42 General Staff, Headquarters 1 Australian Division
- 1/44 General Staff, Headquarters 2 Australian Division
- 1/46 General Staff, Headquarters 3 Australian Division
- 1/48 General Staff, Headquarters 4 Australian Division
- 1/50 General Staff, Headquarters 5 Australian Division
- 1/52 General Staff, Headquarters 6 Australian Division
- 1/66 General Officer Commanding AIF Depots in UK
- 23/1 1 Infantry Brigade
- 23/5 5 Infantry Brigade
- 23/7 7 Infantry Brigade
- 23/8 8 Infantry Brigade
- 35 New Zealand Units

2DRL/1212 Appreciation by Birdwood on life and work of General White
2DRL/0513 Papers of Brigadier Harold Edward 'Pompey' Elliott
3DRL/221 Papers of General Sir Herbert Vaughan Cox
3DRL/606 Diaries, Notebooks and Folders of C E W Bean
3DRL/1400 Papers of General Sir Cyril Brudenell Bingham White

3DRL/2222 Papers of Sir George Foster Pearce
3DRL/2316 Papers of General Sir John Monash
3DRL/2803 Papers of Major General William Holmes
3DRL/3195 Papers of Gunner (later Lieutenant) Colin Kingsmill
3DRL/3376 Papers of Field Marshal Lord William Birdwood (including six diaries)
3DRL/6673 Official History records of C E W Bean
3DRL/7747 Personal, school and family papers of C E W Bean, 1781-1968
PR85/083 Research papers of Dr Guy Verney
Various photographs, postcards and heraldry

Museums Victoria

Various photographs

National Library of Australia

Papers of Ronald Craufurd Munro Ferguson (Lord Novar), 1912-1935, 723209
Papers of Phyllis Birdwood, 1879-1936, 1118392
Photograph album (1915-1922) of Richard Gavin Gardner Casey, Baron Casey, 6573955
Various photographs

National Portrait Gallery

Cast plaster, patinated, bust of Field Marshal the Lord Birdwood, Barbara Tribe, 1938, (Gift of the Estate of the late Barbara Tribe), 2009.47

India

National Archives, New Delhi

Foreign Department, External-B, Nov 1913 – Visit Programme

United Service Institution of India, New Delhi

Various books, papers and medals

New Zealand

Alexander Turnbull Library, Wellington

Letters from Birdwood to Sir Godfrey Williams, (Chief Engineer at Gallipoli), MS-Papers-2189
Correspondence Birdwood and Mrs Malone, MS-Papers-9049-1
Papers relating to the death of William Malone, MS-Papers-9049-4

Archives New Zealand, Wellington

Birdwood visit to New Zealand in 1920, R10 623 386
Correspondence Sir James Allen and Birdwood (1915-1919), R22 319 674
Birdwood appointment as Colonel in Chief 1 New Zealand Mounted Rifles, R22 429 224

Auckland War Memorial Museum

Various photographs

Kippenberger Military Archive, National Army Museum, Waiouru

Bollinger, Second Lieutenant George, Diary, 2003.245
Braithwaite, Brigadier General W G, Papers, 1994.3315
Hampton, W A, Photographs of Wellington Regiment at Gallipoli
Hart, Brig Herbert, Diaries, 1990.1011-1014
Hart, Private Leonard, Diary, 2004.181
Sutherland, Private Peter John, Letters, 1998.1737
Swan, Private James W, DCM, Personal account, 1999.1086
Temperley, Colonel A C, 'A Personal Narrative of The Battle of Chunuk Bair', 1994.3315
Thompson, Peter M, Diary, 1999.803

Pakistan

The Baloch Regimental Museum, Abbottabad

The Baluch Regiment: Regimental News Precis

United Kingdom

British Library, (including India Office Records and Private Papers), London

Correspondence regarding march of a force to Black Mountain, Hazara, in October 1890, L/Mil/&/14698
Expedition against the Hasanzai and Akazai tribes of the Black Mountain, 1891, L/Mil/17/13/53
The India List – Civil and Military.
Indian Army List
The Indian Year Book
Kitchener-Marker papers, MS 52276-8
Rough map of Tirah and surrounding country, 1897, Maps 51820.(27)
Map of Tirah and neighbouring country showing locations of the Afridi, Orakzai, Zaimusht and portion of the Shinwari tribes, 1884, Maps 51820.(23.)
Order of Bath recommendations 1891 – Mirianzai, Manipur and Hazara, L/Mil/7/1300

Papers of Sir George Christopher Birdwood, scholar, administrator in India and surgeon, 1876-1902, Mss Eur F216

Papers of Field Marshal Lord Birdwood, Indian Army, 1883-1949, Mss Eur D686

Papers of Sir Alfred Lyall, Bengal Civil service 1856-1911, Mss Eur F132

Papers of Sir Francis Younghusband, 1863-1942, Mss Eur F197

The Quarterly India List for April 1896. Calcutta, 1896.

The Quarterly Indian Army List for April 1891. Calcutta, 1891.

Queen's India Cadetship Applications, L/Mil/9/293

Photograph Album Gallipoli 1 May – 15 December 1915, Mss Eur A 190

Sketches of movements of Tirah Expeditionary Force, 1897, Maps 15.b.39.

Clifton College Archives, Bristol

Birdwood, ma[jor] (W R) school report October 1879 – December 1882

The Memorial to Old Cliftonians who fell in the South African War Bristol, 1904.

Various correspondence

Imperial War Museum, London

Papers of Colonel C J L Allanson, 10759.

Papers of Field Marshal Lord Birdwood, 22581.

Papers of Major General G P Dawnay, 10403.

Papers of Captain F S Faber, 16620.

Papers of Captain A N McGrigor, 9984.

Joint Services Command and Staff College Library, Shrivenham

Scheme for Special Expeditionary Force. Senior Division Exercise. Camberley Staff College. 1913

Lecture 3 – The August Operations. The Dardanelles Campaign. Camberley Staff College. Vol. 14-3, 1923.

Lecture 4 – The end of the Campaign. The Dardanelles Campaign. Camberley Staff College. Vol. 14-4, 1923.

Liddell Hart Centre for Military Archives, King's College, London

Papers of General Sir Alexander Godley, (1867-1957), GB0099 KCLMA Godley.

Papers of Field Marshal Earl Haig, Autograph diaries and letters home to his wife, 1914-1919, MF 856-865.

Papers of General Sir Ian Hamilton, (1853-1947), GB0099 KCLMA Hamilton.

Papers of Brigadier General Philip Howell, (1877-1916), GB0099 KCLMA Howell.

Haig, FM Earl "Autograph diaries." In FM Earl Haig: Autograph diaries and letters home to his wife, 1914-1919, edited by LHMCA: GB0099 KCLMA MF 856-865, 1914-1919.

The National Archives, Kew

CAB 17/184 General Staff 1906.
CAB 19/33 Dardanelles Commission.
PRO 30/57/64 Correspondence Birdwood and Colonel Fitzgerald.
WO 95/522 War Diaries Fifth Army
WO 95/2763 War Diary 1/5 Battalion Gloucestershire Regiment
WO 222/213 report on Convalescent Homes on Riviera.

National Army Museum, London

Governor-General's Body Guard Digest of Services from 1889, 1954-05-10
Papers of Field Marshal Lord Birdwood, (165-1951), (including fifty-six diaries), 6706-96.
Record of officers who served with Probyn's Horse, 1857-1947, 2005-05-21
Photographs of fellow officers of Birdwood, 1972-11-7.
Photograph album of visit by Viscount Kitchener to Jind State, interspersed with other photographs compiled by Birdwood (1903-1907), 62006—29.
Uniform and equipment items, 11 (Prince of Wales's Own) regiment of Bengal Lancers, 1958-07-60 & 09-77.
Various photograph albums and sketchbook of Black Mountain Expedition (1891).
Various photograph albums of Tirah Expeditionary Force (1897-1898).
Watercolour drawing of William Riddell Birdwood, 11 (Prince of Wales's Own) Bengal Lancers, By Alfred Crowdy Lovett, c. 1894, (NAM 1957-06-28).

Peterhouse Archives, Cambridge

Meeting of the Peterhouse Historical Society, 8 June 1936. Speaker The Master, Sir William Birdwood, *Gallipoli*.
Peterhouse Registers.

The Royal Archives, Windsor

Correspondence of Colonel Sir Clive Wigram, Assistant Private Secretary to HM King George V
RA PS/GV/C/L/2293, 2294.
RA PS/GV/C/N/832, 838,2556, 2561.
RA PS/GV/C/Q/2521
RA PS/PSO/GV/C/P/284

Royal Military Academy Sandhurst Archives, Camberley

Royal Military College Papers, 1884, WO152/54 Box 105.
Serve to Lead (An Anthology) (Camberley, 1959).

Totnes Archives, Totnes (including Plymouth and West Devon Record Office references)

The Honorary Freedom of Borough of Totnes, 1888-1975 (Totnes, 2008).
Papers of the Birdwood family including photographs, family papers, newspaper cuttings and genealogical notes, reference 1390.

Printed Sources

Official reports and command papers

'First Report of the Dardanelles Commission." London: HMSO 1917-1918.
"Final Report of the Dardanelles Commission." London: HMSO, 1919.
House of Lords Debates, 1943 and 1946.
"Report of the Army in India Committee 1919-1920" London: HMSO, 1920.
"Report of the Indian Sandhurst Committee." London: HMSO, 1927.
"Report of the Indian Statutory Commission." London: 1930
Report of the Special Committee to review historical inequalities in commemoration, Maidenhead: CWGC, 2021.
"Indian Round Table Conference 12th November 1930 - 19th January 1931." Calcutta: Government of India, 1931.

Official histories

Aspinall-Oglander, Brig-Gen C F, *Military Operations: Gallipoli Volume I: Inception of the campaign to May 1915.* London, 1929.
———. *Military Operations: Gallipoli Volume II: May 1915 to the evacuation.* London, 1932.
Bean, C E W, ed *The Official History of Australia in the War of 1914-1918, Volume 1.* Sydney, 1921.
———. *The Official History of Australia in the War of 1914-1918, Volume II* Sydney, 1924.
———. *The Official History of Australia in the War of 1914-1918, Volume III.* Sydney, 1929.
———. *The Official History of Australia in the War of 1914-1918, Volume IV.* Sydney, 1933.
———. *The Official History of Australia in the War of 1914-1918, Volume V.* Sydney, 1941.
———. *The Official History of Australia in the War of 1914-1918, Volume VI* Sydney, 1942.
Edmonds, Brig-Gen Sir James E, *The Occupation of Constantinople, 1918-1923* (London, 2013 (reprint of first edition 2010)).
Waite, Major Fred, *The New Zealanders at Gallipoli.* Official History of the New Zealand Effort in the Great War. Vol. I, Auckland, 1921.

Contemporary published works (mostly pre-1939)

Arthur, Sir George, *Life of Lord Kitchener* (London, 1920).
Ashmead-Bartlett, Ellis, *The Uncensored Dardanelles* (London, 1928).
———, *Ashmead-Bartlett's despatches from the Dardanelles* (London, 1923).
Atteridge, A Hilliard, *Wars of the Nineties* (London, 1899).

Asquith, Anthony, and Geoffrey Barkas, *Tell England* (London, 1931).
Austin, Lt Col W S, *The Official History of the New Zealand Rifle Brigade* (Wellington, 1924).

Bean, C E W, ed., *The Anzac Book* (London, 1916).
———, *Lettters from France* (London, 1917).
Birdwood, FM Lord, *Khaki and Gown* (London, 1941).
———, *In My Time. Recollections and Anecdotes.* (London, 1945).
Birdwood, FM Sir W R, *Reminiscences of the Residencies of the Commanders-in-Chief in India* (Bath, 2006 (reprint of 1930 privately published edition)).
Birdwood, Lady, *A visit to Australia and New Zealand* (London, 1922).
Borwick, F, ed., *Clifton College Annals and Register 1862-1925* (Bristol, 1925).
Boyle, Major C A, *The History of Probyn's Horse (5th King Edward's Own Lancers)* (Aldershot, 1929).
Buchan, John, *History of the Battle of the Somme, 1916* (London, 1916).
Buck, E J, *Simla Past and Present* (Shimla, 2015 (reprint of 1925 second edition)).

Calamy, Edmund, *A Continuation of the account of the ministers, lecturers, masters, and fellows of colleges and schoolmasters, who were Ejected and Silenced after the Restoration in 1660, by or before, the Act of Uniformity* (London, 1728).
Callwell, Colonel C E, *Tirah 1897 (*London, 1911).
Callwell, Major General Sir C E, *Dardanelles* (London, 1924).
Christie, O F, *A History of Clifton College 1860-1934.* (Bristol, 1935).
Churchill, Winston S, *The Story of the Malakand Field Force.* (London, 1898).
Churchill, Winston Spencer, *London to Ladysmith via Pretoria* (London, 1900).
Churchill, The Rt Hon Winston S, *Sandhurst Edition of The World Crisis* (London, 1933).
Cooper, Duff, *Haig* (London, 1936)

Godley, General Sir Alexander, *Life of an Irish Soldier* (London, 1939).
Grange, Baroness Ernest de la, *Open house in Flanders, 1914-191,* (London, 1929).

Hamilton, General Sir Ian, *Gallipoli Diary,Vol. I & II* (London, 1920).
Hare, Major General Sir Steuart, *Annals of the King's Royal Rifle Corps: Vol 4 "The K.R.R.C." 1872-1913* (London, 1929).
Harington, General Sir Charles, *Plumer of Messines* (London, 1935).
Hart, B H Liddell, *The Real War.* (London, 1930).
Hutchinson, Colonel H D, The Campaign in Tirah 1897-1898: *An Account of* Kingsford, C L, *The Story Of The Royal Warwickshire Regiment* (London, 1921).

Lloyd George, David, *War Memoirs Volumes I-VI* (London, 1933-6).
Lucas, Sir Charles, *The Empire at War, Vol. III Australia, New Zealand, The Pacific Islands* (London, 1924).

Masefield, John, *Gallipoli* (London, 1916).
Mockler-Ferryman, Major A F, *Annals of Sandhurst* (London, 1900).
Morgenthau, Henry, *Secrets of the Bosphorus* (London, 1918).

Nevinson, Henry W, *The Dardanelles Campaign* (London, 1918).
North, John, *Gallipoli: The Fading Vision* (London, 1936).

Powles, Colonel C G, ed., *The History of the Canterbury Mounted Rifles 1914-1919* (Christchurch, 1928).

Shadwell, Captain L J, *Lockhart's Advance through Tirah* (London, 1898).
Sheppard, Samuel T, *The Byculla Club, 1833-1916, A History* (Bombay, 1916).
Street, A G, *The Gentlemen of the Party* (London, 1936).

Thompson, Edward, and G T Garrat, *Rise and Fulfilment of British Rule in India* (London, 1934).

Younghusband, Captain G J, and Younghusband, Captain Frank E, *The Relief of Chitral* (London, 1895).

Other Secondary Works

Adam-Smith, Patsy, *The ANZACS*. (Southbank, Victoria, 1978).
Ah, Adelaide Kow, *William McKenzie: Anzac padre* (London 1949).
Ahmed, Major General Rafiuddin, *History of the Baloch Regiment 1820-1939* (Abbottabad, 1998).
Andrews, E M, *The ANZAC Illusion: Anglo-Australian Relations during World War 1* (Cambridge, 1993).
Anglesey, The Marquess of, *A History of the British Cavalry Volume 4: 1899-1913* (London, 1986).
Australian Dictionary of Biography

Barnett, Correlli, *The Swordbearers: Studies in Supreme Command in the First World War* (London, 1986).
Barua, Pradeep, *Gentlemen of the Raj: the Indian Army Officer Corps, 1817-1949* (Westport, CT, 2003).
Bashford, Alison and Macintyre, Stuart, eds, *The Commonwealth of Australia -The Cambridge History of Australia* (Port Melbourne, 2013).
Beachcroft, S P, ed., *Clifton College Register, 1862 to 1962* (Bristol, 1962).
Bean, C E W, ed., *The Anzac Book Book* (Sydney, 2010 (Third edition)).
———, *Two Men I Knew* (Sydney, 1957).
Beaumont, Joan, *Broken Nation* (Crowsnest, 2013).
Beckett, Ian F W, and Steven J Corvi, eds, *Haig's Generals* (Barnsley, 2006).
Beckett, Ian F W, *A British Profession of Arms:The Politics of Command in the Late Victorian Army* (Oaklahoma, 2018).
Billington, Rachel, *Glory – A story of Gallipoli* (London, 2015).
Blackburn, Kevin, *War, Sport and the Anzac Tradition (*Basingstoke, 2016).
Blake, Robert, *The Private Papers of Douglas Haig 1914-1919* (London, 1952).
Bollard, Robert, *In the shadow of Gallipoli: The hidden story of Australia in WWI* (Sydney, 2013).
Bond, Brian, and Nigel Cave, *Haig: A Reappraisal 70 Years On* (London, 1999).

Bou, Jean, ed., *The AIF in Battle* (Melbourne, 2016).
———, and Dennis, Peter, with Dalgleish, Paul, *The Australian Imperial Force – The Centenary History of Australia and the Great War Volume 5* (South Melbourne, 2016).
Bowen, H V, Margarette Lincoln, and Nigel Rigby, eds, *The Worlds of the East India Company* (Woodbridge, 2002).
Braga, Stuart, *Kokoda Commander: a life of Major-General "Tubby" Allen* (Melbourne, 2004).
Brenchley, Fred, and Brenchley, Elizabeth, *Myth Maker: Ellis Ashmead-Bartlett: The Englishman who Sparked Australia's Gallipoli Legend* (Brisbane, 2005).
Bridge, Carl, *William Hughes* (London, 2011).
Broadbent, Harvey, *Gallipoli: The Fatal Shore* (Camberwell, 20050.
Bryer, Robin, *Jack: A literary biography of John Connell (John Henry Robertson 1909-1965)* (Milton Keynes, 2010).
Bush, Eric, *Gallipoli* (London, 1975).

Cameron, David and Donlon, Denise, "A Preliminary Archaeological Survey of the ANZAC Gallipoli Battlefields of 1915." *Australasian Historical Archaeology* 23 (2005), 131-138.
Cameron, David W, *The August Offensive at ANZAC 1915* (Sydney, 2011).
Carlyon, Les, *Gallipoli* (Sydney, 2001).
———, *The Great War* (Sydney, 2006).
Carver, Field Marshal Lord, *The Boer War* (London, 1999).
Çelik, Kenan, ed., *The Gallipoli Campaign International Perspective 85 Years On* (Çanakkale, 2013).
Chamberlain, Max, "The Wilmansrust affair." *Journal of the Australian War Memorial* 6, no. April (1985): 47-55.
Chanin, Eileen, *Capital Designs* (Melbourne, 2018).
Charlton, Peter, *Pozieres, 1916: Australians on the Somme* (London, 1986).
Chasseaud, Peter, and Peter Doyle, *Grasping Gallipoli: Terrains, Maps and Failure at the Dardanelles, 1915* (Stroud, 2005).
Chevenix Trench, Charles, *The Indian Army and the King's Enemies 1900-1947* (London, 1988).
Chhina, Rana T S, and Chandra, Yashaswini, *Right of the Line: The President's Bodyguard* (new Delhi, 2015).
Chhina, Rana T S, *India and the Great War* (New Delhi, 2015).
Connell, John, *Auchinleck* (London, 1959).
———, *Wavell Scholar and Soldier* (London, 1964).
Connell, John, and Roberts, Brigadier Michael, *Wavell Supreme Commander* (London, 1969).
Connor, John, *Anzac and Empire: George Foster Pearce and the Foundations of Australian Defence* (Melbourne, 2011).
Coombs, Rose, *Before Endeavours Fade.*(London, 1990).
Corrigan, Gordon, *Sepoys in the Trenches: The Indian Corps on the Western Front 1914-15* (Stroud, 1999).
Coulthard-Clark, Chris, *Encyclopaedia of Australia's Battles* (Crowsnest, 2010).
Crawford, John, and McGibbon, Ian, eds, *New Zealand's Great War: New Zealand, the Allies and the First World War* (Auckland, 2007).
———, and Peter Cooke, eds, *No Better Death: The Great War diaries and letters of William G Malone* (Auckland, 2014).

Crawley, Rhys, *Climax at Gallipoli: The failure of the August Offensive* (Oklahoma, 2014).
———, and LoCiciero, Michael, *Gallipoli: New Perspectives on the Mediterranean Expeditionary Force, 1915-16* (Warwick, 2018)
Cunneen, Christopher, *King's Men: Australia's Governor-Generals from Hopetoun to Isaacs* (Sydney, 1983).

Dancocks, D G, *Sir Arthur Currie* (Toronto, 1983).
Das, Santanu, ed., *Race, Empires and First World War Writing* (New York, 2011).
De Bellis, Dianne Kaye, *Stories of Australian Deserters in World War 1* (University of South Australia, 2014).
Delaney, Douglas E, & Gardner, Nikolas, eds, *Turning Point 1917: : The British Empire at War* (Vancouver, 2017).
Dilks, David, *Curzon in India, Volume 1* (London, 1969).
———, *Curzon in India, Volume 2* (London, 1970).
Diver, Maud, *The Unsung: A record of British services in India* (Edinburgh, 1945).
Dixon, Norman, *On the Psychology of Military Incompetence* (London, 1994).
Duckers, Peter, *The British-Indian Army 1860-1914* (Princes Risborough, 2003).
Dunbar, Sir George, *India at War* (London,1941).

Edgar, Peter, *To Villers-Bretonneux with Brigadier-General William Glasgow DSO and the 13th Australian Infantry Brigade* (Loftus, NSW, 2006).
Edwardes, Michael, *High Noon of Empire, India under Curzon* (London, 1965).
Ekins, Ashley, ed., *Gallipoli: A Ridge Too Far* (Wollombi, 2013).
Elford, F G. "Herbert Ward Wilson, OBE, MC, CdeG, MSc." *The Educational Magazine, Victoria*, Vol 13, no 3, Apr 1956: 97-108.
Elliott, Major General J G, *The Frontier 1839-1947* (London, 1968).
Erickson, Edward J, *Gallipoli The Ottoman Campaign* (Barnsley, 2010).
———, *Gallipoli: Command under Fire* (Oxford, 2015).
Evans, Geoffrey, *Slim as Military Commander* (London, 1969).

Farr, Don, *The Silent General: Horne of the First Army, A Biography of Haig's Trusted Great War Comrade-in-Arms* (Solihull, 2007).
Farrar-Hockley, Anthony, *Goughie* (St Albans, 1975).
Faught, C Brad, *Kitchener Hero and Anti-Hero* (London, 2016).
Ferguson, Bernard, *Wavell Potrait of a Soldier* (London, 1961).
Fewster, Kevin, ed., *Bean's Gallipoli: the diaries of Australia's official war correspondent* (Crowsnest, 1983).
Fewster, Kevin, Başarin, Hatice Hürmüz and Başarin, Vecihi, A Turkish view of Gallipoli: Canakkale (Crowsnest, 2003).
Fewster, Kevin, 'Politics, Pageantry and Purpose: The 1920 Tour of Australia by the Prince of Wales'. *Labour History*, 38 (1980), 59-66.
Fitzhardinge, L F, "W M Hughes and the Treaty of Versailles." *Journal of Commonwealth Political Studies* 5, no. 2 (1967): 130-42.
Fitzsimmons, Peter, *Gallipoli* (North Sydney, 2014).

———, *Victory at Villers-Bretonneux: Why a French Town will never forget the Amzacs* (North Sydney, 2016).
Fox-Godden, Aimée, *Learning to Fight: Military Innovation and Change in the British Army, 1914-1918* (Cambridge, 2018).
Frame, Tom, *The Shores of Gallipoli* (Alexandria, NSW, 2000).
Fraser, George MacDonald, *Quartered Safe Out Here* (London, 2000).
French, David, *Raising Churchill's Army: The British Army and the War against Germany, 1919-1945* (Oxford, 2000.
———, and Holden-Reid, Brian, eds, *The British General Staff: Reform and Innovation, c. 1890-1939.* (London, 2002).
———, *Military Identities: The Regimental System, the British Army, and the British People, c. 1870-2005 (*Oxford, 2005).
French, Patrick, *Younghusband: The Last Great Imperial Adventurer* (London, 1994).

Gammage, Bill, *The Broken Years: Australian soldiers in the Great War* (Canberra, 1974).
Gaylor, John, *Sons of John Company: The Indian and Pakistan Armies 1903-91* (Tunbridge Wells, 1992).
Gilbert, Martin, *Winston S. Churchill: The Challenge of War, 1914–1916* (London, 1971).
———, First World War (London, 1994).
———, "Churchill and Gallipoli." In *Gallipoli: Making history*, edited by Jenny Macleod. London, 2004.
Gilmour, David, *Curzon* (London, 1994).
Glen, Frank, *Bowler of Gallipoli: Witness to the ANZAC Legend* (Canberra, 2004).
Gooding, Janda, *Gallipoli Revisited: In the Footsteps of Charles Bean and The Australian Historical Mission* (Richmond, Victoria, 2009).
Goradia, Nayana, *Lord Curzon, The Last of the British Moghuls* (Delhi, 1993).
Gray, Anne, *Henry Fullwood War Paintings* (Canberra, 1983).
Greenwood, Alexander, *Field-Marshal Auchinleck* (Durham, 1990).
Gray, John H, *From the Uttermost Ends of the Earth: The New Zealand Division on the Western Front 1916-1918* (Christchurch, 2011).
Grey, Jeffrey, *A Military History of Australia* (Cambridge, 1999).
Griffith, Paddy, *Battle Tactics of the Western Front: The British Army's Art of Attack, 1916-1918* (New Haven, 1994).
Grint, Keith, *Leadership, Management and Command - Rethinking D-Day* (London, 2008).
———. "Problems, problems, problems: The social construction of 'leadership'." *Human Relations* 58 (1) (2005): 1467-94.
Groom, Winston, *A Storm in Flanders: The Ypres Salient, 1914-1918: Tragedy and Triumph on the Western Front* (New York, 2002).
Guest, Freddie, *Indian Cavalryman* (London, 1959).

Hall, Brain N, "Technological Adaptation in a Global Conflict: The British Army and Communications beyond the Western Front, 1914-1918," *The Journal of Military History* 78, no.1 (2014): 37-71.
Hamid, Major General S Shahid, *So they rode and fought* (Tunbridge Wells, 1983).

Hampton, Meleah, *Attack on the Somme: 1st Anzac Corps and the Battle of Pozières Ridge, 1916* (Solihull, 2016).
———, "Hubert Gough, the Anzacs and the Somme: A Descent into Pointlessness" *British Journal for Military History* 2, issue 3, (2016), 47-61.
Harris, J P, *Douglas Haig and the First World War* (Cambridge, 2009).
Harris, Paul, *General Sir Herbert Lawrence: Haig's Chief of Staff* (Warwick, 2019).
Hart, Peter, *Gallipoli* (London, 2011).
———, *The Great War* (London, 2013.
———, *The Last Battle: Endgame on the Western Front, 1918* (London, 2018).
———, *The Gallipoli Evacuation* (Manly, 2020).
Haythornthwaite, Philip J, *The Colonial Wars Source Book* (London, 2000).
Heathcote, T A, *The Military in British India: The Development of British Land Forces in South Asia, 1600-1947.* Manchester, 1995.
———, *Dictionary of Field Marshals of The British Army* (Barnsley, 1999).
Hickey, Michael, *Gallipoli* (London, 1995).
Hilton, Richard, *The North-West Frontier* (London, 1957).
Hodgkinson, Peter E, Westerman, William F, "'Fit to Command a Battalion': The Senior Officers' School 1916-18" *Journal of the Society for Army Historical Research* 93, issue 374, (2015), 120-138.
Holbrook, Carolyn, *ANZAC: The Unauthorised Biography* (Sydney, 2014).
Holden, Robert, *And the Band played On: How Music Lifted the Anzac Spirit in the Battlefields of the First World War* (Richmond, Victoria, 2014).
Holbrook, Carolyn, *Anzac: The Unauthorised Biography,* (NewSouth, Sydney, 2014).
Holburn, Vanessa, *The Amritsar Massacre: The British Empire's Worst Atrocity* (Barnsley, 2019).
Holdsworth, Angela, and Christopher Pugsley, eds, *Sandhurst : A Tradition of Leadership* (London, 2005).
Holmes, Richard, *Sahib: The British Soldier in India 1750–1914* (London, 2005).
Horner, David, "Australian Military Biographies." In *Ranging Shots: New Directions in Australian Military History*, edited by Carl Bridge. London,1998.
Hurst, James, *The Landing in the Dawn* (Solihull, 2018).
Hyatt, A M J, *General Sir Arthur Currie: A Military Biography* (Toronto, 1987).

Inglis, K S, *Sacred Places: War Memorials in the Australian Landscape* (Carlton, 2005).

James, Robert Rhodes, *Gallipoli* (London, 1965).
Jeffreys, Alan, ed., *The Indian Army in the First World War: New Perspectives* (Solihull, 2018).
Jog, N G, *Churchill's blind spot: India,* (Bombay, 1944).
Judd, Denis, *Empire: The British Imperial Experience from 1765 to the Present,* (I B Taurus, 2012).

Kaye, M M, *Golden Afternoon* (London, 1997).
Keegan, John, *The Mask Of Command: A Study of Generalship* (London, 1987).
———, *The First World War* (London, 1998).
King, Peter, *The Viceroy's Fall* (London, 1986).
Knighton, C S, ed., *Clifton College: Foundation to Evacuation, Bristol Record Society's Publication Vol 65* (Bristol, 2012).

Lack, John, Inglis, K S, and Winter, Jay, *ANZAC Remembered: Selected Writings by K. S. Inglis.* (Melbourne, 1998).
Laffin, John, *Digger: The legend of the Australian Soldier* (London, 1959).
———, *British Butchers & Bunglers of World War One* (Stroud, 1988).
———, *We Will Remember Them: Australian Epitaphs of World War 1* (Kenthurst, NSW, 1995).
Lee, Celia, and John Lee, *Winston & Jack: The Churchill Brothers* (London, 2007).
Lee, John, *A Soldier's Life: General Sir Ian Hamilton 1853-1947* (London, 2000).
———, "William Birdwood." In *Haig's Generals*, edited by Ian F W Beckett and Steven J Corvi. (Barnsley, 2006).
Lee, Roger, *British Battle Planning in 1916 and the Battle of Fromelles* (Farnham, 2015).
Lewin, Ronald, *Slim: The Standardbearer* (London, 1976).
Liddle, Peter H, ed., *Passchendaele in Perspective: The Third battle of Ypres* (London, 1997).
Lloyd, Nick, *The Amritsar Massacre* (London, 2011).
———, *Hundred Days: The End of the Great War* (London, 2013).
LoCicero, Michael, ed., *"Two Sides of the Same Bad Penny?" Gallipoli and the Western Front : A Comparison* (Warwick, 2018).
Low, D A, *Congress and the Raj,* (New Delhi, 2004).
Lyman, Robert, *Slim, Master of War: Burma, 1942-5: Burma and the Birth of Modern Warfare* (London, 2004).

MacDonald, Andrew, *Passchendaele: The Anatomy of a Tragedy* (Sydney, 2013).
Macleod, Jenny, "General Sir Ian Hamilton and the Dardanelles Commission" *War in History,* 8,(4), 2001), 418-441.
———, "The Rise and Fall of Anzac Day: 1965 and 1990 Compared.," *War & Society,* 20, no. 1 (2002): 149-68.
———, *Reconsidering Gallipoli* (Manchester, 2004).
———, ed., *Gallipoli: making history* (London, 2004).
———,*Gallipoli* (Oxford, 2015).
Magnus, Philip, *Kitchener, Portrait of an Imperialist* (London, 1958).
Marshall-Cornwall, General Sir James, *Haig as a Military Commander* (London, 1973).
Mason, Philip, *A Matter of Honour* (London, 1974).
McCarthy, Dudley, *Gallipoli to the Somme: the story of C E W Bean* (London, 1983).
McClenaghan, Tony, *For The Honour of My House: The Contribution of the Indina Princely States to the First World War* (Warwick, 2019).
McKernan, Michael, *Gallipoli: A Short History* (Crowsnest, 2010).
McMullin, Ross, *Pompey Elliott at War* (Melbourne, 2018).
Mead, Gary, *The Good Soldier: The Biography of Douglas Haig* (London, 2007).
Millar, John Dermot, *The Soul of Anzac* (North Melbourne, 2015).
Miller, Russel, *Uncle Bill: The Authorised Biography of Field Marshal Viscount Slim* (London, 2013).
Miller, Charles, *Khyber: British India's North West Frontier* (London, 1977).
Moon, Penderel, ed., *Wavell The Viceroy's Journal* (Oxford, 1973).
Moon, Sir Penderel, *The British Conquest and Dominion of India* (New Delhi, 1999).
Moorehead, Alan, *Gallipoli* (London, 1956).
———, *Gallipoli* (London, 2015).

Moreman, T R, *The Army in India and the Development of Frontier Warfare, 1849-1947.* (Basingstoke, 1998).
Muirhead, J A O, ed., *Clifton College Register, 1862 to 1947* (Bristol, 1948).

Nath, Asok, *Izzat: Historical Records and Iconography of Indian Cavalry Regiments 1750-2007* (New Delhi, 2009).
———, *Sowars and Sepoys in the Great War 1914-1918* (Dhaka, 2014).
Newman, Steve, *Gallipoli: Then and Now* (Old Harlow, 2000).
Nicolson, Harold, *King George the Fifth His Life and Reign* (London, 1952).

Oberoi, Harjot, "Sikh fundamentalism." In *Indian Political Thought*, edited by Aakash Singh and Mohapatra (Abingdon, 2010).
Odgers, George, *Diggers: The Australian Army, Navy and Air Force in Eleven Wars Volume 1 From 1860 to 5 June 1944* (Sydney, 1994).
Oxford Dictionary of National Biography

Pakenham, Thomas, *The Boer War* (London, 1979).
Parker, Sarah E, *Grace & Favour* (Hampton Court Palace, 2005).
Parkinson, Roger, *The Auk: Auchinleck, victor at Alamein* (London, 1977).
Pedersen, Peter, *Monash as: Military Commander* (Melbourne, 1985).
———,*The Anzacs: Gallipoli to the Western Front* (Melbourne, 2007).
———, with Chris Roberts, *ANZACS on the Western Front: The Australian War Memorial Battlefield Guide* (Milton, Queensland, 2012).
———, *Anzacs on the Western Front* (Milton, Queensland, 2012).
———, *Anzac Treasures: The Gallipoli Collection of the Australian War Memorial* (Crowsnest, 2014).
Philpott, William, *Bloody Victory: The Sacrifice on the Somme* (London, 2009).
———, *Attrition:Fighting the First World War* (London, 2014).
Pollock, John, *Kitchener* (London, 2001).
Powell, Geoffrey, *Plumer: The Soldier's General* (London, 1990).
Price, Val, *The Honorary Freedom of the Borough of Totnes 1888 to 1975* (Totnes, 2008).
Prior, Robin, *Churchill's World Crisis as History* (Beckenham, 1983).
———, and Trevor Wilson, *Command on the Western Front: The Military Careeer of Sir Henry Rawlinson (1914-1918)* (Oxford, 1992).
———, *The Somme* (Sydney, 2006).
———, *Gallipoli: the end of the myth* (London, 2009).
Pugsley, Christopher, *The ANZAC Experience* (Auckland, 2004).
———, *Haig and the implementation of tactical doctrine on the Western Front* (Sandhurst, 2011).
———, *Gallipoli The New Zealand Story* (Auckland, 2014).
———, *Gallipoli The New Zealand Story* (Auckland, 2022).

Radley, Kenneth, *Get Tough, Stay Tough: Shaping The Canadian Corps, 1914-1918* (Solihull, 2014).
Ransford, Oliver,*The Battle of Spion Kop* (London, 1969).

Reid, C Lestock, *Commerce and Conquest: The Story of the Honourable East India Company* (London, 1947).
Rhodes James, Robert, *Gallipoli* (London, 1989).
Robbins, Simon, *British Generalship during the Great War: the military career of Sir Henry Horne (1861-1929)* (Farnham, 2010).
———, *British Generalship on the Western Front 1914-18: defeat into victory* (Abingdon, 2005).
Roberts, Chris, *The Landing at ANZAC 1915* (Sydney, 2011).
Robertson, John, *The Tragedy & Glory of Gallipoli: Anzac & Empire* (Sydney, 1990).
Rutledge, Martha, ed.,*Socks from Bungendore* (West Geelong, 2015).
Roy, Kaushik, *The Army in British India: From Colonial Warfare to Total War 1857-1947* (London, 2013).
Royle, Trevor, *The Kitchener Enigma* (London, 1985).

Sadler, Peter S, *The Paladin: A Life of Major General Sir John Gellibrand* (Melbourne, 2000).
Sagona, Antonio, Mithat Atabay, C J Makie, Ian McGibbon, and Richard Reid, eds, *Anzac Battlefield*. (Port Melbourne, 2016).
Saunders, Antony, *Raiding on the Werstern Front* (Barnsley, 2102).
Scott, Douglas, ed., *Douglas Haig: The Preparatory Prologue Diaries & Letters 1861 - 1914* (Barnsley, 2006).
Sebag-Montefiore, Hugh, *Somme: Into the Breach* (London, 2016).
Seldon, Anthony and Walsh, David, *Public Schools and the Great War: The Gneration Lost* (Barnsley, 2013).
Senior, Michael, *Haking, A Dutiful Soldier* (Barnsley, 2012).
Seal, Graham, *Inventing Anzac: The Digger and National Mythology*, (Brisbane, University of Queensland Press, 2004).
Serle, G, *John Monash* (Melbourne, 1983).
Sheffield, Gary, and Till, Geoffrey, *Challenges of High Command in the Twentieth Century* (Camberley, 1999).
———, and Dan Todman, eds, *Command and Control on the Western Front* (Stroud, 2004).
———, and John Bourne, eds, *Douglas Haig: war diaries and letters, 1914-1918* (London, 2005).
———, *The Chief: Douglas Haig and the British Army* (London, 2011).
———, *Command and Morale on the Western Front* (Barnsley, 2014).
Shepperd, Alan, *Sandhurst: The Royal Military Academy Sandhurst and its Predecessors* (London, 1980).
Simon, Brian, and Ian Bradley, eds, *The Victorian Public School* (Dublin, 1975).
Simpson, Andy, *Directing Operations: British Corps Command on the Western Front 1914-1918* (Stroud, 2006).
Singh, Major General V K, *Leadership in the Indian Army: Biographies of Twelve Soldiers* (New Delhi, 2005).
Sixsmith, E K G, *Douglas Haig* (Worthing, 1976).
Skeen, General Sir Andrew, *Passing It On* (Aldershot, 1943).
Slim, FM Sir William, *Defeat into Victory* (London, 1956).
———, *Unofficial History* (London, 1959).
Smithers, A J, *Sir John Monash* (London, 1973).
Souter, Gavin, *Lion and Kangaroo* (Sydney, 1976).

Spear, Percival, *India, a modern history* (Ann Arbor, 1961).
Stanley, Peter, *Bad Characters: Sex, Crime, Mutiny, Murder and the Australian Imperial Force* (Sydney, 2010).
———, *War Without End* (Sydney, 2014).
———, *Die in Battle, Do Not Despair: The Indians on Gallipoli, 1915* (Solihull, 2015).
———, ed., *Charles Bean: Man, Myth, Legacy* (Sydney, 2017).
———, *The Terriers in India: British Territorials 1914-19* (Warwick, 2019).
Stein, Burton, *A History of India* (Oxford, 1998).
Stephens, Chris, *Bristol's Australian Pioneer* (Bristol, 2016).
Stevenson, Robert, *To Win the Battle: The 1st Australian Division in the Great War, 1914–1918* (Melbourne, 2013).
———, *The War With Germany – The Centenary History of Australia and the Great War Volume 3* (South Melbourne, 2015).
Stewart, Captain P F, *The History of XII Royal Lancers (Prince of Wales's)* (London, 1950).
Strachan, Hew, *The Politics of the British Army* (Oxford, 1997).
———, ed., *Military Lives* (Oxford 2002).
———, *The First World War* (London, 2003).
Swinson, Arthur, *North-West Frontier* (London, 1967).

Terraine, John, *Douglas Haig The Educated Soldier* (London, 1963).
Thomson, Alistair, 'Popular Gallipoli history and the representation of Australian military manhood', *History Australia*, 16:3 (2019), 518-533,
Trafford, Cheryl, ed., *The Best School of All* (London, 2009).
Travers, Tim, *The Killing Ground* (London, 1987).
———, *Gallipoli 1915* (Stroud, 2001).
Tripodi, Christian, *Edge of Empire – The British Political Officer and Tribal Administration on the North-West Frontier 1877-1947* (Farnham, 2011).

Urban, Mark, *Generals: Ten British Commanders who Shaped the World* (London, 2005).

Walker, Jonathan, *The Blood Tub: General Gough and the Battle of Bullecourt, 1917* (Staplehurst, 1998).
Wallace, R L, *The Australians at the Boer War* (Canberra, 1976).
Warner, Philip, *Auchinleck The Lonely Soldier* (London, 1981).
———, *Field Marshal Earl Haig* (London, 1991).
Wavell, General Sir Archibald. *Allenby A Study in Greatness* (London, 1940).
———, *Generals and Generalship* (Harmondsworth, 1941).
———, FM Viscount, *The Good Soldier* (Bombay, 1947).
———, *Other Men's Flowers* (London, 1971).
Wearne, Sarah, and James Kerr, *To Our Brothers: Memorials to a Lost Generation in British Schools.* (Warwick, 2018).
Weeks, Col H E, *History of the 5th Royal Gurkha Rifles (Frontier Force) 1858 to 1928* (Uckfield, 2009).
Westerman, William, *Soldiers and Gentlemen: Australian Battalion Commanders in the Great War, 1914-1918* (Cambridge, 2017).

Wilcox, Craig, "Australia's South African war 1899-1902." *Scientia Militaria* 30, no. 1 (2000): 1-12.
———, *Australia's Boer War: the war in South Africa, 1899-1902* (South Melbourne, 2002).
Wilson, Jon, *India Conquered* (London, 2016).
Winrow, Andrew, 'Reactionary or Reformer? Major General Douglas Haig: Inspector General of Cavalry India 1903-1906', *Durbar, Journal of Indian Military History Society,* Volume 26, No 4, Winter 2009.
Winter, Denis, *Haig's Command: A Reassessment* (London, 1991).
———, *25 April 1915: The Inevitable Tragedy* (St Lucia, Queensland, 1994).
Williams, Jeffery, *Byng of Vimy* (London, 1983).Wilson, Jon, *India Conquered* (London, 2016).
Winterbottom, Derek, *Henry Newbolt and The Spirit of Clifton* (Bristol, 1986).
———, *John Percival: The Great Educator* (Bristol, 1993).
———, *Bertrand Hallward, First Vice-Chancellor of the University of Nottingham 1948-1965: A Biography* (Nottingham, 1995).
Wolpert, Stanley, *A New History of India* (Oxford, 1982).
Wray, Christopher, *Pozières: Echoes of a Distant Battle* (Cambridge, 2015).

Young, G M, *Stanley Baldwin* (London, 1952).

Newspapers and Journals

The Age
Argus
Aussie
The Canberra Times
Daily Express
Daily Mail
Daily Mirror
The Daily Telegraph
Devon and Exeter Gazette
Digger
Durbar
Exeter and Plymouth Gazette
The Gallipolian
Gazette of India
Geraldton Guardian and Express
Hobart Mercury
Illustrated Weekly of India
Illustrated Western Daily News
London Gazette
The Mail
The Pioneer
Portrait
Reveille
Sabretache

Scientia Militaria
The Tablet
Taunton Courier, and Western Advertiser
The Times
The Times of India
Western Daily Press

Unpublished Sources

Beckett, R T, 'An imperial force?: the AIF in the United Kingdom , 1914-1918' (King's College London, PhD thesis, 2008).

De Bellis, Dianne Kaye, 'Stories of Australian Deserters in World War 1' (University of South Australia, PhD thesis, 2014).

Harris, Clive, A study of the Operational Techniques of the British IX Corps and the Australia Corps during the Breaking of the Hindenburg Line 29 September 1918, (University of Wolverhampton, MA Dissertation, 2016).

Millar, John Dermot, 'A study in the limitations of command: General Sir William Birdwood and the AIF 1914-1918' (University of New South Wales, PhD thesis, 1993).

Verney, Guy, 'The Army High Command and Australian Defence Policy, 1901-1918' (University of Sydney, PhD thesis, 1985).

Media

Gallipoli: The Fatal Shore, Australian Broadcasting Corporation Television Documentary, 1988.

The Boys Who Came Home: Recollections of Gallipoli, Australian Broadcasting Corporation Television Documentary, 1990.

Revealing Gallipoli, Wain, Fimeri, 2005.

Coronation Durbar at Delhi, Paul, R.W, British Film Institute Library, 1903.

Gallipoli, Weir, Peter, 1981.

Index

Index of Places

Index of People

Index of Military Formations & Units

Miscellaneous